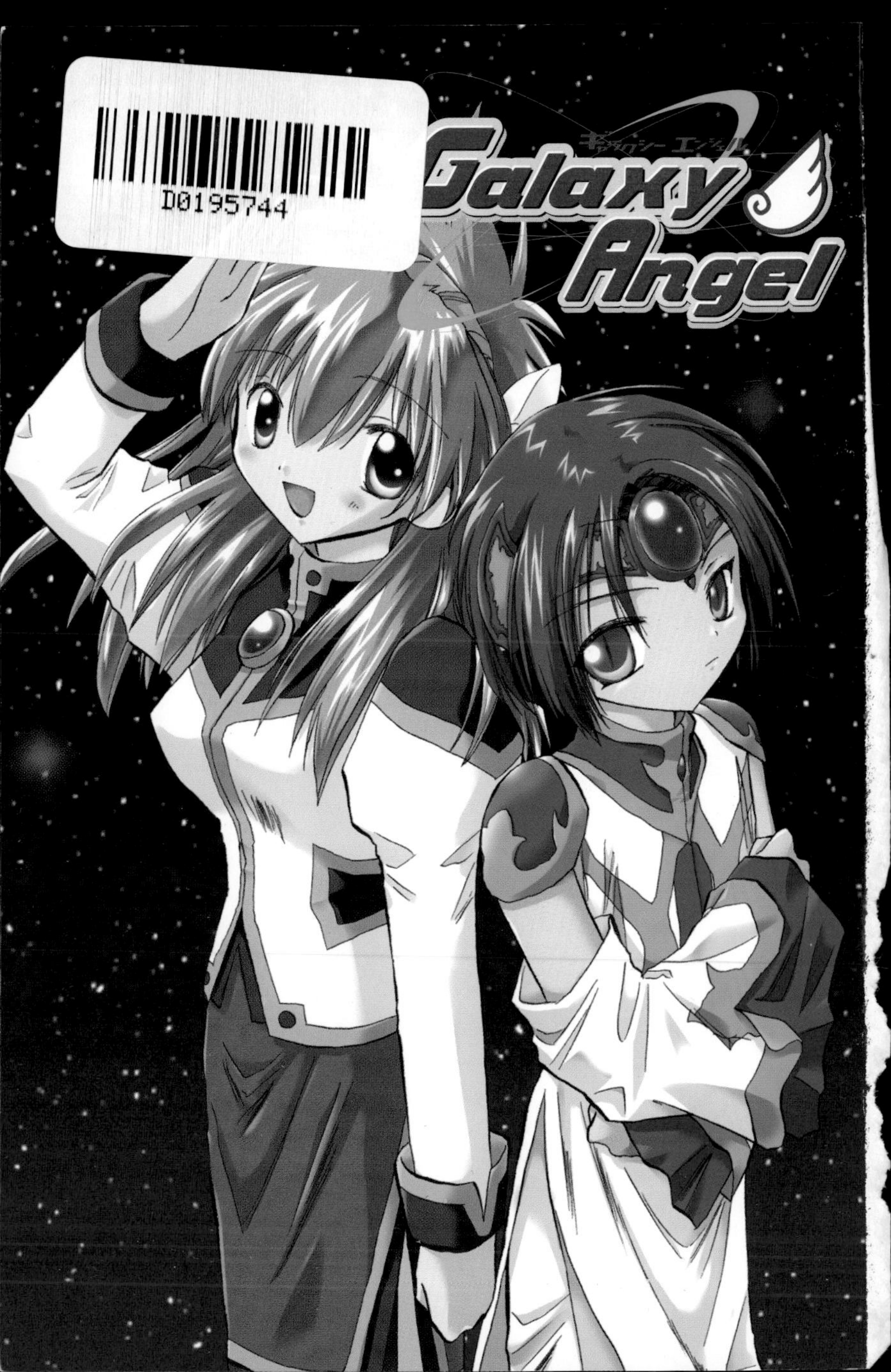
ギャラクシーエンジェル
Galaxy Angel

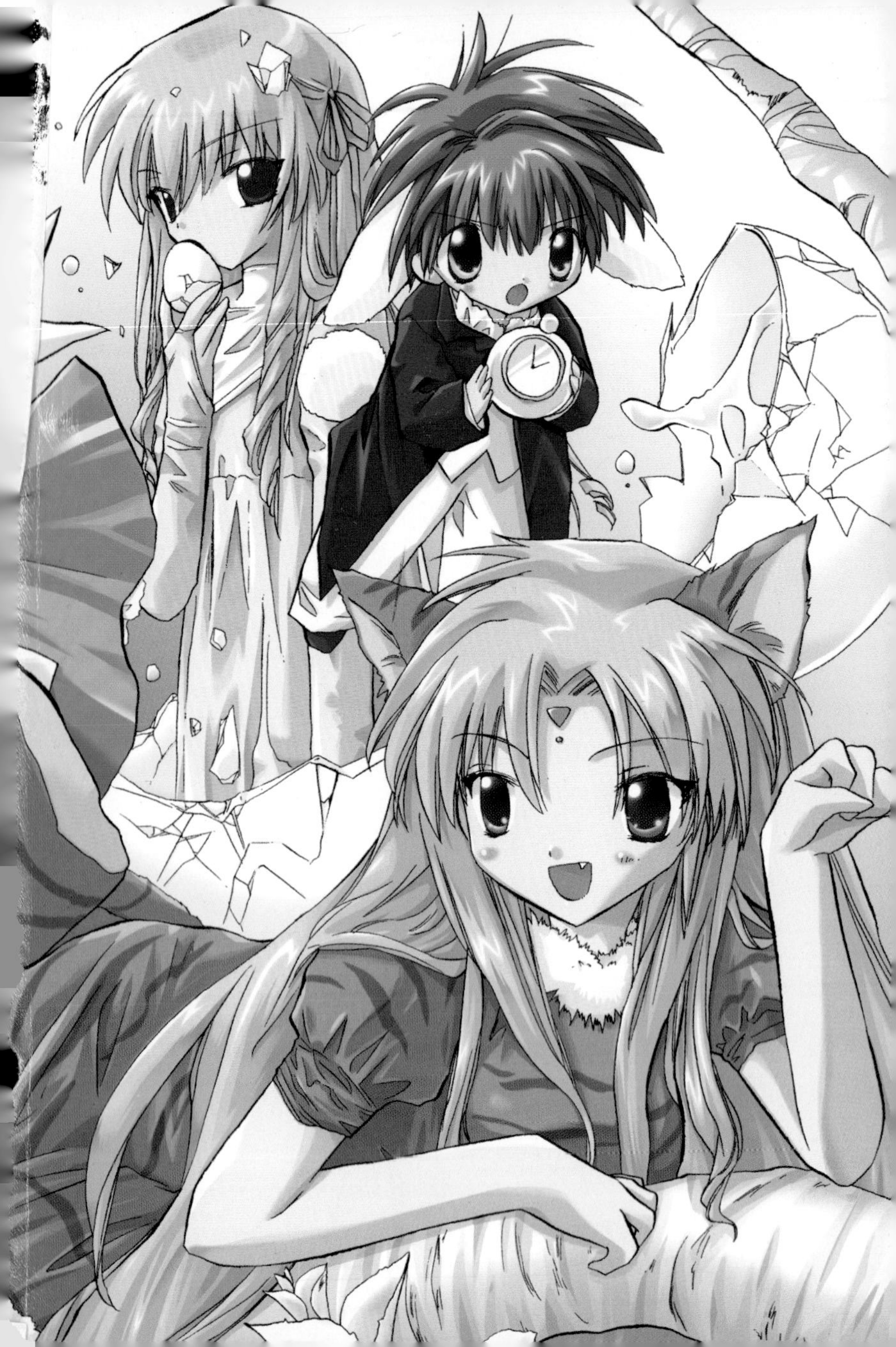

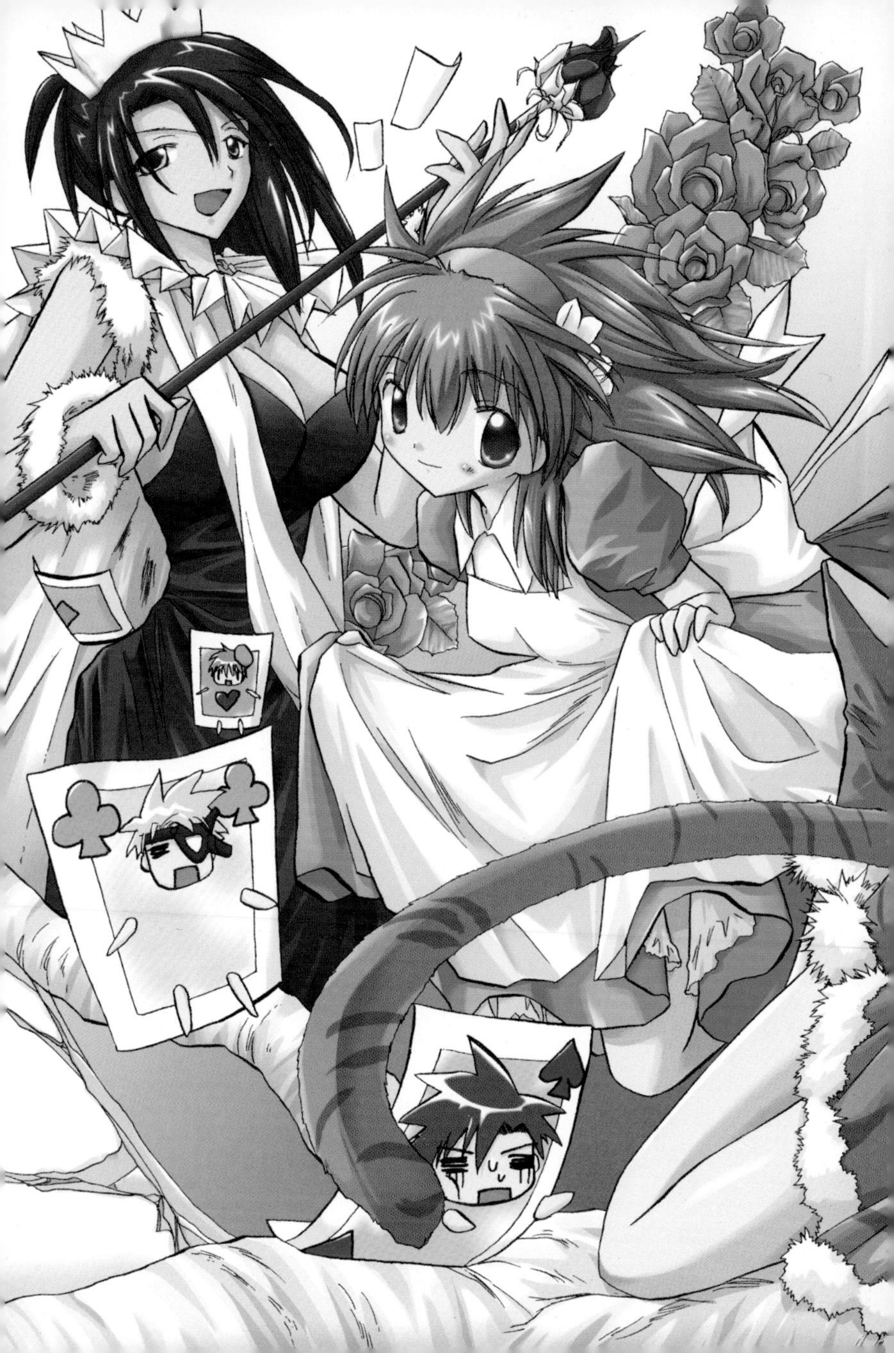

CONTENTS

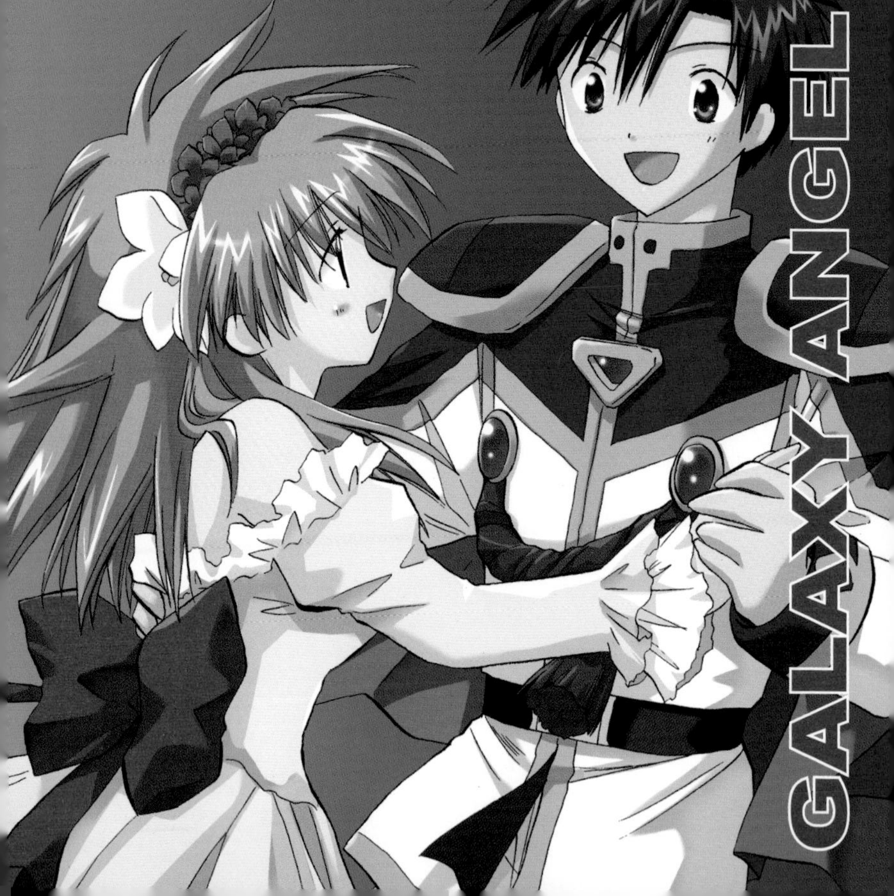

GALAXY ANGEL

ギャラクシー エンジェル

Galaxy Angel ④

by Kanan
Supervised by Ryo Mizuno
Original Concept by BROCCOLI

brought to you by
BROCCOLI BOOKS
A DIVISION OF BROCCOLI INTERNATIONAL USA

Other titles available from Broccoli Books

Galaxy Angel™ Volume 4

English Adaptation Staff
Translation: Koji Tajii
English Adaptation: Jason R. Grissom
Touch-Up, & Lettering: Fawn Lau
Cover & Graphic Supervision: Chris McDougall

Editor: Dietrich Seto
Sales Manager: Ardith D. Santiago
Managing Editor: Shizuki Yamashita
Publisher: Hideki Uchino

Email: editor@broccolibooks.com
Website: www.bro-usa.com

A (**B**) BROCCOLI BOOKS Manga
Broccoli Books is a division of Broccoli International USA, Inc.
12211 W. Washington Blvd, Suite 110, Los Angeles CA 90066

© 2003, 2004 BROCCOLI
© 2003, 2004 Kanan
Supervised by Ryo Mizuno
All Rights Reserved. First published in Japan in 2003 by KADOKAWA SHOTEN PUBLISHING
CO., LTD., Tokyo.
English translation rights arranged with KADOKAWA SHOTEN PUBLISHING CO., LTD.
through BROCCOLI Co., Ltd.

ISBN: 1-932480-43-9

Published by Broccoli International USA, Inc.
First printing, December 2004

All illustrations by Kanan with the exception of pg. 199, Trick Master by IKUSABUNE.

BROCCOLI INTERNATIONAL USA

www.bro-usa.com

10 9 8 7 6 5 4 3 2 1
Printed in the United States

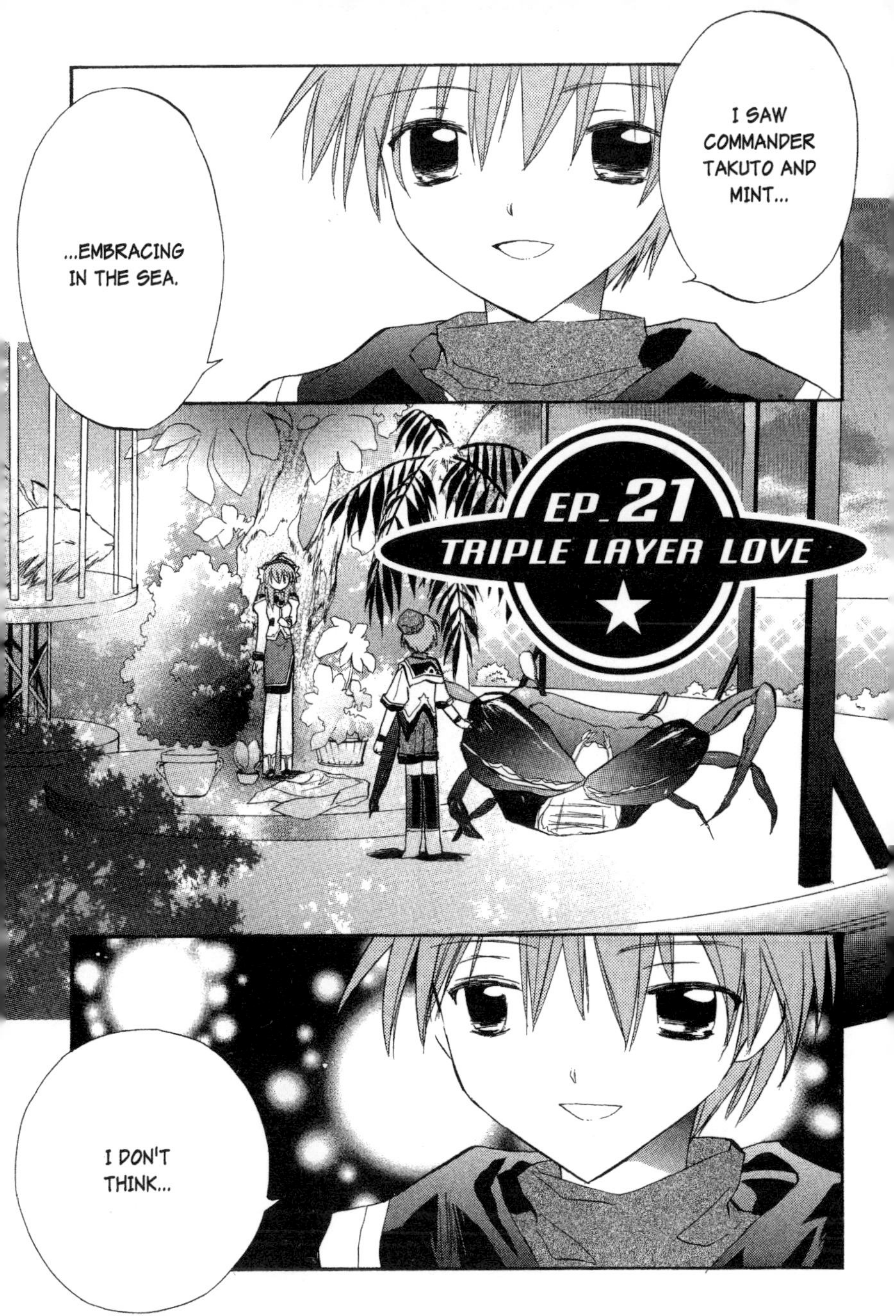
I SAW COMMANDER TAKUTO AND MINT...
...EMBRACING IN THE SEA.
EP_21
TRIPLE LAYER LOVE
I DON'T THINK...

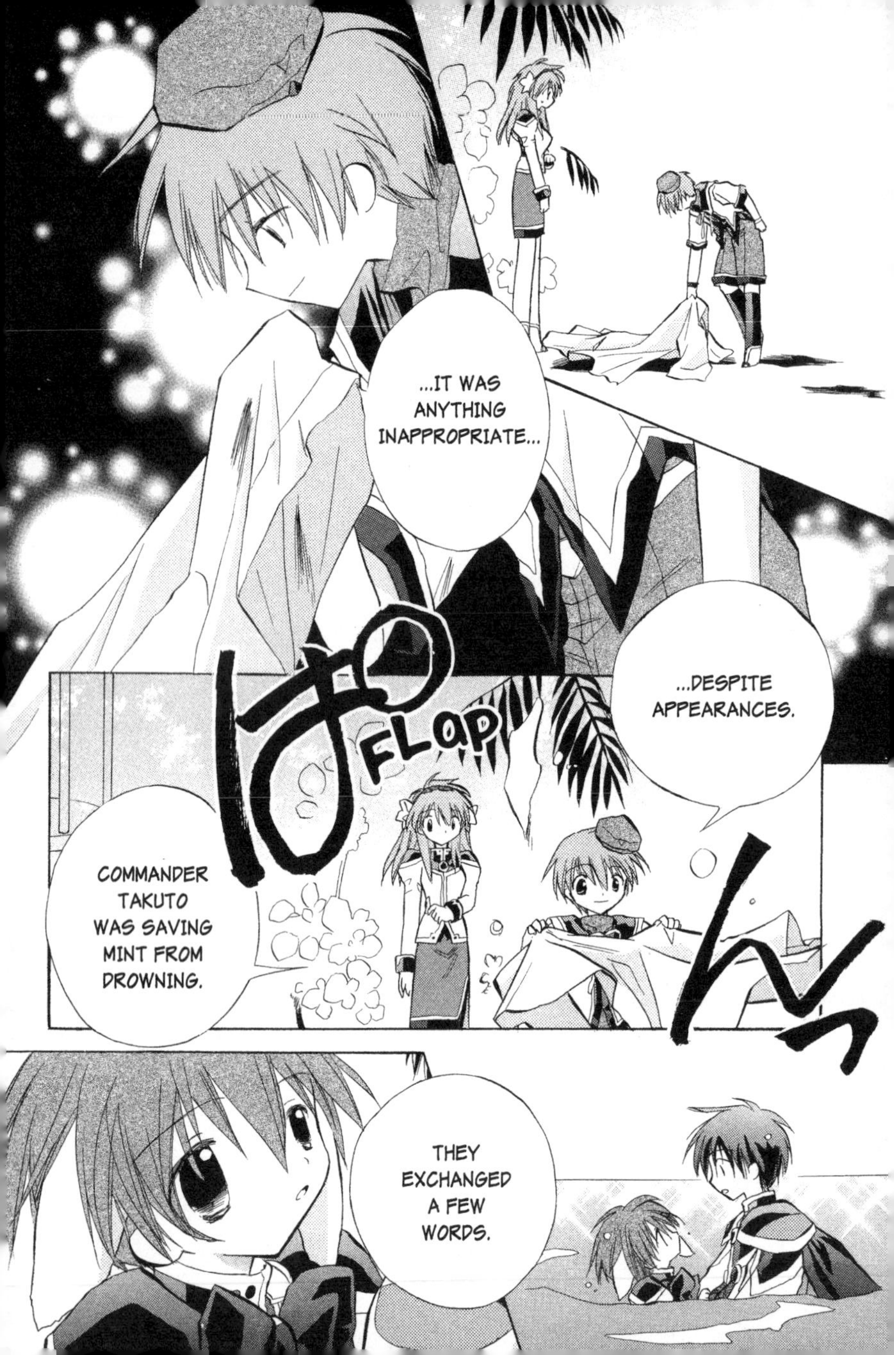
...IT WAS ANYTHING INAPPROPRIATE...
...DESPITE APPEARANCES.
FLAP
COMMANDER TAKUTO WAS SAVING MINT FROM DROWNING.
THEY EXCHANGED A FEW WORDS.

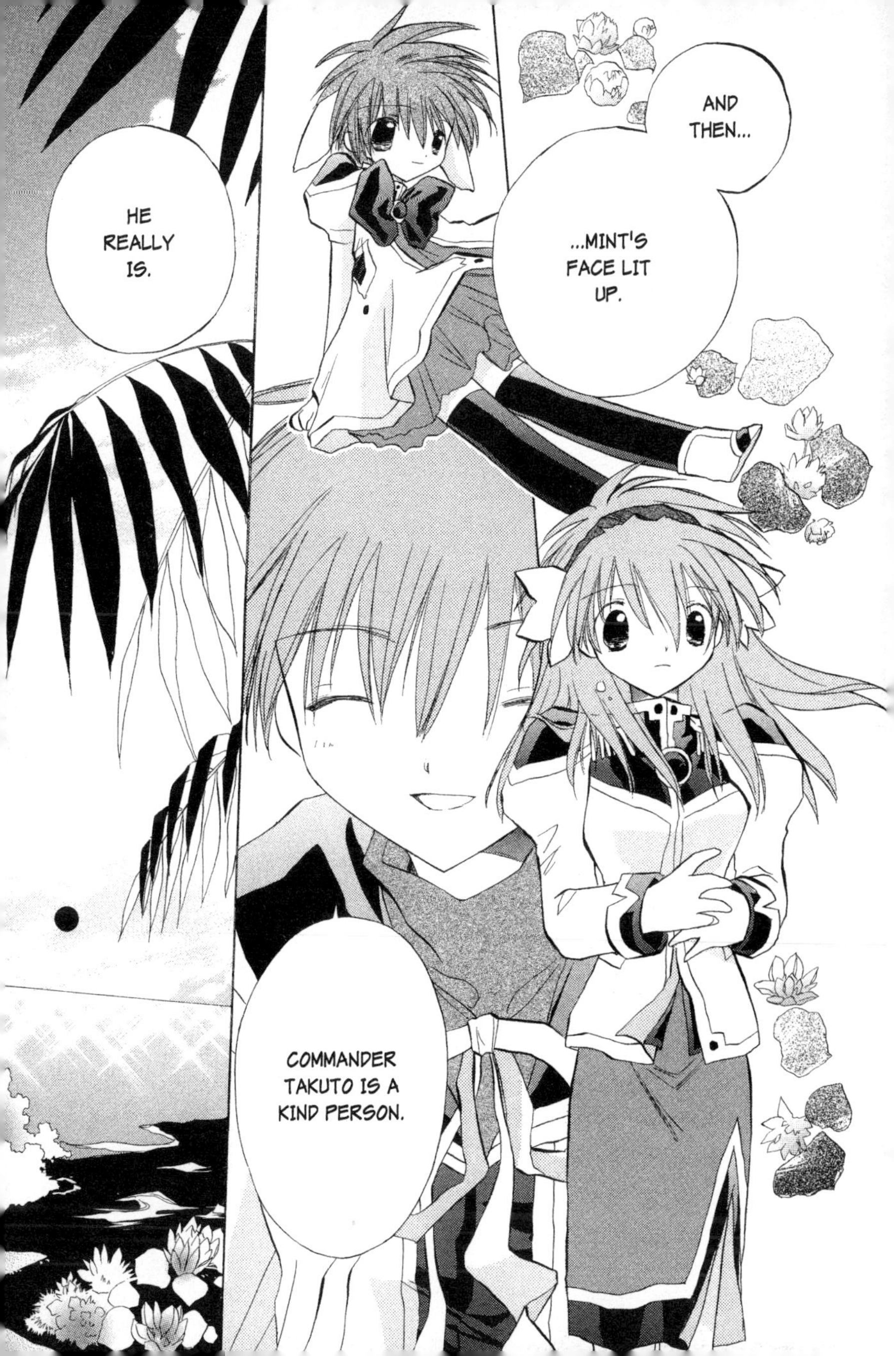
AND THEN...
...MINT'S FACE LIT UP.
COMMANDER TAKUTO IS A KIND PERSON.
HE REALLY IS.

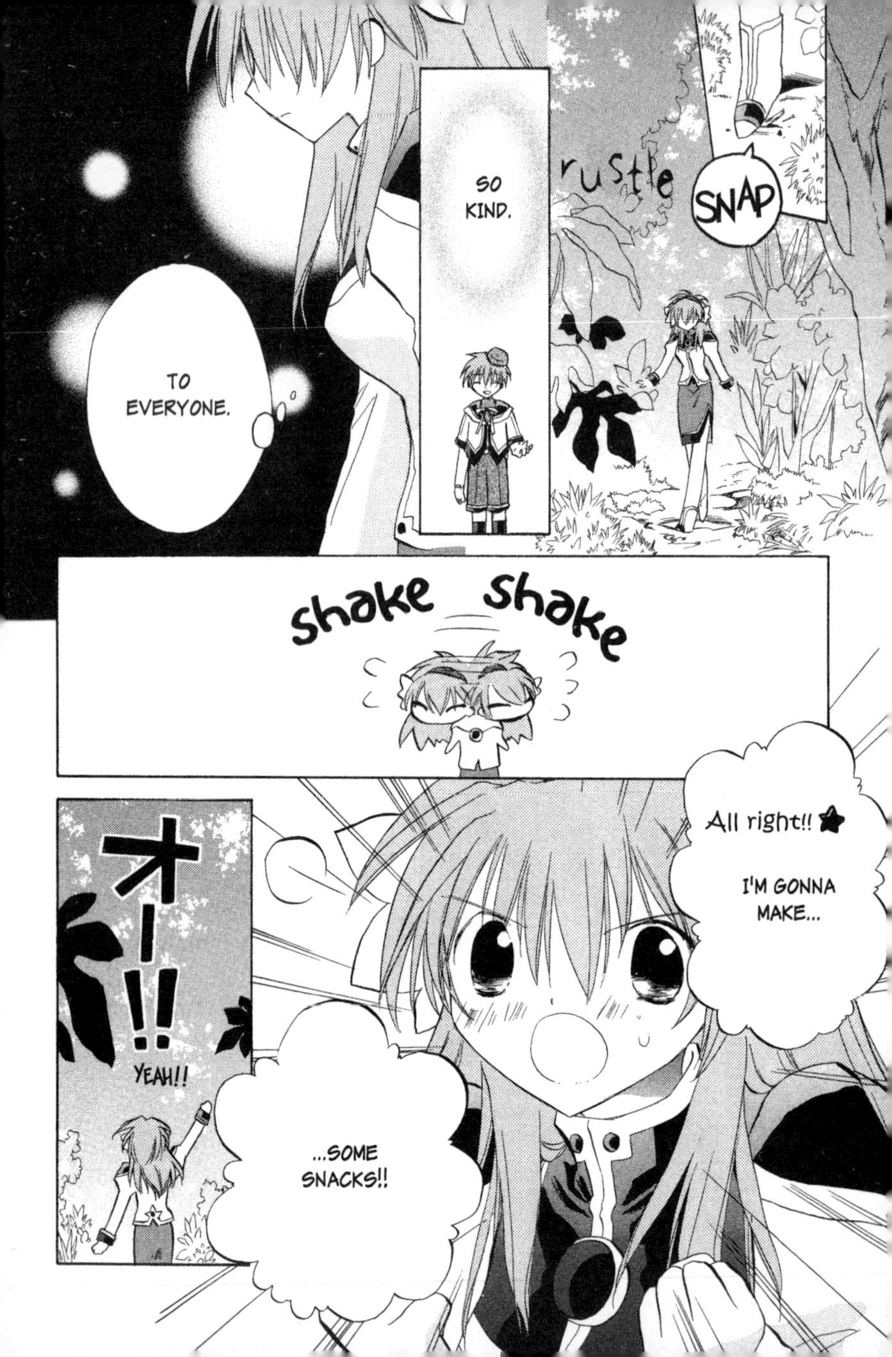
rustle
SNAP
SO KIND.
TO EVERYONE.
shake shake
All right!!
I'M GONNA MAKE...
...SOME SNACKS!!
オー!!
YEAH!!

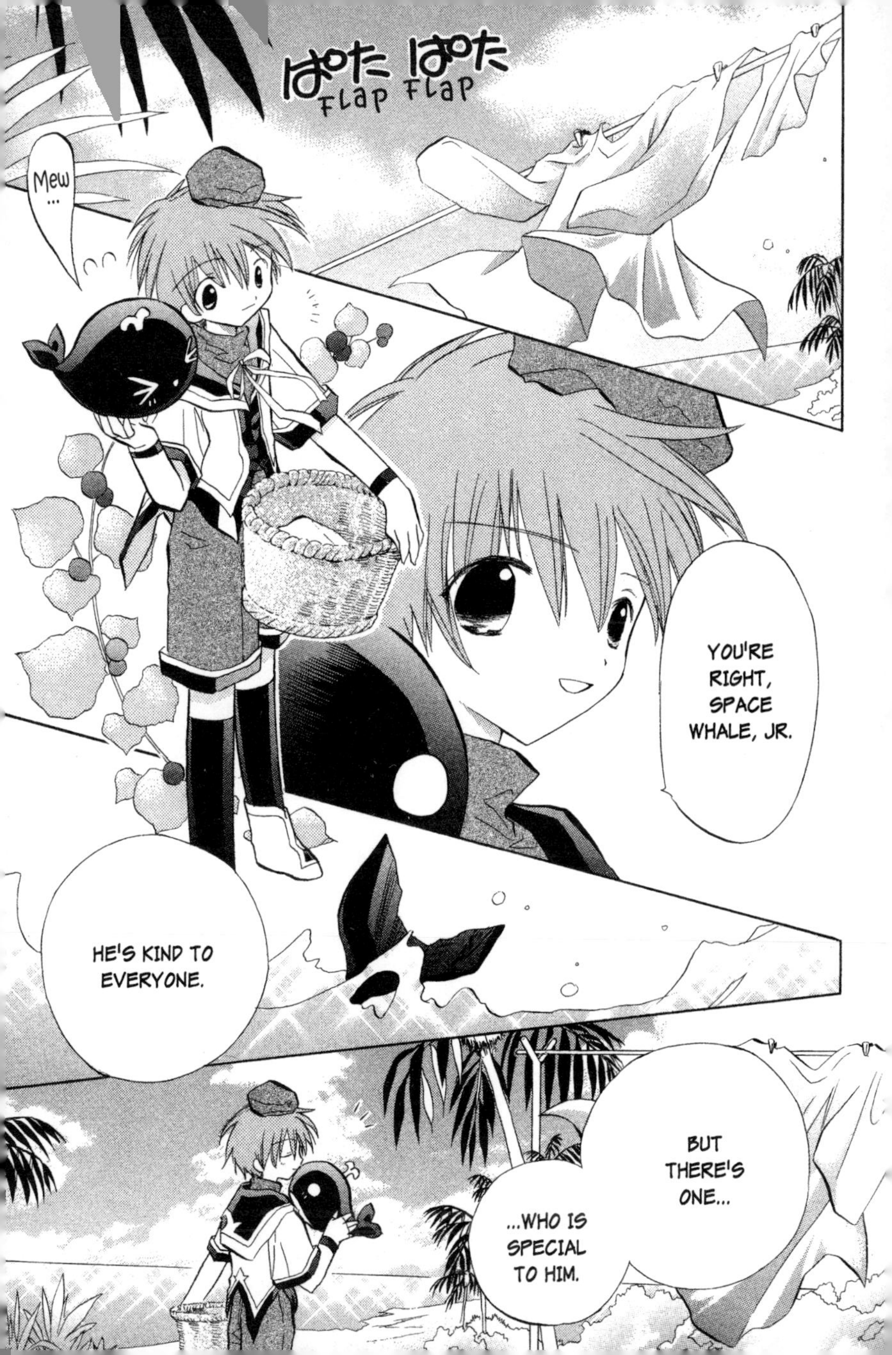
ぱた ぱた
Flap Flap
Mew ...
YOU'RE RIGHT, SPACE WHALE, JR.
HE'S KIND TO EVERYONE.
BUT THERE'S ONE...
...WHO IS SPECIAL TO HIM.

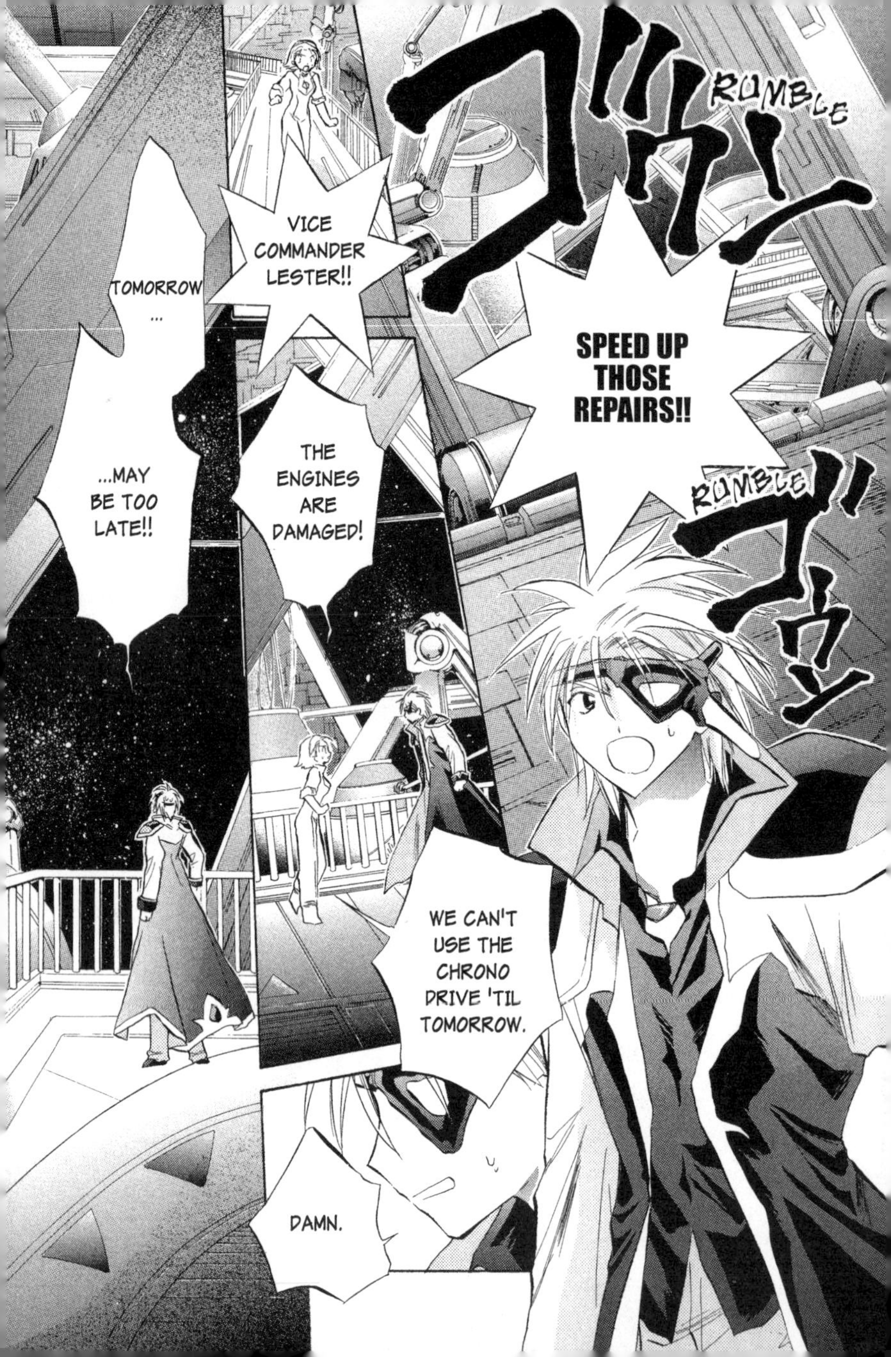
RUMBLE
SPEED UP THOSE REPAIRS!!
RUMBLE
WE CAN'T USE THE CHRONO DRIVE 'TIL TOMORROW.
VICE COMMANDER LESTER!!
THE ENGINES ARE DAMAGED!
TOMORROW ...
...MAY BE TOO LATE!!
DAMN.

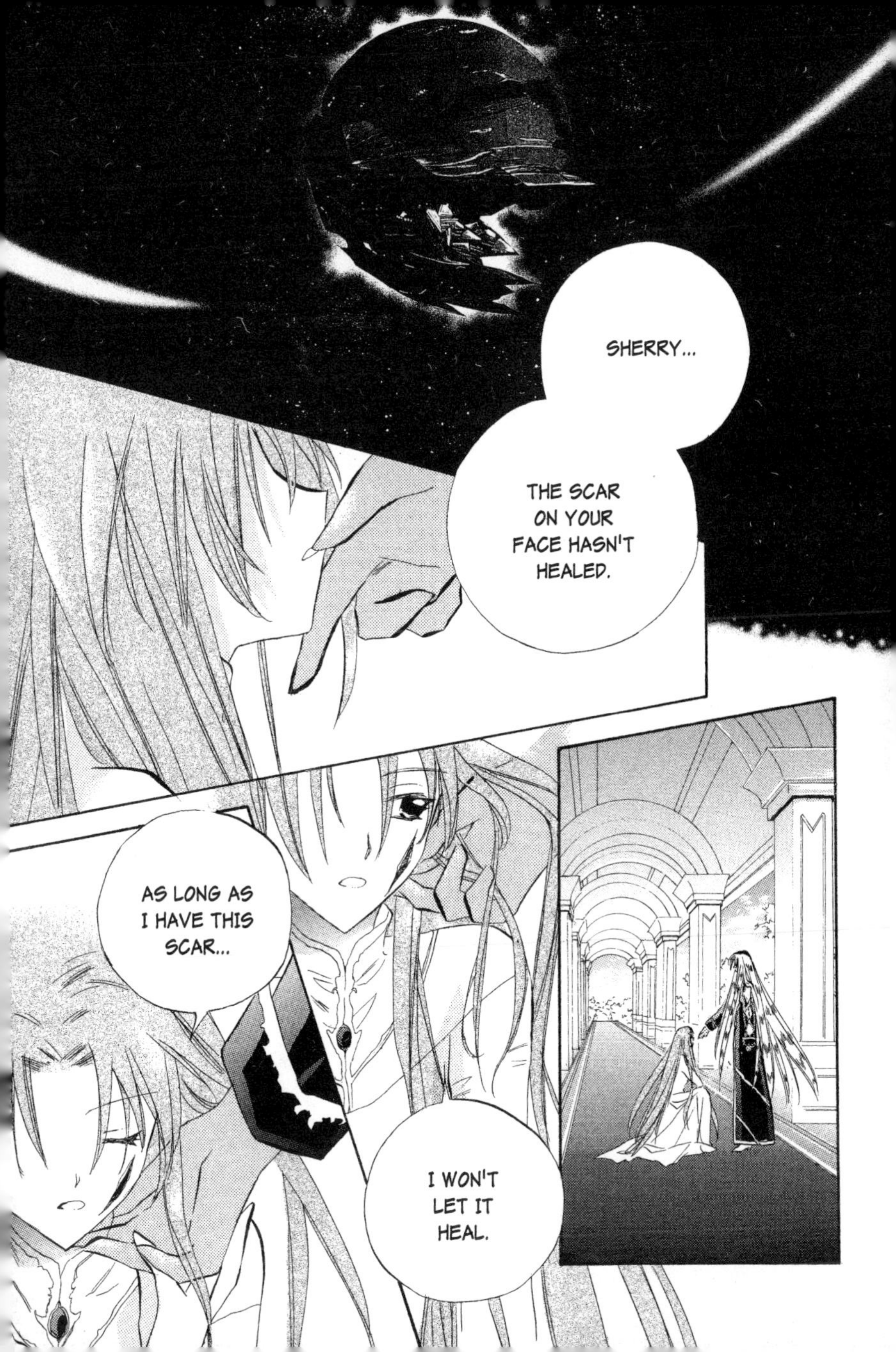
SHERRY...
THE SCAR ON YOUR FACE HASN'T HEALED.
AS LONG AS I HAVE THIS SCAR...
I WON'T LET IT HEAL.

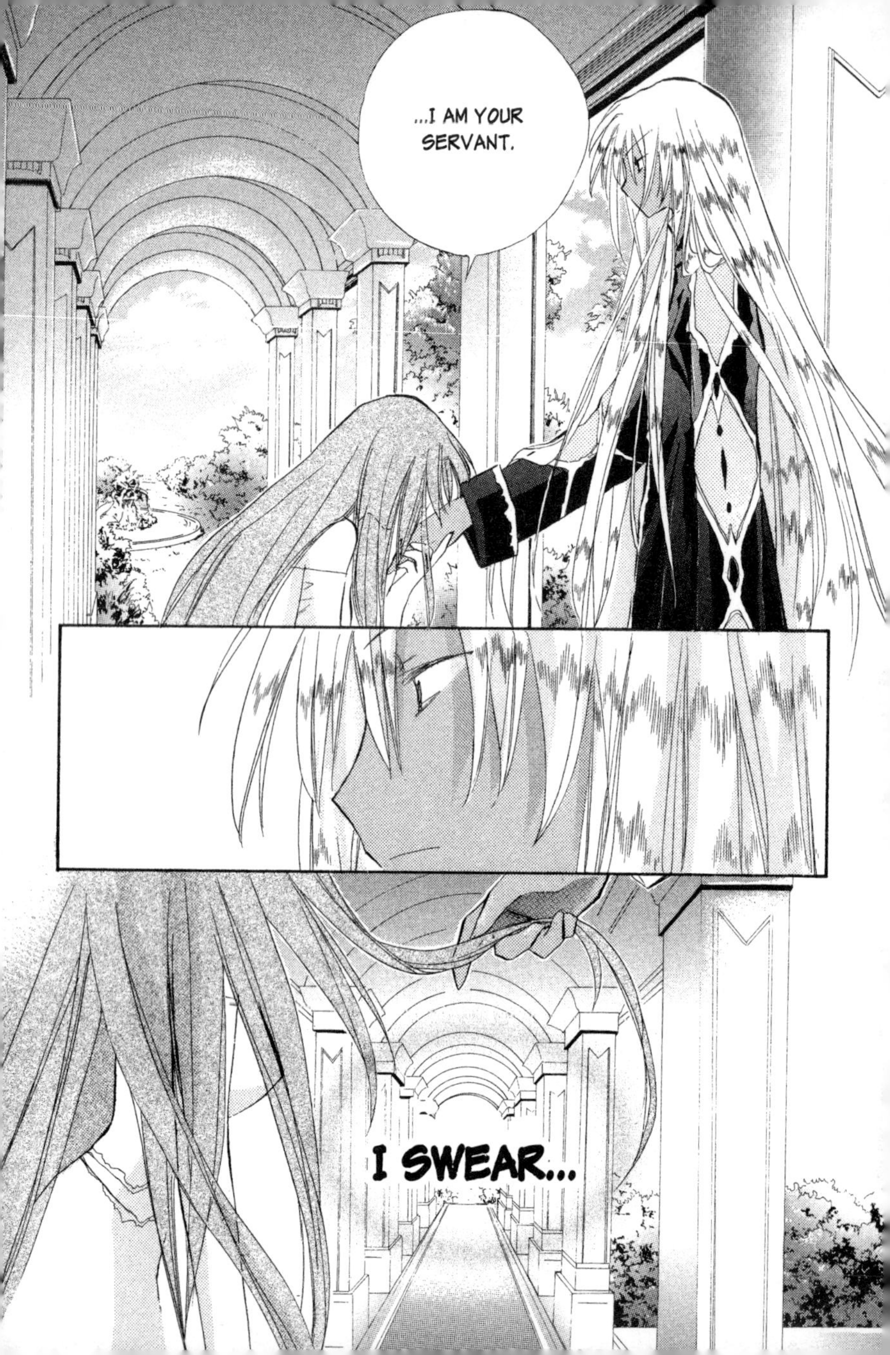
...I AM YOUR SERVANT.
I SWEAR...

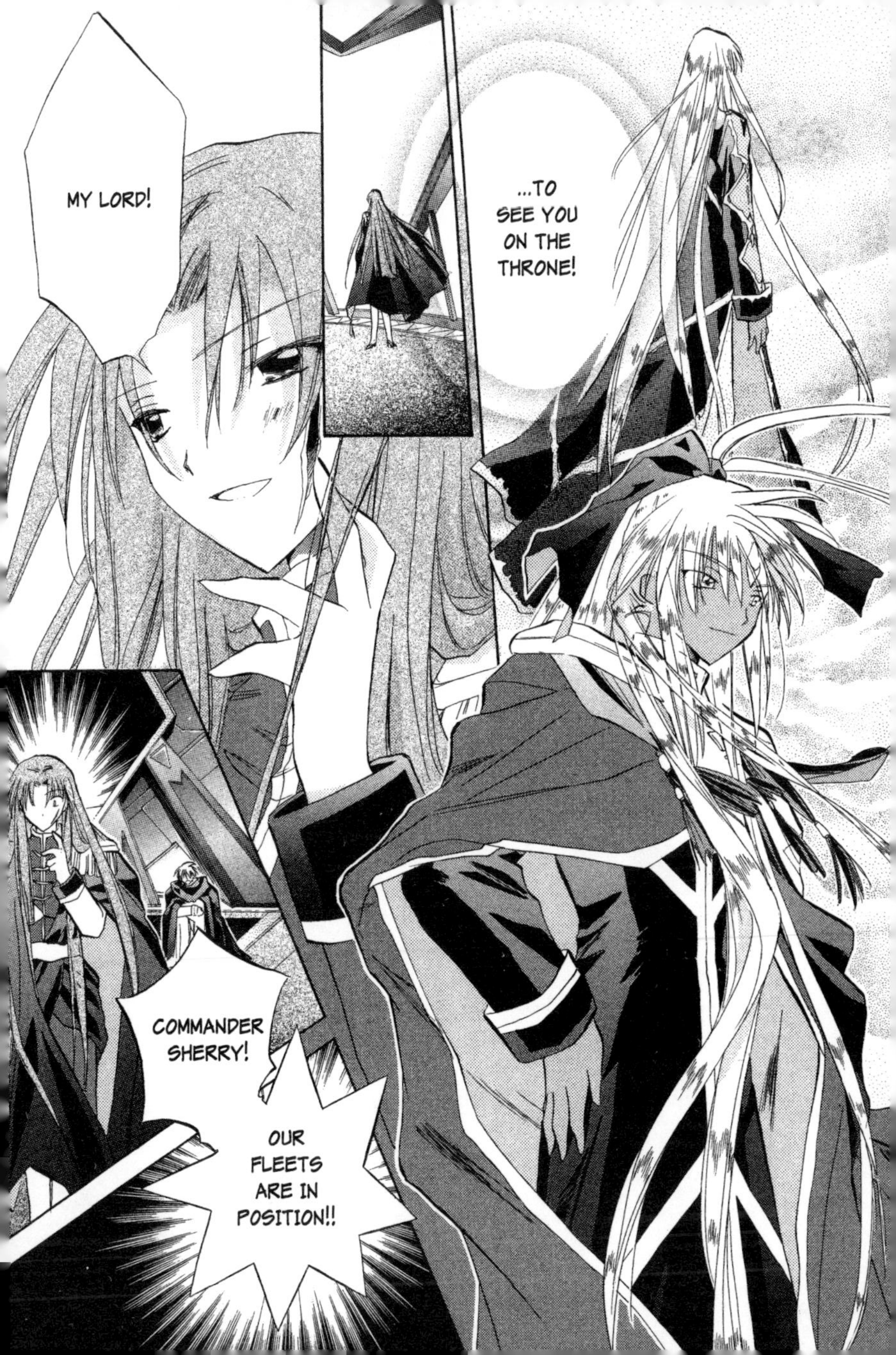
...TO SEE YOU ON THE THRONE!
MY LORD!
COMMANDER SHERRY!
OUR FLEETS ARE IN POSITION!!

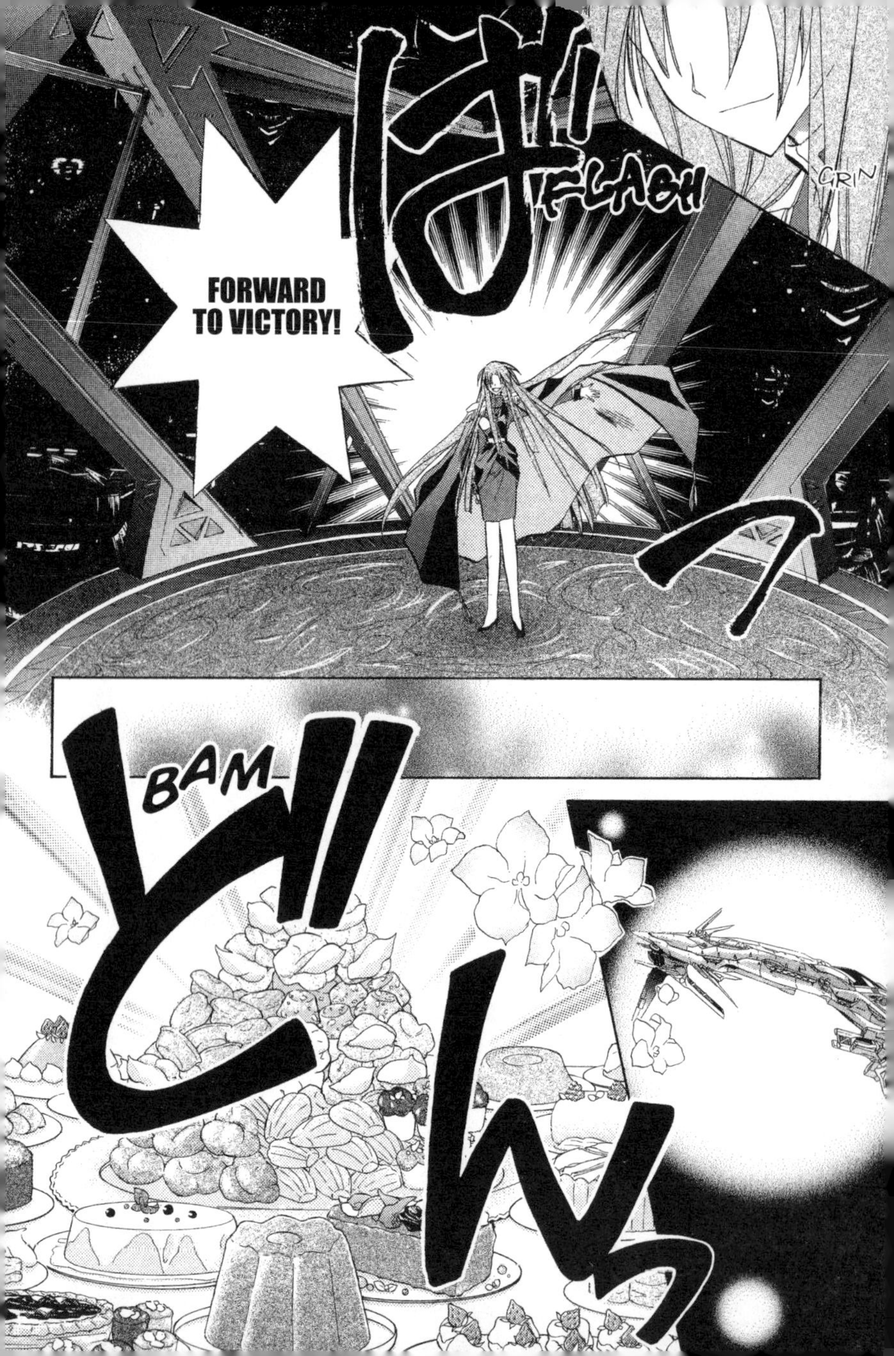
GRIN
FLASH
FORWARD TO VICTORY!
BAM

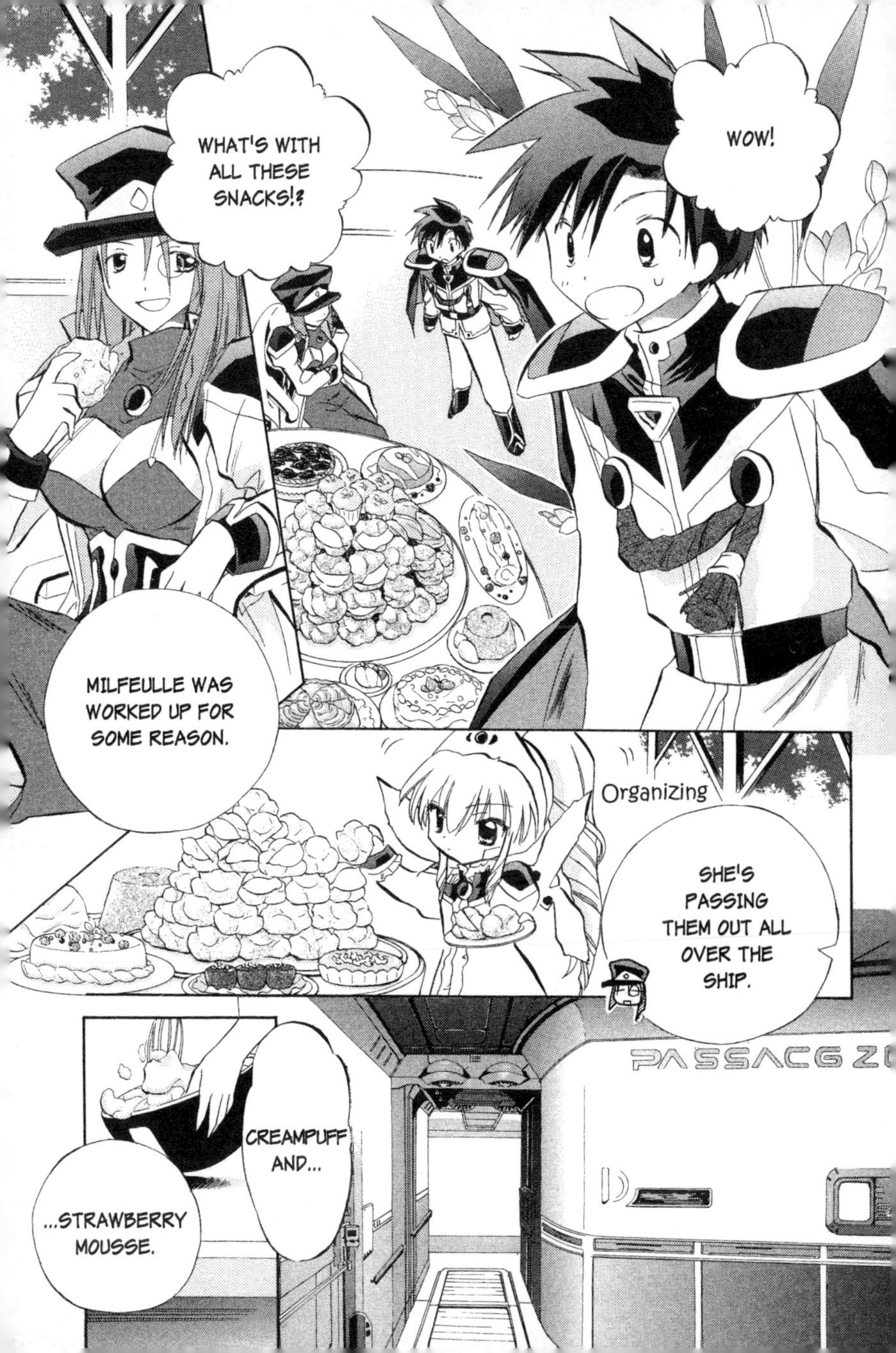
WOW!
WHAT'S WITH ALL THESE SNACKS!?
MILFEULLE WAS WORKED UP FOR SOME REASON.
Organizing
SHE'S PASSING THEM OUT ALL OVER THE SHIP.
CREAMPUFF AND...
...STRAWBERRY MOUSSE.

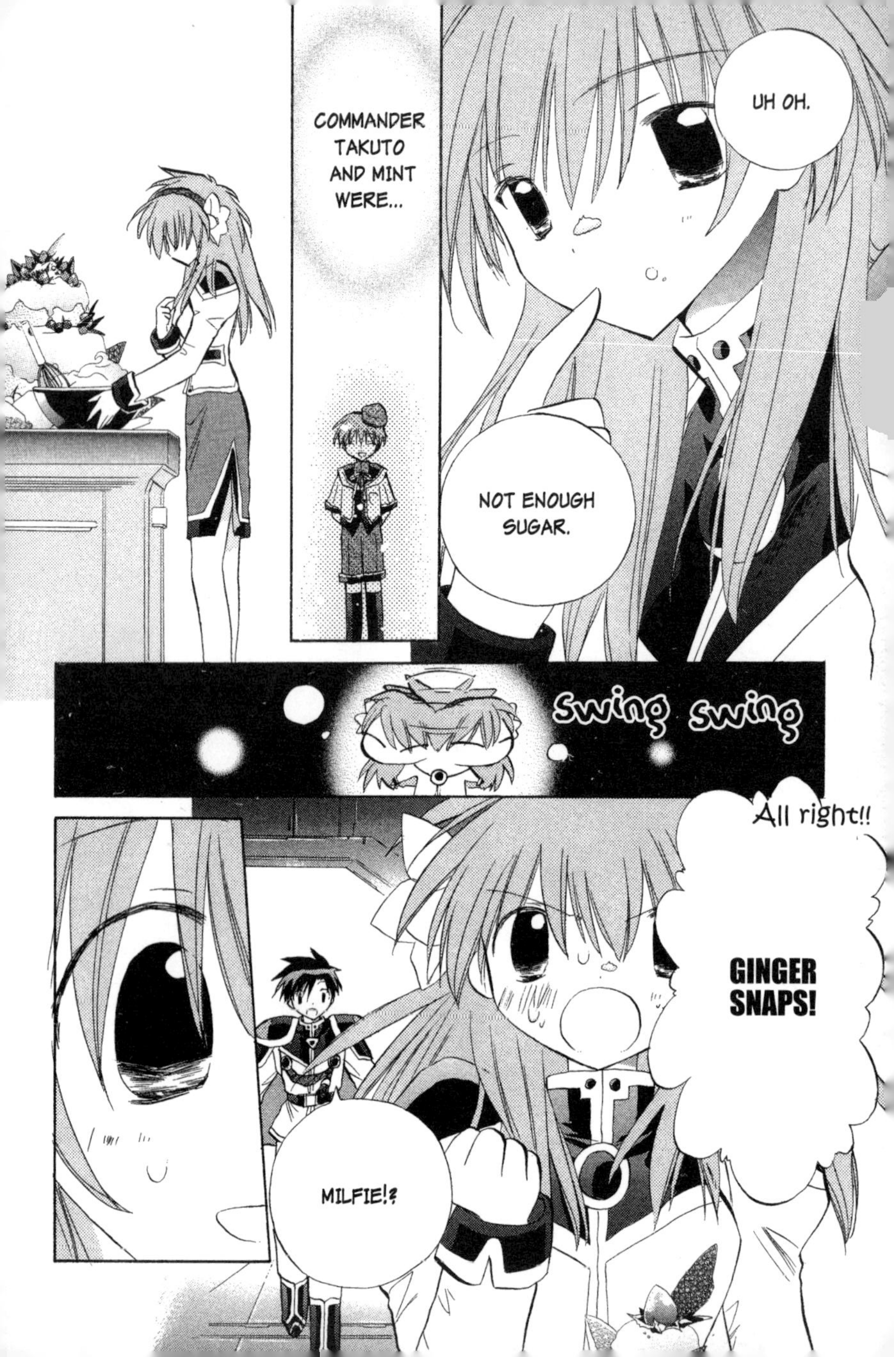
UH OH.
NOT ENOUGH SUGAR.
COMMANDER TAKUTO AND MINT WERE...
swing swing
All right!!
GINGER SNAPS!
MILFIE!?

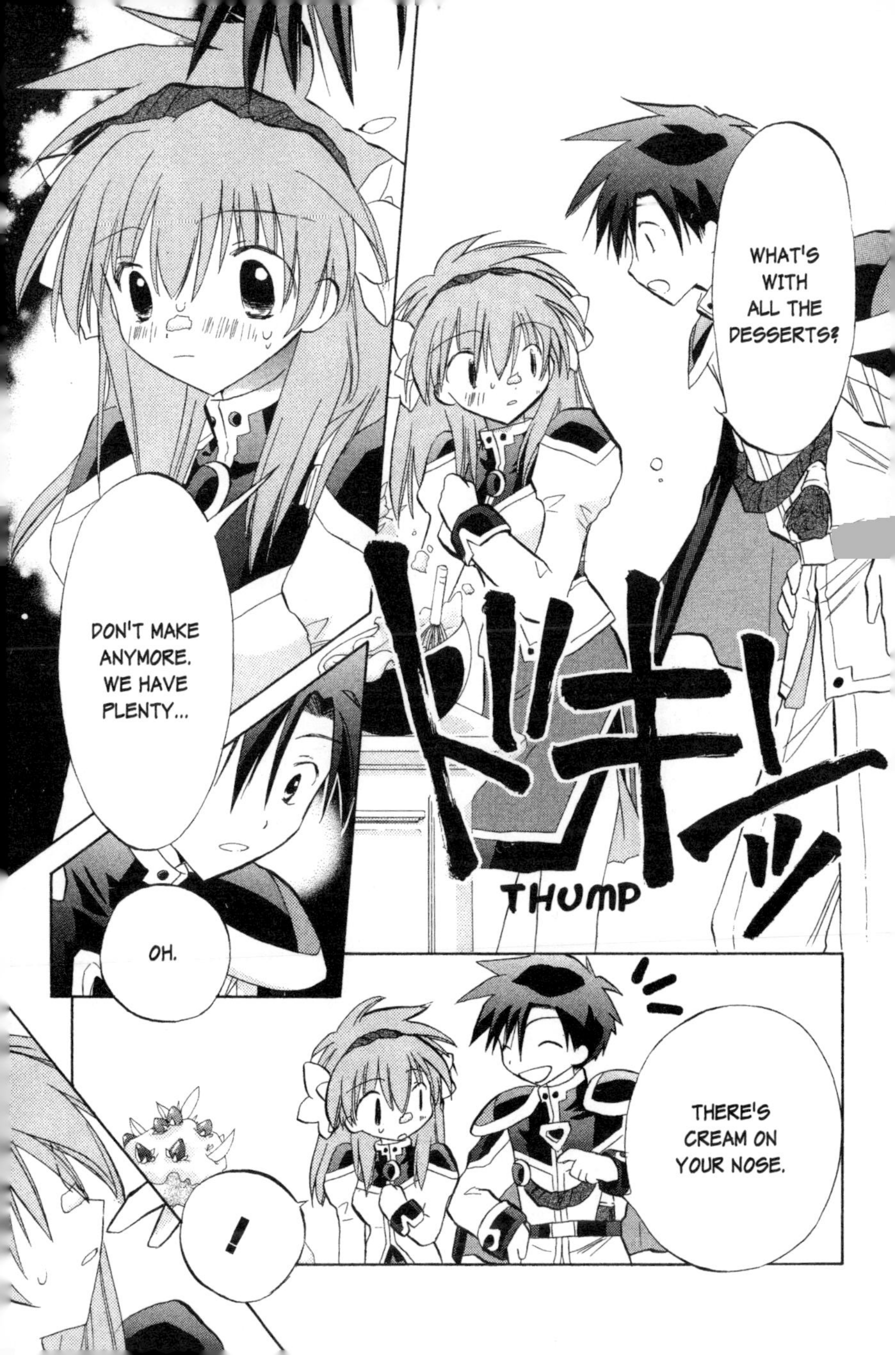
WHAT'S WITH ALL THE DESSERTS?
THUMP
DON'T MAKE ANYMORE. WE HAVE PLENTY...
OH.
THERE'S CREAM ON YOUR NOSE.
!

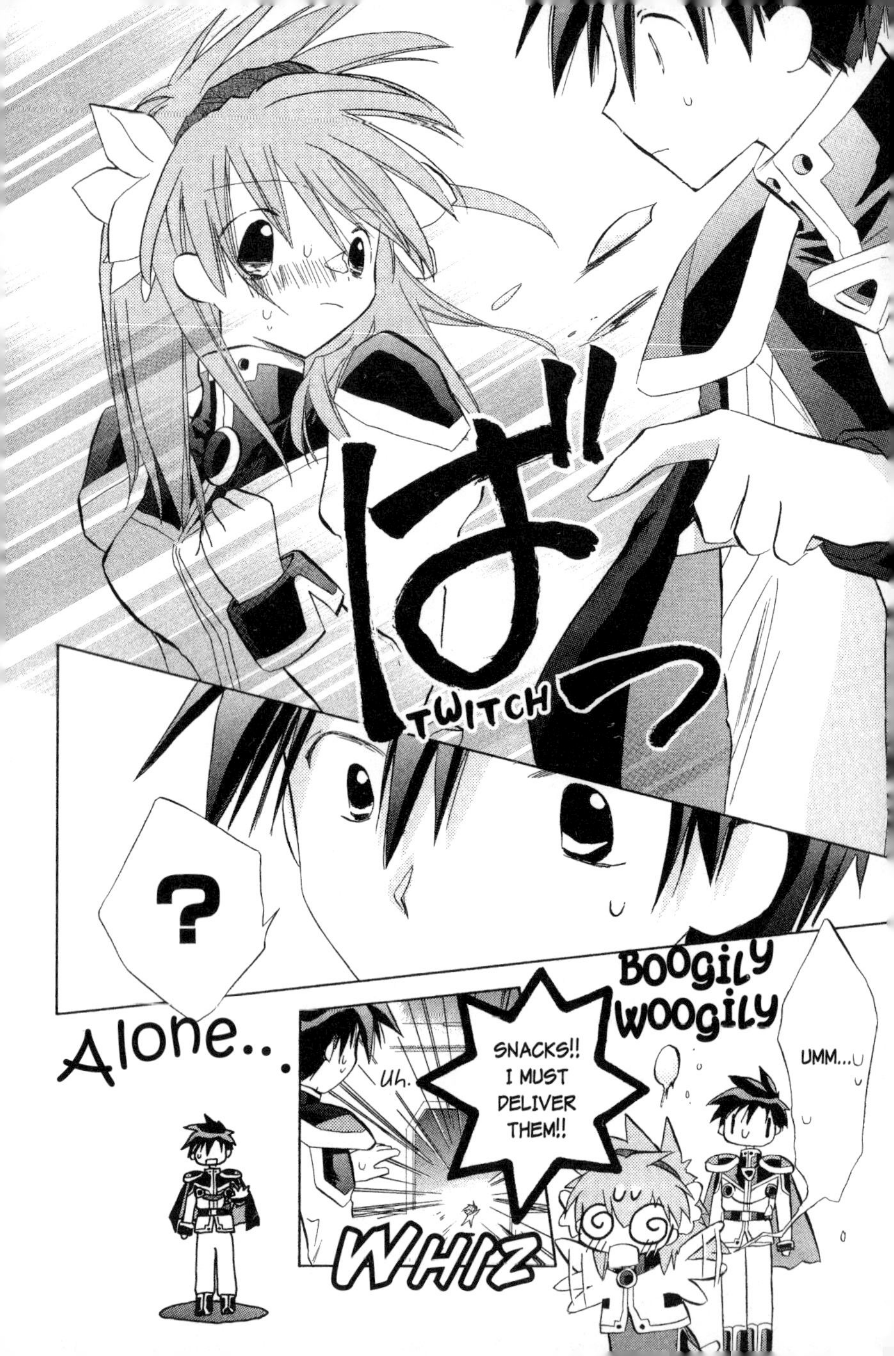
ぱっ
TWITCH
?
UMM...
BOOGILY WOOGILY
SNACKS!! I MUST DELIVER THEM!!
Uh.
WHIZ
Alone...

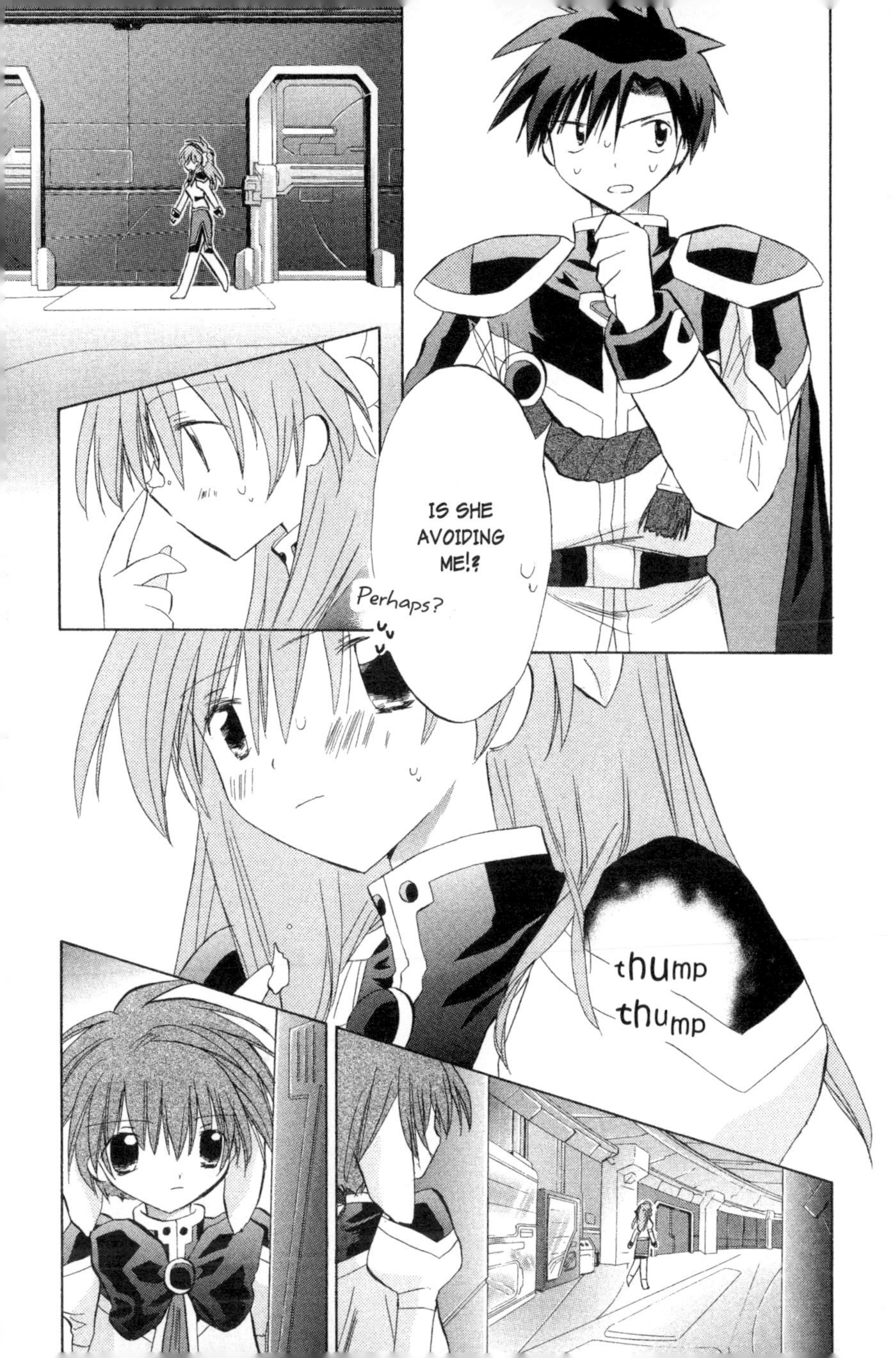
IS SHE AVOIDING ME!?
Perhaps?
thump thump

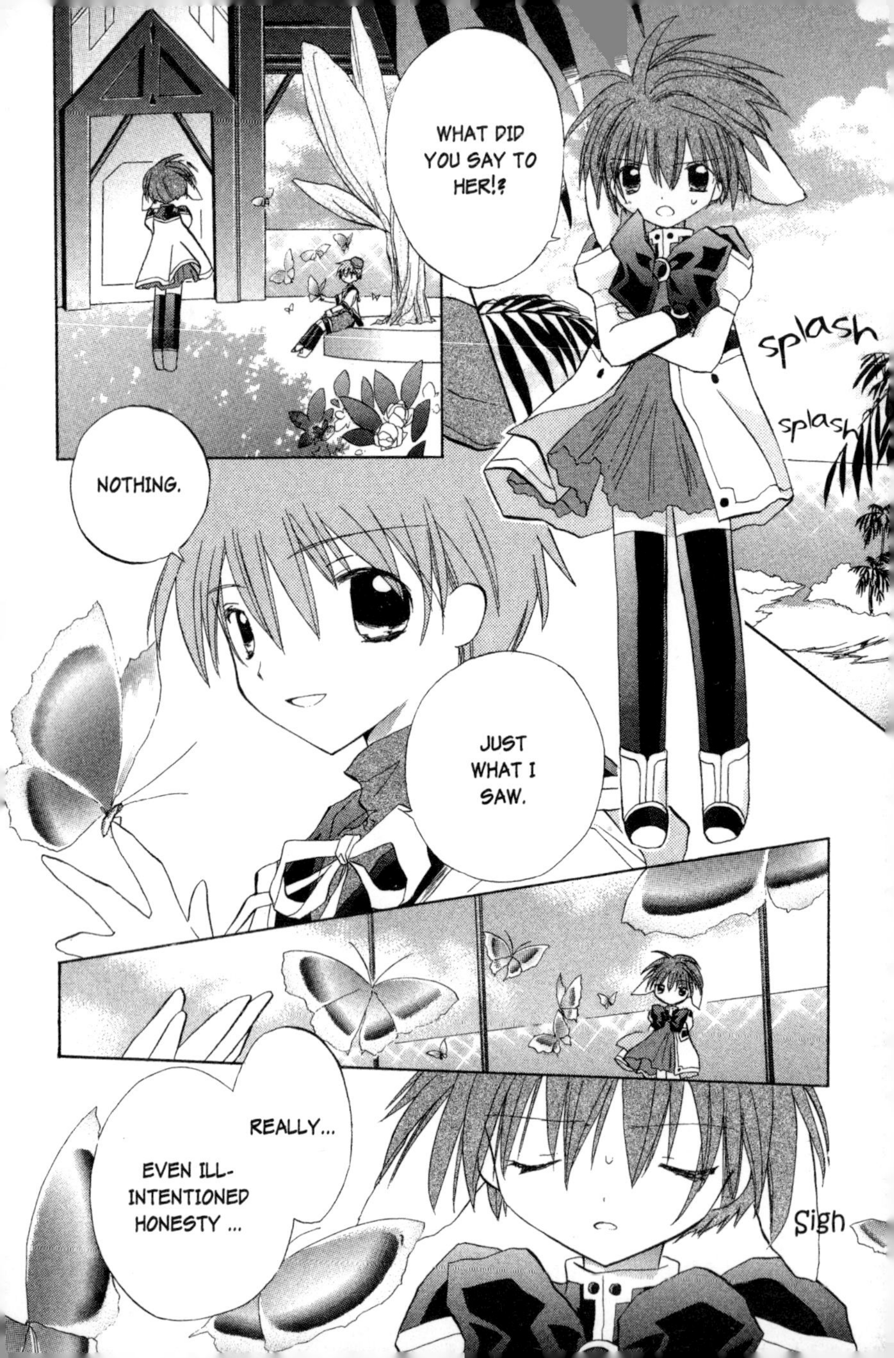
WHAT DID YOU SAY TO HER!?
splash
splash
NOTHING.
JUST WHAT I SAW.
REALLY...
EVEN ILL-INTENTIONED HONESTY ...
Sigh

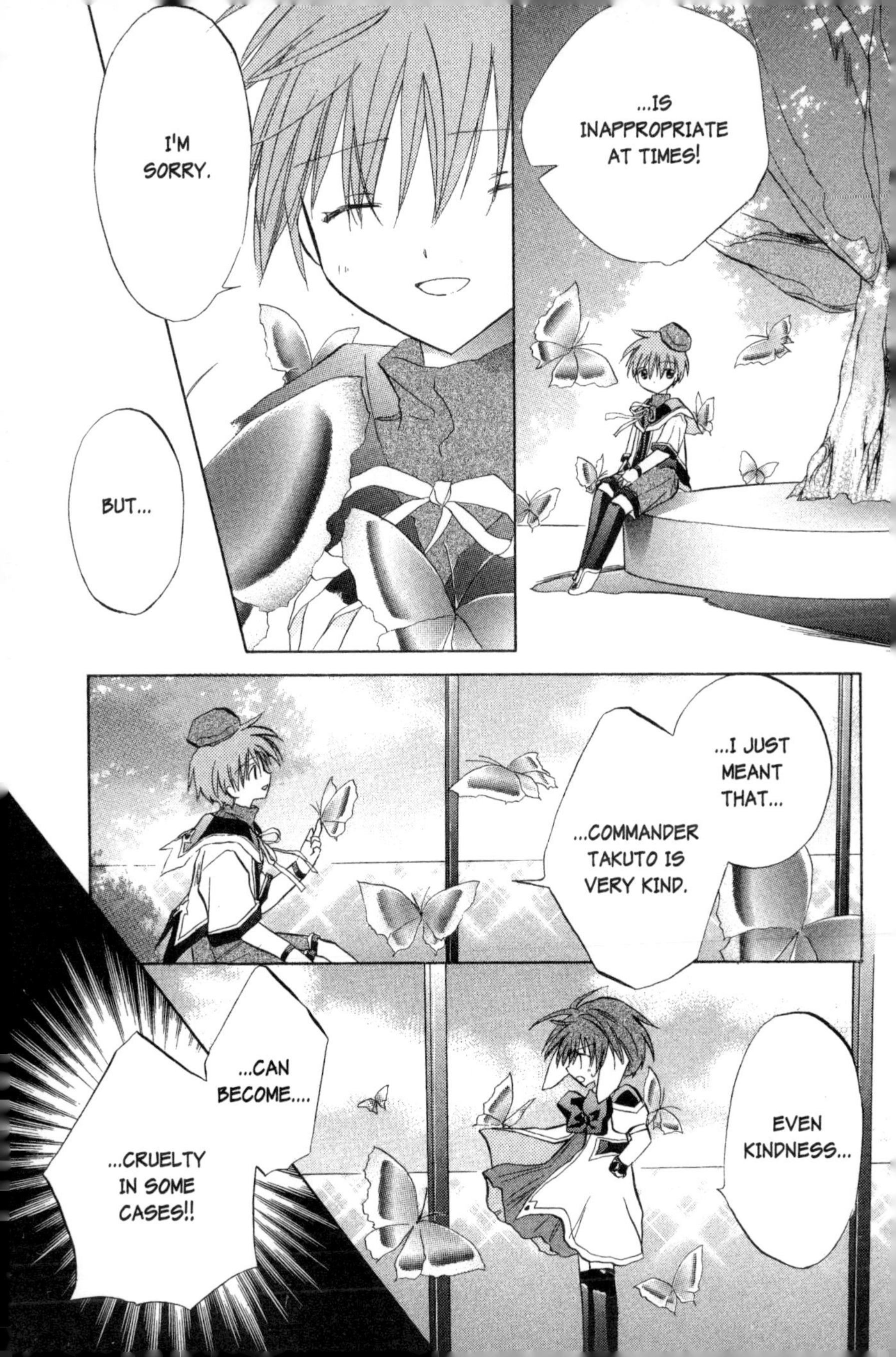
...IS INAPPROPRIATE AT TIMES!
I'M SORRY.
BUT...
...I JUST MEANT THAT...
...COMMANDER TAKUTO IS VERY KIND.
EVEN KINDNESS...
...CAN BECOME....
...CRUELTY IN SOME CASES!!

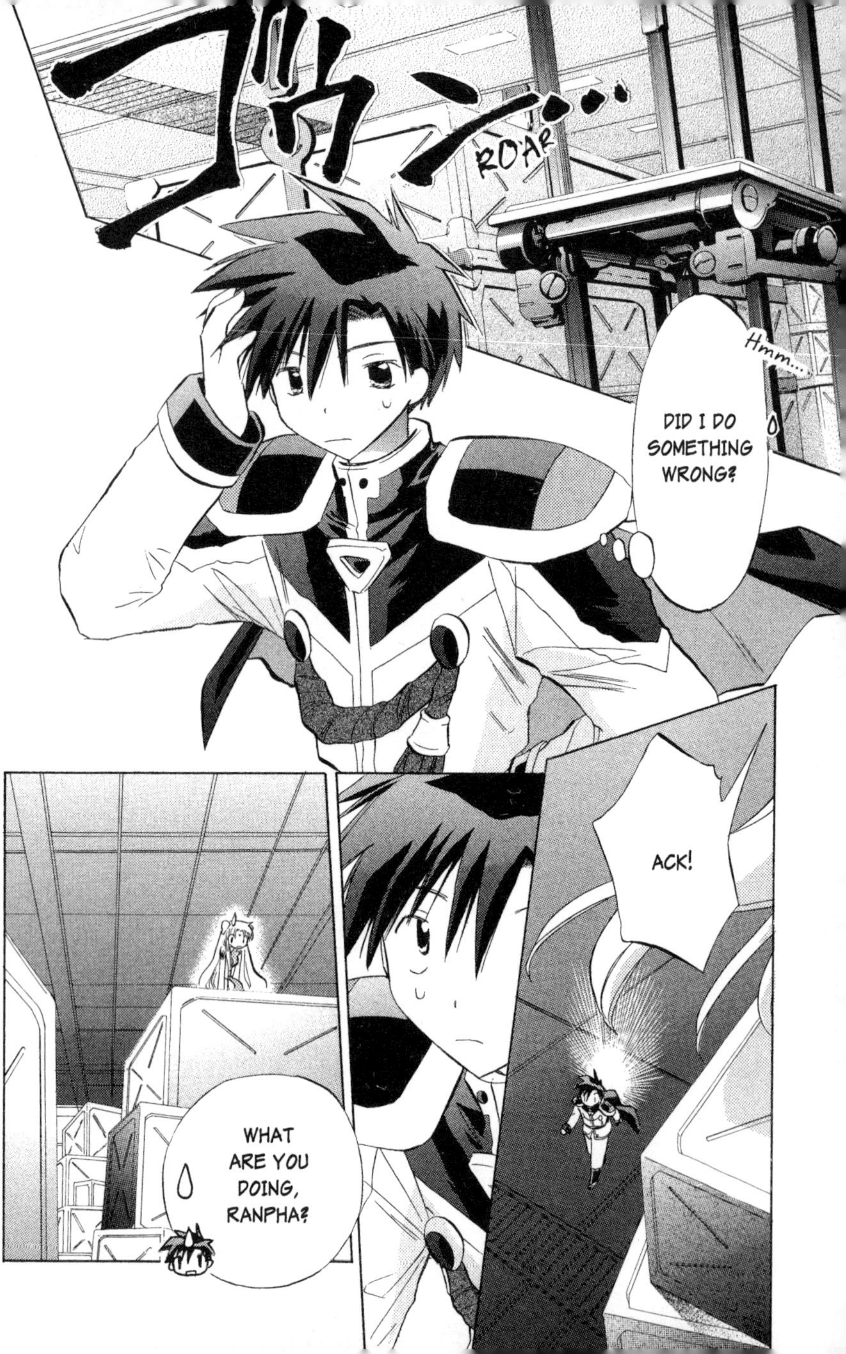
ROAR
Hmm...
DID I DO SOMETHING WRONG?
ACK!
WHAT ARE YOU DOING, RANPHA?

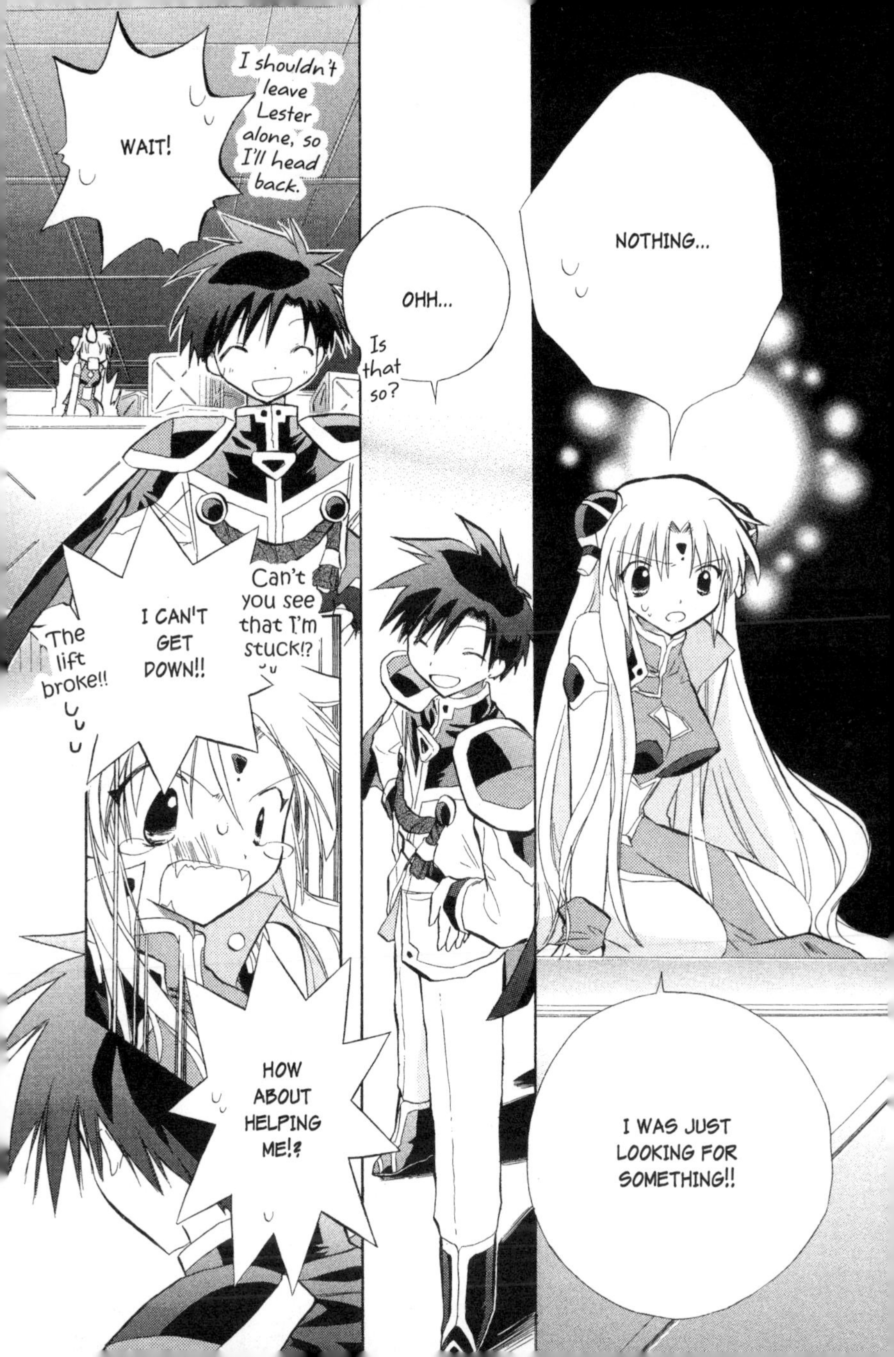
NOTHING...
I WAS JUST LOOKING FOR SOMETHING!!
OHH...
Is that so?
I shouldn't leave Lester alone, so I'll head back.
WAIT!
Can't you see that I'm stuck!?
I CAN'T GET DOWN!!
The lift broke!!
HOW ABOUT HELPING ME!?

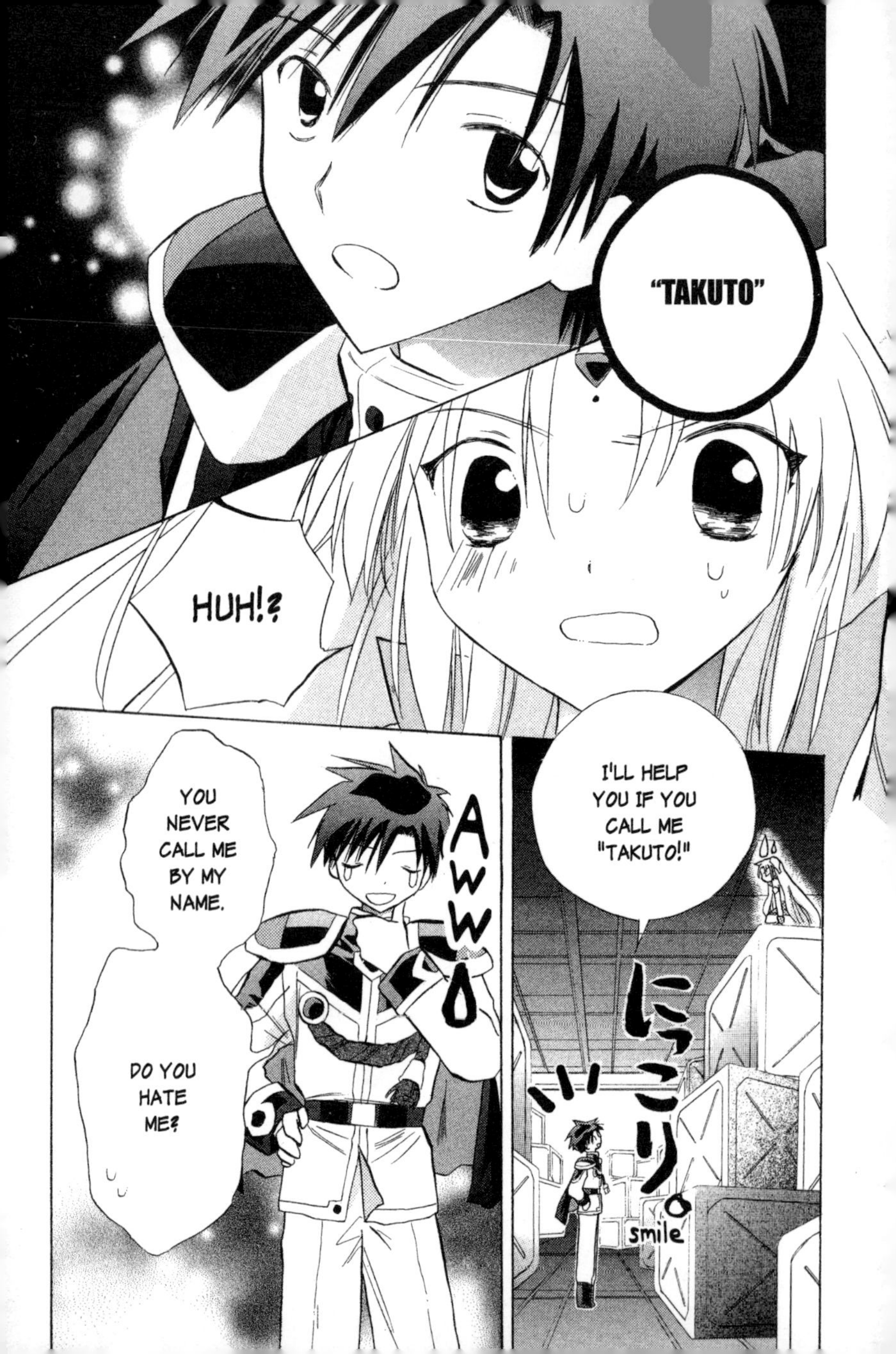
"TAKUTO"
HUH!?
I'LL HELP YOU IF YOU CALL ME "TAKUTO!"
にっこり
smile
YOU NEVER CALL ME BY MY NAME.
DO YOU HATE ME?
AWWW

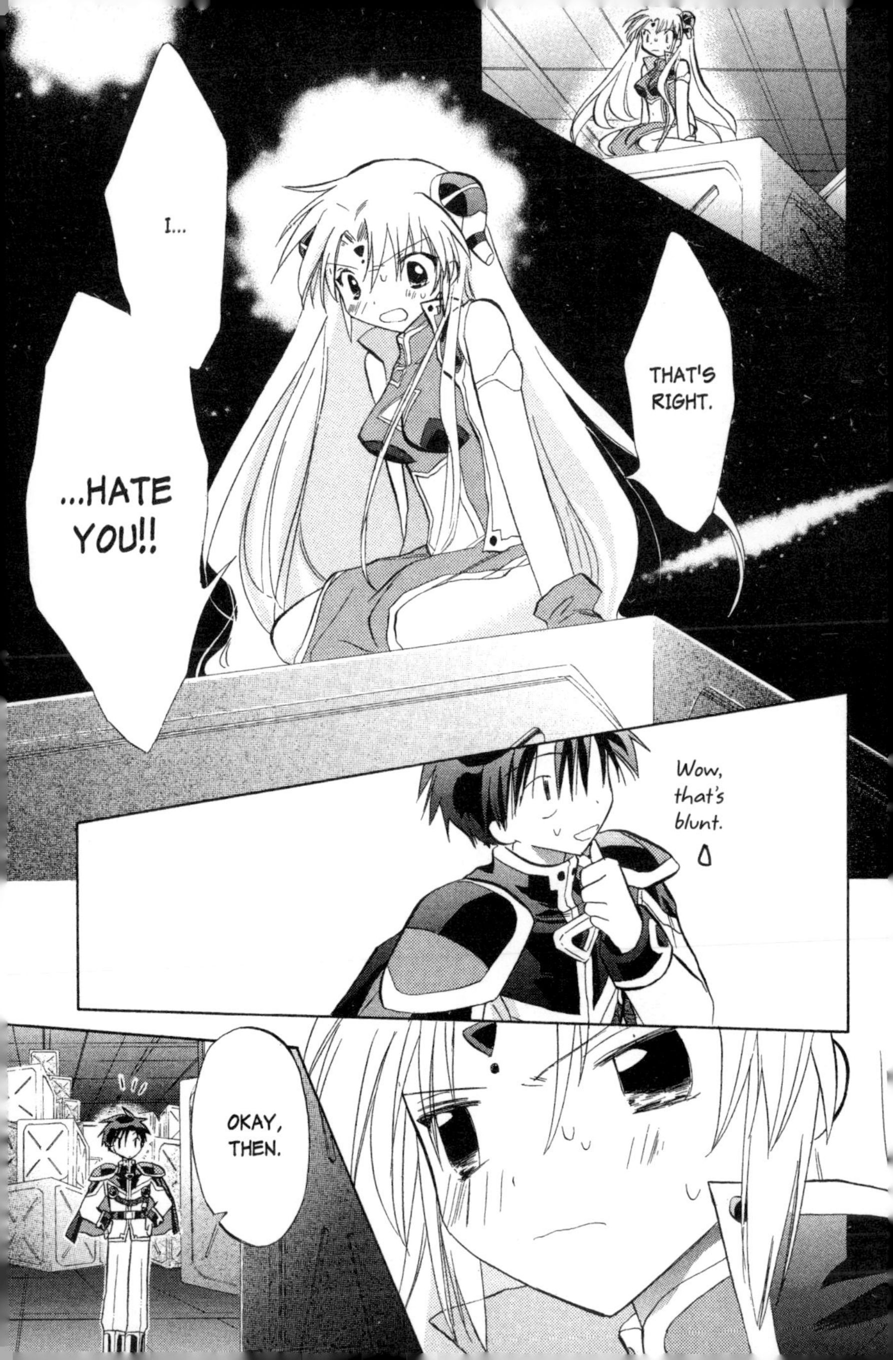
THAT'S RIGHT.
I...
...HATE YOU!!
Wow, that's blunt.
OKAY, THEN.

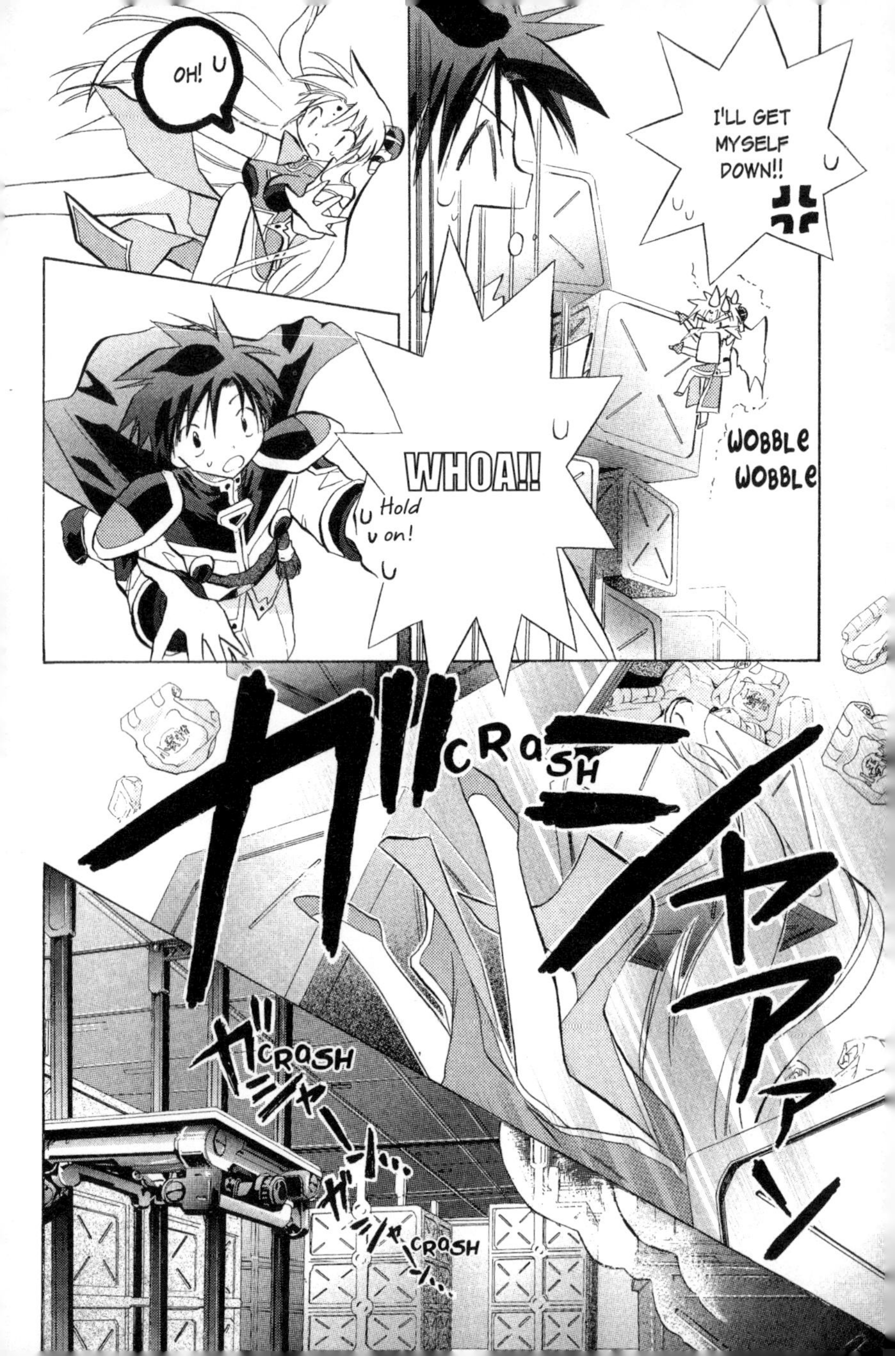

I'LL GET MYSELF DOWN!!
WOBBLE WOBBLE
OH!
WHOA!!
Hold on!
CRASH
CRASH
CRASH

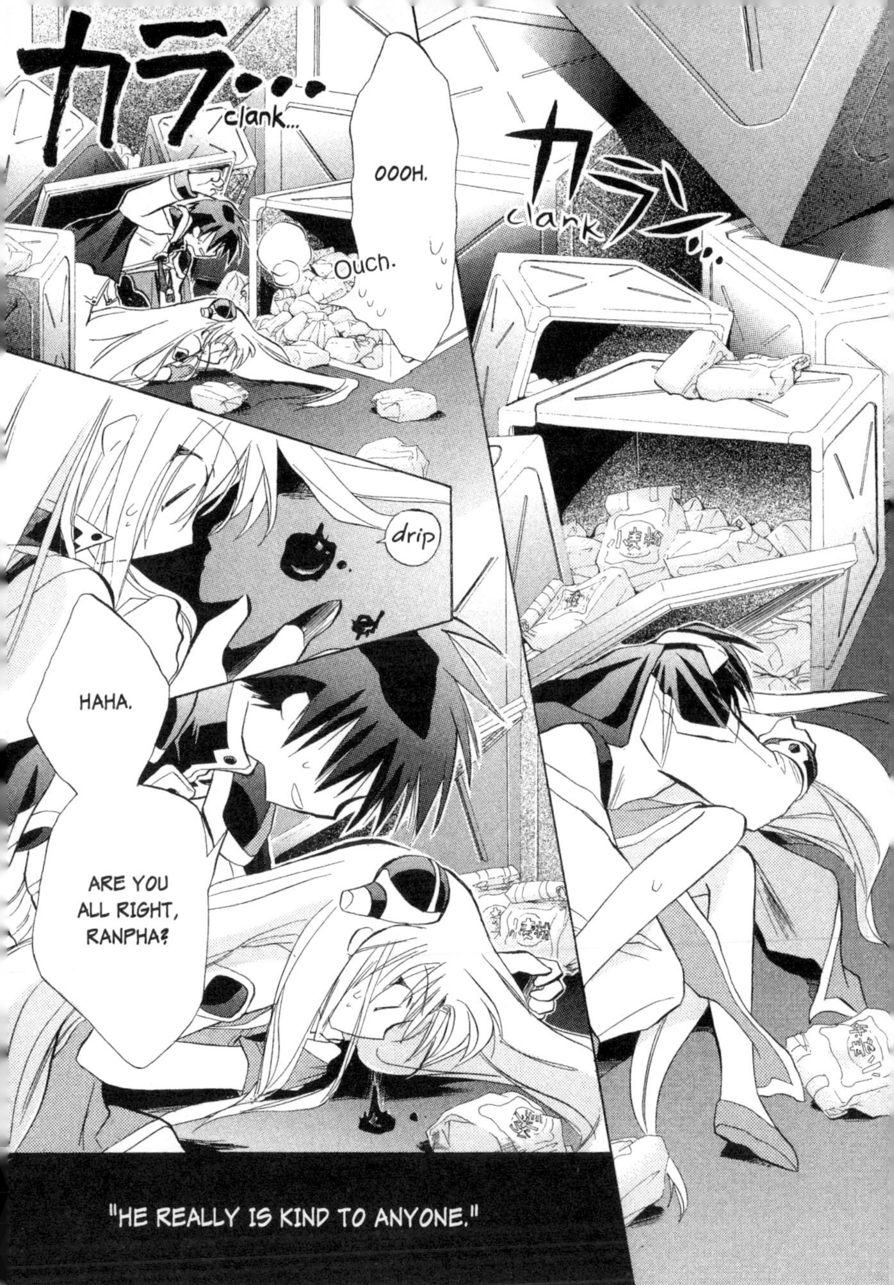

カラン…
clank
カラ…
clank…
OOOH.
Ouch.
drip
HAHA.
ARE YOU ALL RIGHT, RANPHA?
"HE REALLY IS KIND TO ANYONE."

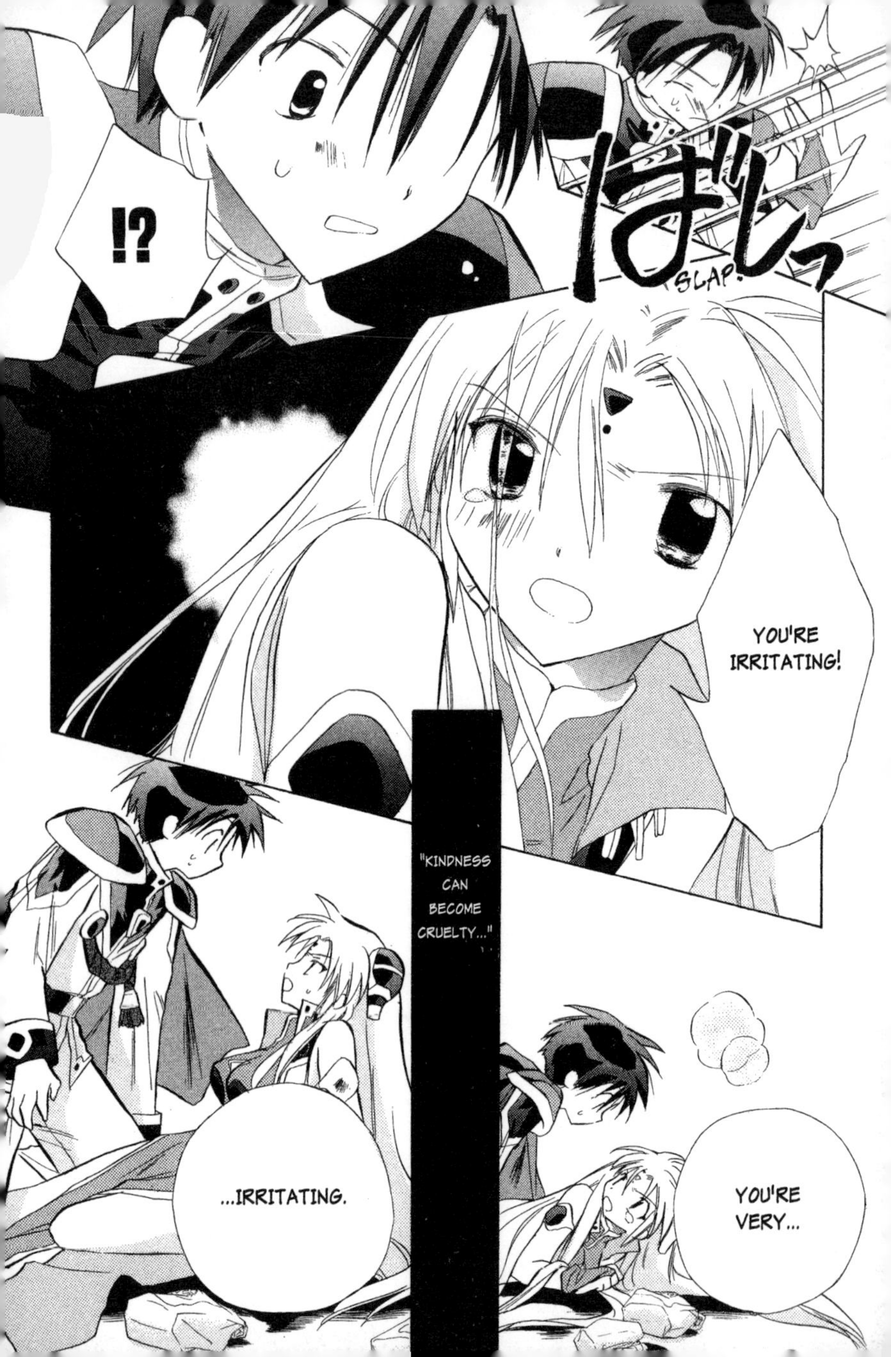
ばしっ
SLAP!
!?
YOU'RE IRRITATING!
"KINDNESS CAN BECOME CRUELTY..."
YOU'RE VERY...
...IRRITATING.

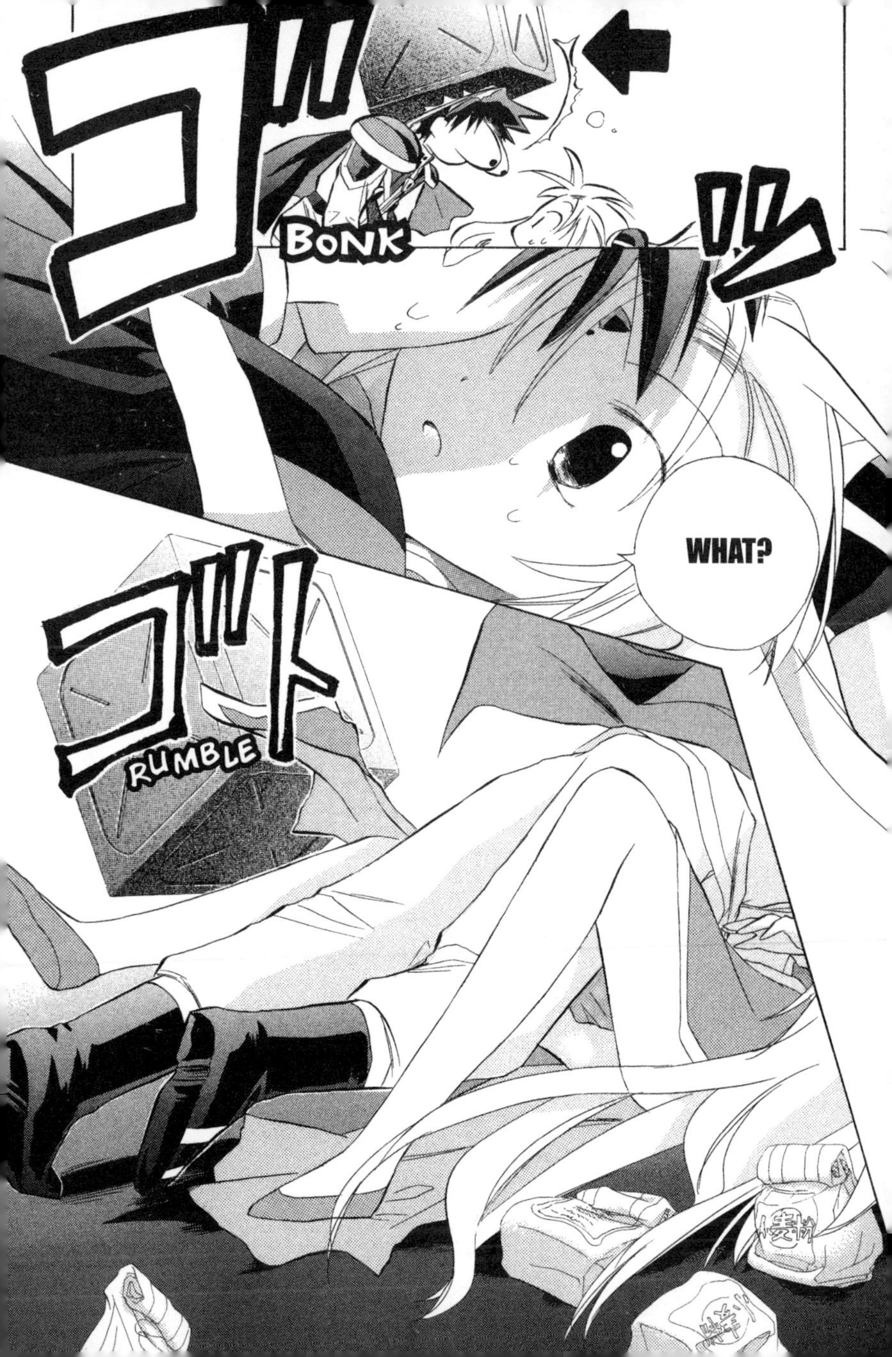
BONK
WHAT?
RUMBLE

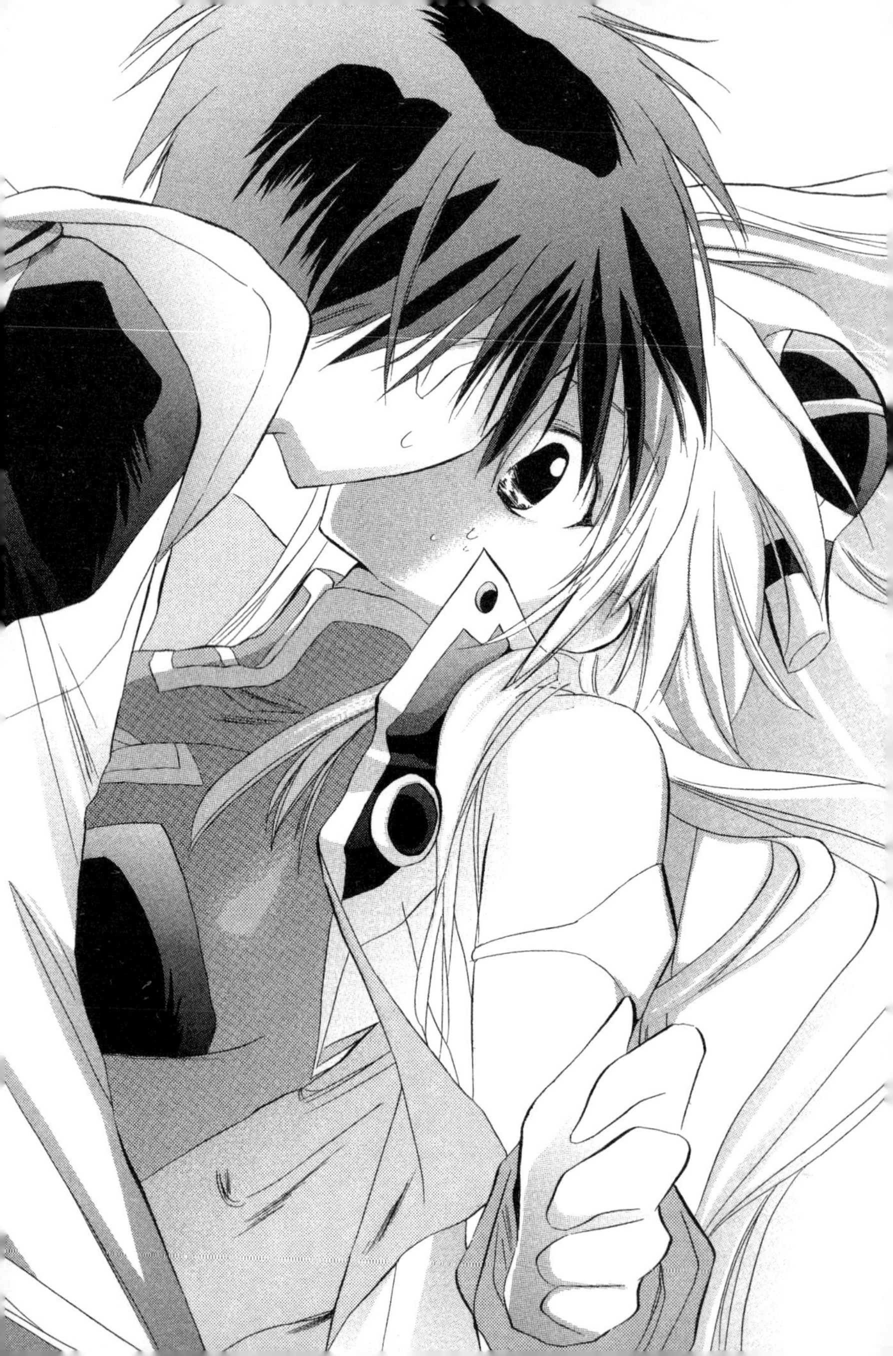

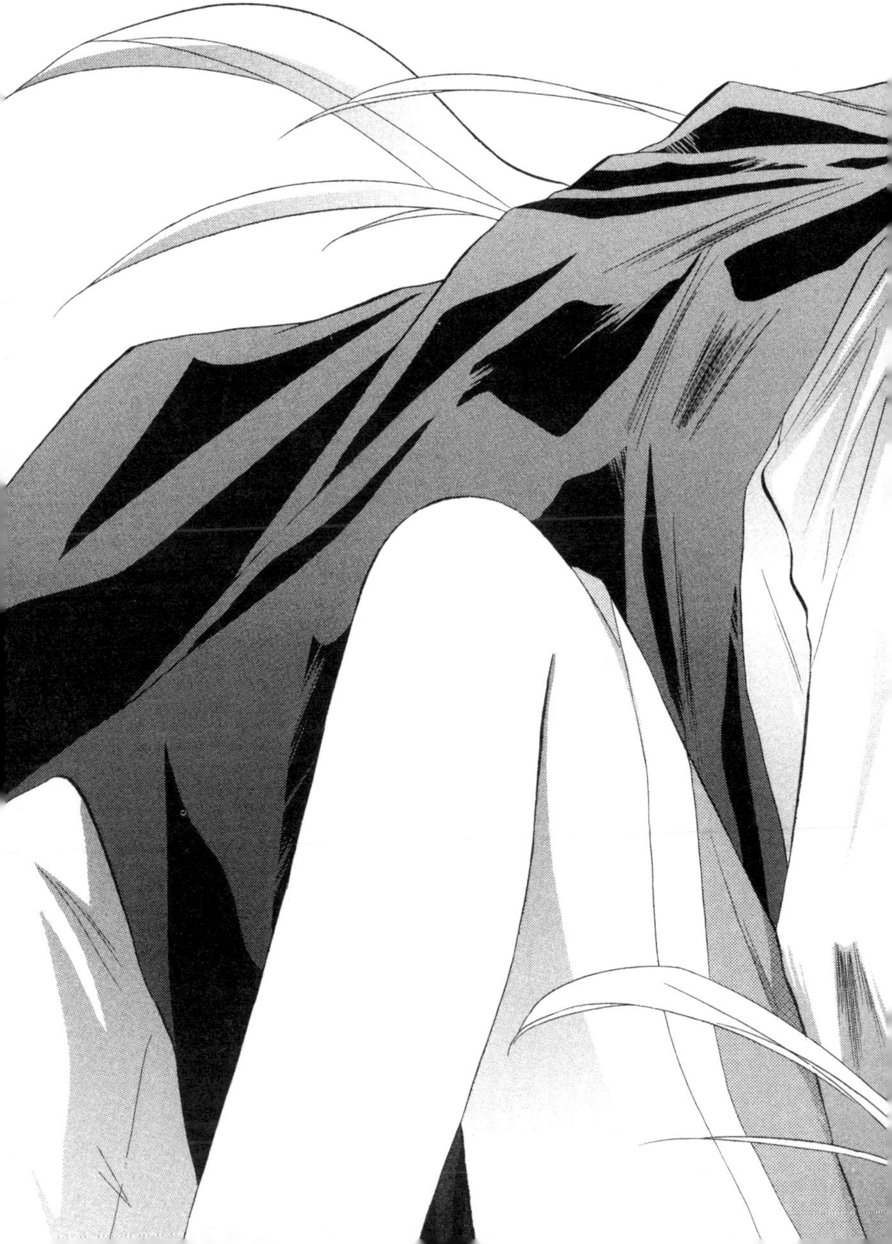

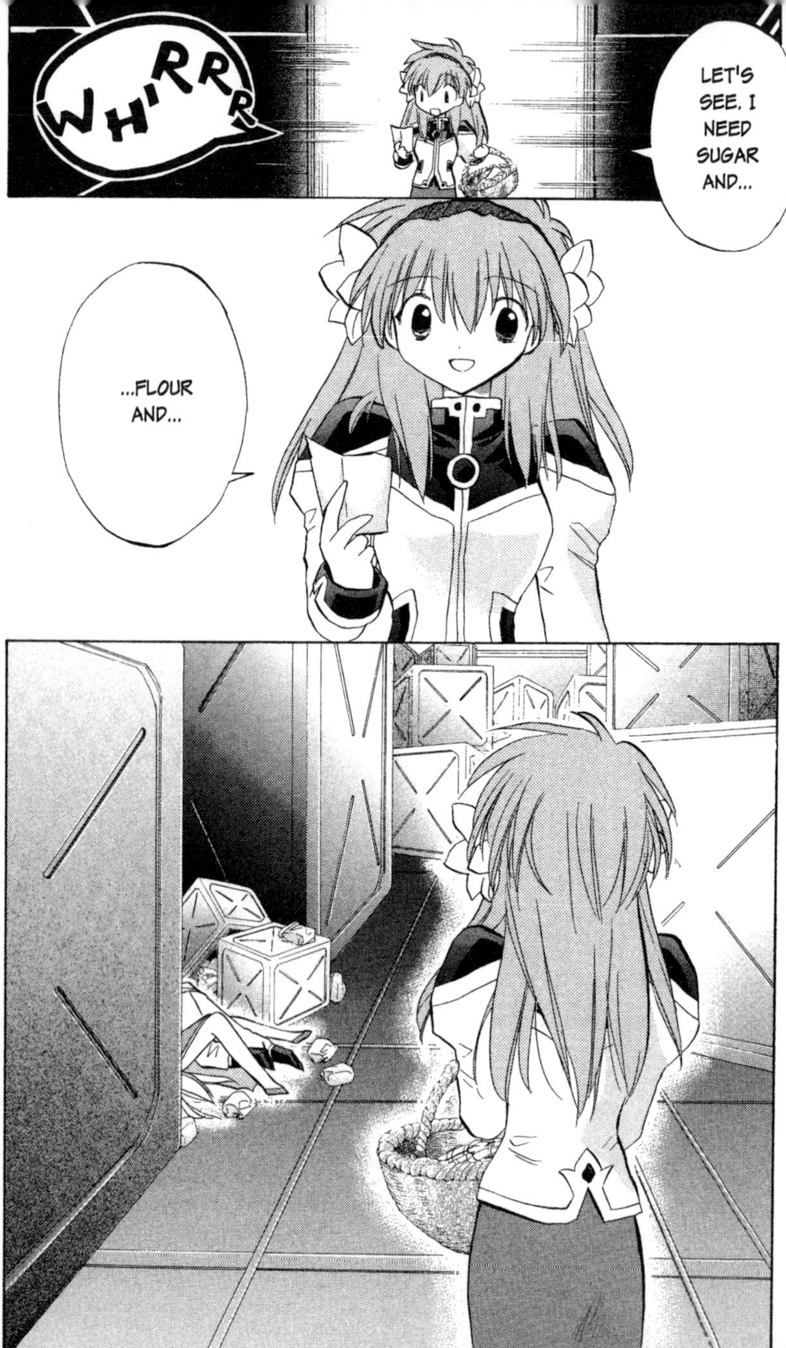
LET'S SEE. I NEED SUGAR AND...
WHIRRR
...FLOUR AND...

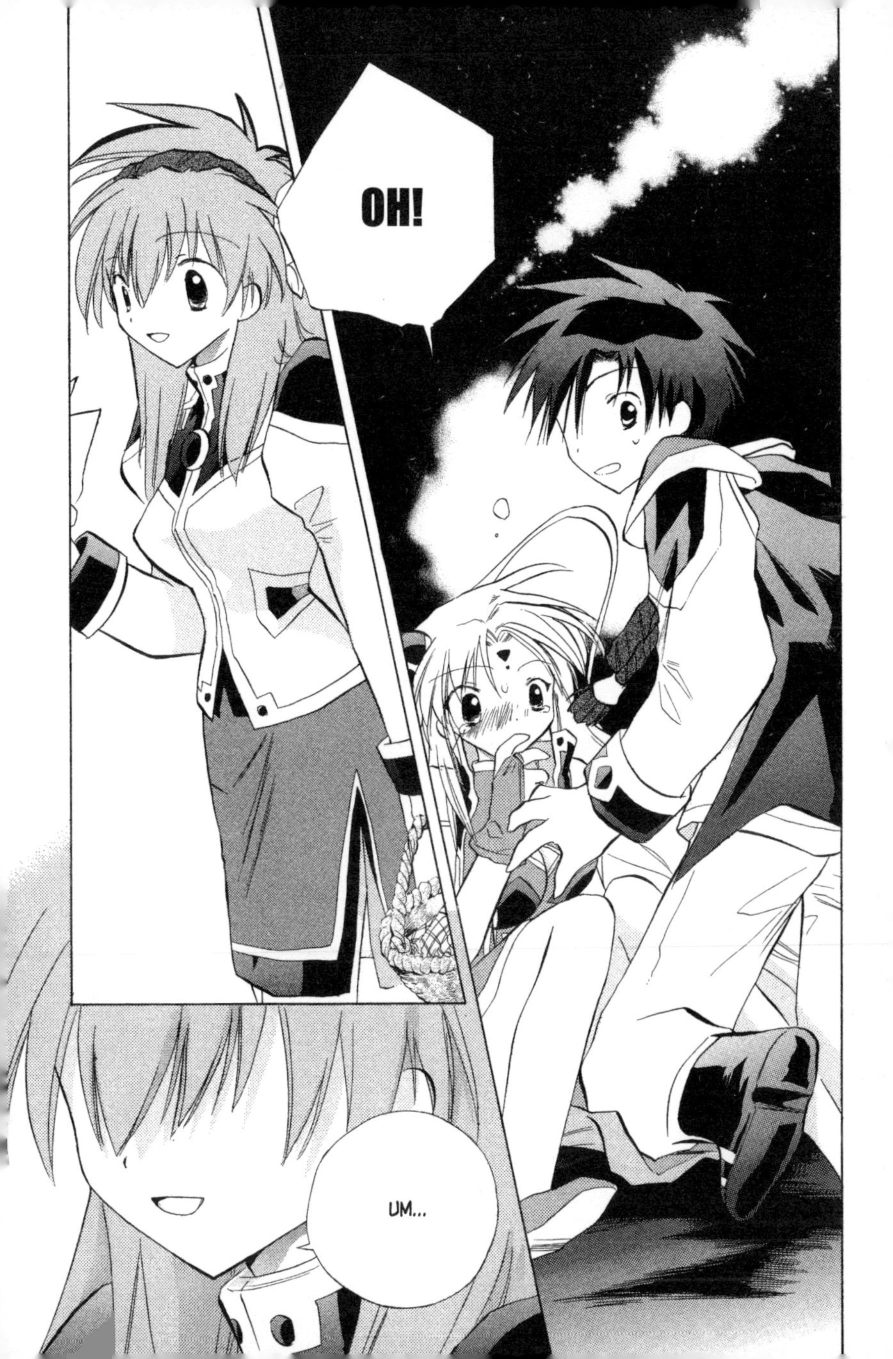
OH!
UM...

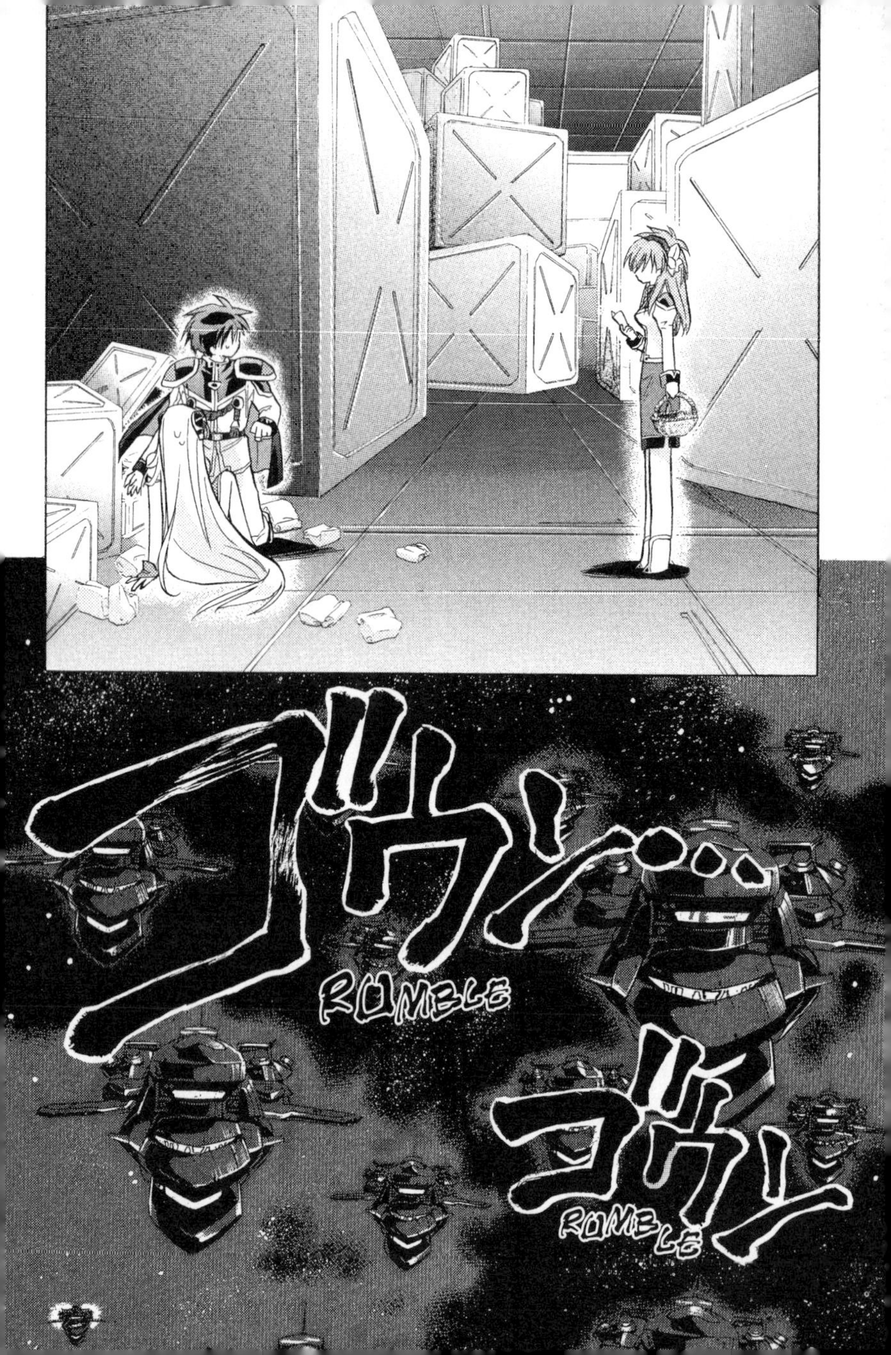
ゴウン…
RUMBLE
ゴウン
RUMBLE

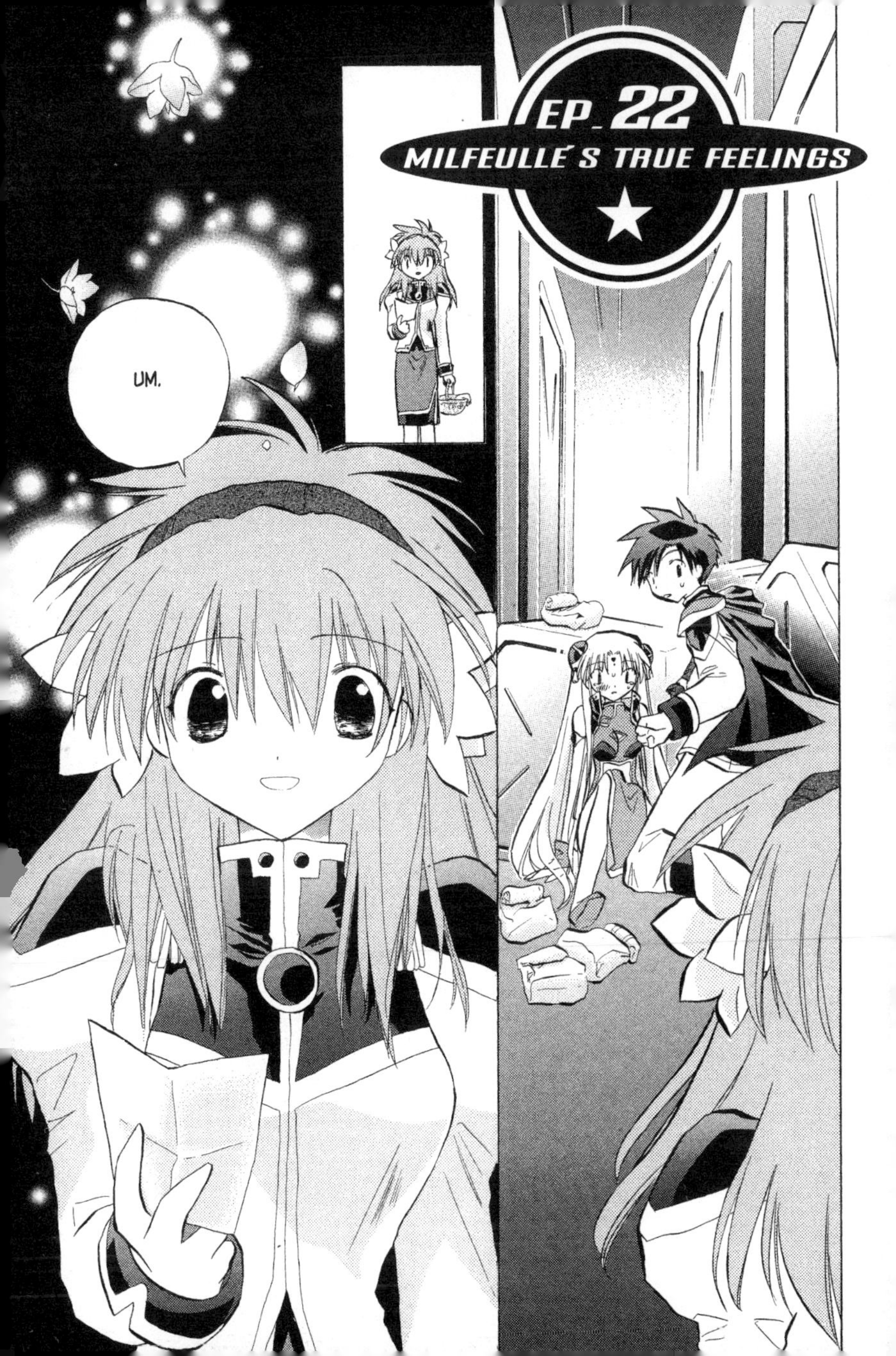
EP_22
MILFEULLE'S TRUE FEELINGS
UM.

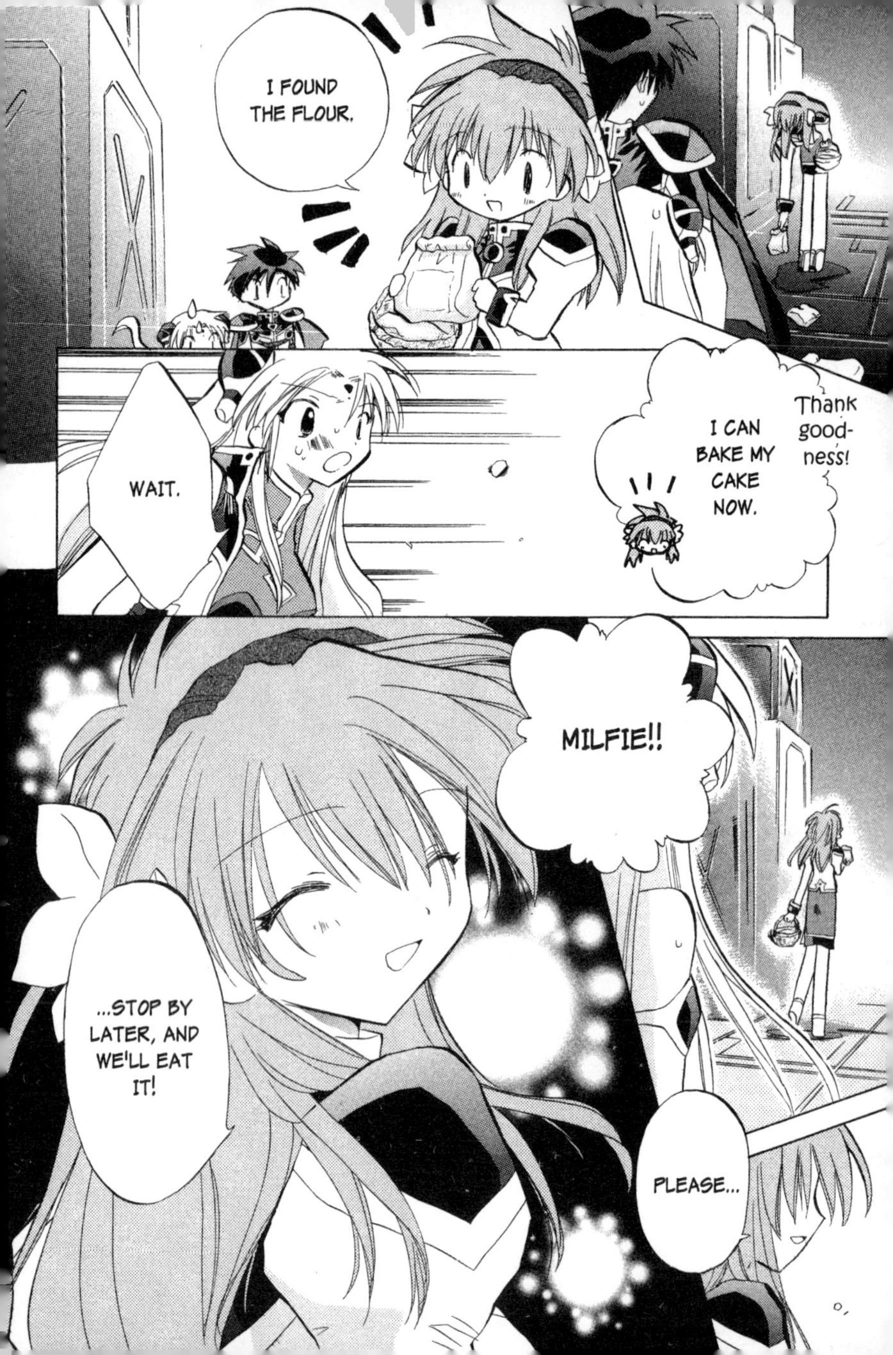
I FOUND THE FLOUR.
Thank goodness!
I CAN BAKE MY CAKE NOW.
WAIT.
MILFIE!!
PLEASE...
...STOP BY LATER, AND WE'LL EAT IT!

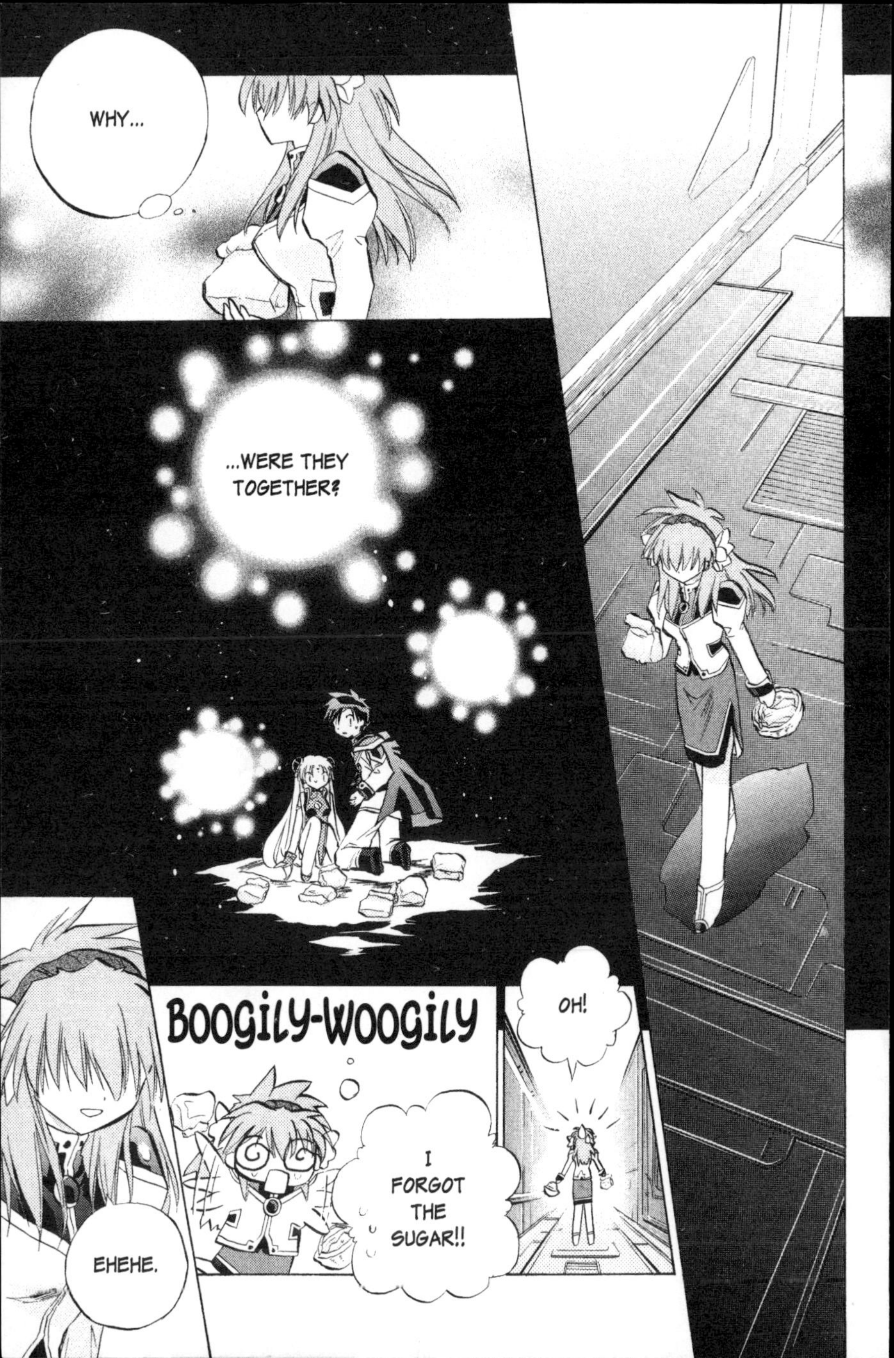
WHY...
...WERE THEY TOGETHER?
OH!
BOOGILY-WOOGILY
I FORGOT THE SUGAR!!
EHEHE.

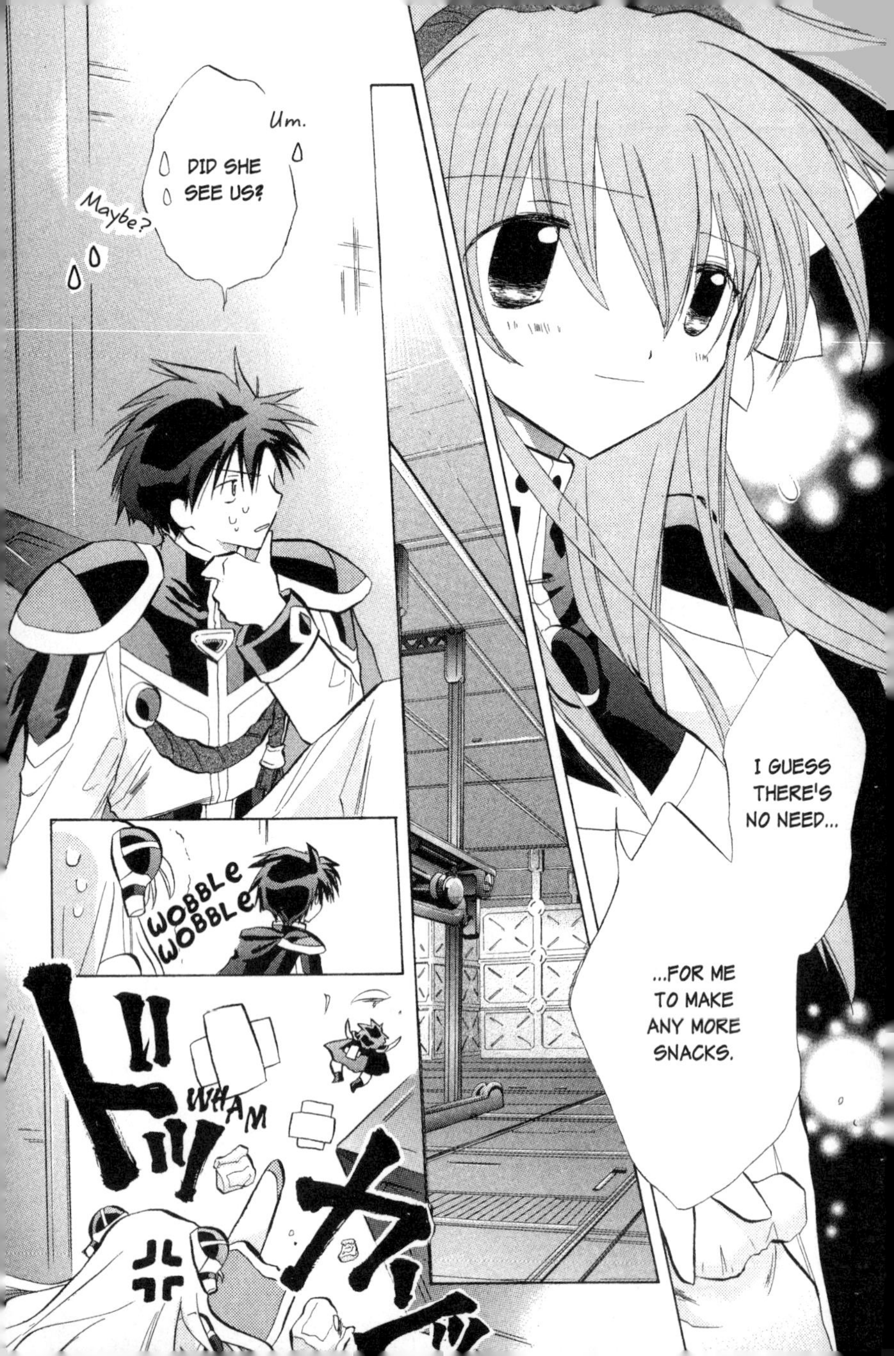
I GUESS THERE'S NO NEED...
...FOR ME TO MAKE ANY MORE SNACKS.
Um.
DID SHE SEE US?
Maybe?
WOBBLE WOBBLE
WHAM

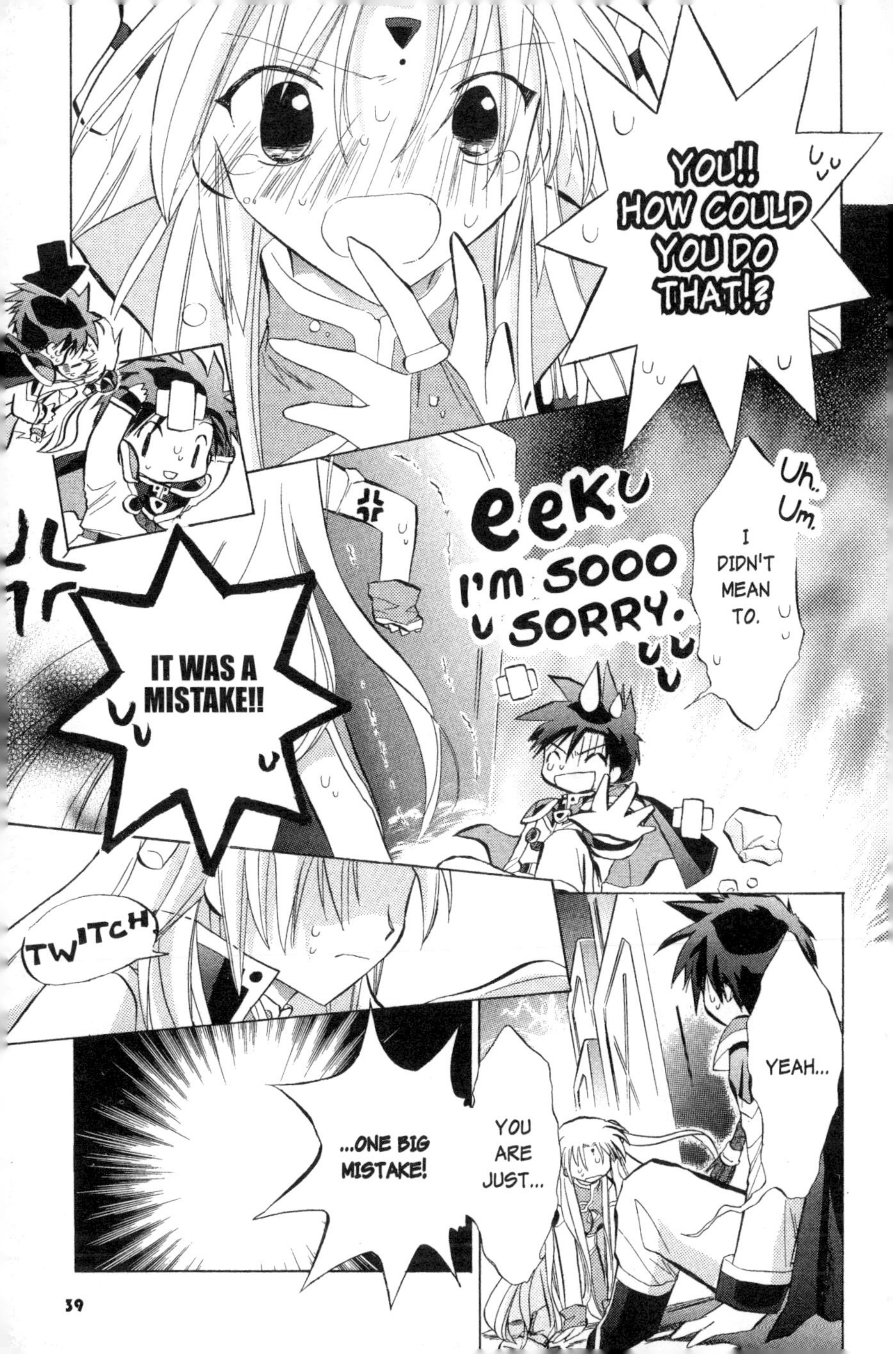
YOU!! HOW COULD YOU DO THAT!?
Uh.. Um.
I DIDN'T MEAN TO.
eek I'm SOOO SORRY.
IT WAS A MISTAKE!!
YEAH...
TWITCH
YOU ARE JUST...
...ONE BIG MISTAKE!

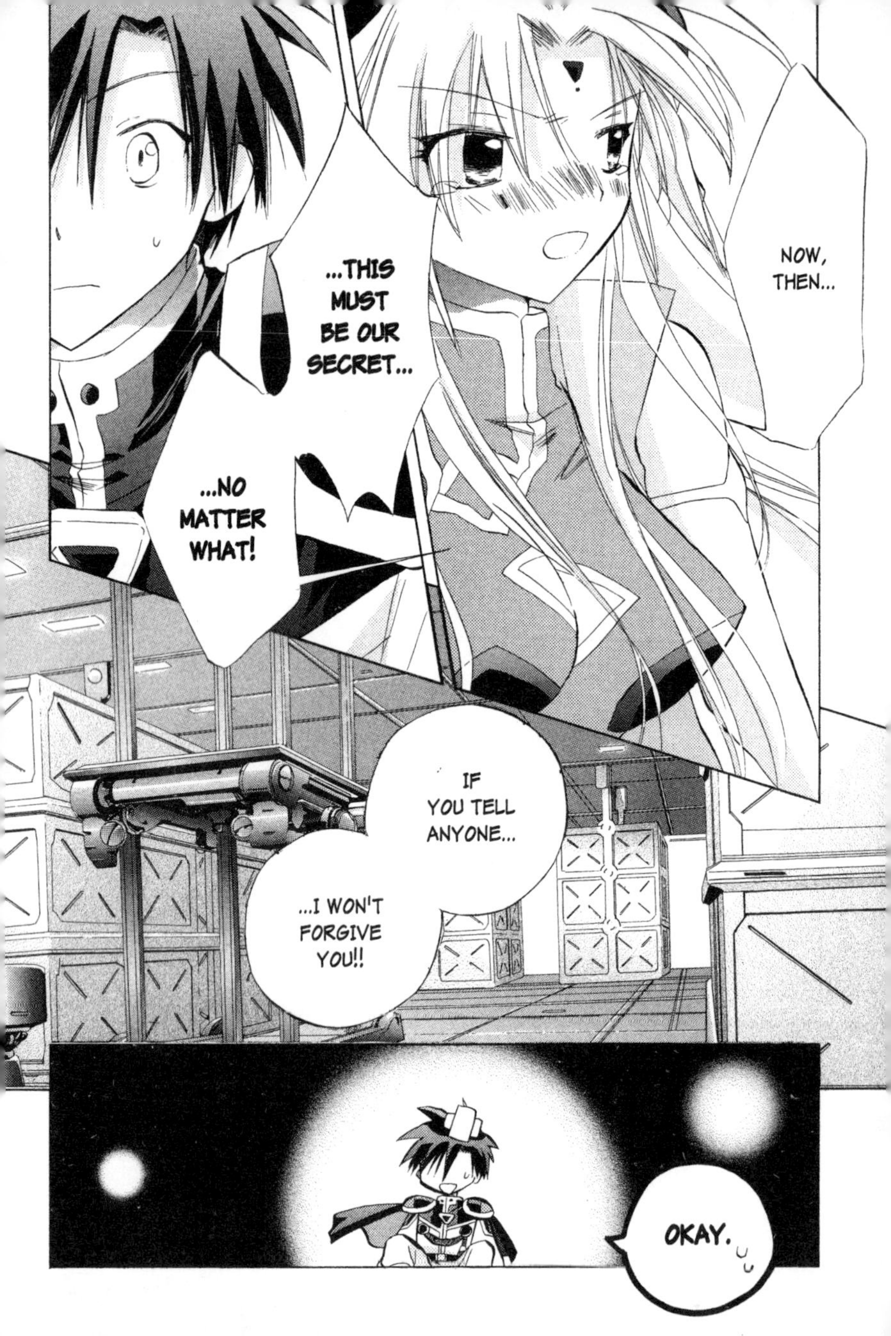
NOW, THEN...
...THIS MUST BE OUR SECRET...
...NO MATTER WHAT!
IF YOU TELL ANYONE...
...I WON'T FORGIVE YOU!!
OKAY.

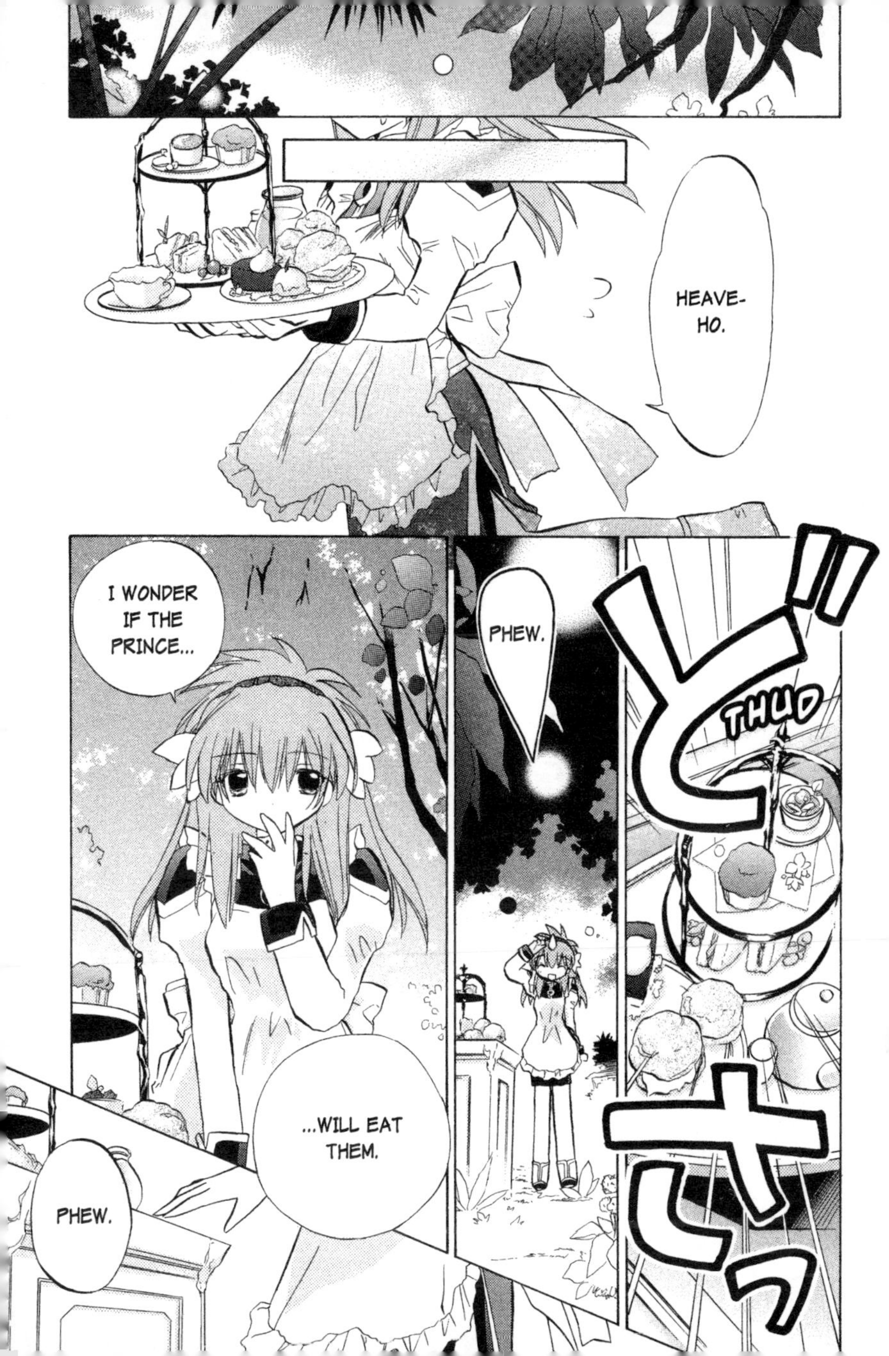
HEAVE-HO.
どさっ
THUD
PHEW.
I WONDER IF THE PRINCE...
...WILL EAT THEM.
PHEW.

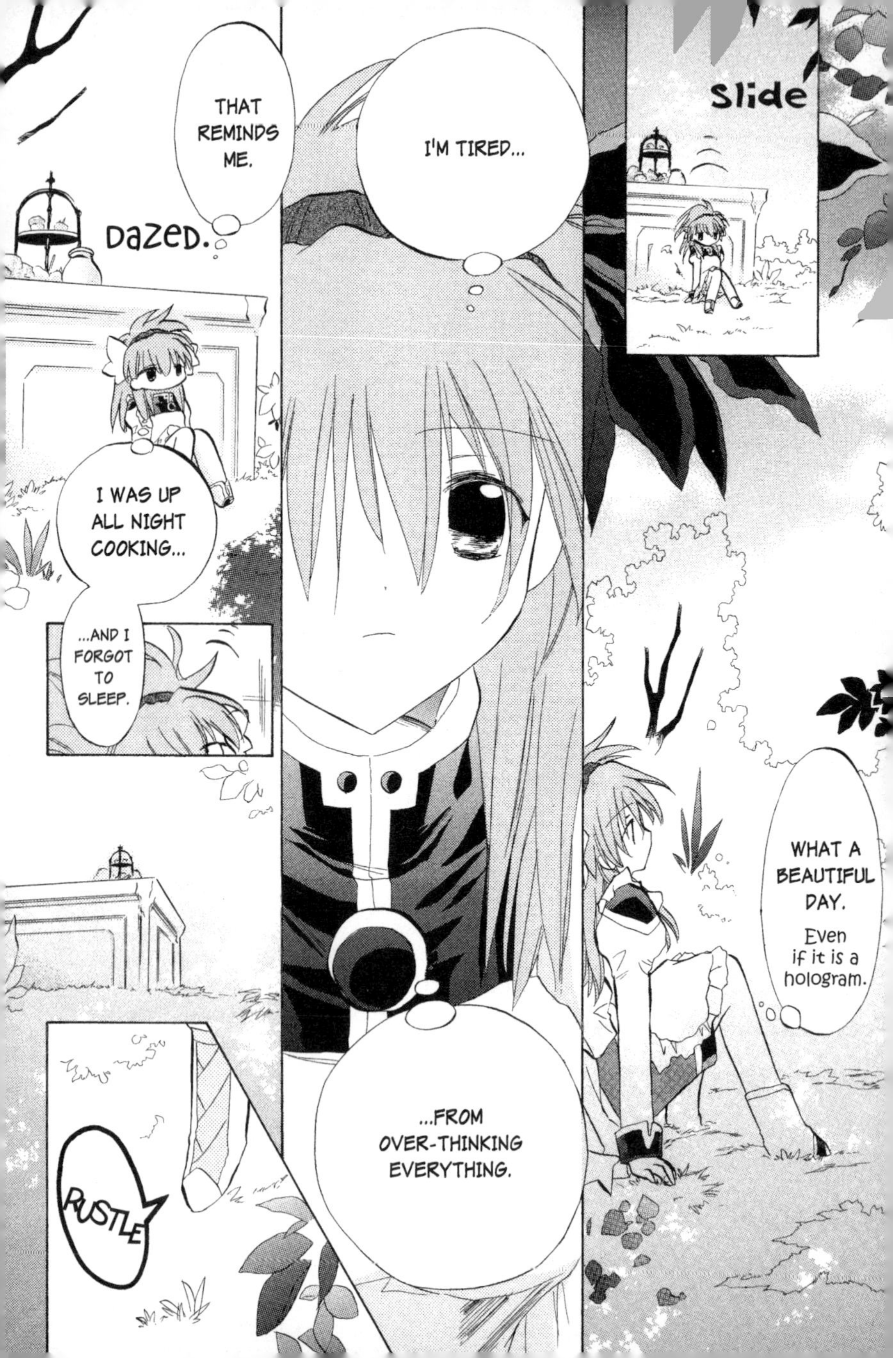

Slide
WHAT A BEAUTIFUL DAY.
Even if it is a hologram.
I'M TIRED...
...FROM OVER-THINKING EVERYTHING.
THAT REMINDS ME.
Dazed.
I WAS UP ALL NIGHT COOKING...
...AND I FORGOT TO SLEEP.
RUSTLE

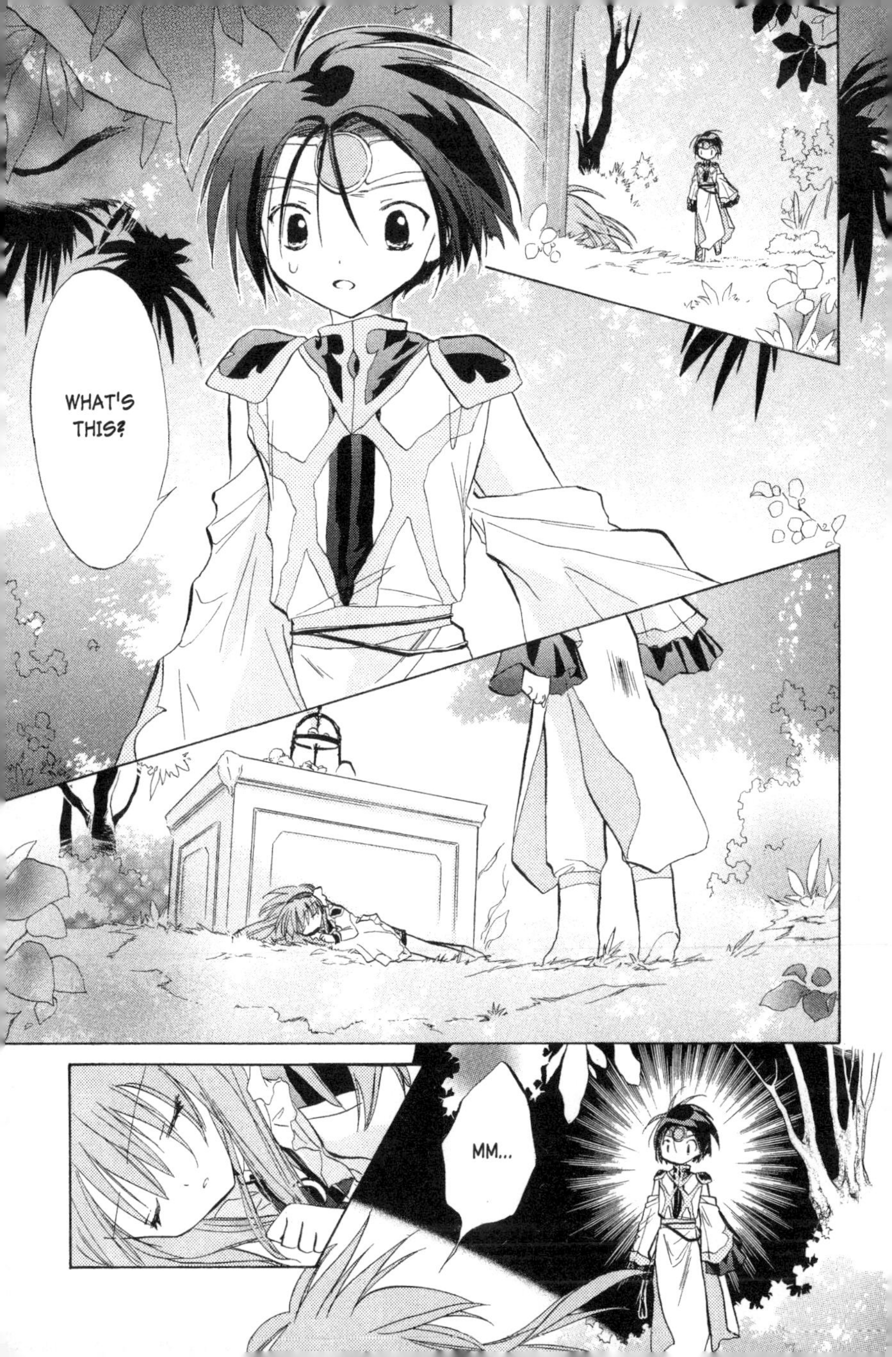
WHAT'S THIS?
MM...

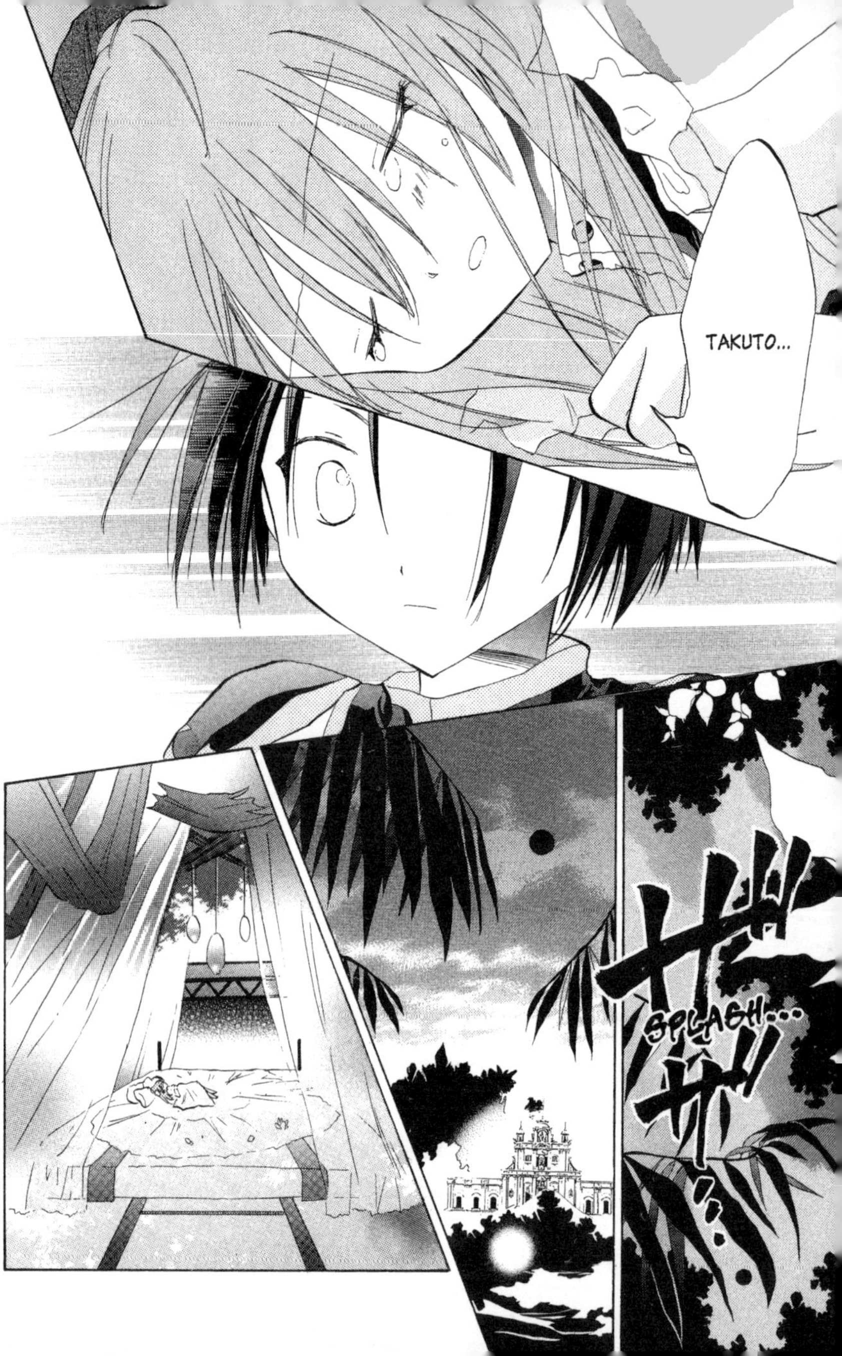
TAKUTO...
SPLASH...

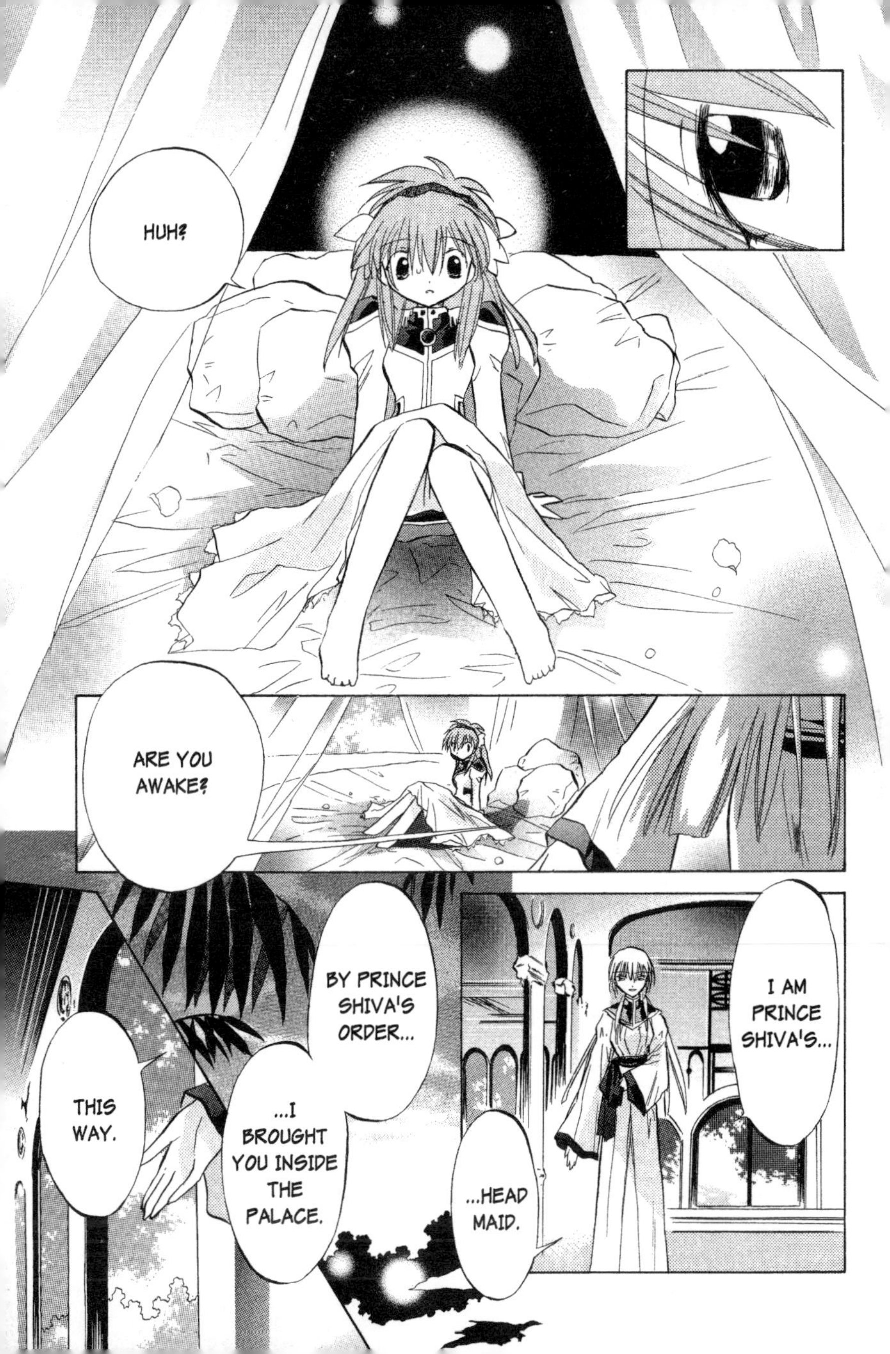
HUH?
ARE YOU AWAKE?
I AM PRINCE SHIVA'S...
...HEAD MAID.
BY PRINCE SHIVA'S ORDER...
...I BROUGHT YOU INSIDE THE PALACE.
THIS WAY.

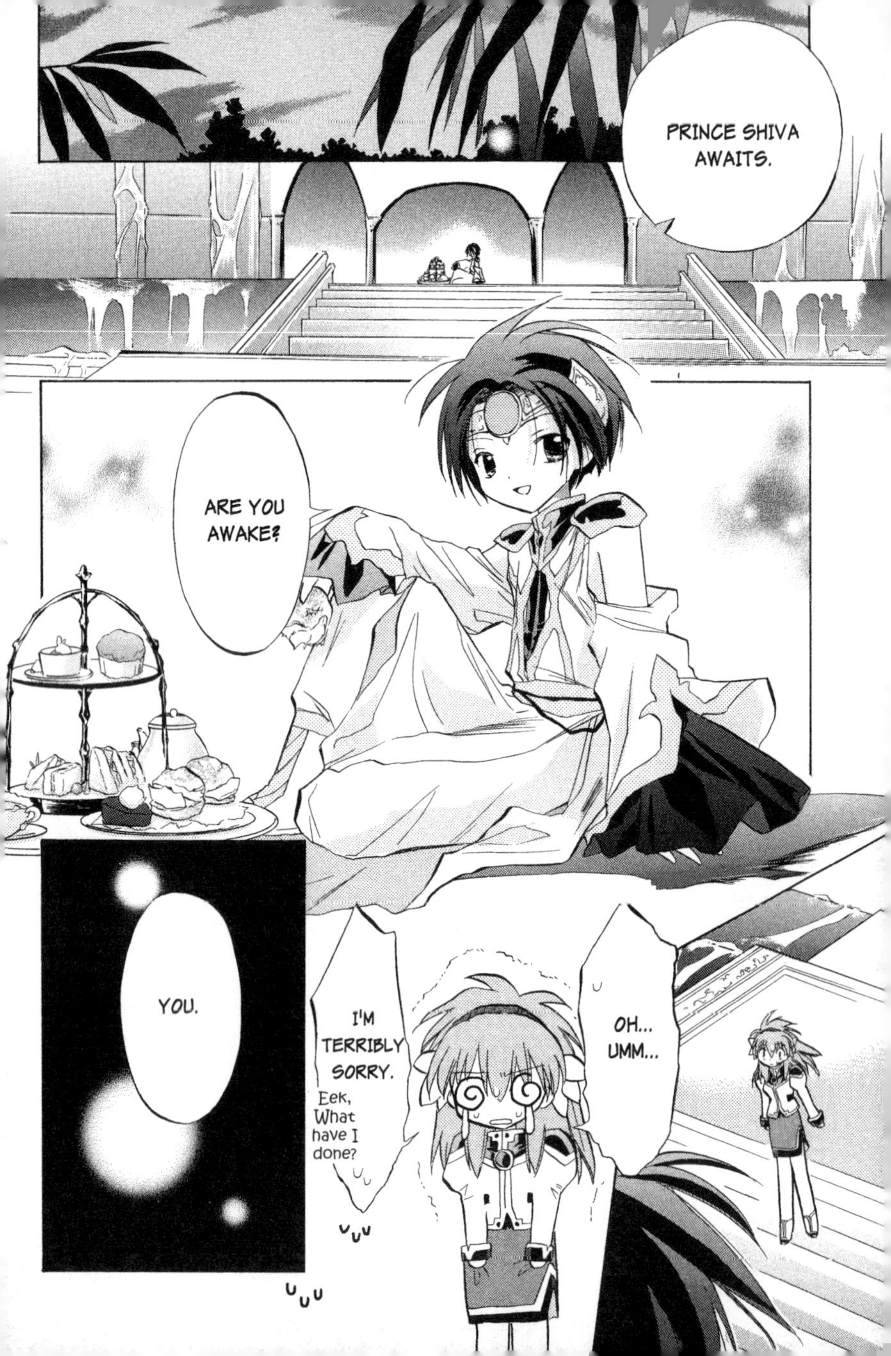
PRINCE SHIVA AWAITS.
ARE YOU AWAKE?
OH... UMM...
I'M TERRIBLY SORRY.
Eek, What have I done?
YOU.

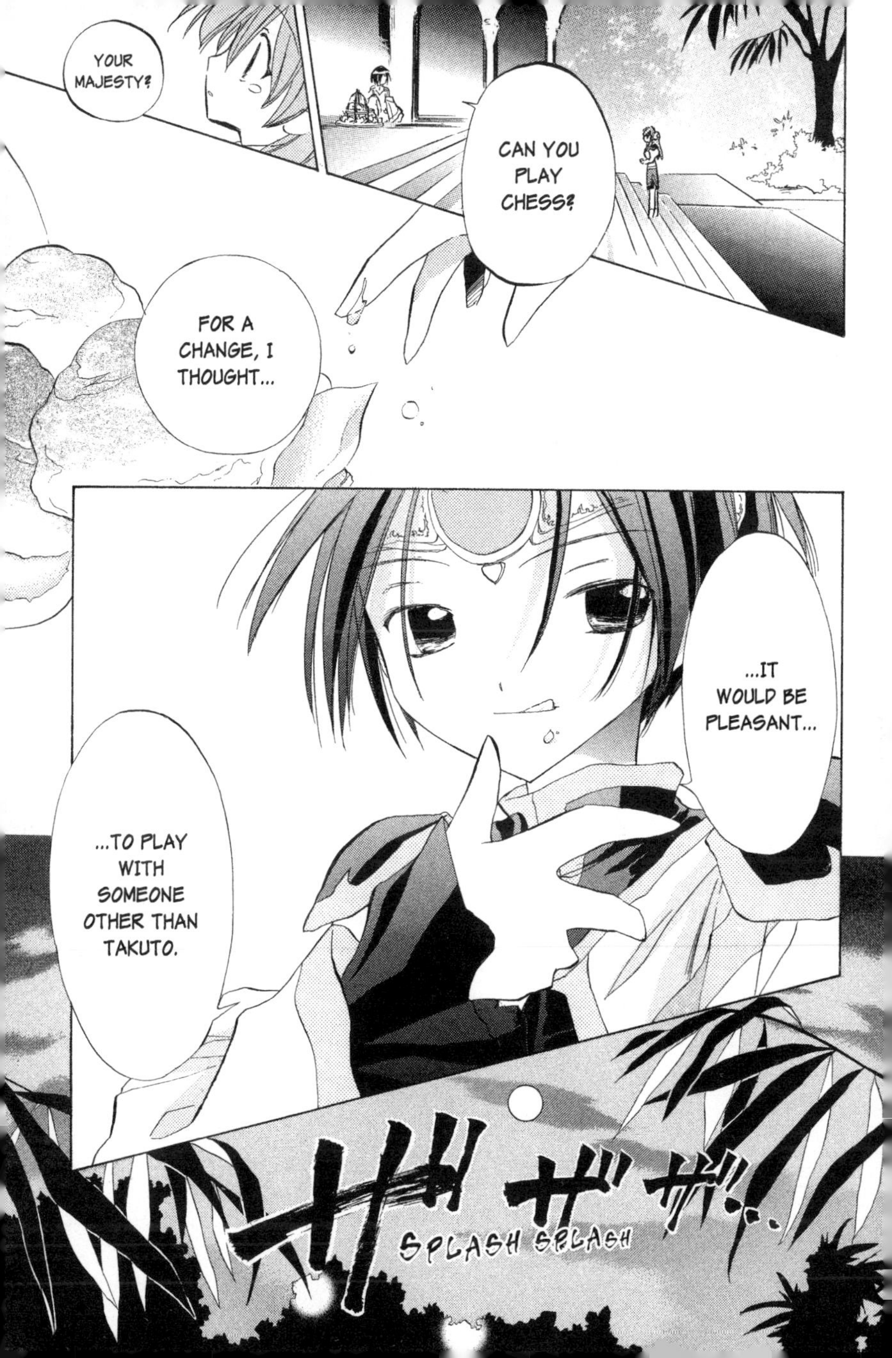

YOUR MAJESTY?
CAN YOU PLAY CHESS?
FOR A CHANGE, I THOUGHT...
...IT WOULD BE PLEASANT...
...TO PLAY WITH SOMEONE OTHER THAN TAKUTO.
ザザザ...
SPLASH SPLASH

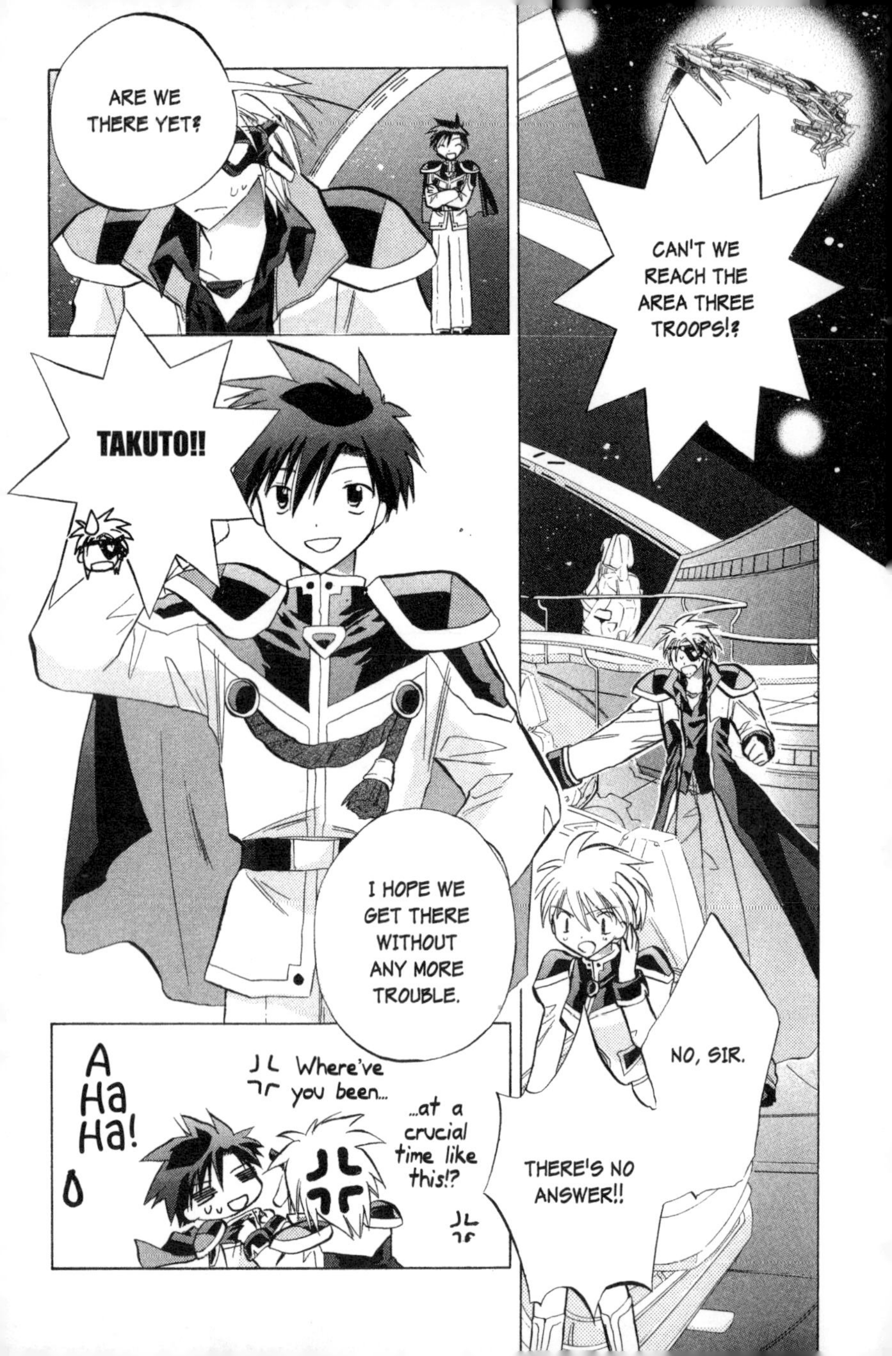
CAN'T WE REACH THE AREA THREE TROOPS!?
NO, SIR.
THERE'S NO ANSWER!!
ARE WE THERE YET?
TAKUTO!!
I HOPE WE GET THERE WITHOUT ANY MORE TROUBLE.
Where've you been...
...at a crucial time like this!?
A Ha Ha!

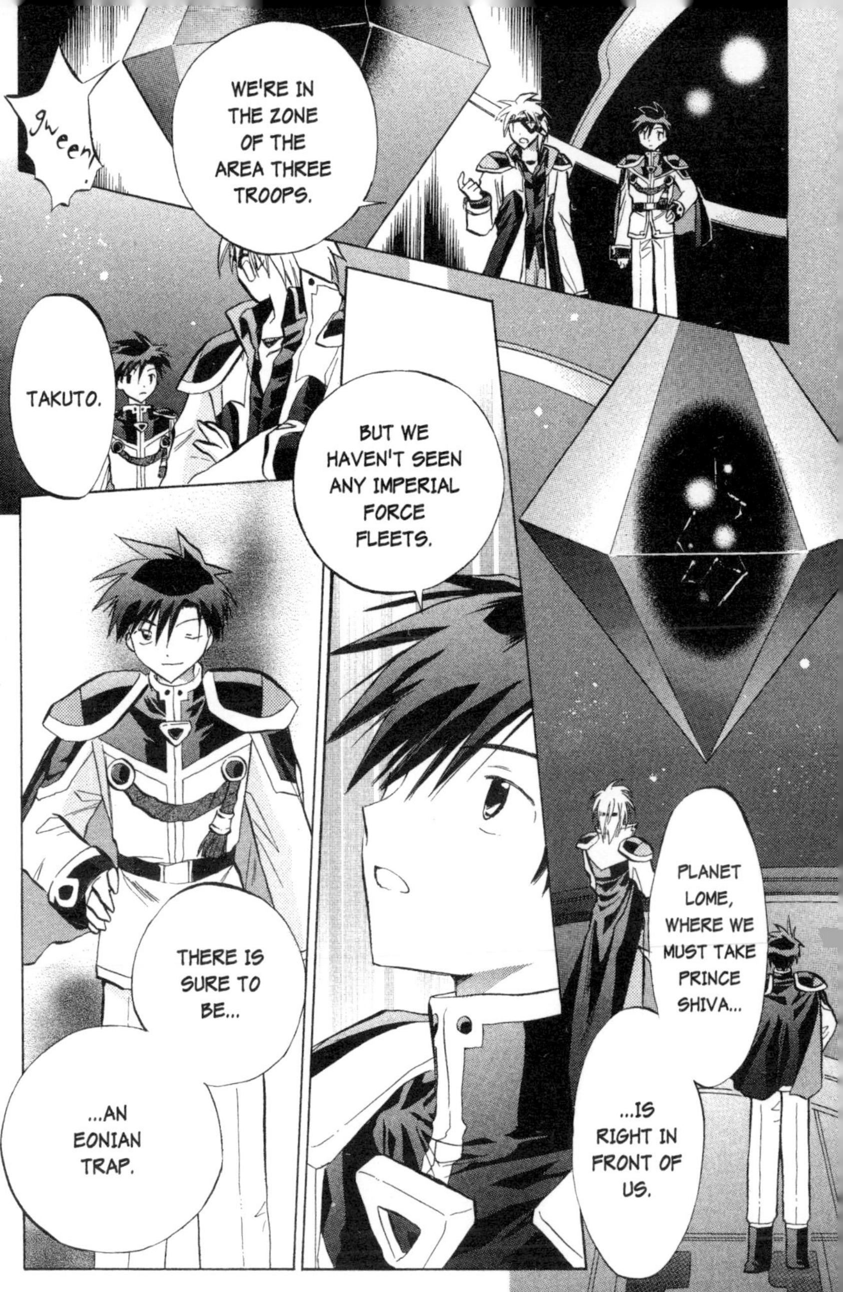
gweeen!
WE'RE IN THE ZONE OF THE AREA THREE TROOPS.
BUT WE HAVEN'T SEEN ANY IMPERIAL FORCE FLEETS.
PLANET LOME, WHERE WE MUST TAKE PRINCE SHIVA...
...IS RIGHT IN FRONT OF US.
TAKUTO.
THERE IS SURE TO BE...
...AN EONIAN TRAP.

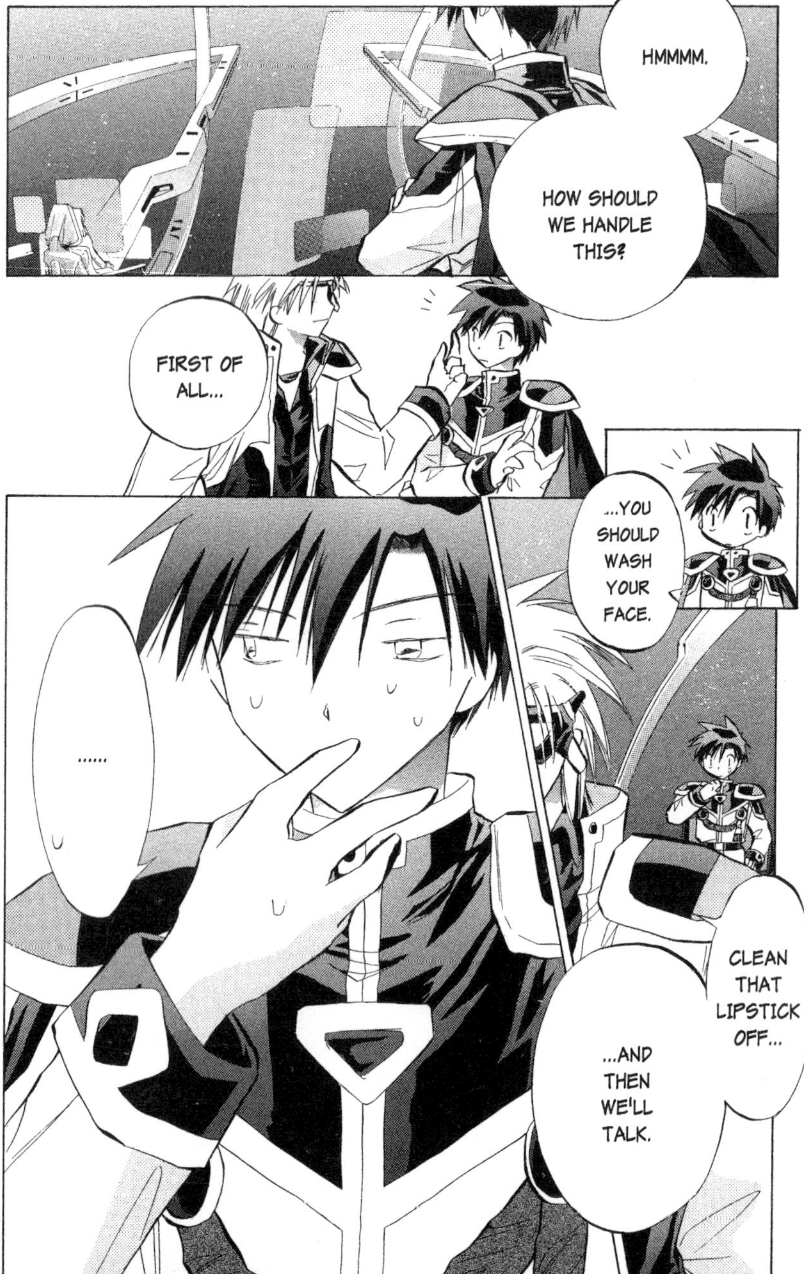
HMMMM.
HOW SHOULD WE HANDLE THIS?
FIRST OF ALL...
...YOU SHOULD WASH YOUR FACE.
......
CLEAN THAT LIPSTICK OFF...
...AND THEN WE'LL TALK.

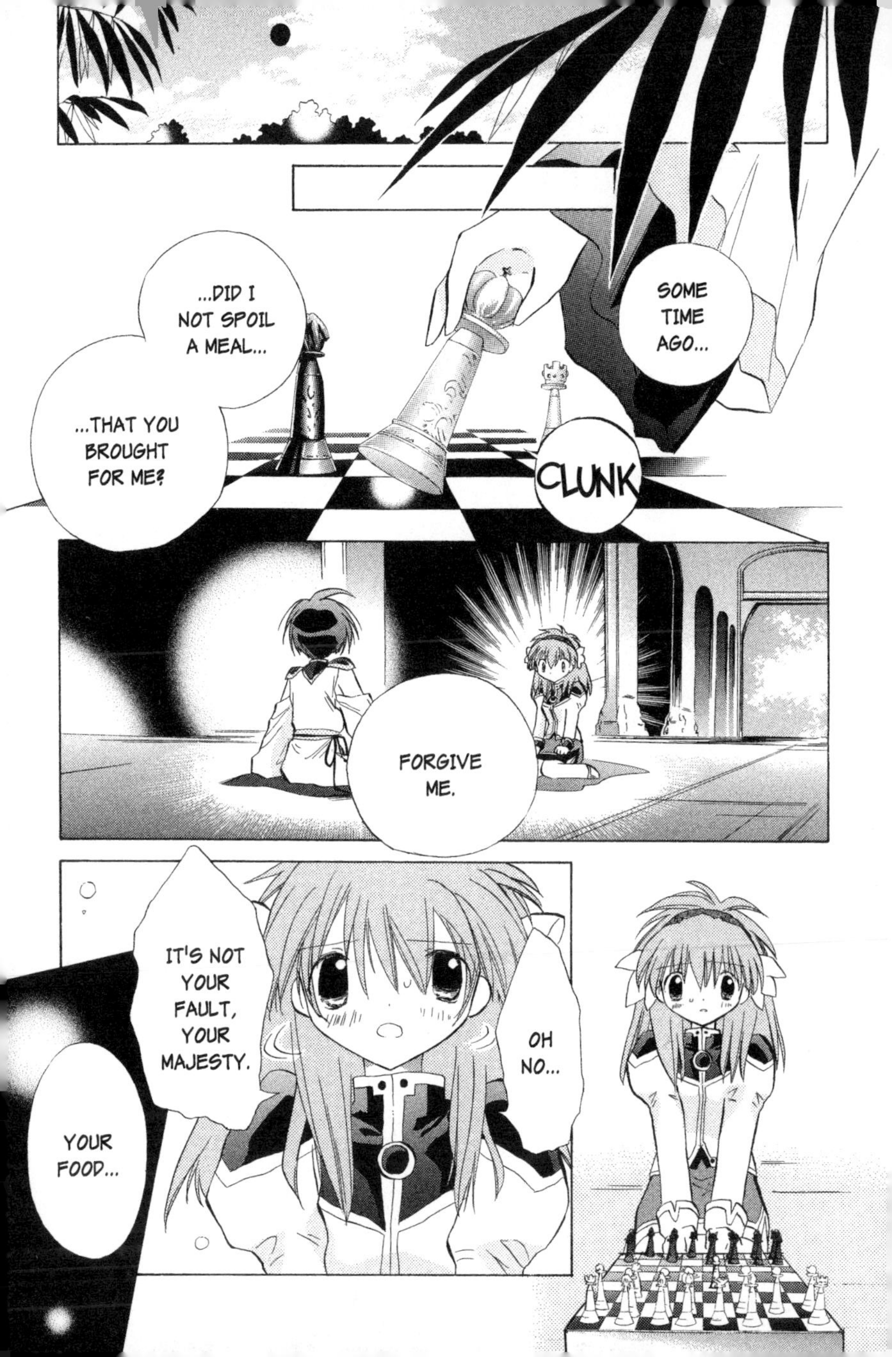
SOME TIME AGO...
...DID I NOT SPOIL A MEAL...
CLUNK
...THAT YOU BROUGHT FOR ME?
FORGIVE ME.
OH NO...
IT'S NOT YOUR FAULT, YOUR MAJESTY.
YOUR FOOD...

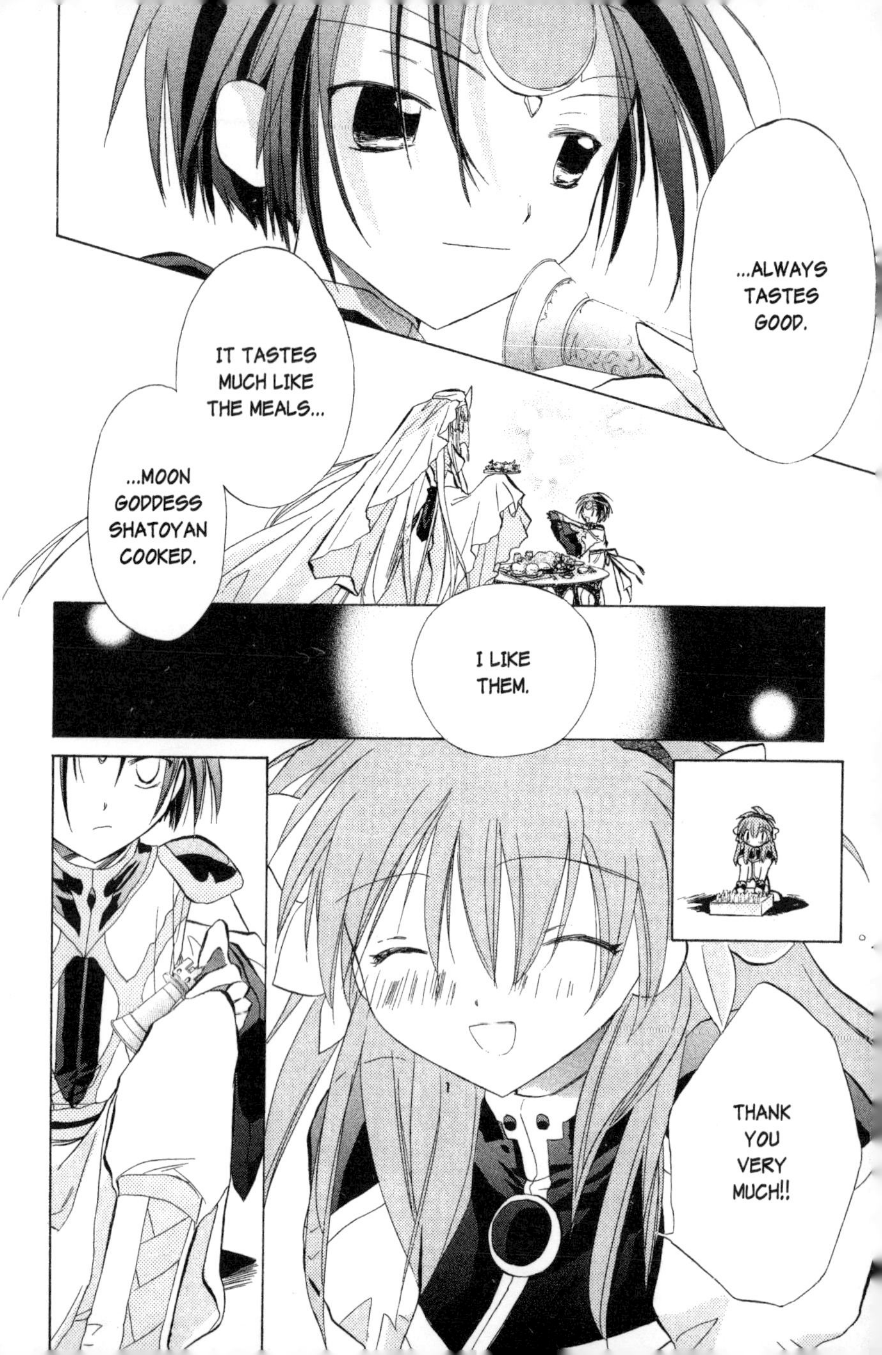
...ALWAYS TASTES GOOD.
IT TASTES MUCH LIKE THE MEALS...
...MOON GODDESS SHATOYAN COOKED.
I LIKE THEM.
THANK YOU VERY MUCH!!

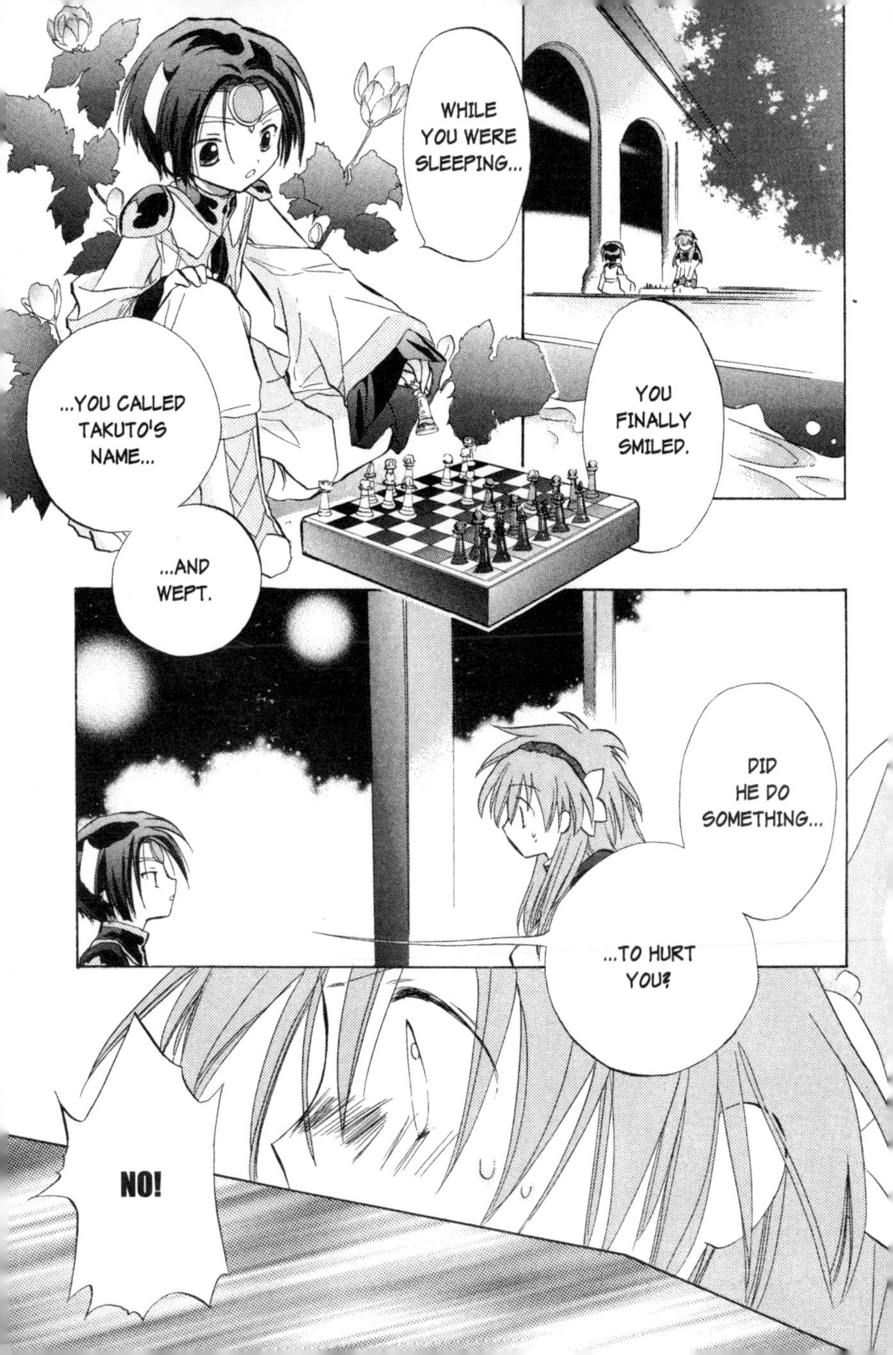
WHILE YOU WERE SLEEPING...
YOU FINALLY SMILED.
...YOU CALLED TAKUTO'S NAME...
...AND WEPT.
DID HE DO SOMETHING...
...TO HURT YOU?
NO!

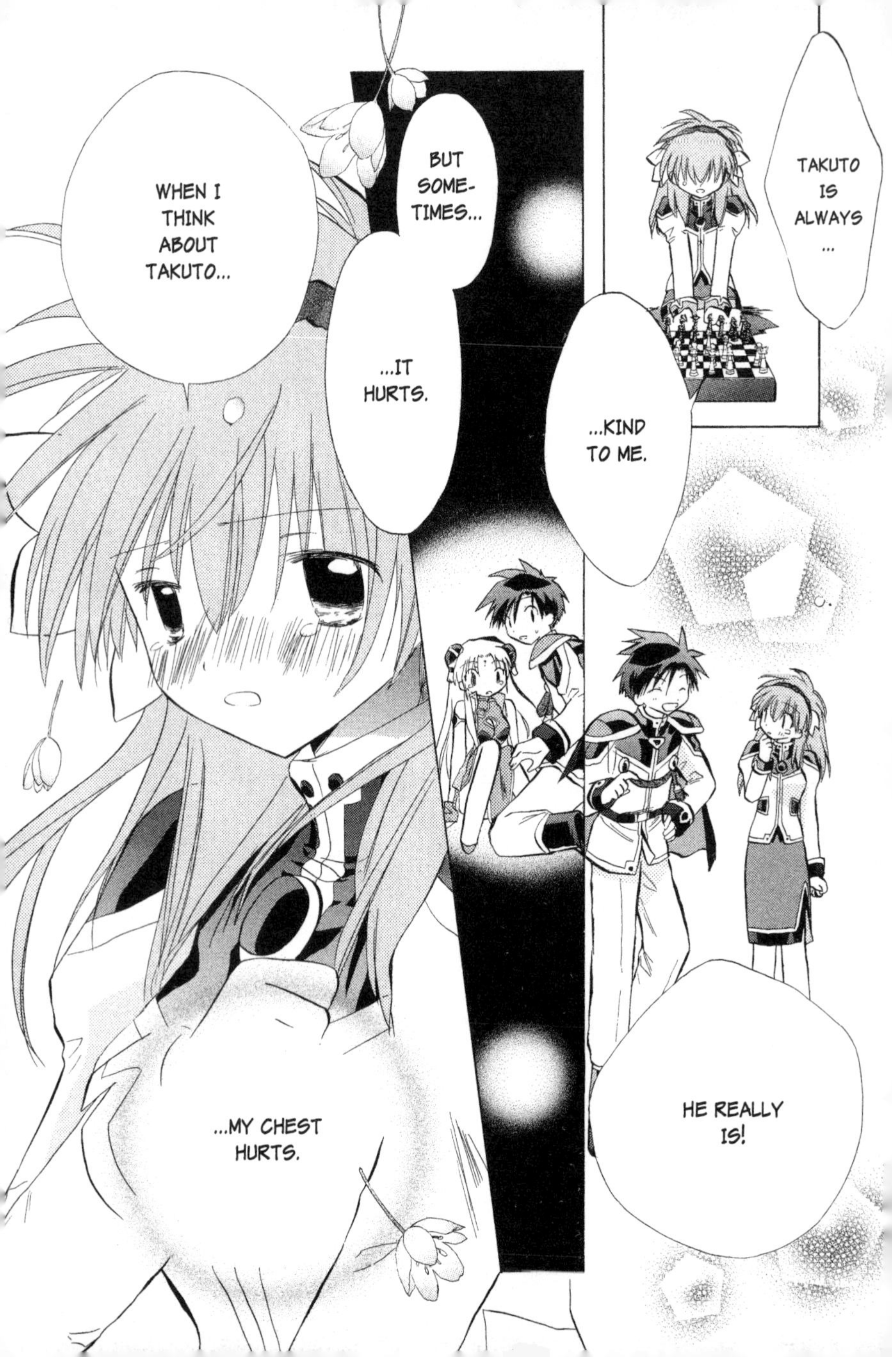
TAKUTO IS ALWAYS ...
...KIND TO ME.
HE REALLY IS!
WHEN I THINK ABOUT TAKUTO...
BUT SOME-TIMES...
...IT HURTS.
...MY CHEST HURTS.

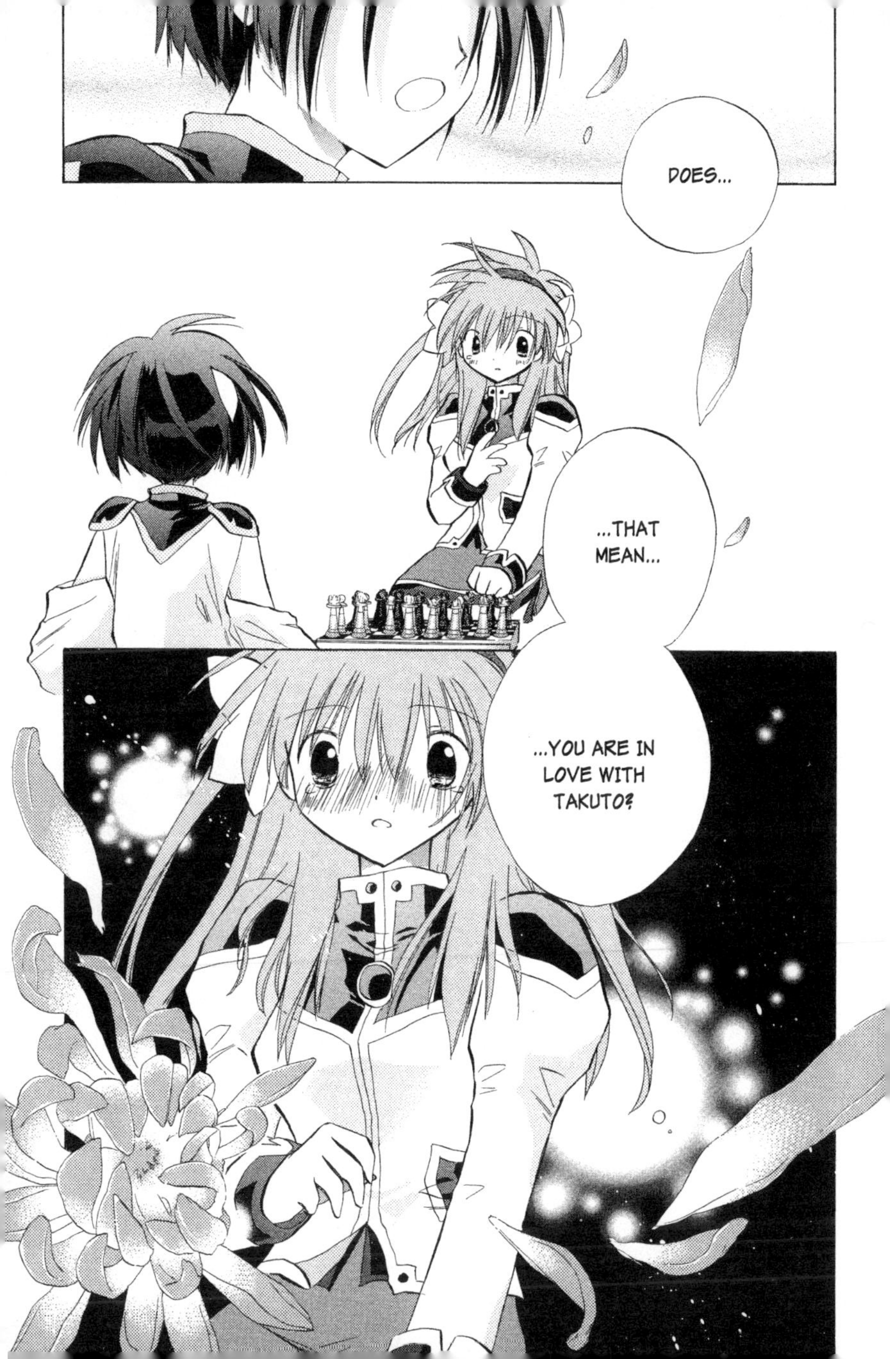
DOES...
...THAT MEAN...
...YOU ARE IN LOVE WITH TAKUTO?

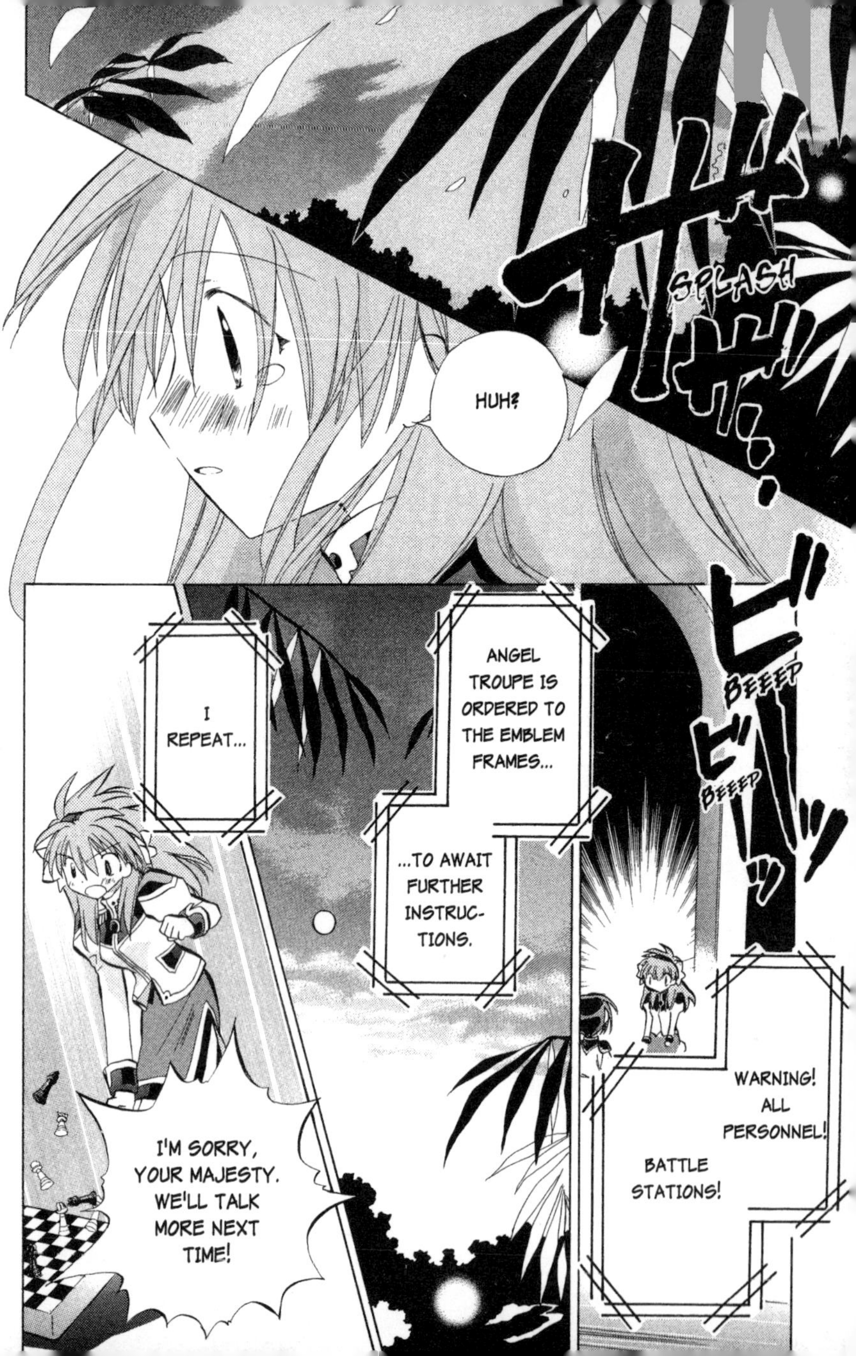
SPLASH
HUH?
BEEEEP
BEEEP
WARNING! ALL PERSONNEL!
BATTLE STATIONS!
ANGEL TROUPE IS ORDERED TO THE EMBLEM FRAMES...
...TO AWAIT FURTHER INSTRUC-TIONS.
I REPEAT...
I'M SORRY, YOUR MAJESTY. WE'LL TALK MORE NEXT TIME!

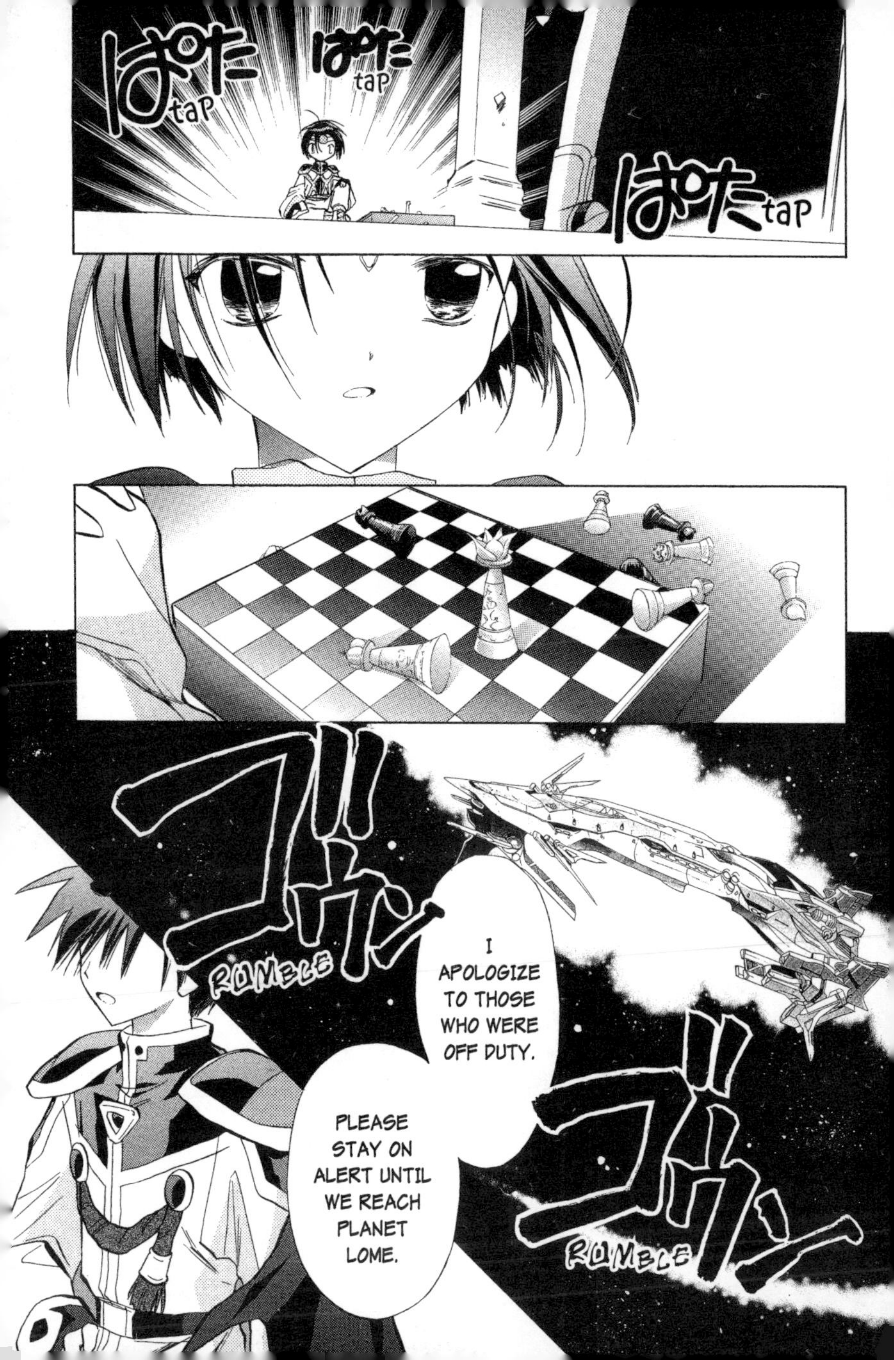
ぱた tap
ぱた tap
ぱた tap
ゴヴン RUMBLE
I APOLOGIZE TO THOSE WHO WERE OFF DUTY.
PLEASE STAY ON ALERT UNTIL WE REACH PLANET LOME.
ゴヴン RUMBLE

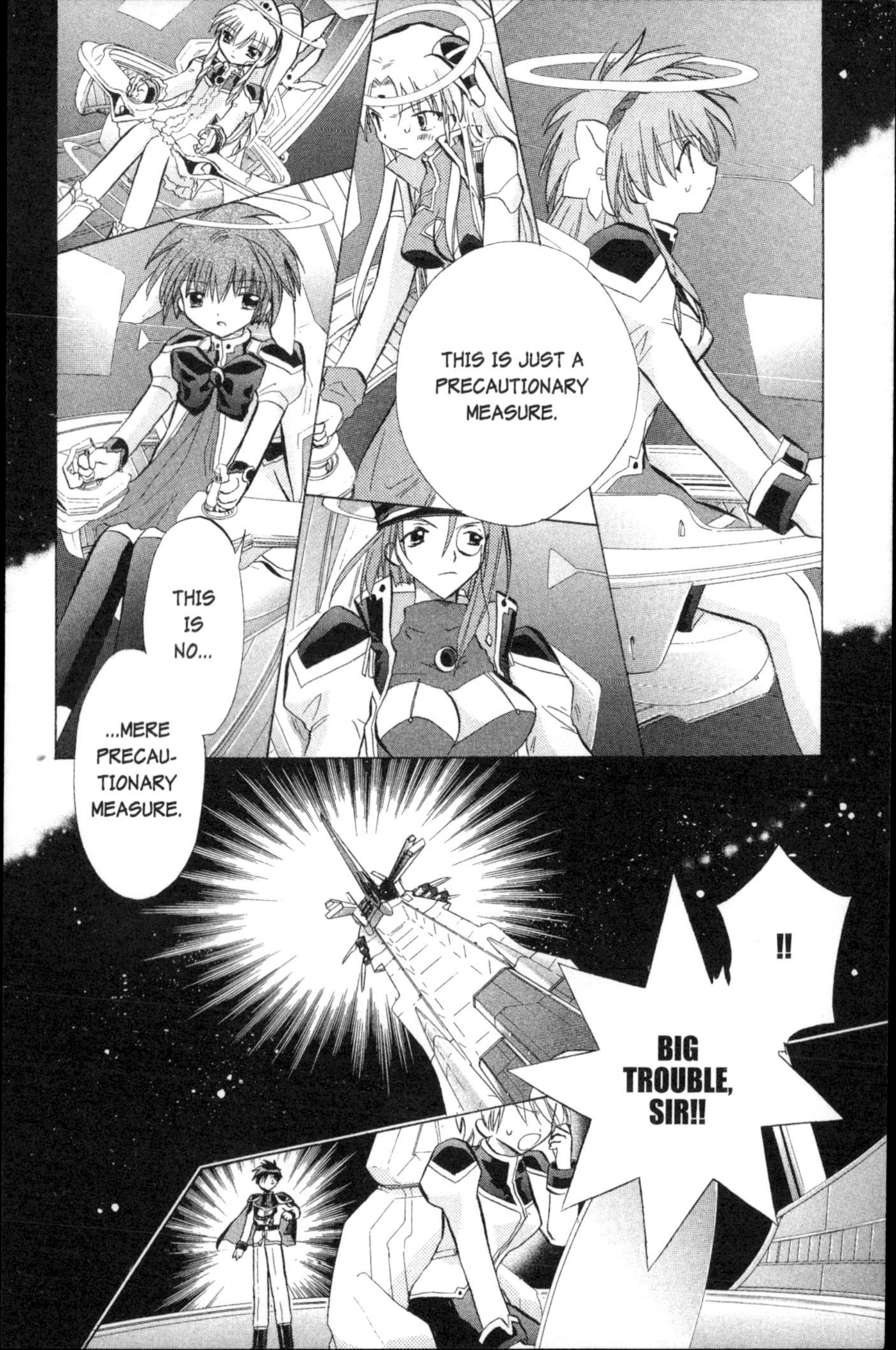
THIS IS JUST A PRECAUTIONARY MEASURE.
THIS IS NO...
...MERE PRECAU-TIONARY MEASURE.
!!
BIG TROUBLE, SIR!!

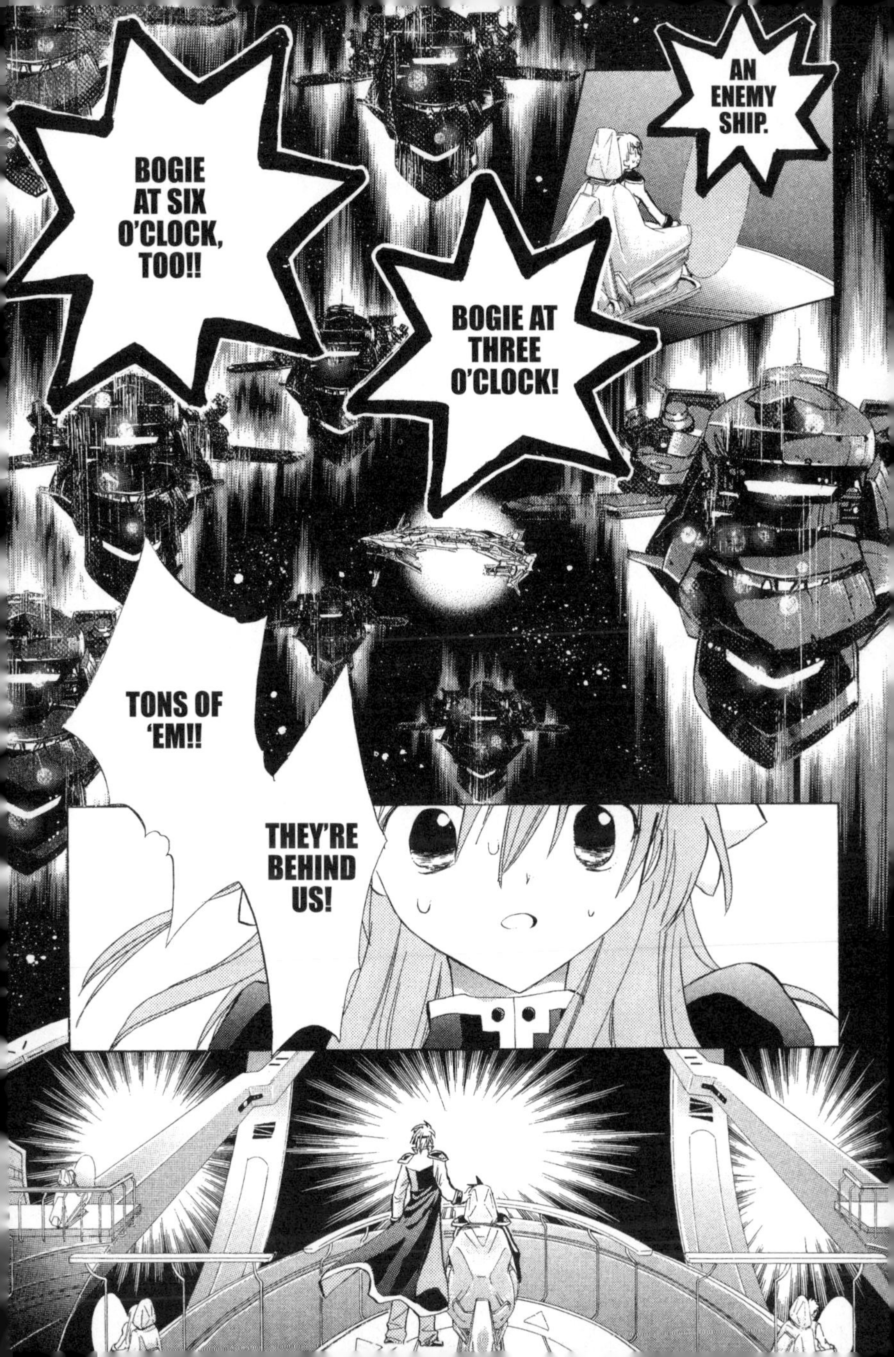
AN ENEMY SHIP.
BOGIE AT THREE O'CLOCK!
BOGIE AT SIX O'CLOCK, TOO!!
TONS OF 'EM!!
THEY'RE BEHIND US!

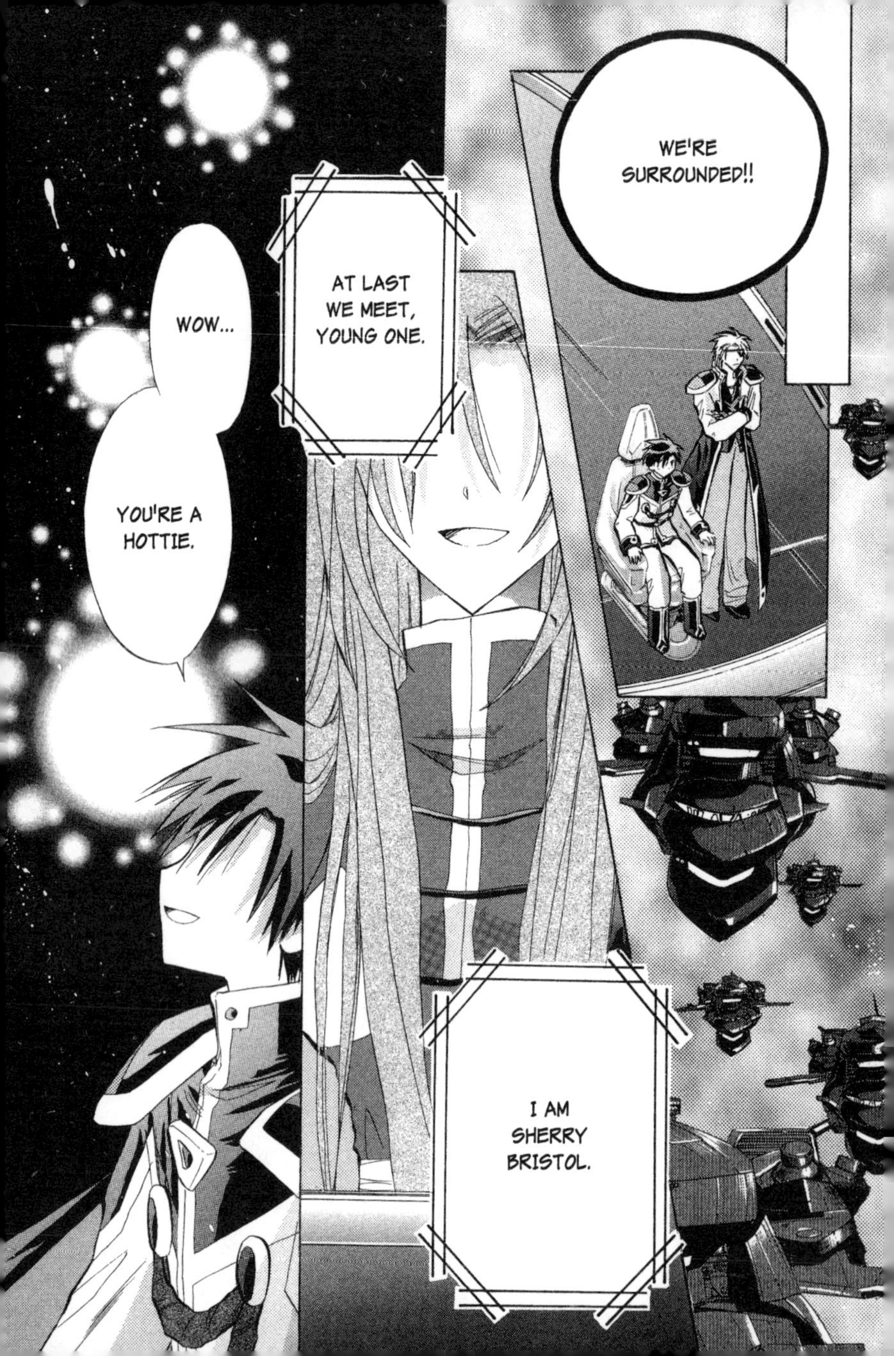

WE'RE SURROUNDED!!
AT LAST WE MEET, YOUNG ONE.
I AM SHERRY BRISTOL.
WOW...
YOU'RE A HOTTIE.

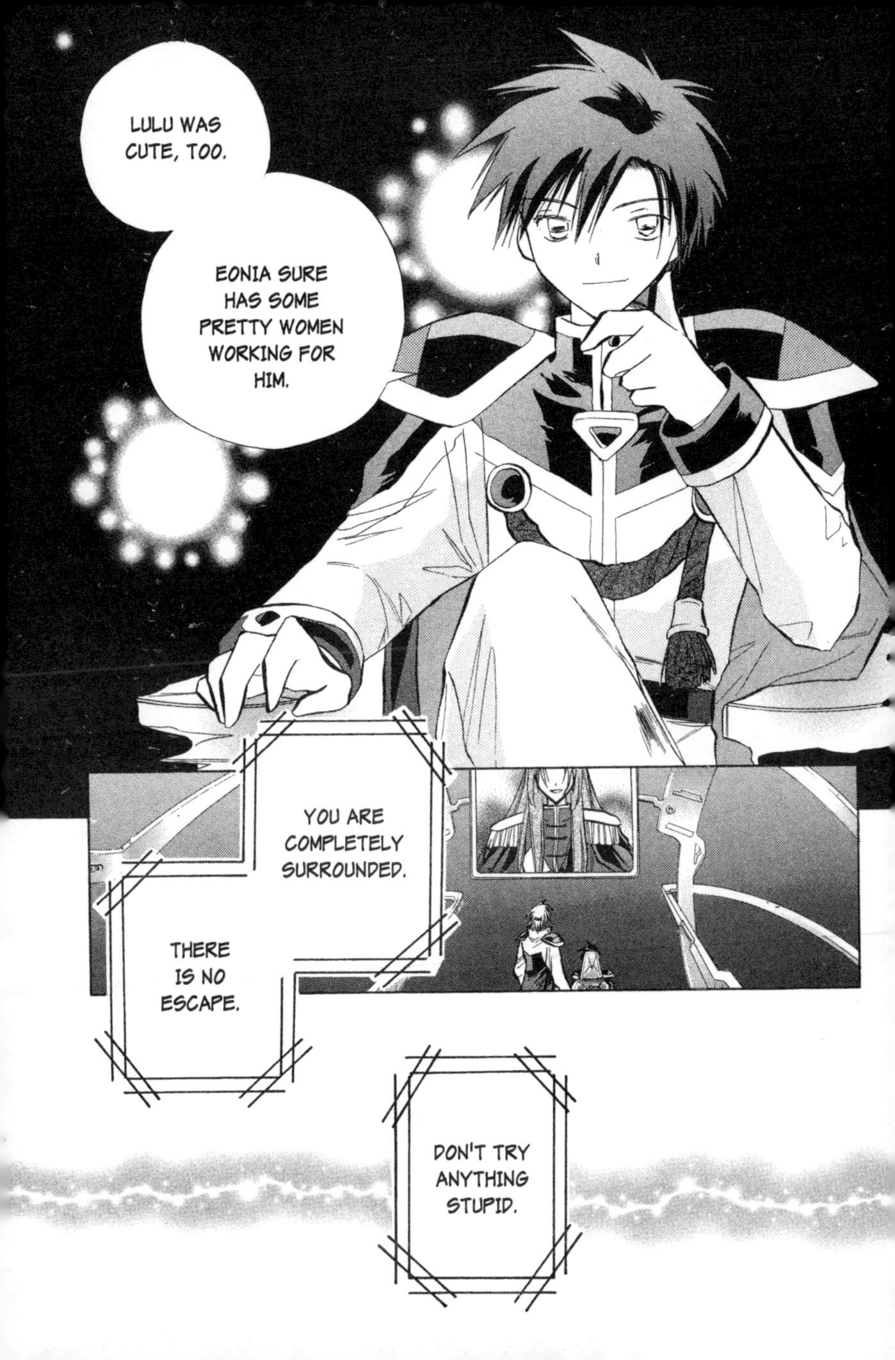
EONIA SURE HAS SOME PRETTY WOMEN WORKING FOR HIM.
LULU WAS CUTE, TOO.
YOU ARE COMPLETELY SURROUNDED.
THERE IS NO ESCAPE.
DON'T TRY ANYTHING STUPID.

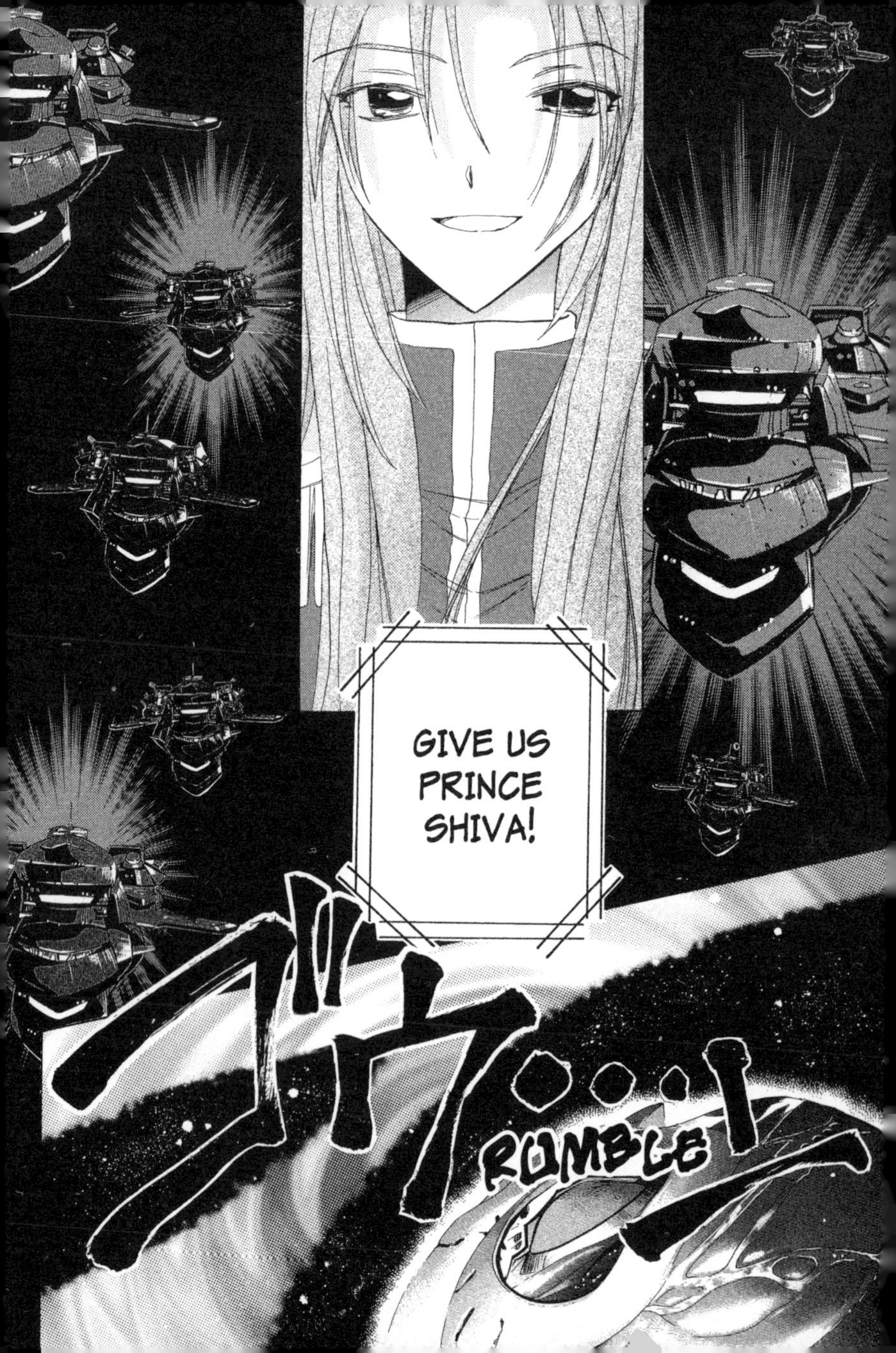
GIVE US PRINCE SHIVA!
RUMBLE

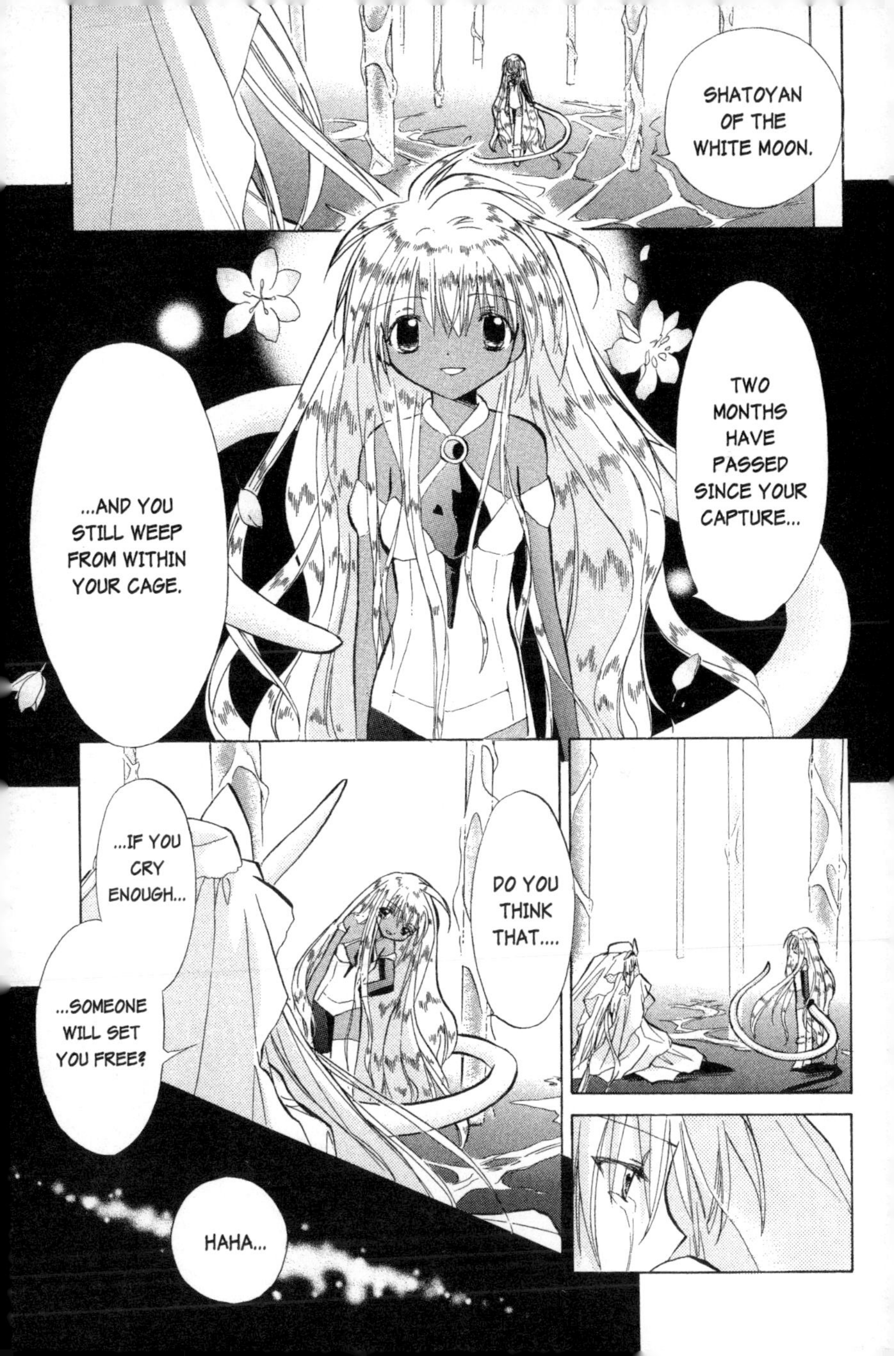
SHATOYAN OF THE WHITE MOON.
TWO MONTHS HAVE PASSED SINCE YOUR CAPTURE...
...AND YOU STILL WEEP FROM WITHIN YOUR CAGE.
DO YOU THINK THAT....
...IF YOU CRY ENOUGH...
...SOMEONE WILL SET YOU FREE?
HAHA...

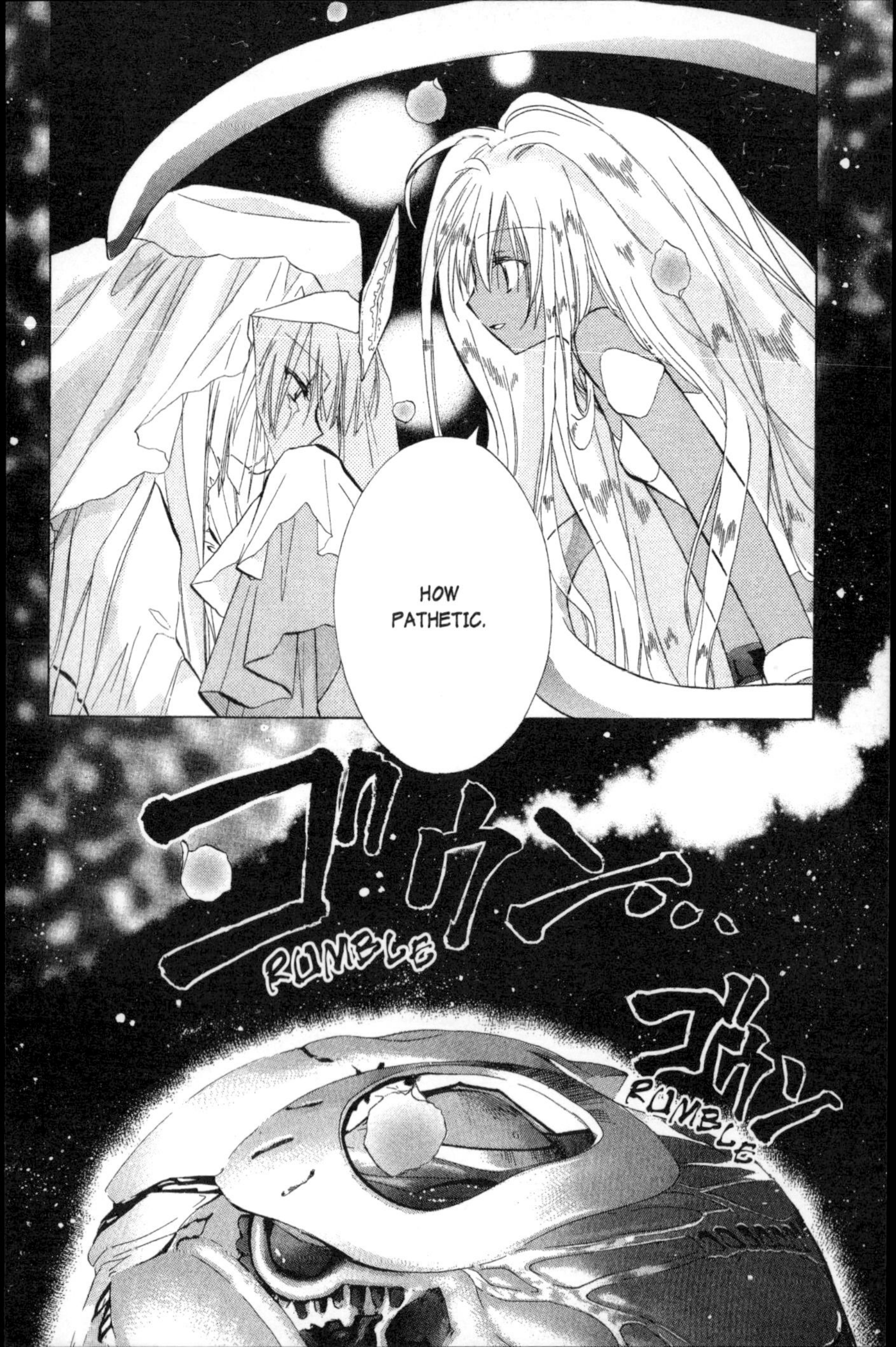
HOW PATHETIC.
ゴウン…
RUMBLE
ゴウン
RUMBLE

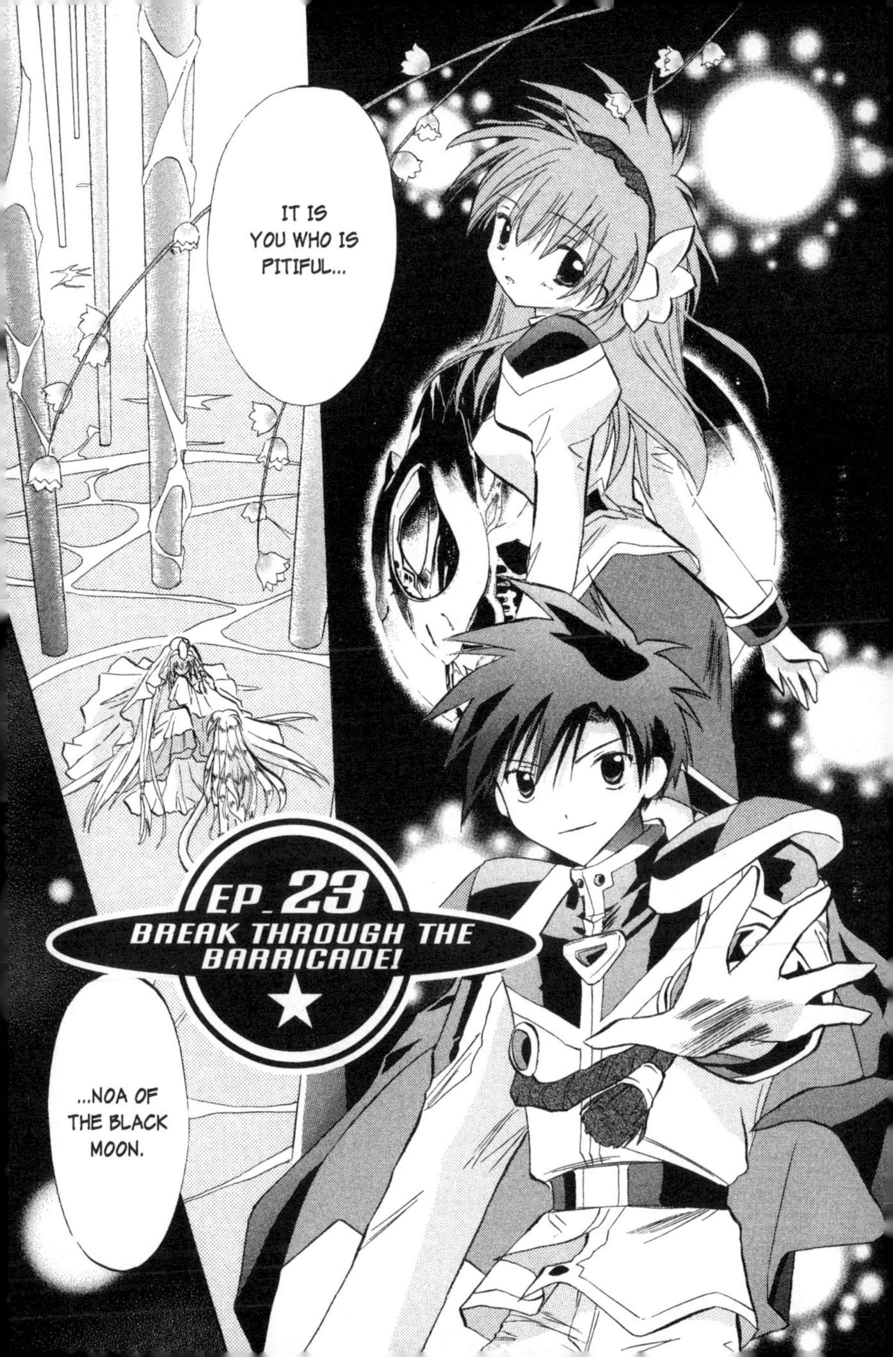

IT IS YOU WHO IS PITIFUL...
EP_23
BREAK THROUGH THE BARRICADE!
...NOA OF THE BLACK MOON.

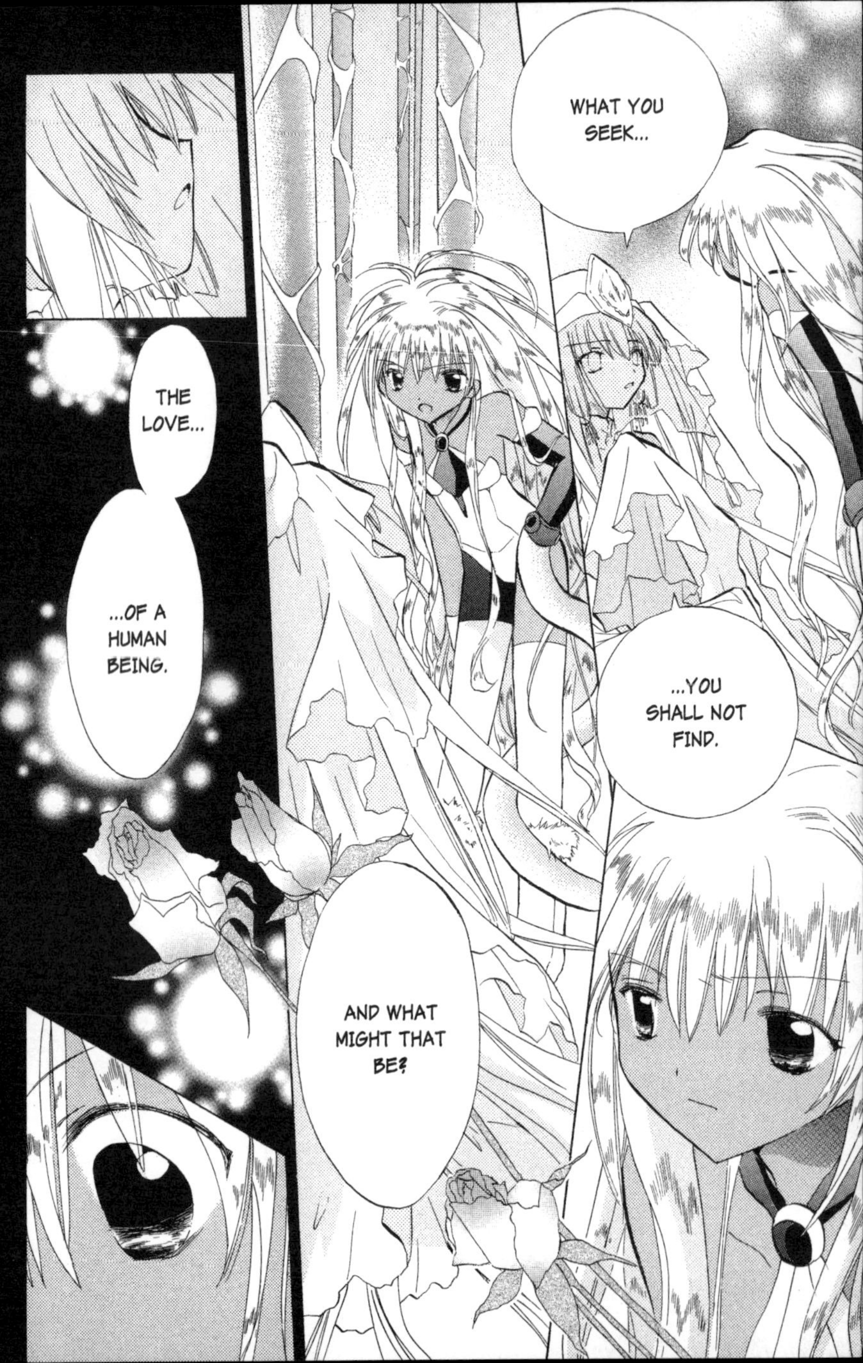
WHAT YOU SEEK...
...YOU SHALL NOT FIND.
AND WHAT MIGHT THAT BE?
THE LOVE...
...OF A HUMAN BEING.

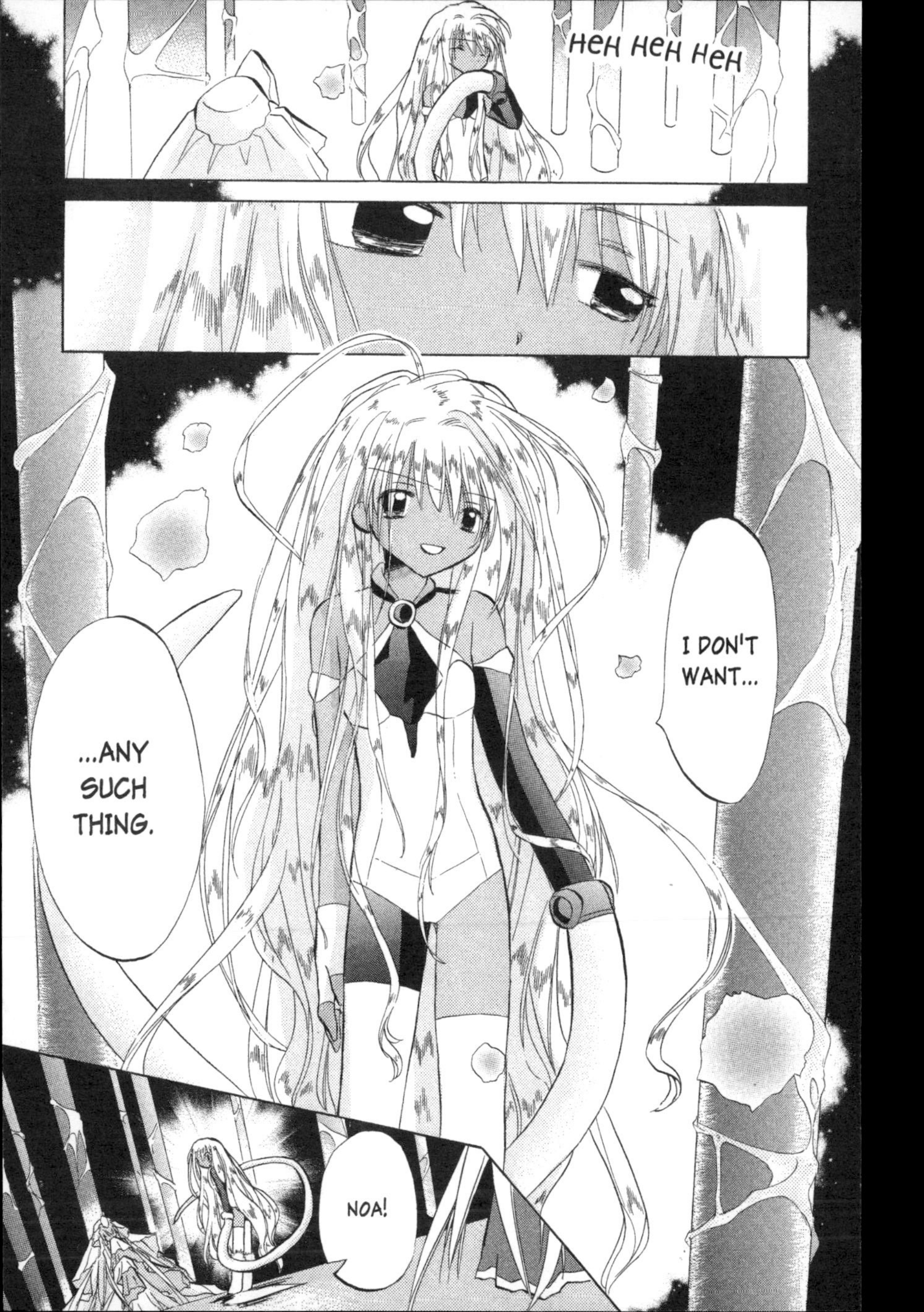
HEH HEH HEH
I DON'T WANT...
...ANY SUCH THING.
NOA!

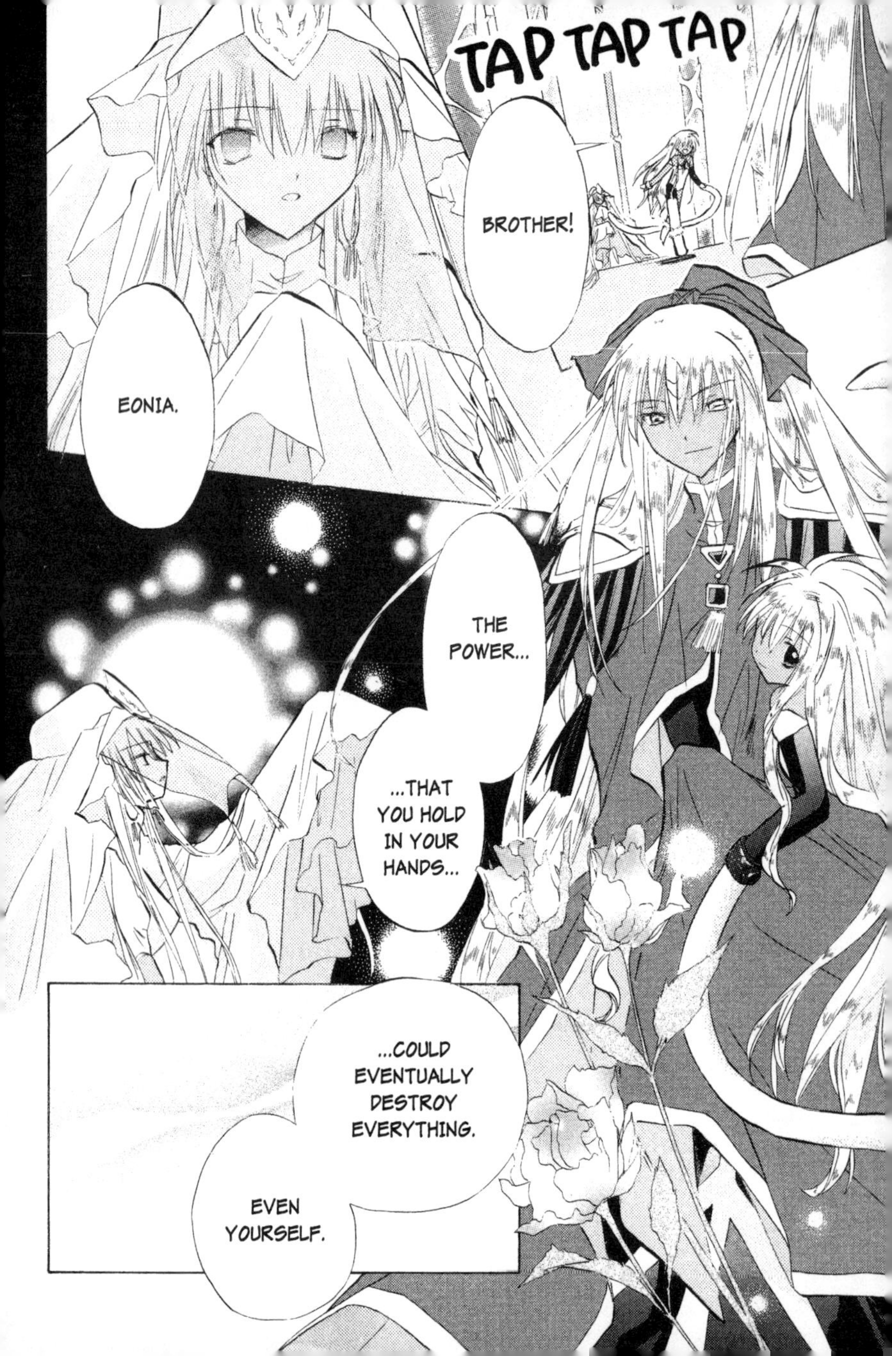
TAP TAP TAP
BROTHER!
EONIA.
THE POWER...
...THAT YOU HOLD IN YOUR HANDS...
...COULD EVENTUALLY DESTROY EVERYTHING.
EVEN YOURSELF.

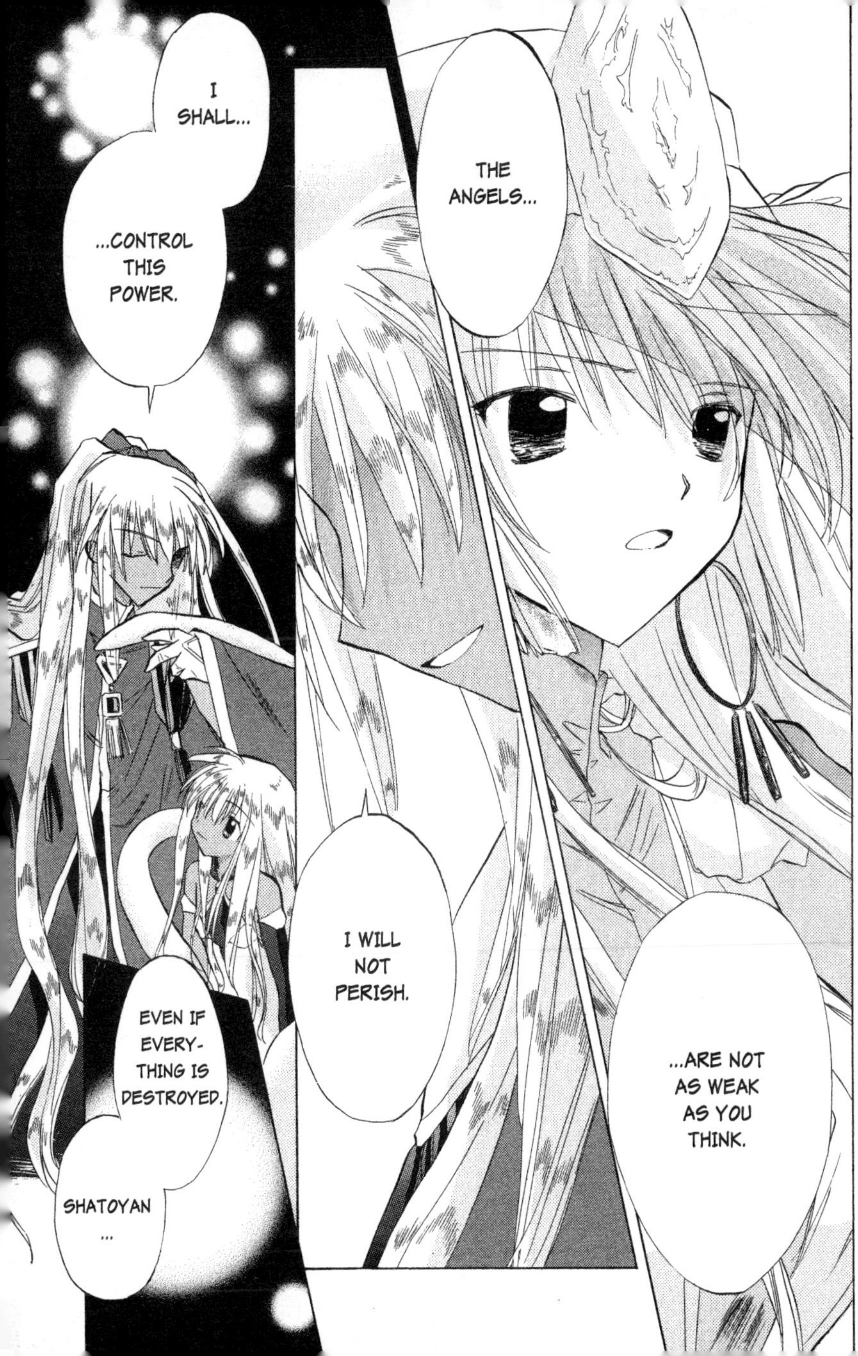
THE ANGELS...
...ARE NOT AS WEAK AS YOU THINK.
I WILL NOT PERISH.
I SHALL...
...CONTROL THIS POWER.
EVEN IF EVERY-THING IS DESTROYED.
SHATOYAN ...

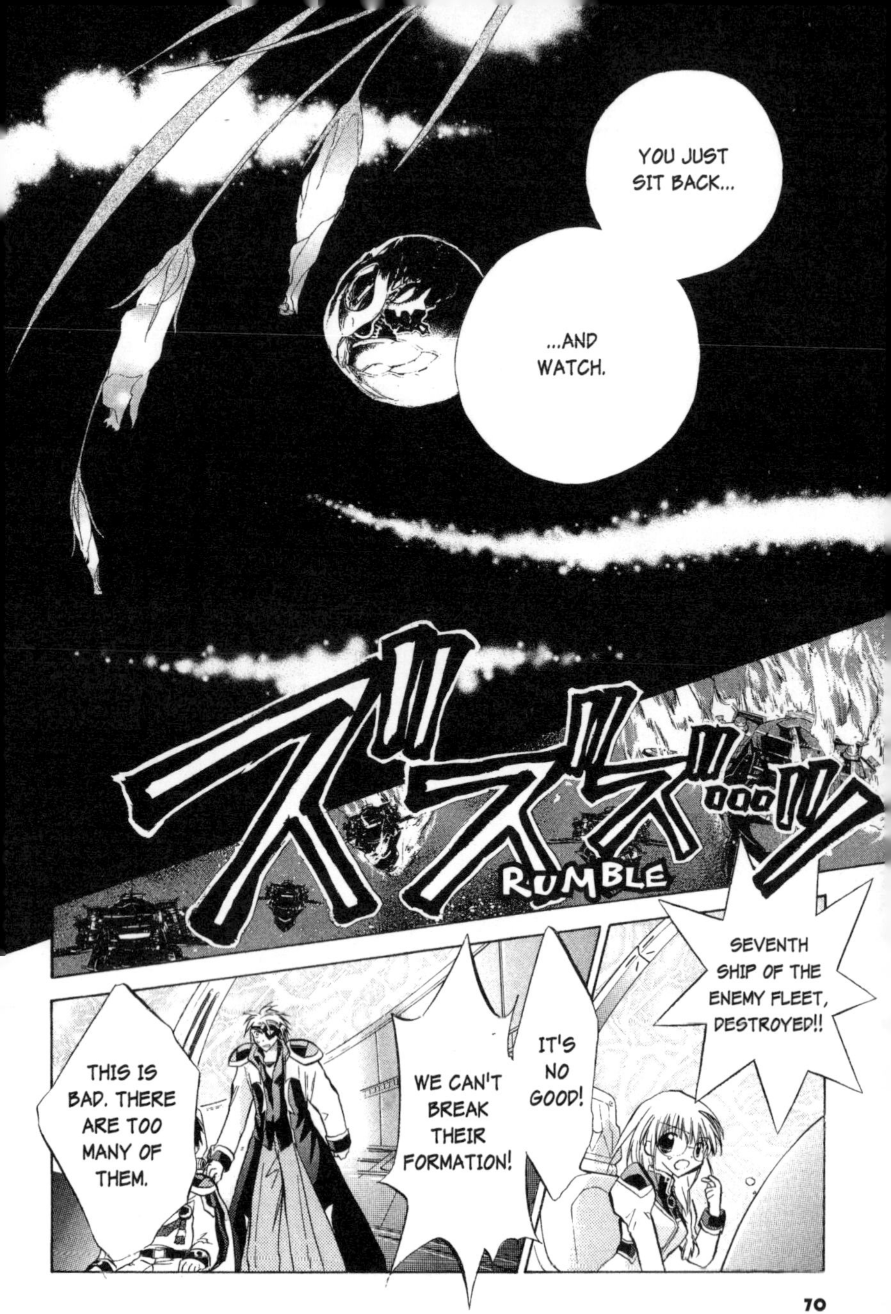
YOU JUST SIT BACK...
...AND WATCH.
ズズズ…ッ
RUMBLE
SEVENTH SHIP OF THE ENEMY FLEET, DESTROYED!!
IT'S NO GOOD!
WE CAN'T BREAK THEIR FORMATION!
THIS IS BAD. THERE ARE TOO MANY OF THEM.

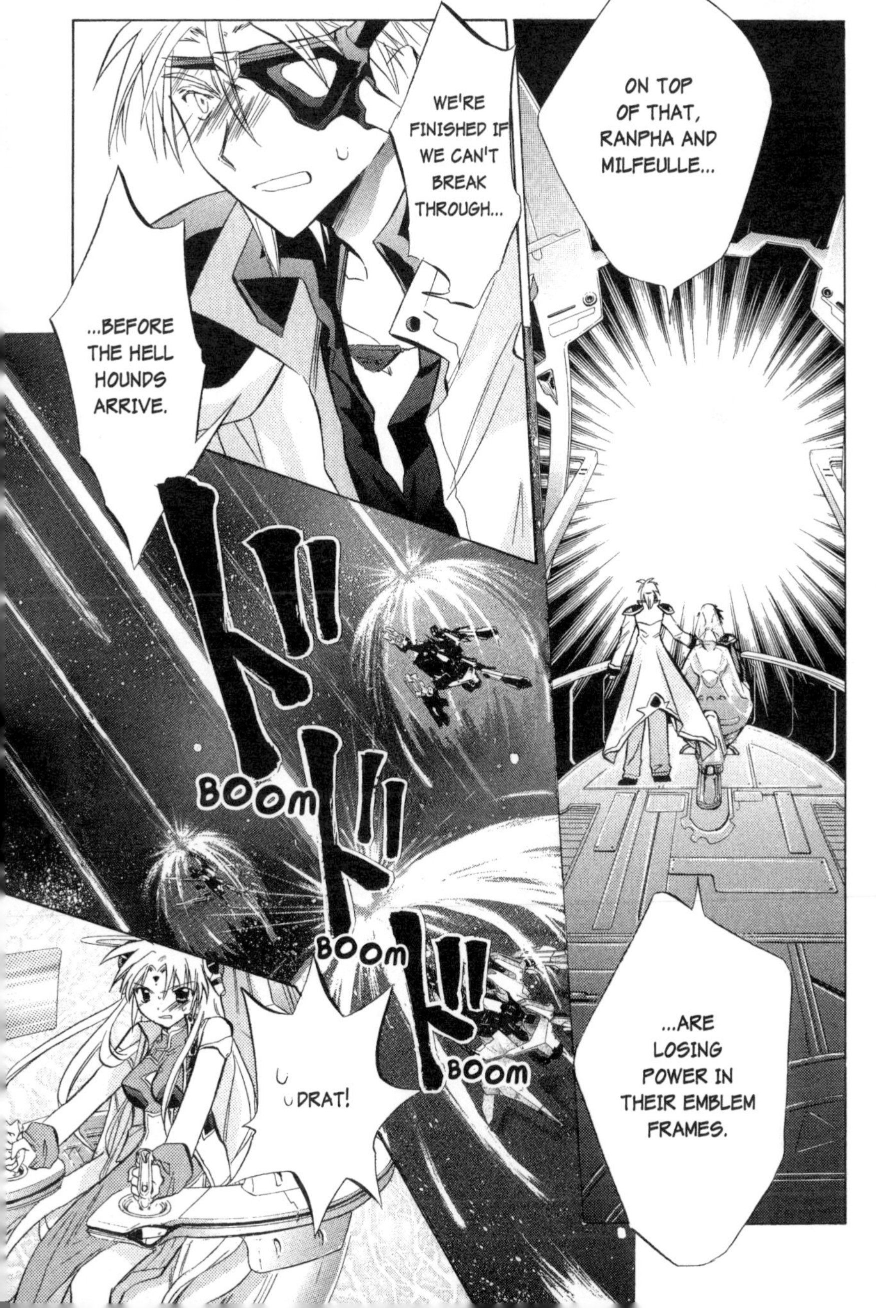
ON TOP OF THAT, RANPHA AND MILFEULLE...
...ARE LOSING POWER IN THEIR EMBLEM FRAMES.
WE'RE FINISHED IF WE CAN'T BREAK THROUGH...
...BEFORE THE HELL HOUNDS ARRIVE.
BOOM
BOOM
BOOM
DRAT!

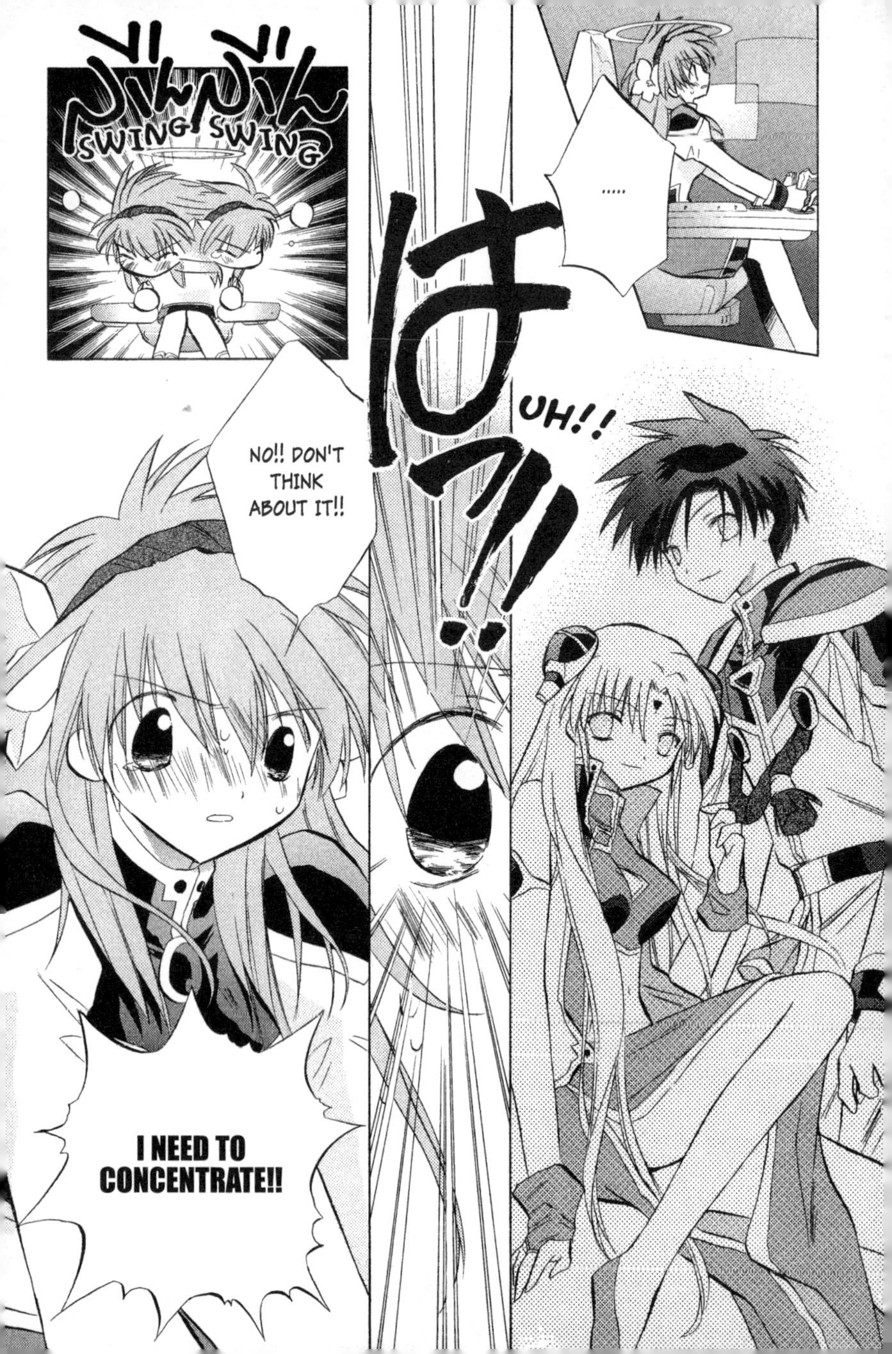
.....
ぶんぶん
SWING SWING
はっ!!
UH!!
NO!! DON'T THINK ABOUT IT!!
I NEED TO CONCENTRATE!!

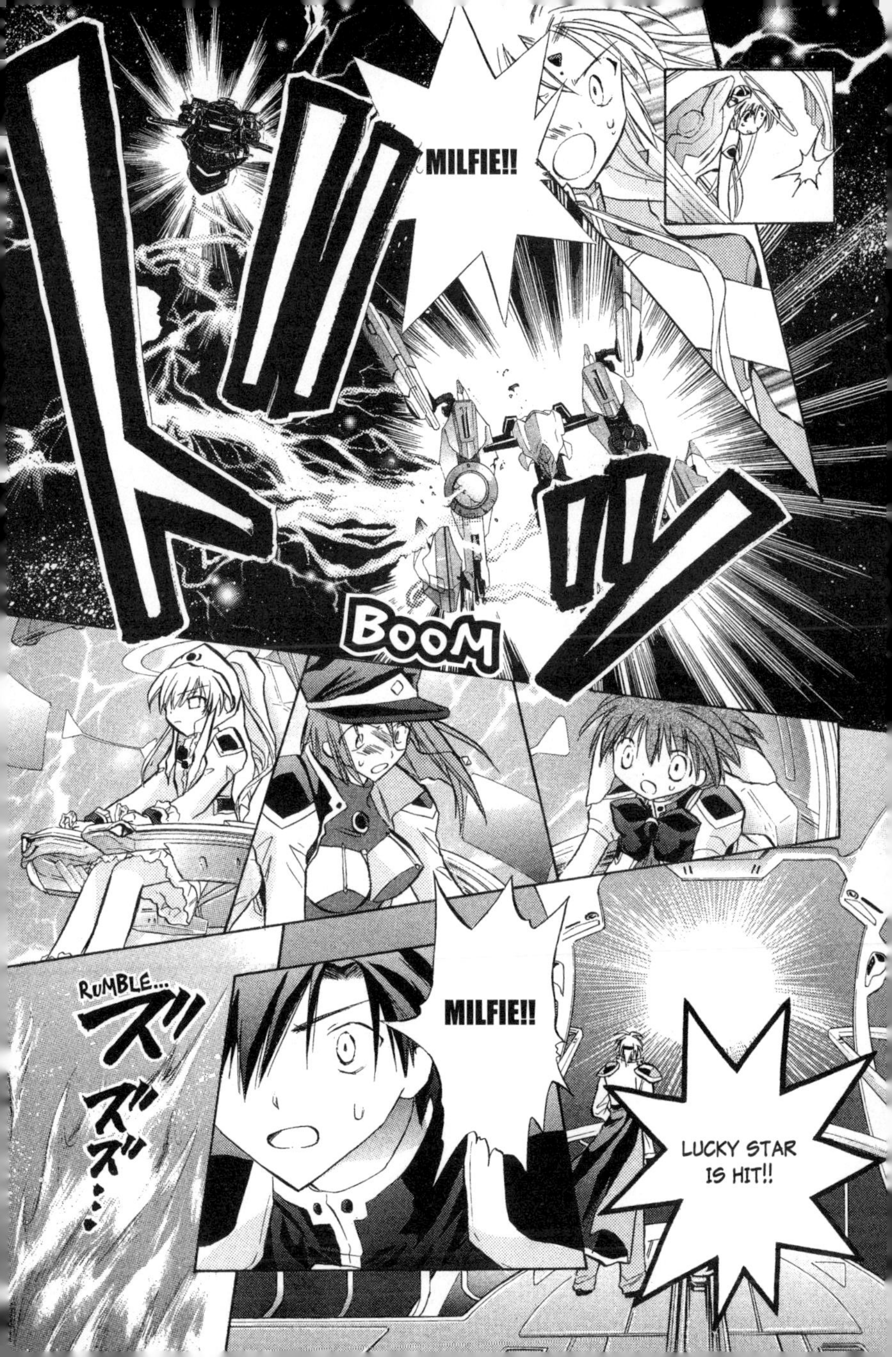

MILFIE!!
BOOM
LUCKY STAR IS HIT!!
MILFIE!!
RUMBLE...
ズズズ...

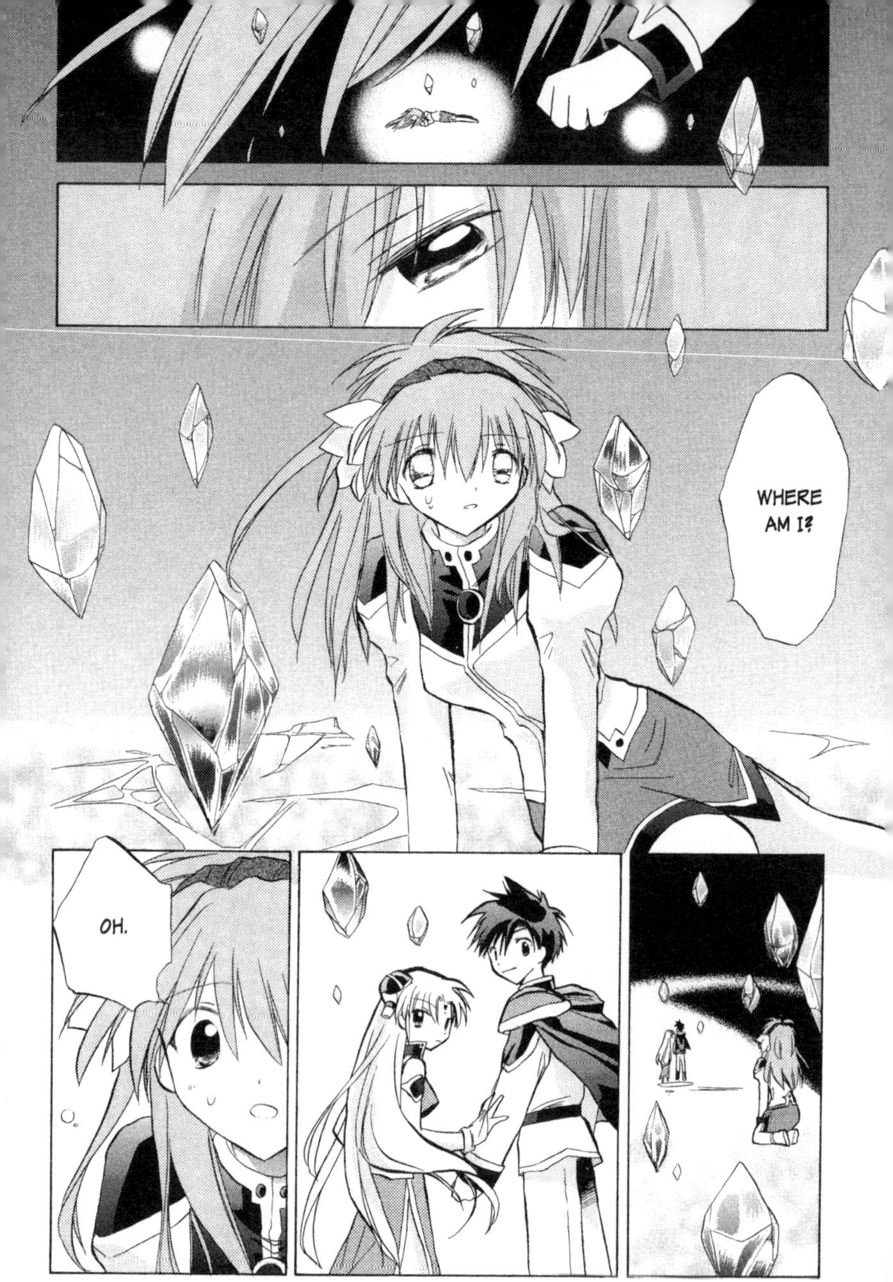
WHERE AM I?
OH.

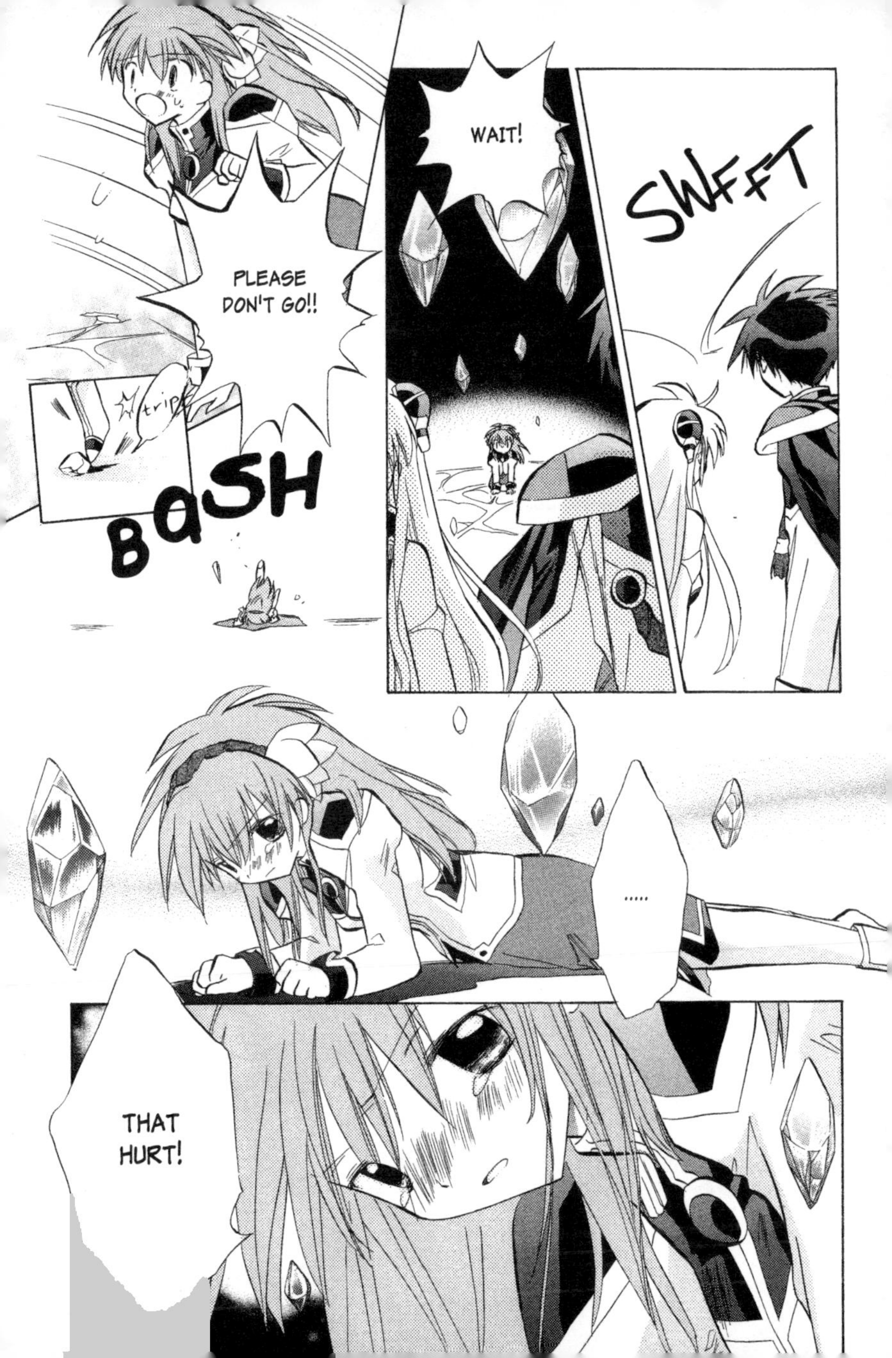
SWFFT
WAIT!
PLEASE DON'T GO!!
trip
BASH
.....
THAT HURT!

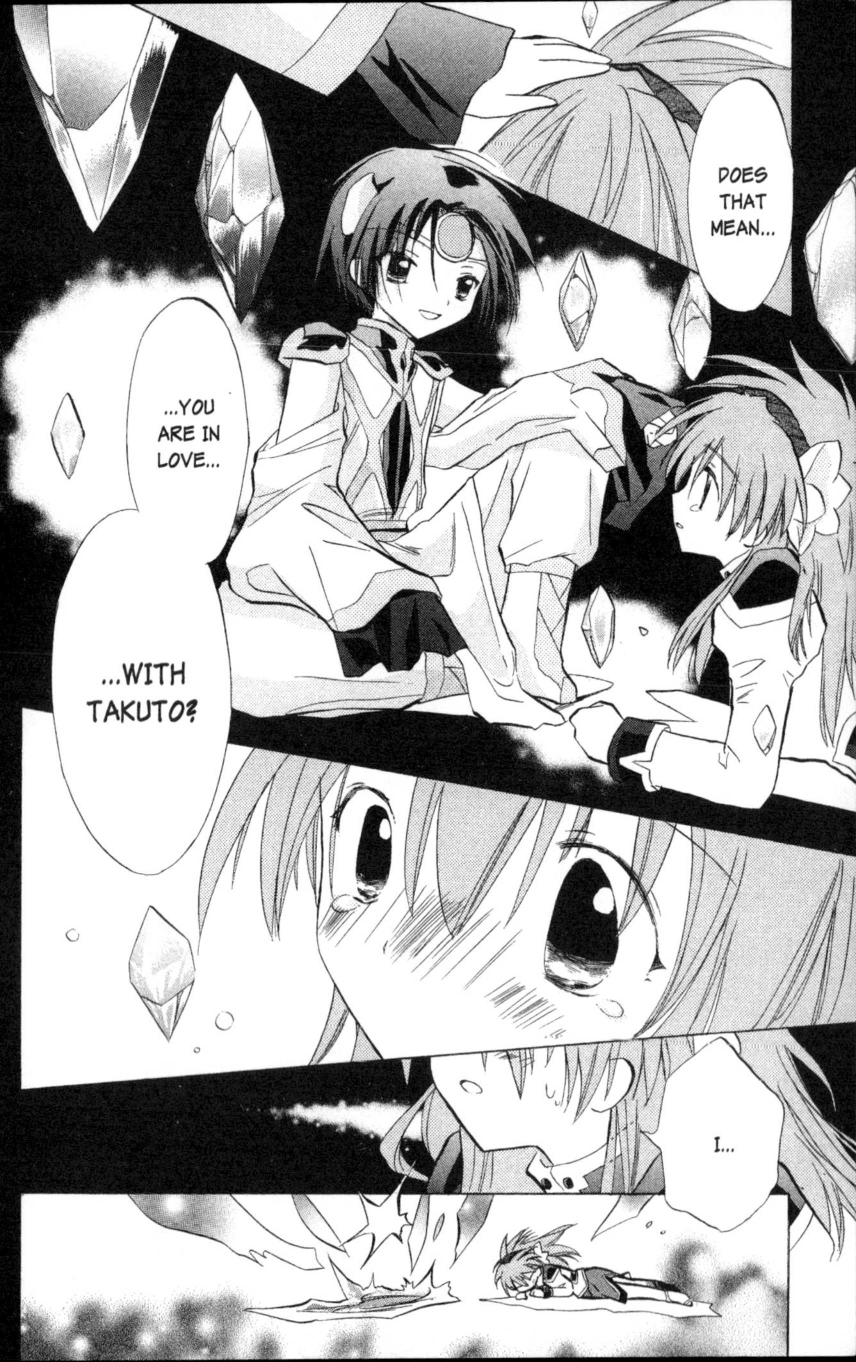
DOES THAT MEAN...
...YOU ARE IN LOVE...
...WITH TAKUTO?
I...

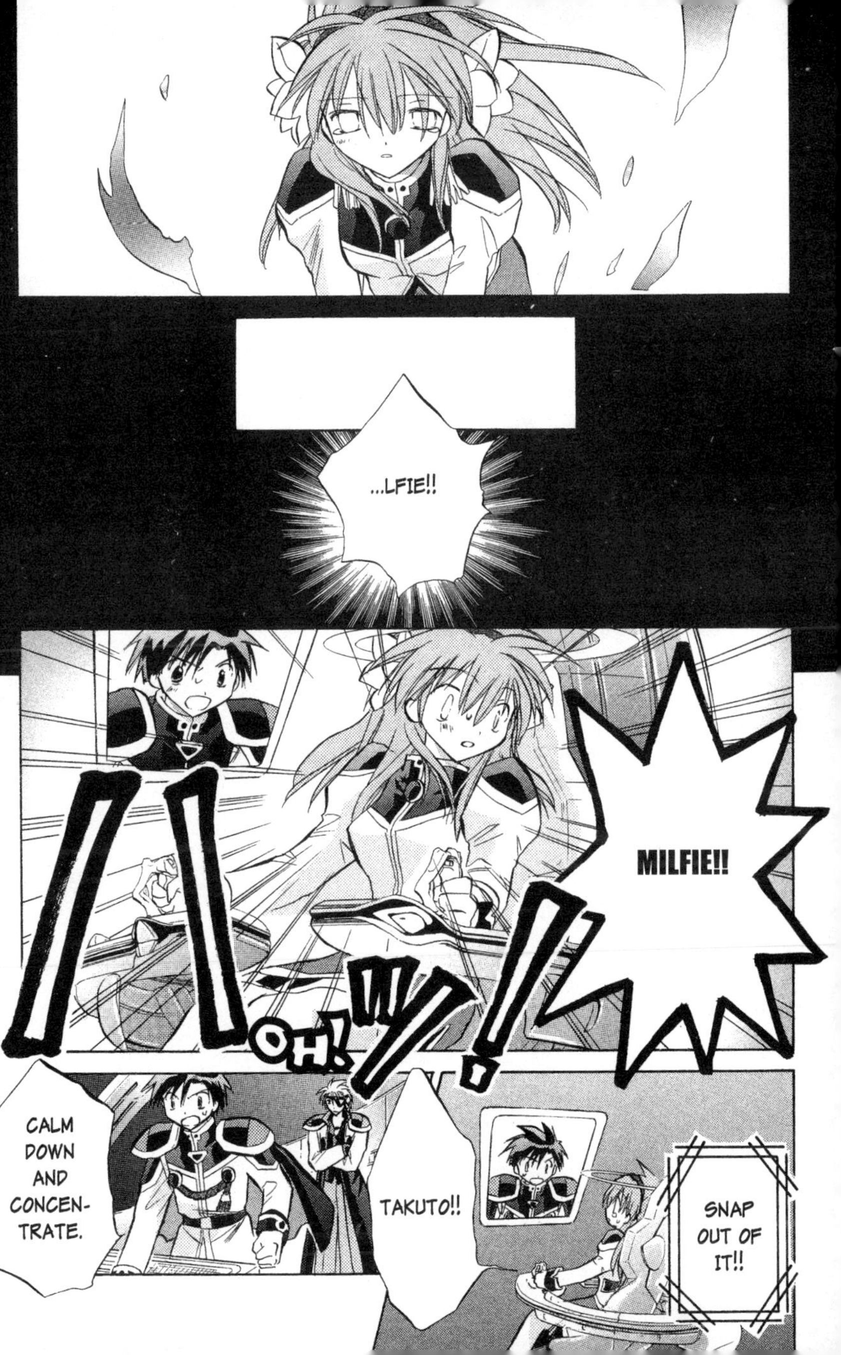

...LFIE!!
MILFIE!!
OH!
SNAP OUT OF IT!!
TAKUTO!!
CALM DOWN AND CONCEN-TRATE.

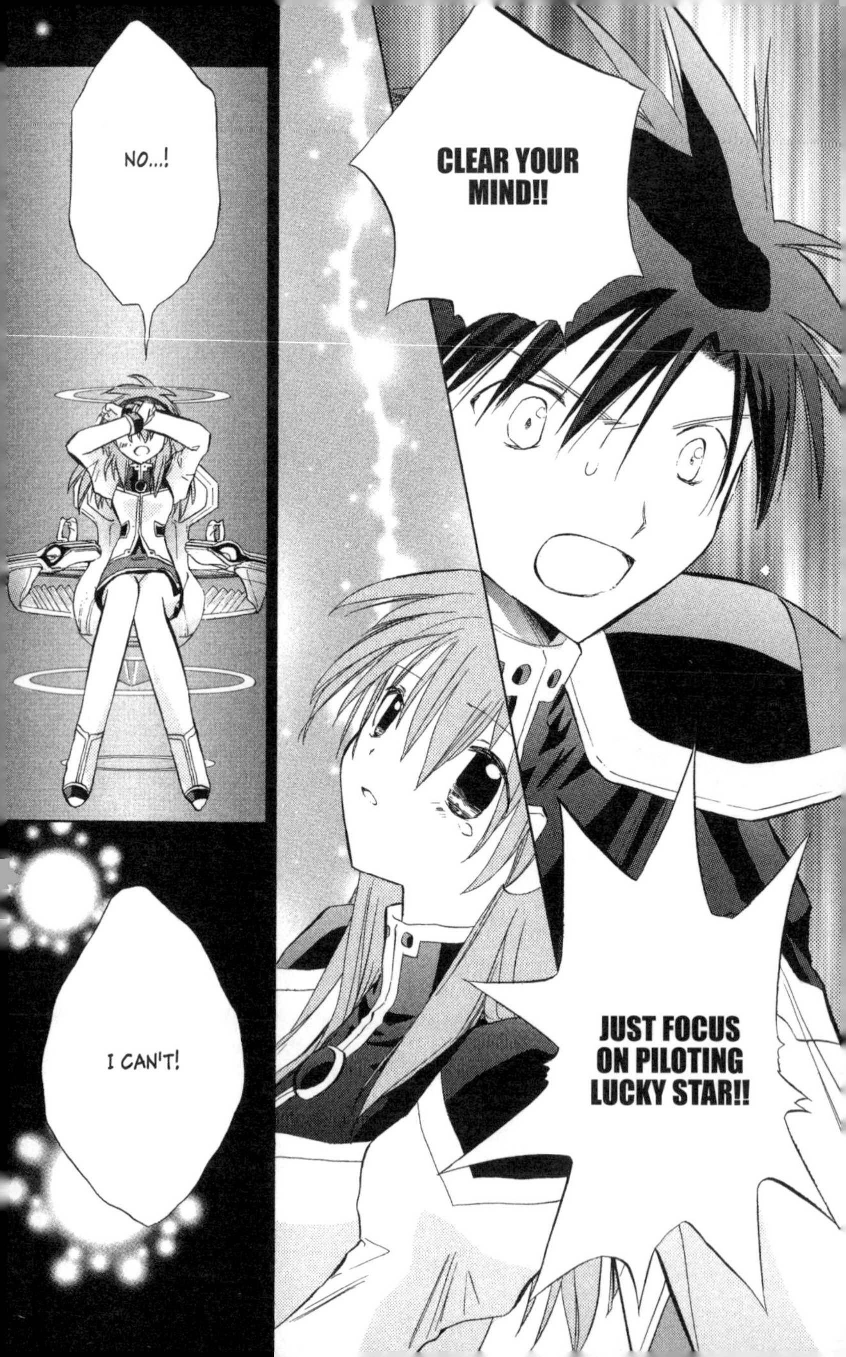
CLEAR YOUR MIND!!
JUST FOCUS ON PILOTING LUCKY STAR!!
NO...!
I CAN'T!

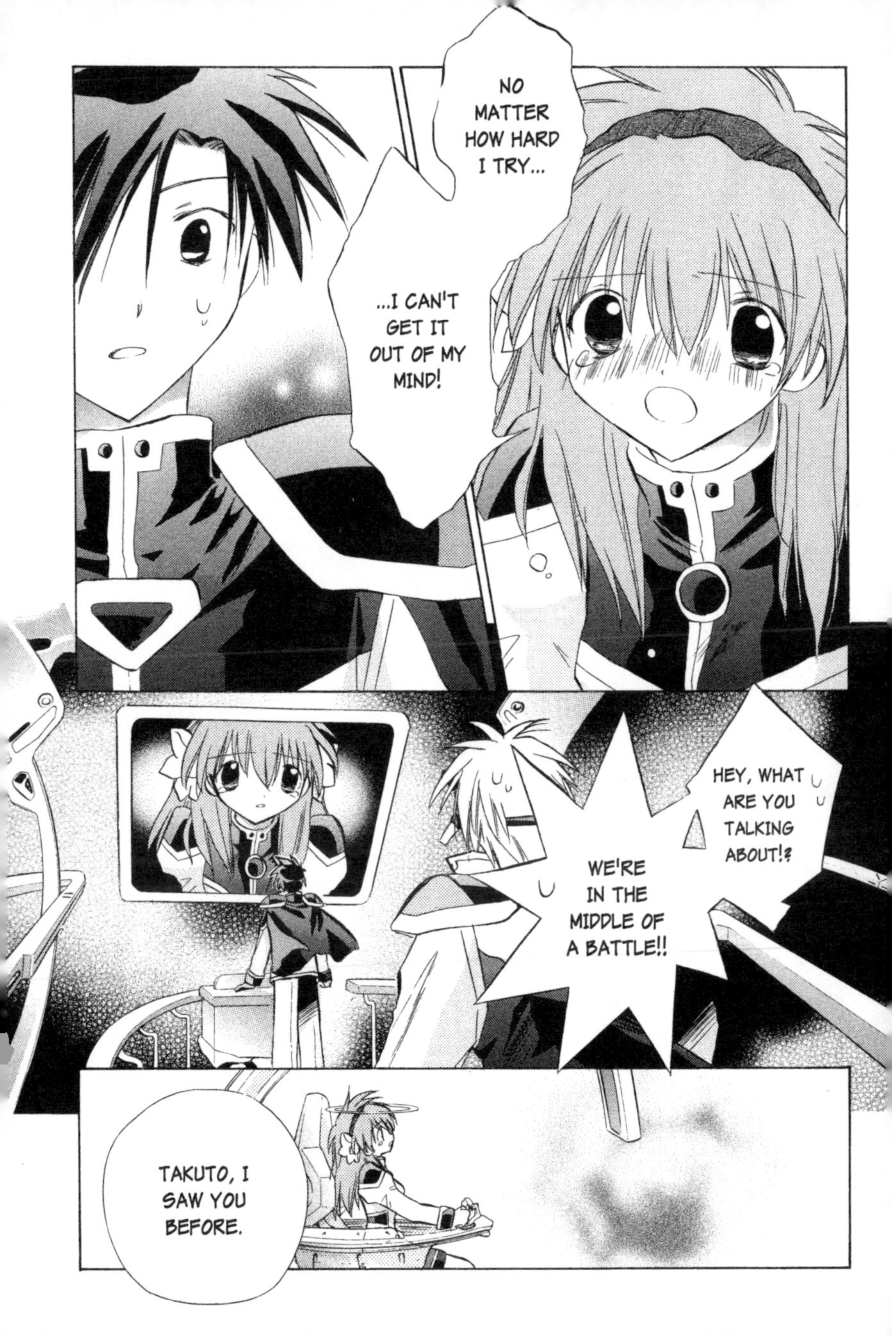
NO MATTER HOW HARD I TRY...
...I CAN'T GET IT OUT OF MY MIND!
HEY, WHAT ARE YOU TALKING ABOUT!?
WE'RE IN THE MIDDLE OF A BATTLE!!
TAKUTO, I SAW YOU BEFORE.

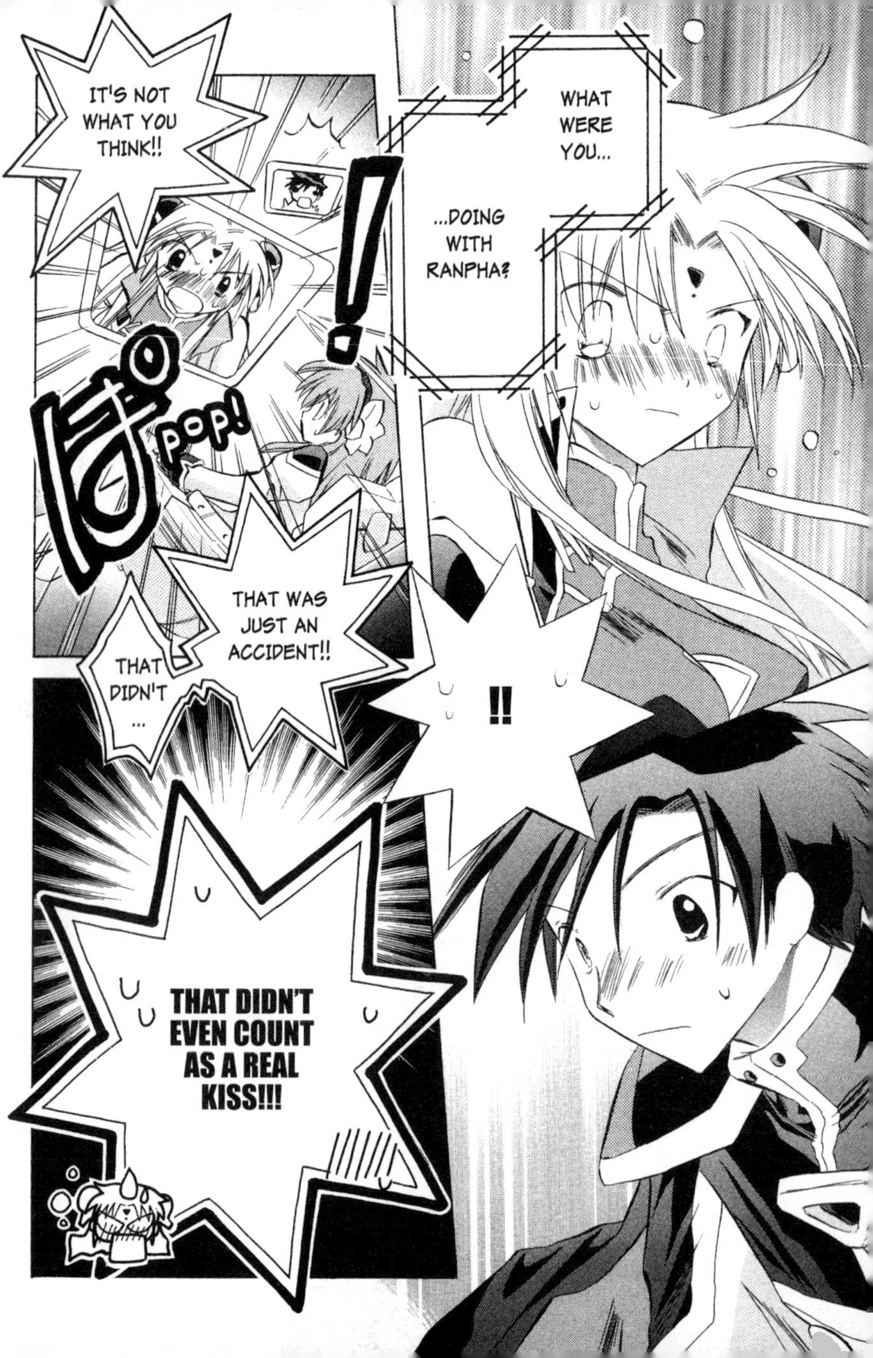
WHAT WERE YOU...
...DOING WITH RANPHA?
IT'S NOT WHAT YOU THINK!!
!
ぽ
POP!
THAT WAS JUST AN ACCIDENT!!
THAT DIDN'T ...
!!
THAT DIDN'T EVEN COUNT AS A REAL KISS!!!

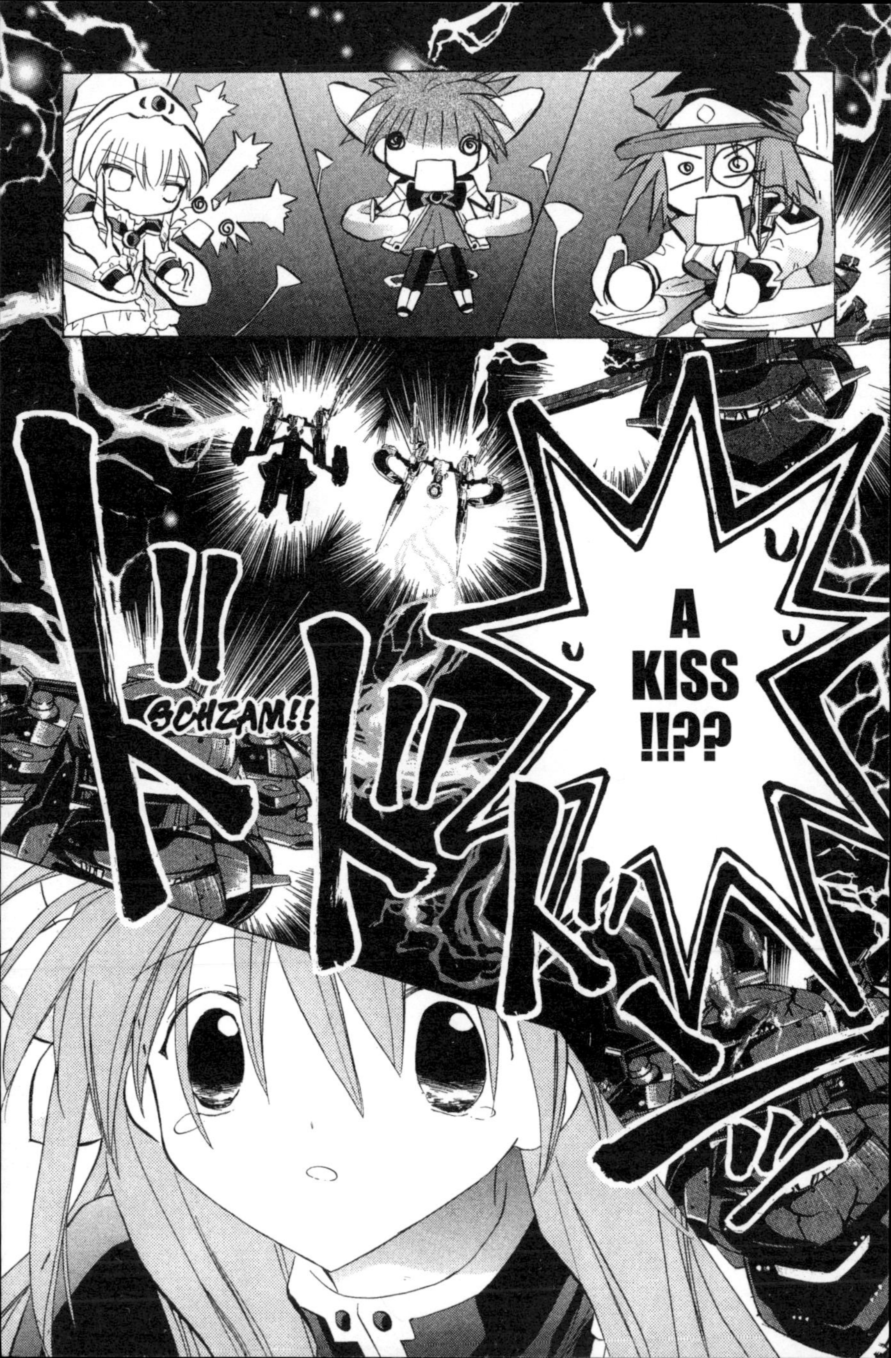
A KISS !!??
SCHZAM!!

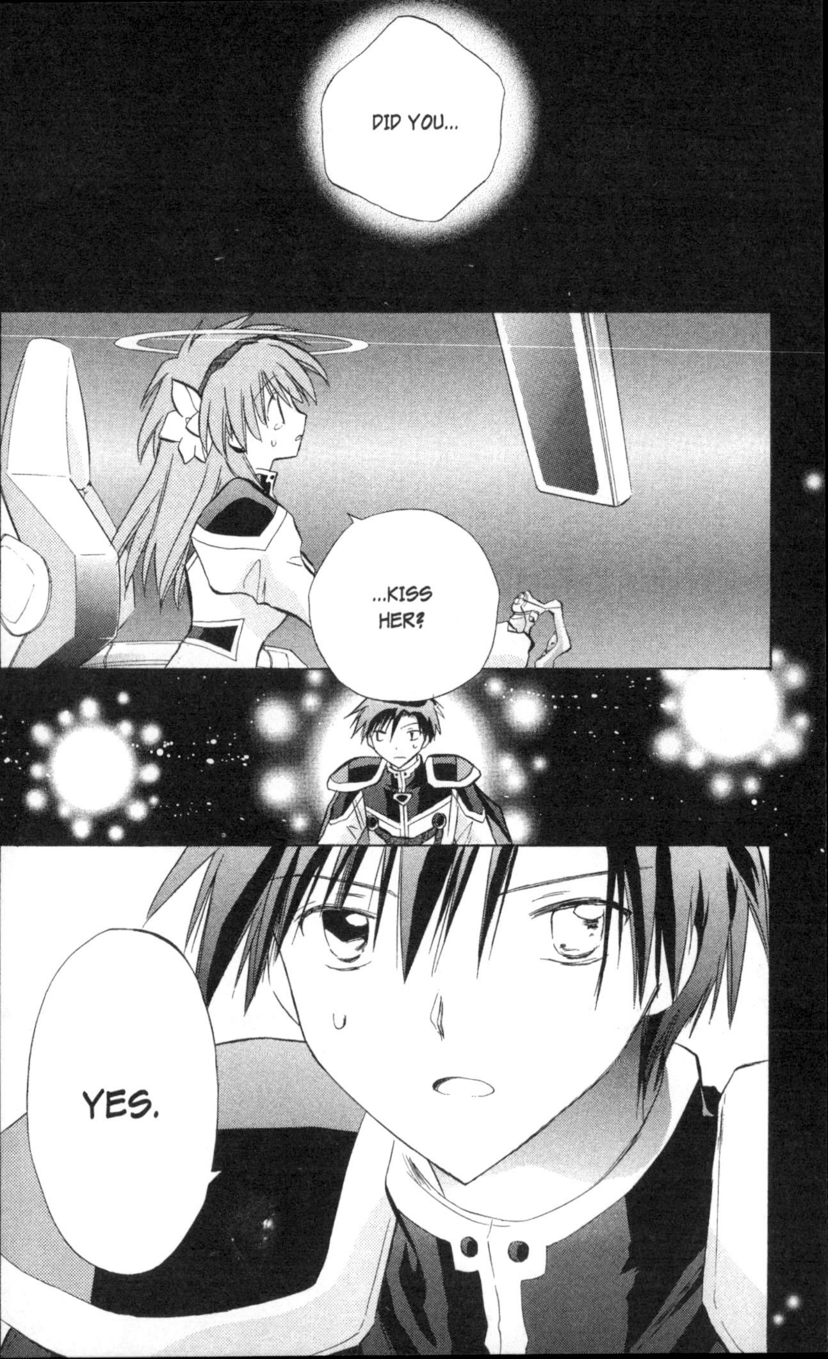
DID YOU...
...KISS HER?
YES.

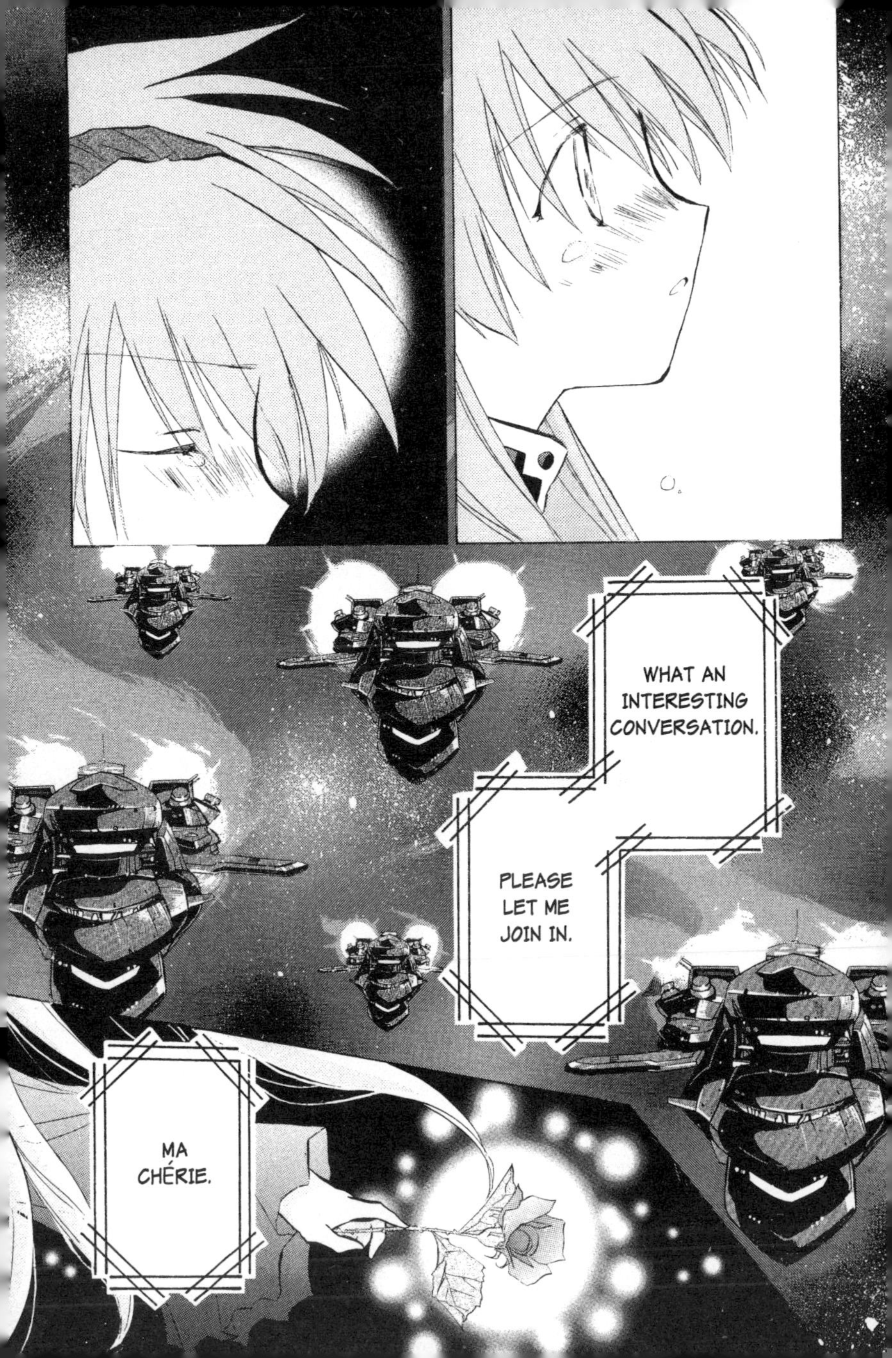
WHAT AN INTERESTING CONVERSATION.
PLEASE LET ME JOIN IN.
MA CHÉRIE.

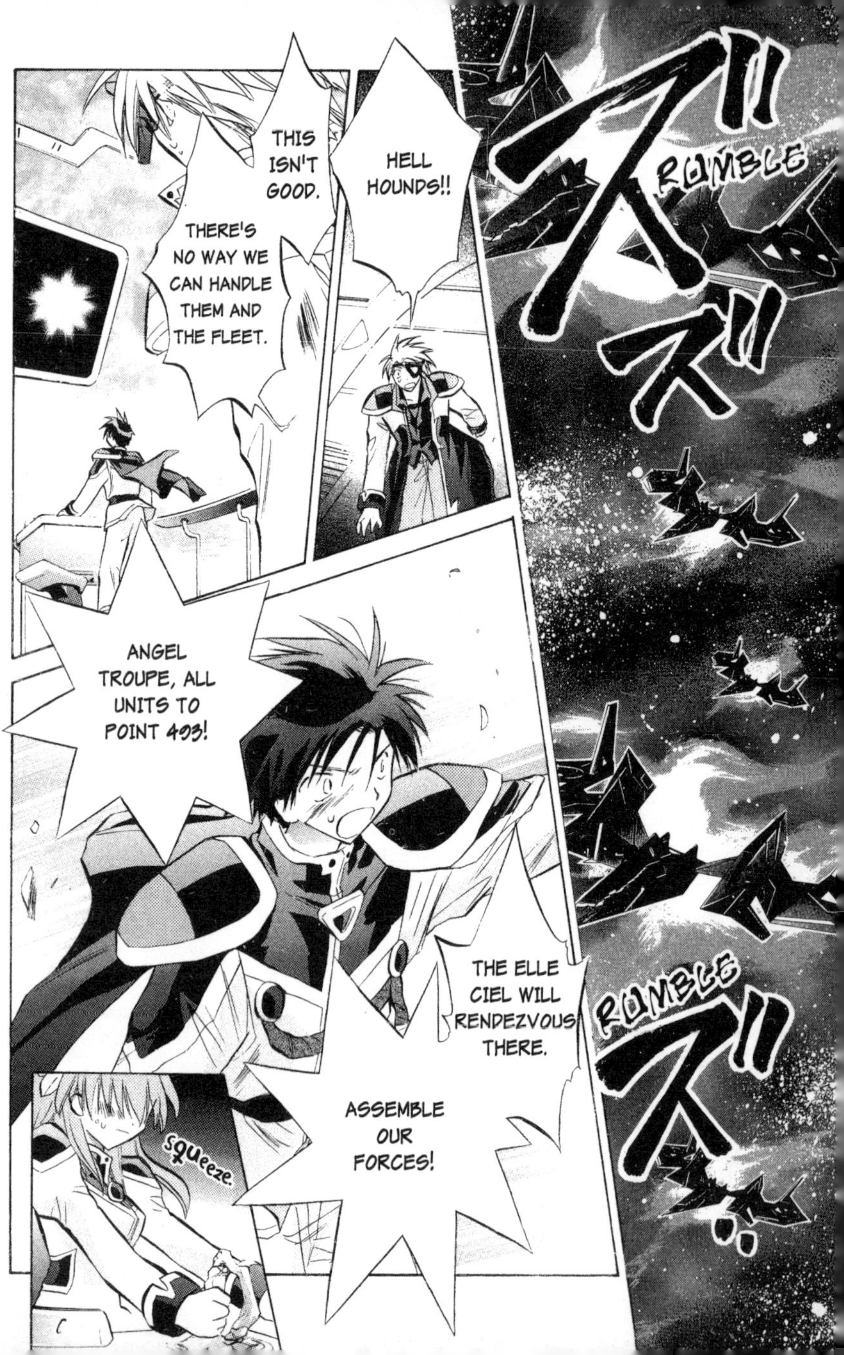
RUMBLE
RUMBLE
HELL HOUNDS!!
THIS ISN'T GOOD.
THERE'S NO WAY WE CAN HANDLE THEM AND THE FLEET.
ANGEL TROUPE, ALL UNITS TO POINT 493!
THE ELLE CIEL WILL RENDEZVOUS THERE.
ASSEMBLE OUR FORCES!
squeeze.

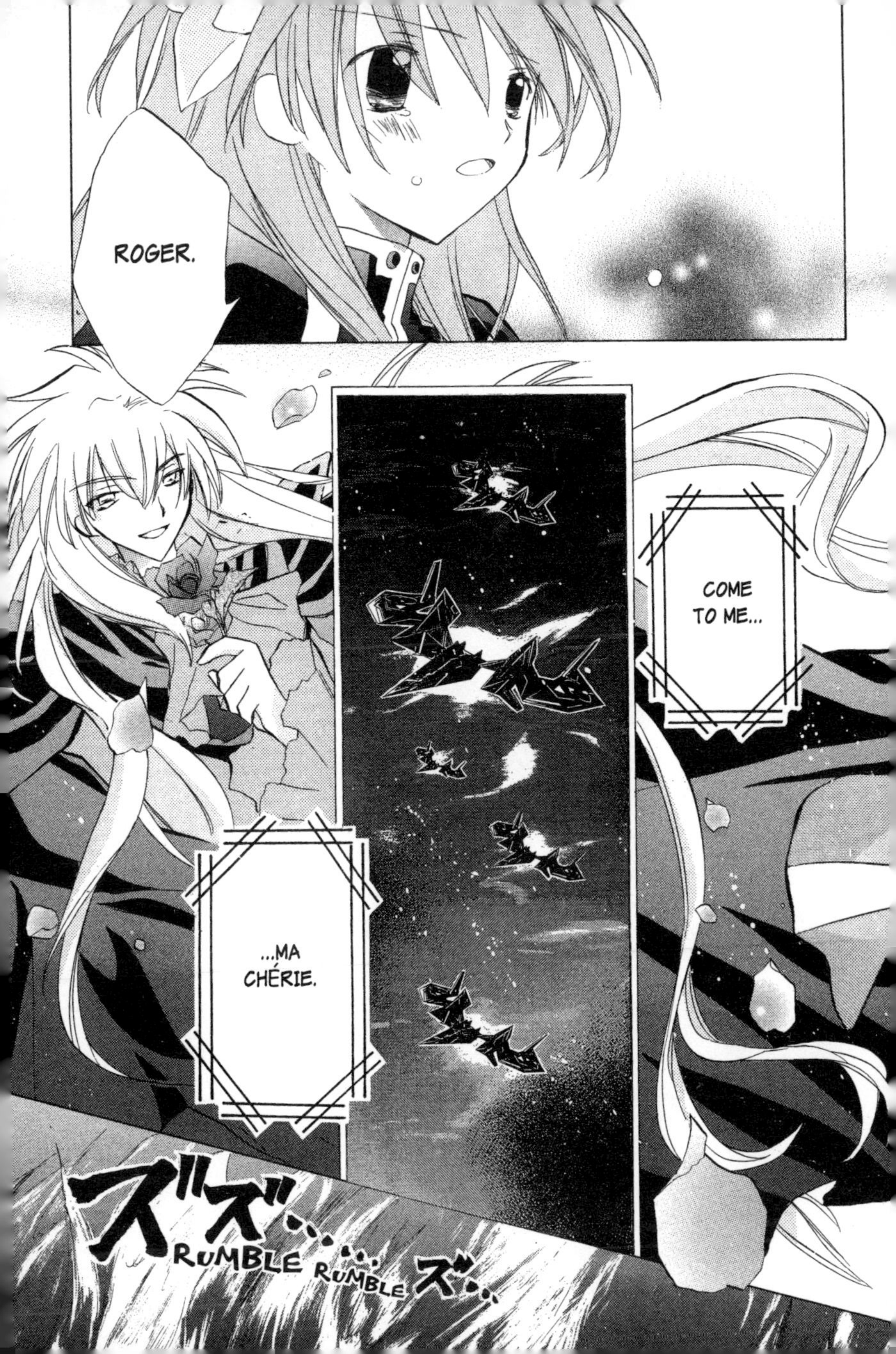
ROGER.
COME TO ME...
...MA CHÉRIE.
ズズ...
RUMBLE RUMBLE
ズ...

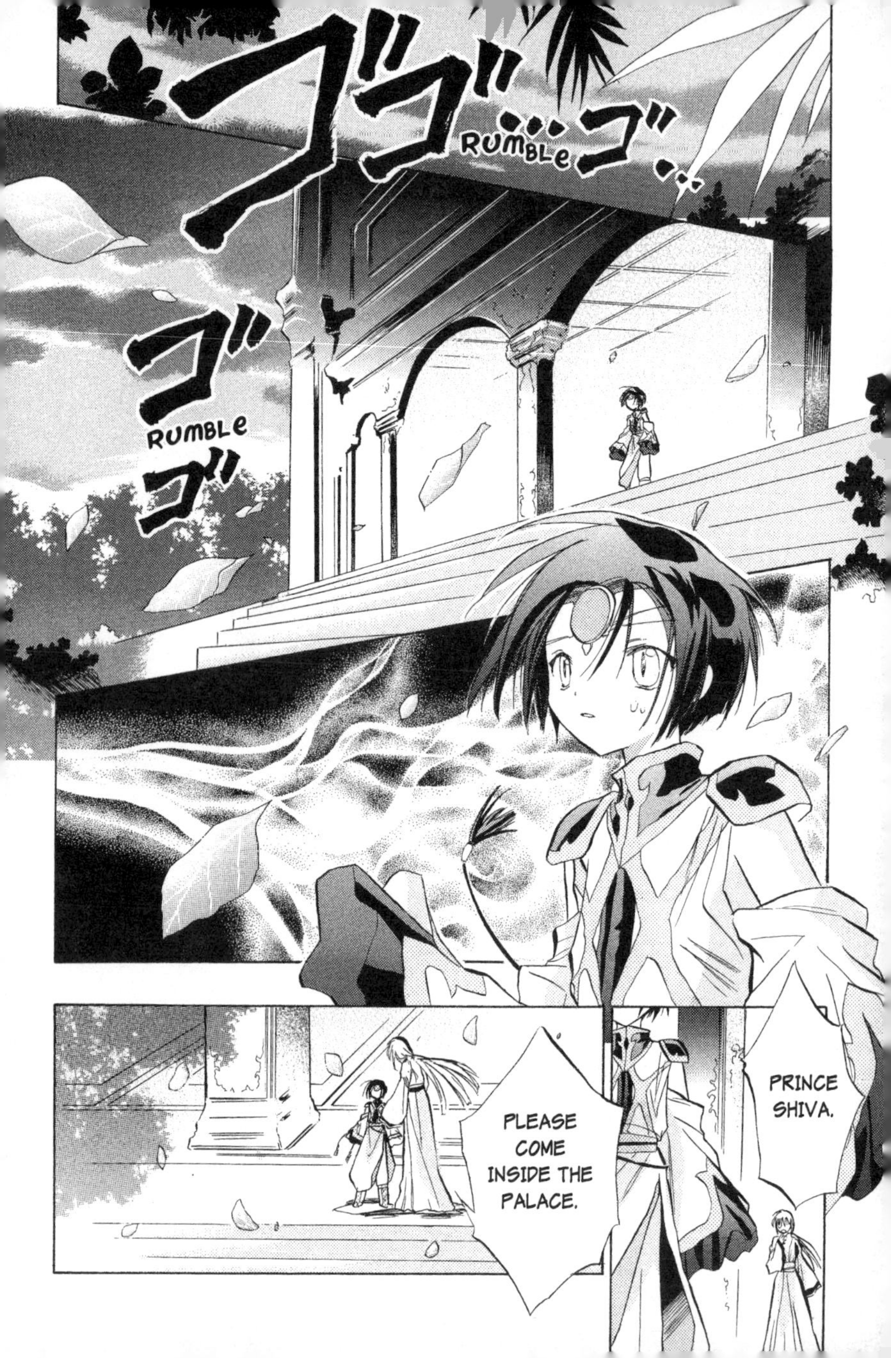
ゴゴ…
RUMBLE
ゴ…
ゴ
RUMBLE
ゴ
PRINCE SHIVA.
PLEASE COME INSIDE THE PALACE.

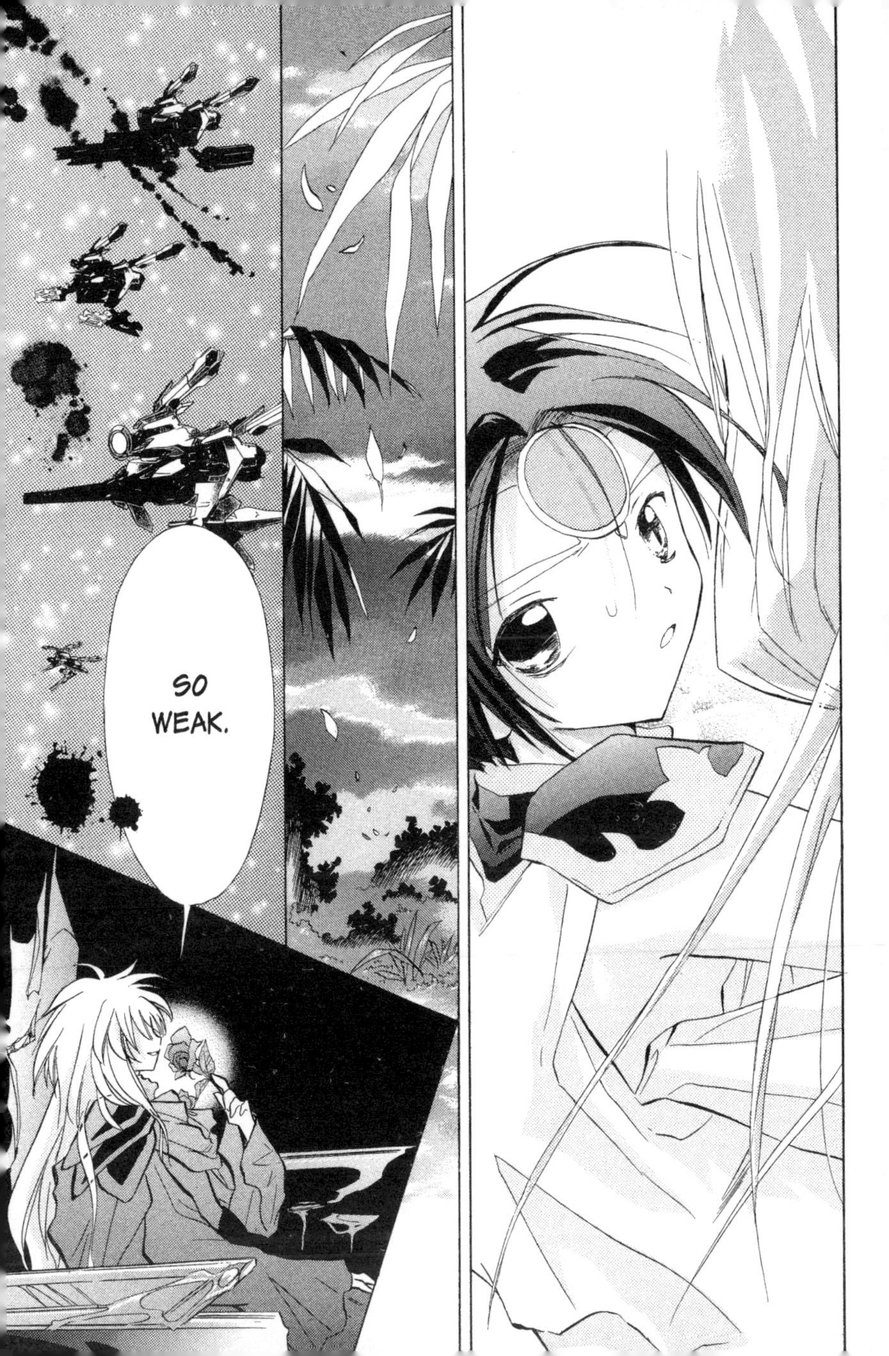
SO WEAK.

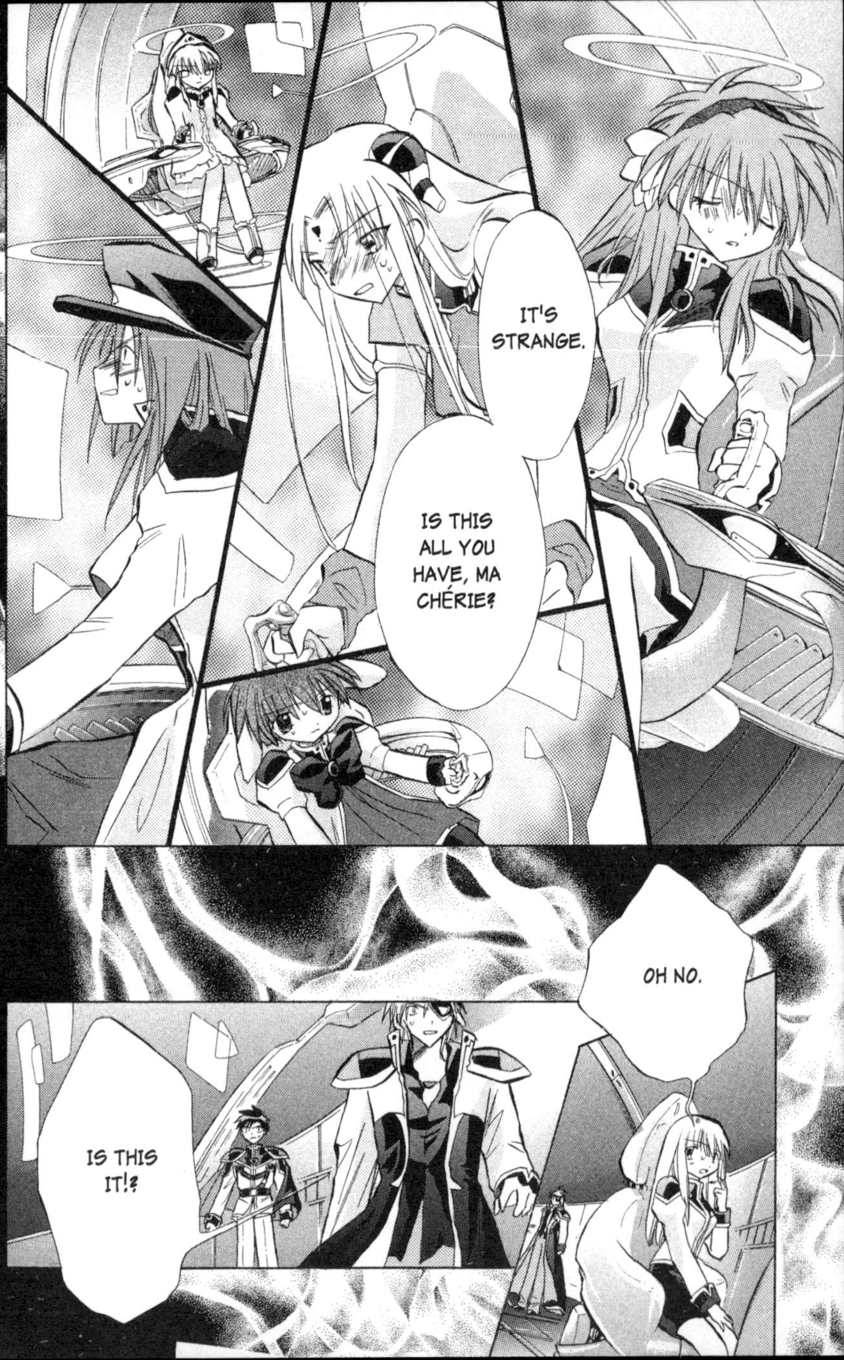
IT'S STRANGE.
IS THIS ALL YOU HAVE, MA CHÉRIE?
OH NO.
IS THIS IT!?

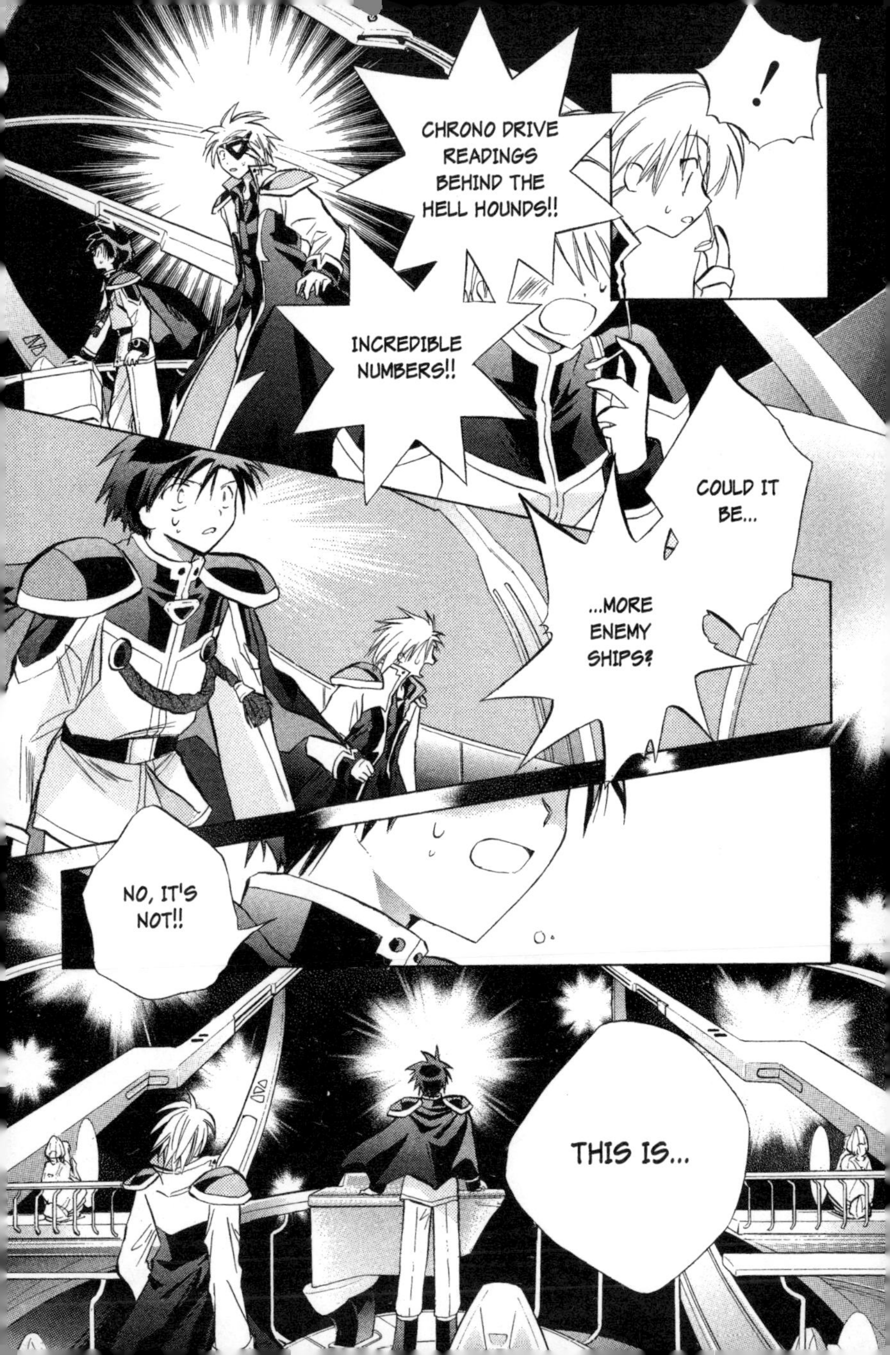
!
CHRONO DRIVE READINGS BEHIND THE HELL HOUNDS!!
INCREDIBLE NUMBERS!!
COULD IT BE...
...MORE ENEMY SHIPS?
NO, IT'S NOT!!
THIS IS...

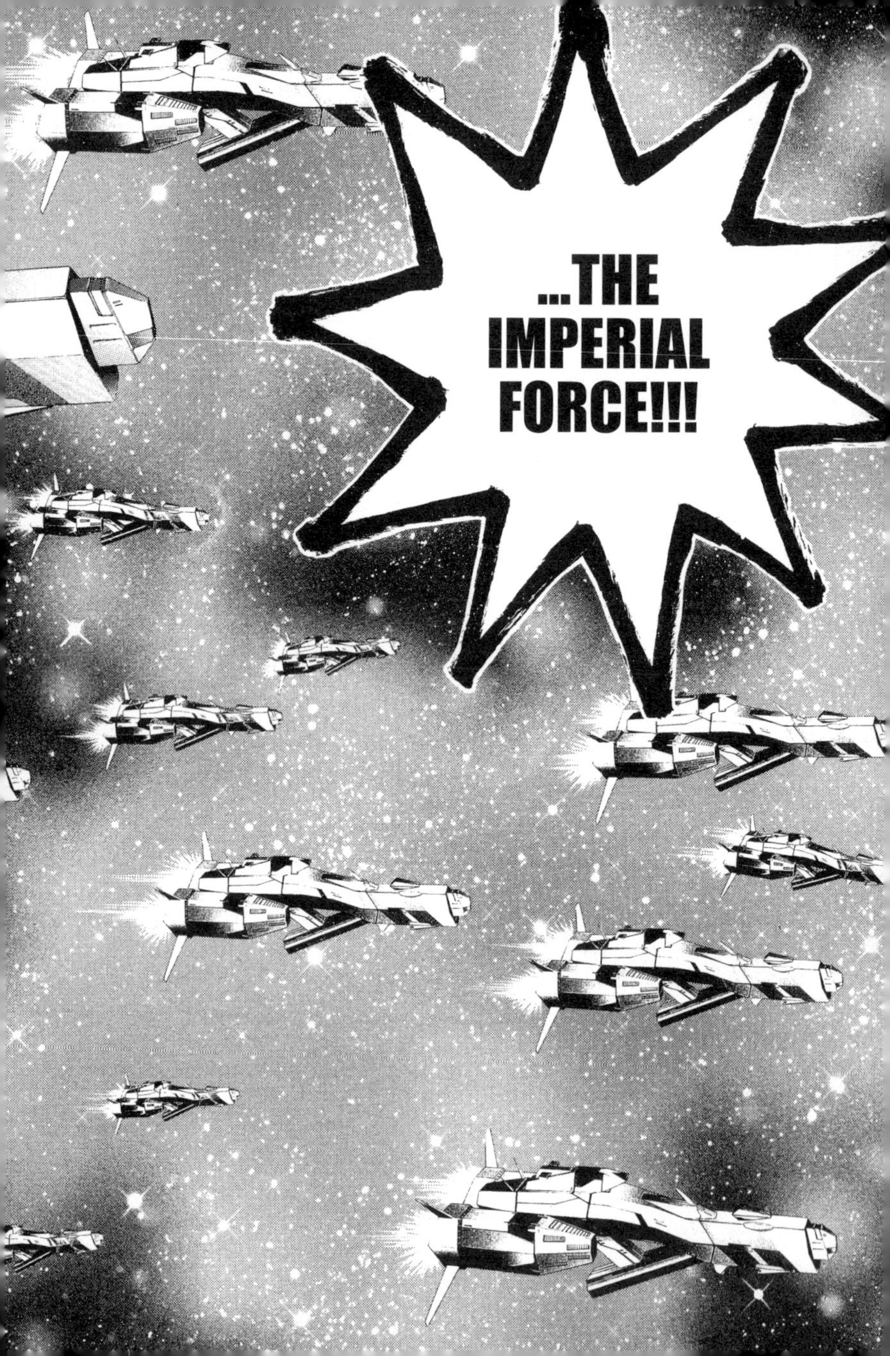
...THE IMPERIAL FORCE!!!

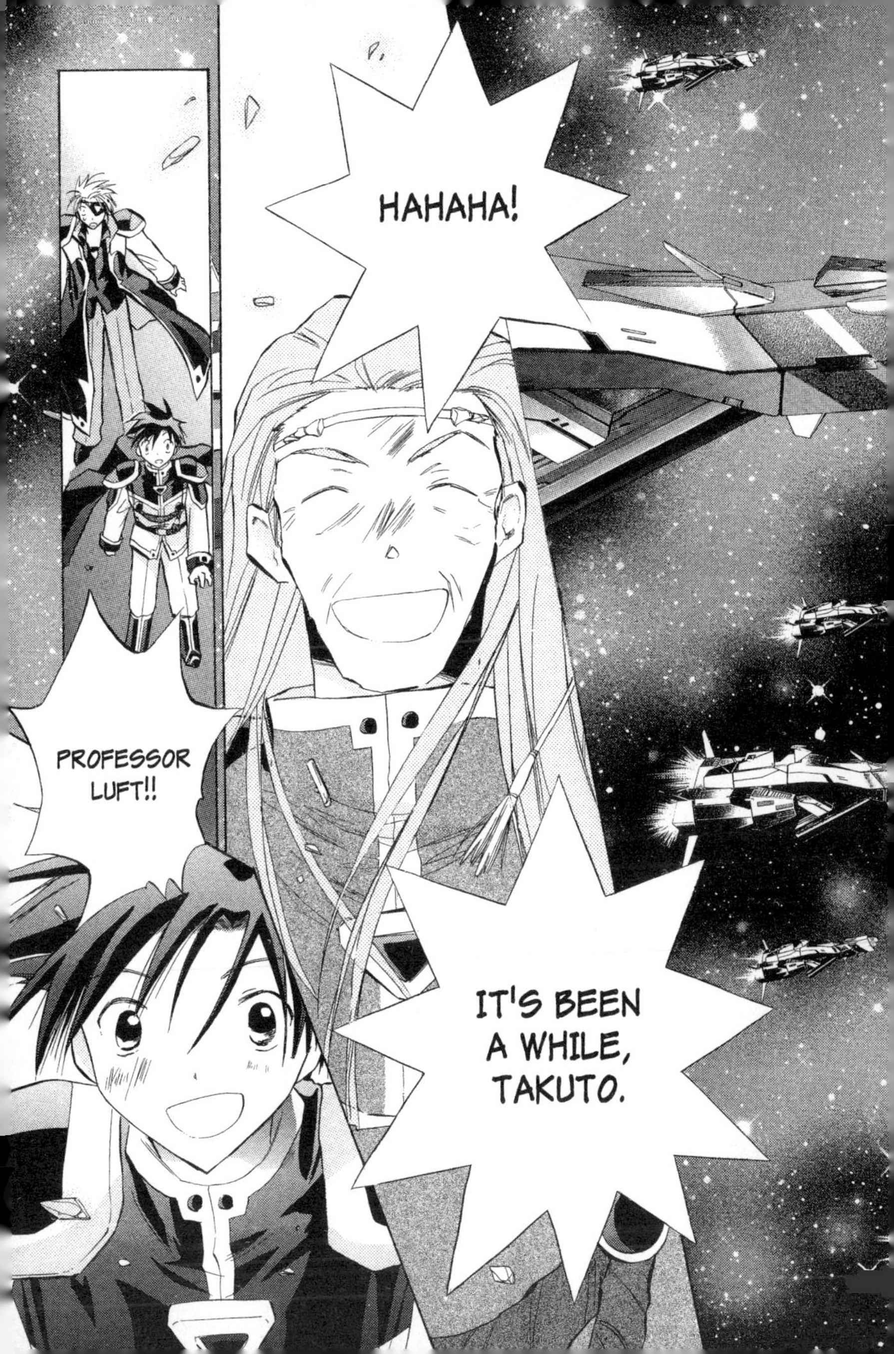
HAHAHA!
PROFESSOR LUFT!!
IT'S BEEN A WHILE, TAKUTO.

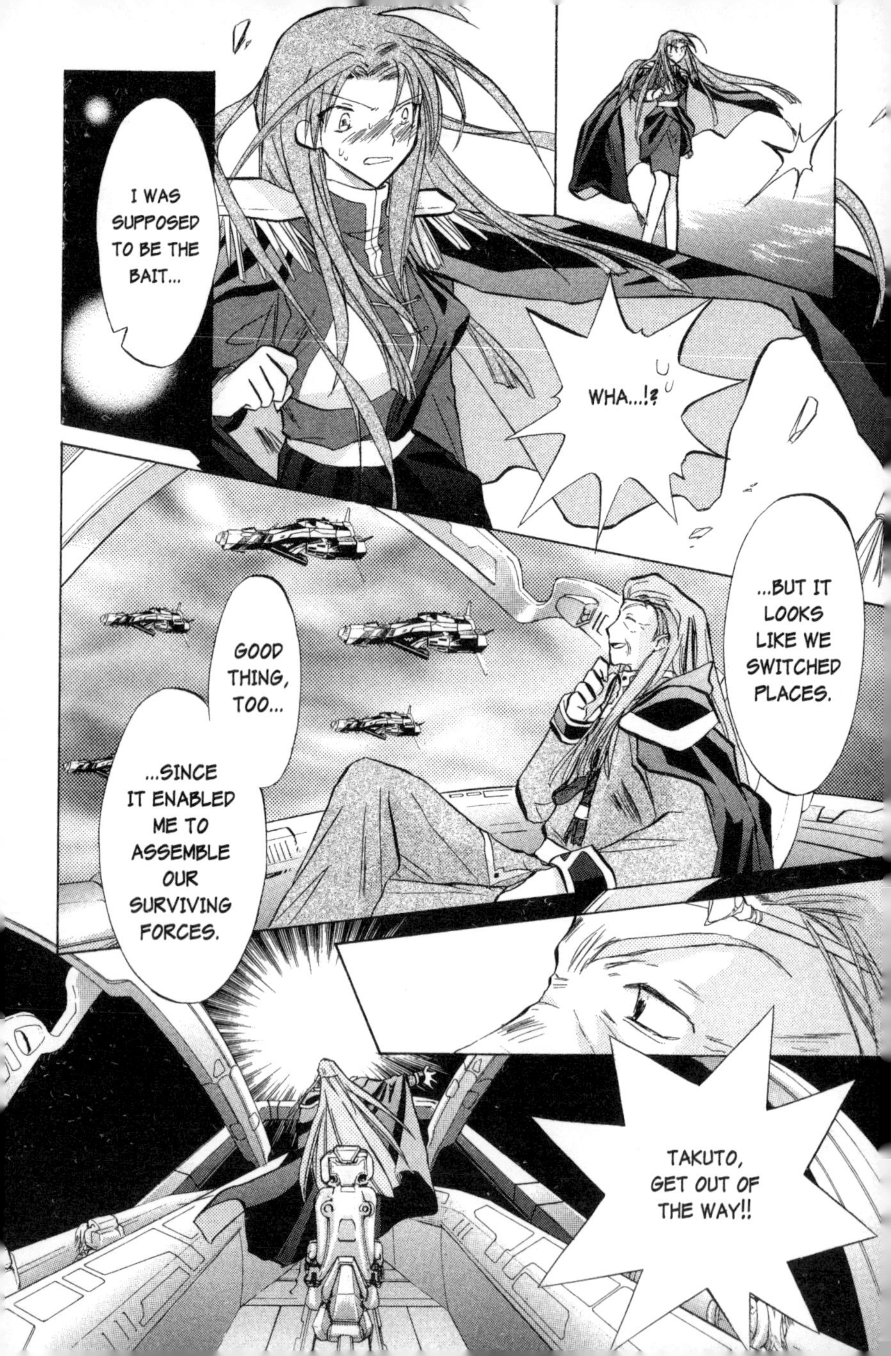
I WAS SUPPOSED TO BE THE BAIT...
WHA...!?
...BUT IT LOOKS LIKE WE SWITCHED PLACES.
GOOD THING, TOO...
...SINCE IT ENABLED ME TO ASSEMBLE OUR SURVIVING FORCES.
TAKUTO, GET OUT OF THE WAY!!

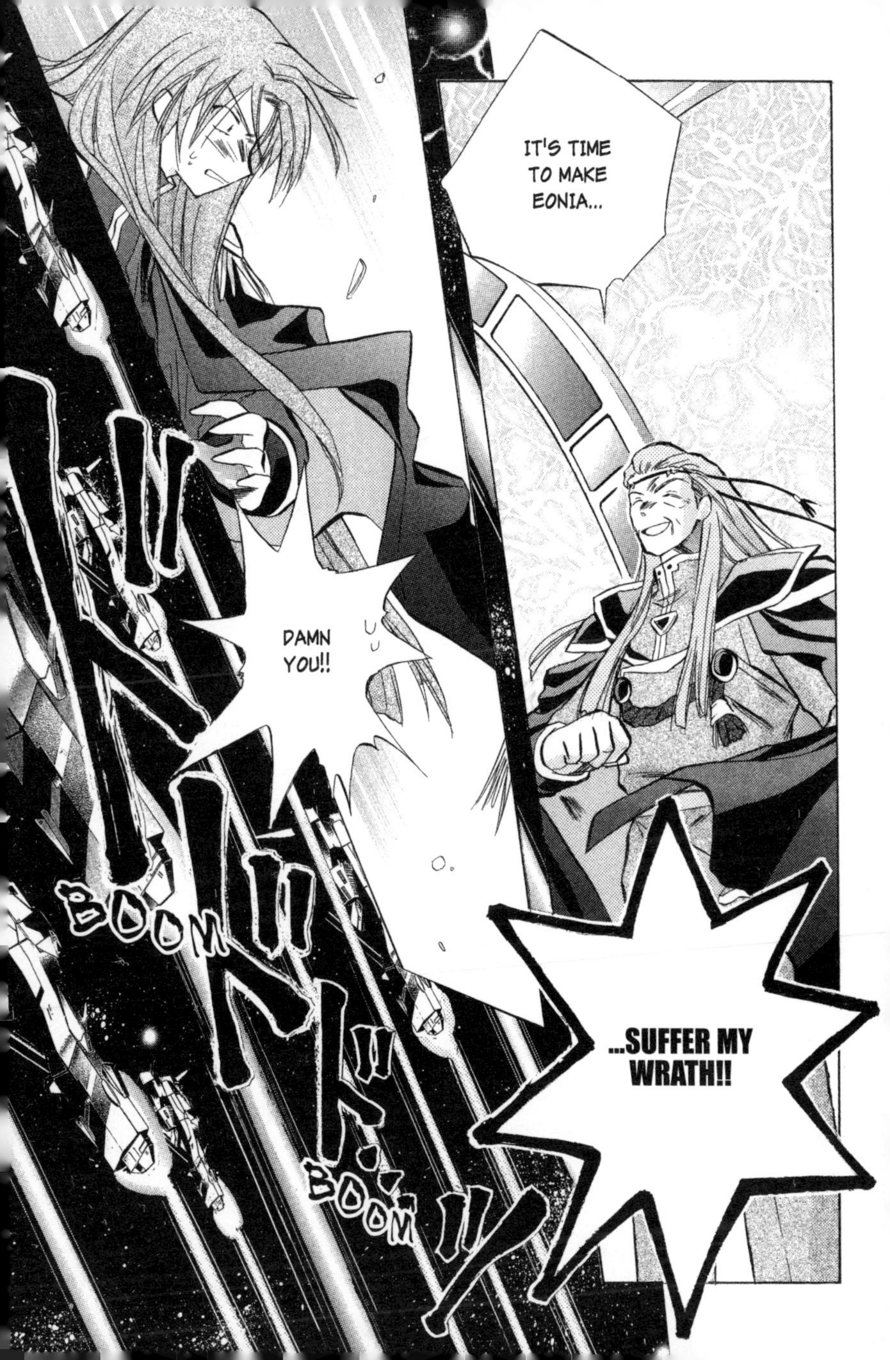
IT'S TIME TO MAKE EONIA...
...SUFFER MY WRATH!!
DAMN YOU!!
BOOM
BOOM

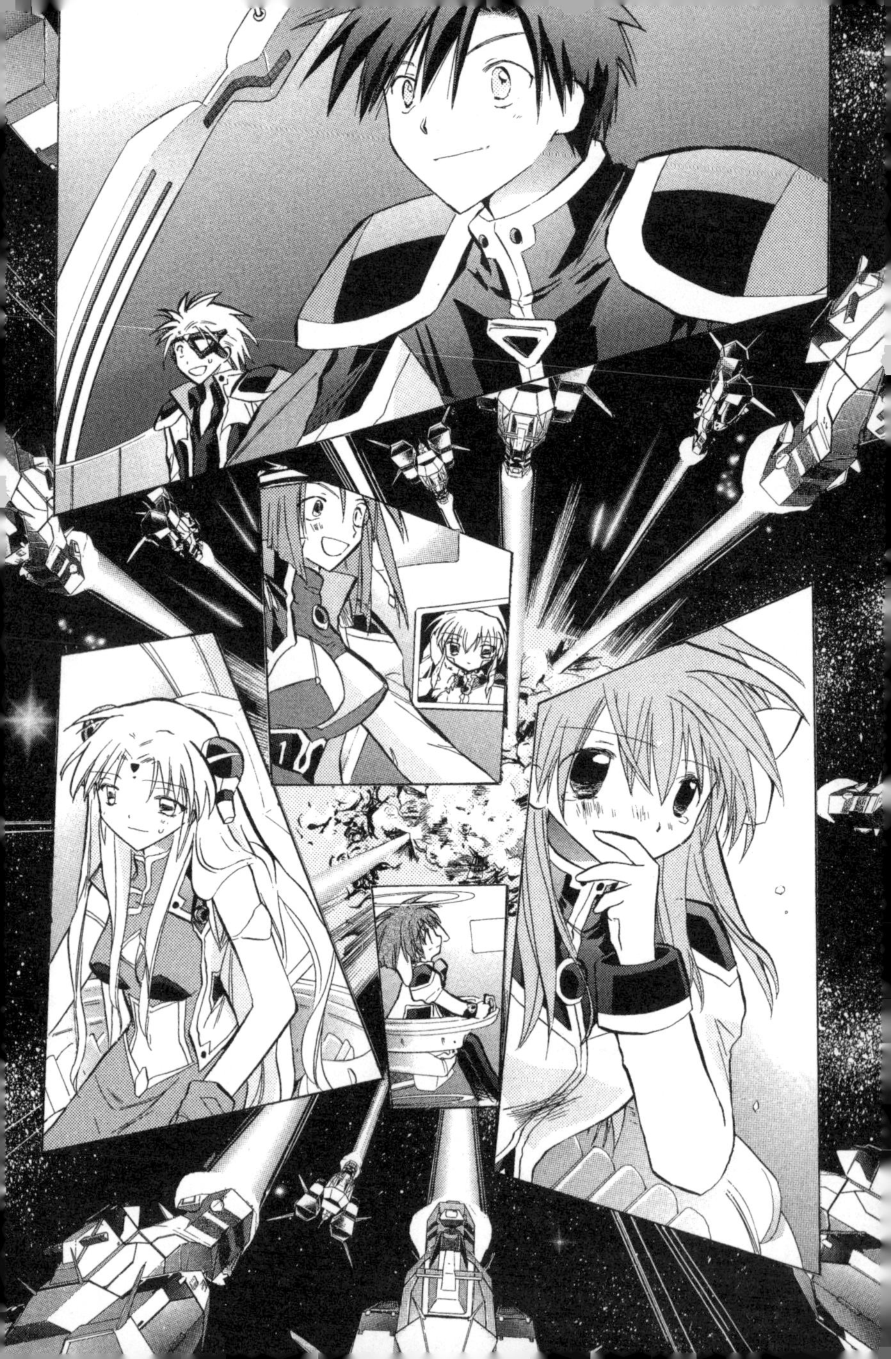

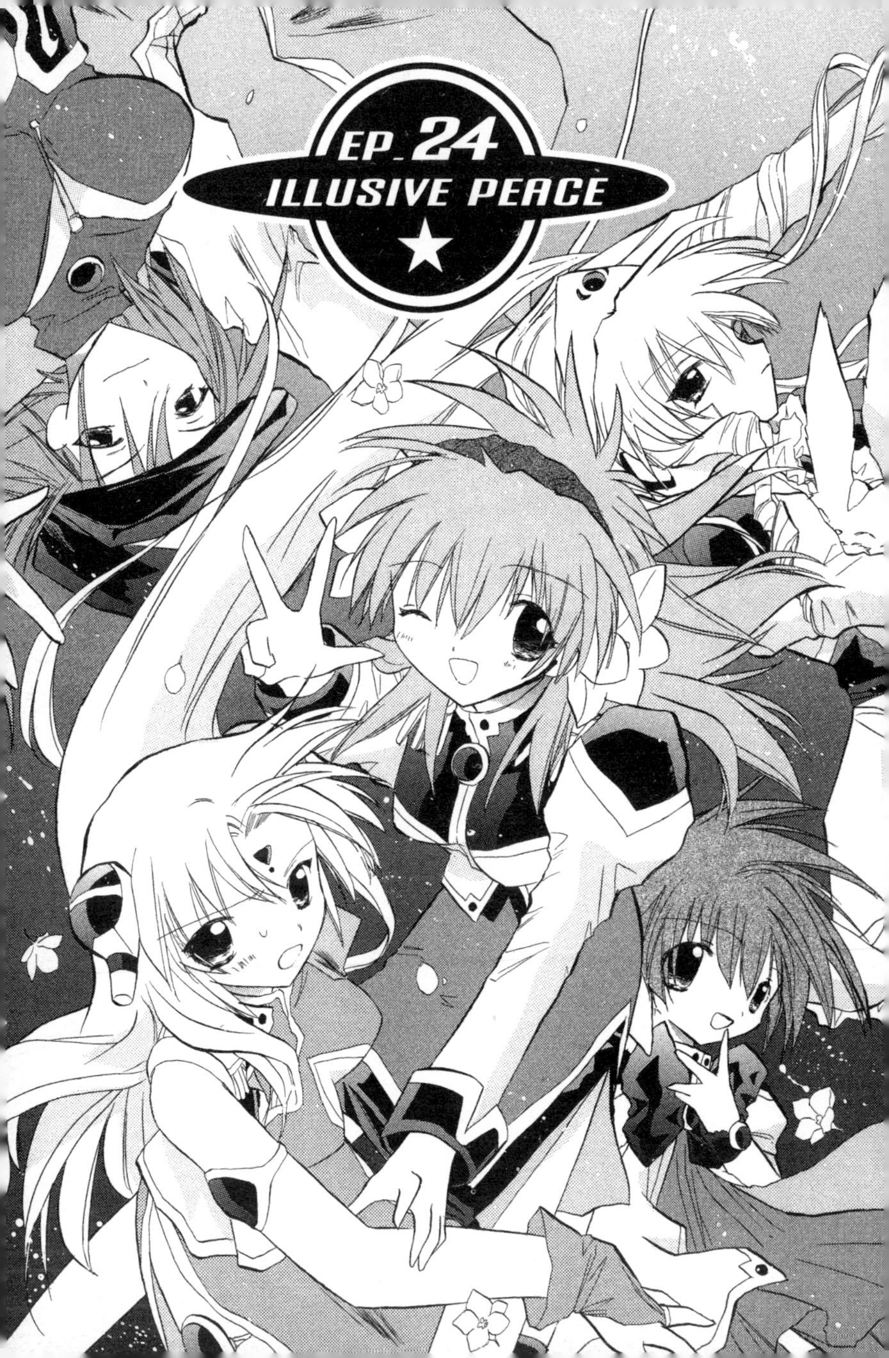
EP_24
ILLUSIVE PEACE

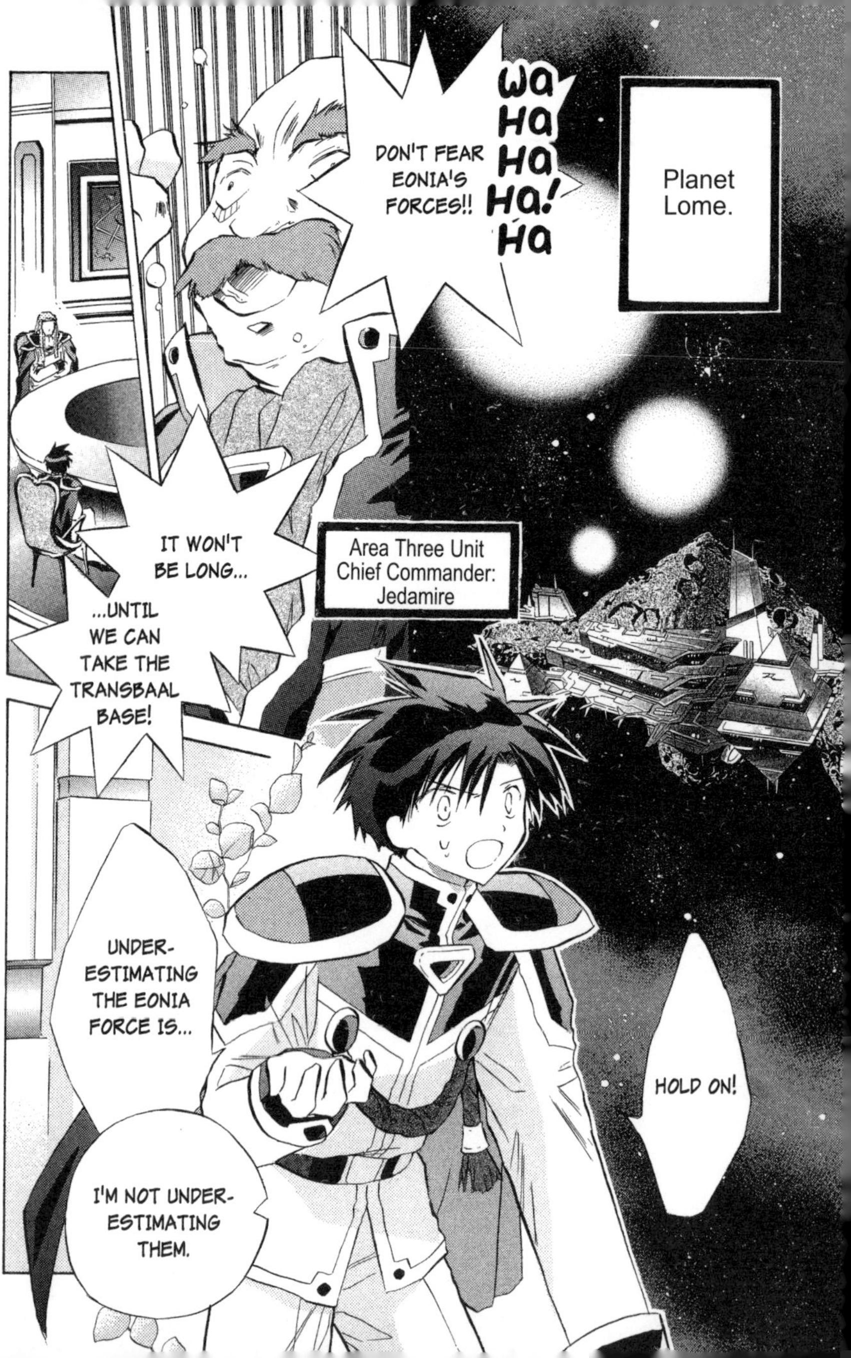
Planet Lome.
WA HA HA HA! HA
DON'T FEAR EONIA'S FORCES!!
Area Three Unit Chief Commander: Jedamire
IT WON'T BE LONG...
...UNTIL WE CAN TAKE THE TRANSBAAL BASE!
HOLD ON!
UNDER-ESTIMATING THE EONIA FORCE IS...
I'M NOT UNDER-ESTIMATING THEM.

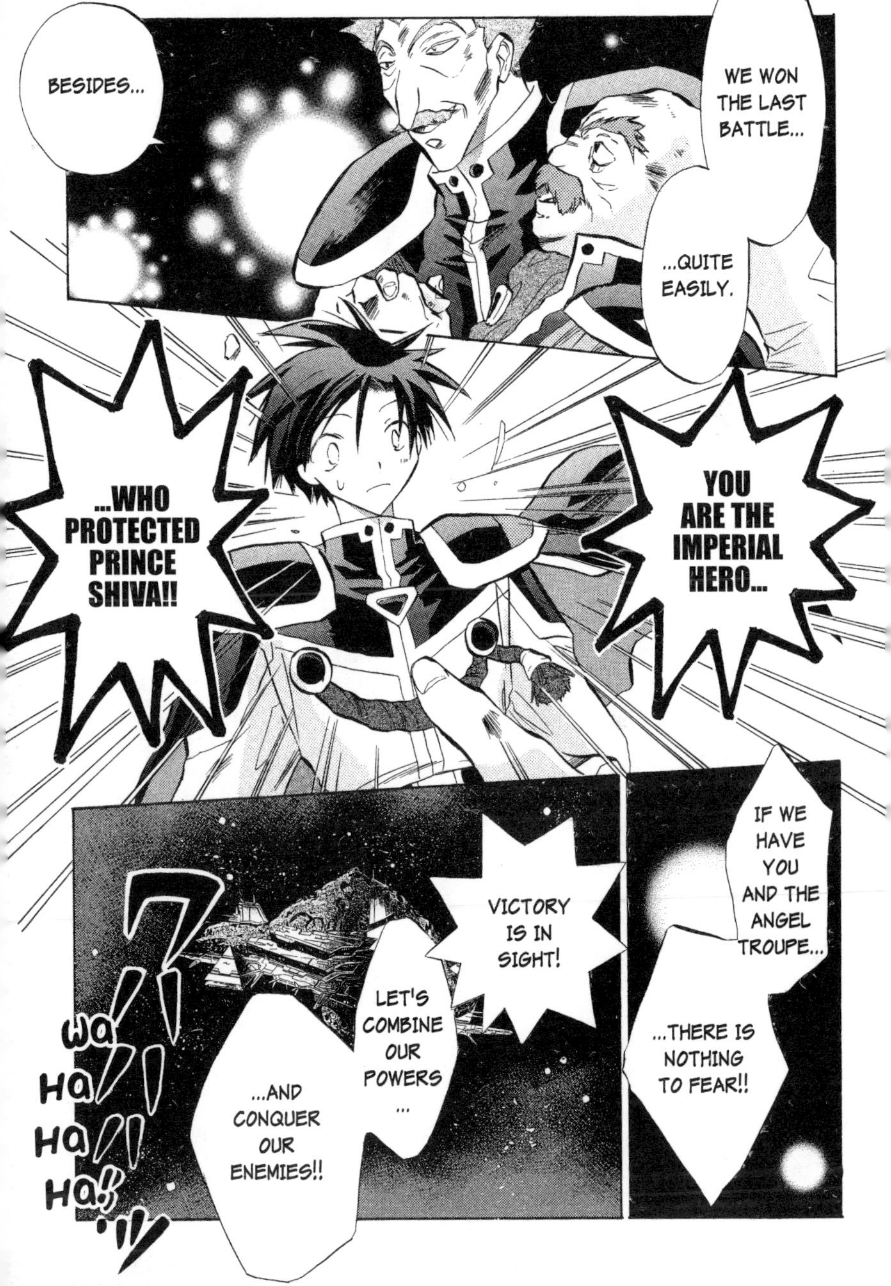
WE WON THE LAST BATTLE...
...QUITE EASILY.
BESIDES...
YOU ARE THE IMPERIAL HERO...
...WHO PROTECTED PRINCE SHIVA!!
IF WE HAVE YOU AND THE ANGEL TROUPE...
...THERE IS NOTHING TO FEAR!!
VICTORY IS IN SIGHT!
LET'S COMBINE OUR POWERS ...
...AND CONQUER OUR ENEMIES!!
Wa Ha Ha Ha!!

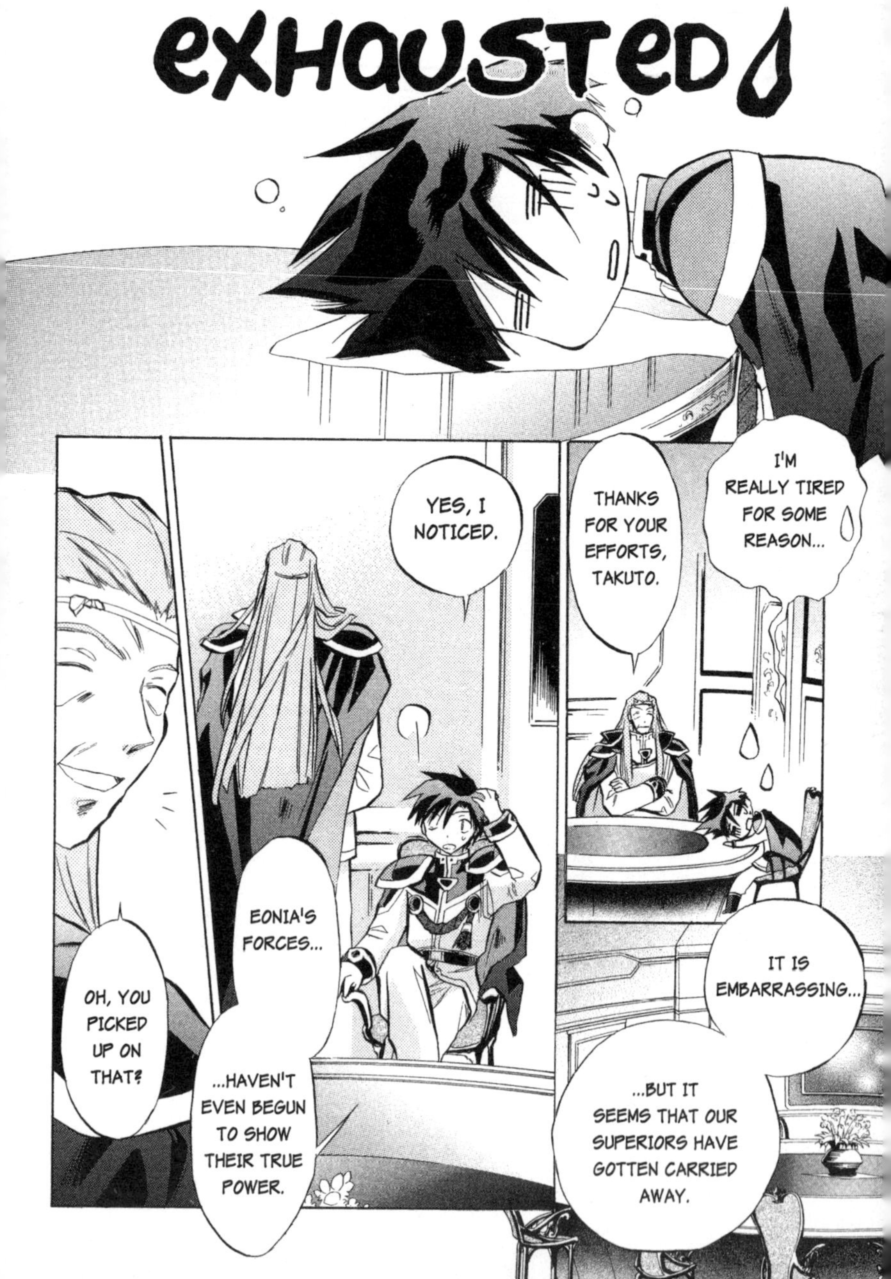
exhausted
I'M REALLY TIRED FOR SOME REASON...
THANKS FOR YOUR EFFORTS, TAKUTO.
YES, I NOTICED.
EONIA'S FORCES...
...HAVEN'T EVEN BEGUN TO SHOW THEIR TRUE POWER.
OH, YOU PICKED UP ON THAT?
IT IS EMBARRASSING...
...BUT IT SEEMS THAT OUR SUPERIORS HAVE GOTTEN CARRIED AWAY.

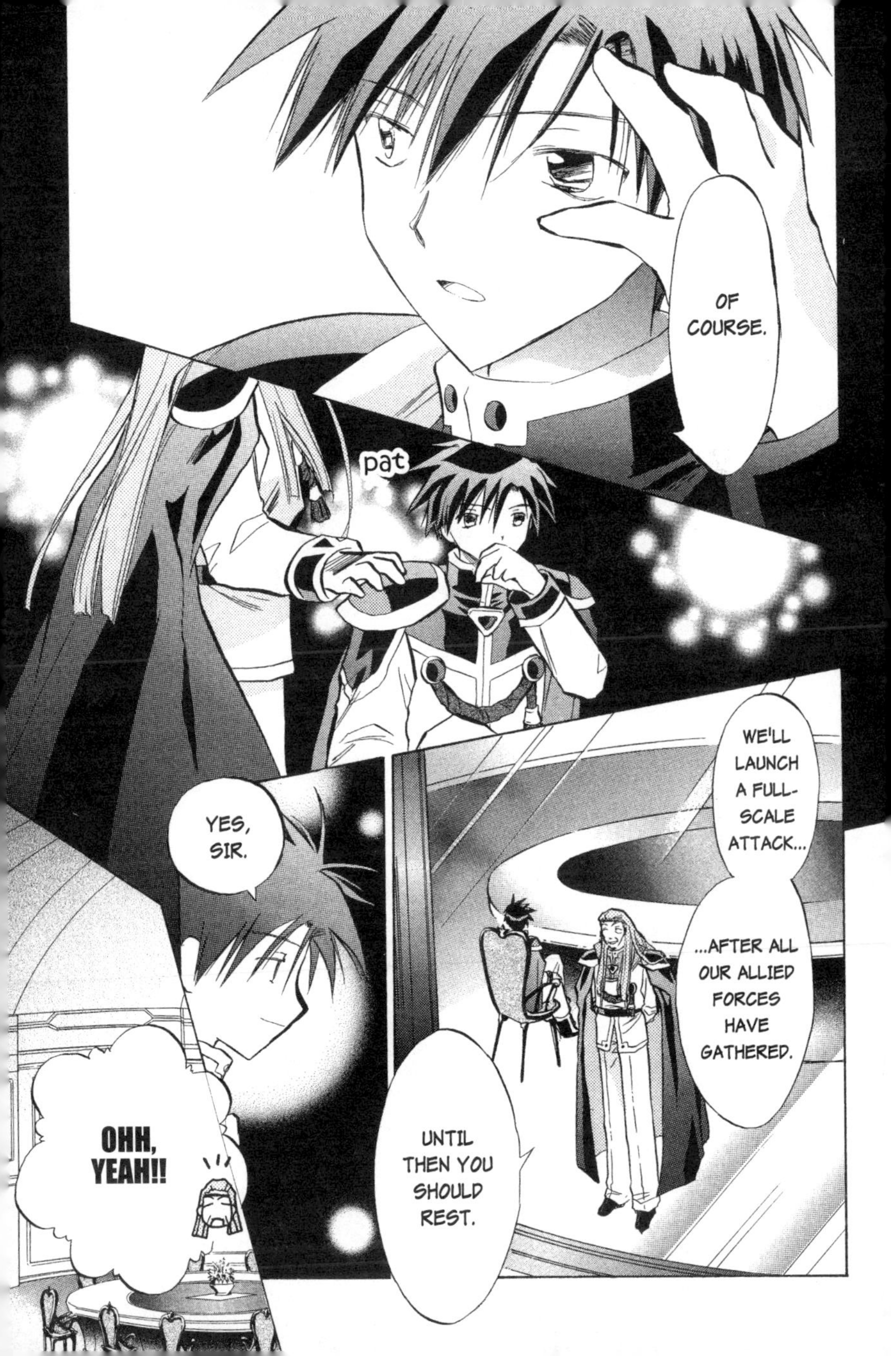
OF COURSE.
pat
WE'LL LAUNCH A FULL-SCALE ATTACK...
...AFTER ALL OUR ALLIED FORCES HAVE GATHERED.
UNTIL THEN YOU SHOULD REST.
YES, SIR.
OHH, YEAH!!

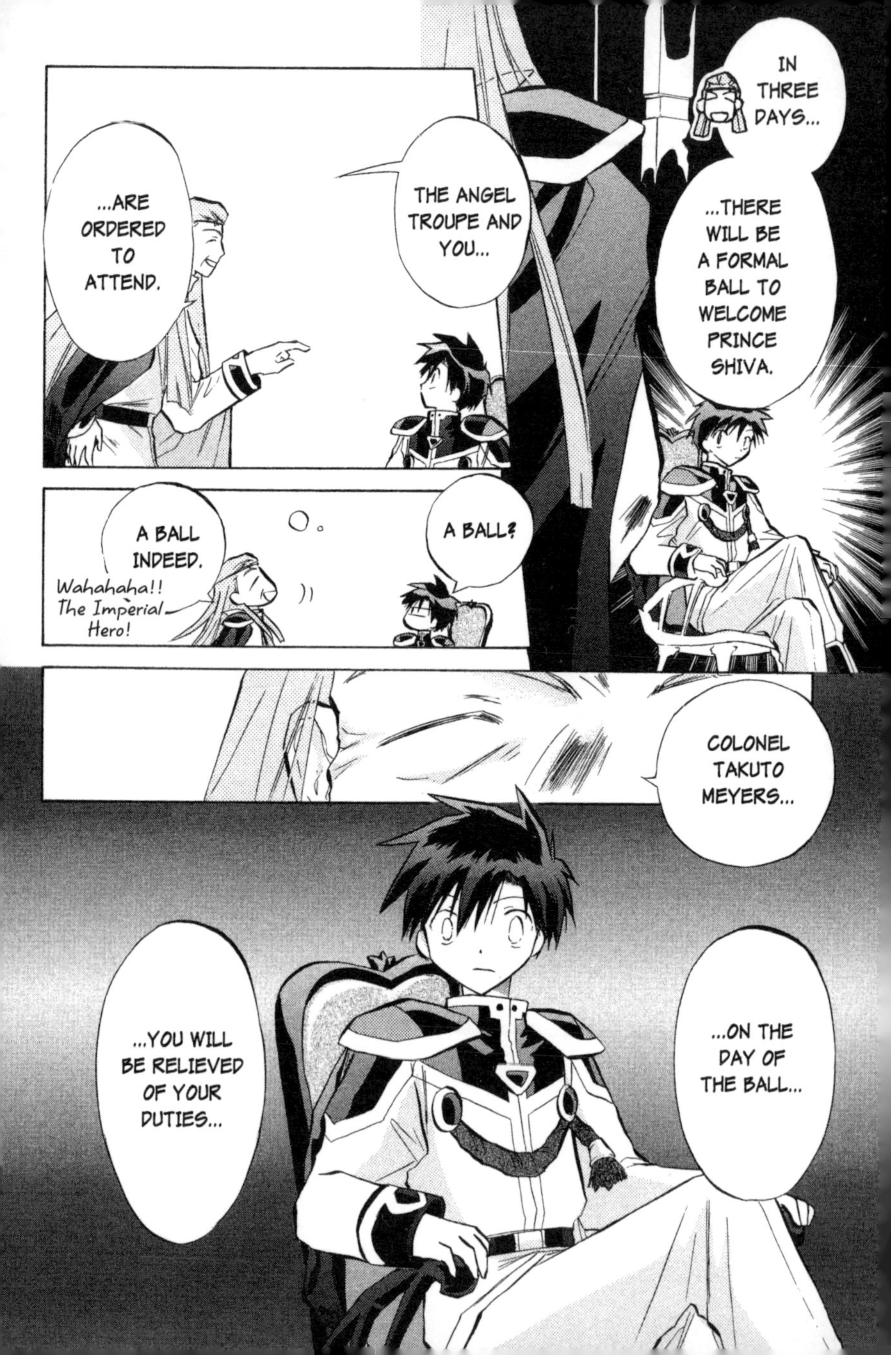
IN THREE DAYS...
...THERE WILL BE A FORMAL BALL TO WELCOME PRINCE SHIVA.
THE ANGEL TROUPE AND YOU...
...ARE ORDERED TO ATTEND.
A BALL?
A BALL INDEED.
Wahahaha!! The Imperial Hero!
COLONEL TAKUTO MEYERS...
...ON THE DAY OF THE BALL...
...YOU WILL BE RELIEVED OF YOUR DUTIES...

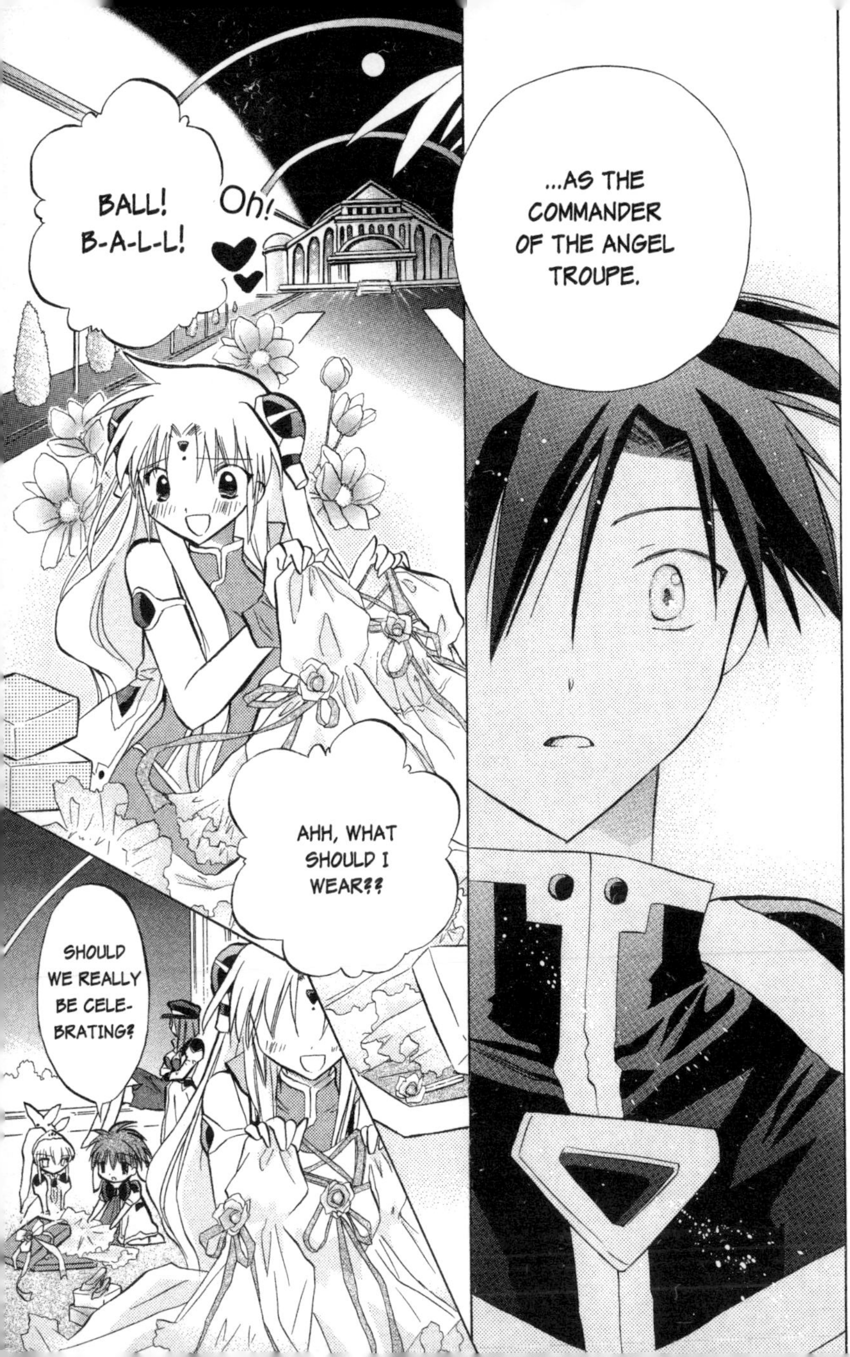
...AS THE COMMANDER OF THE ANGEL TROUPE.
Oh!
BALL! B-A-L-L!
AHH, WHAT SHOULD I WEAR??
SHOULD WE REALLY BE CELE-BRATING?

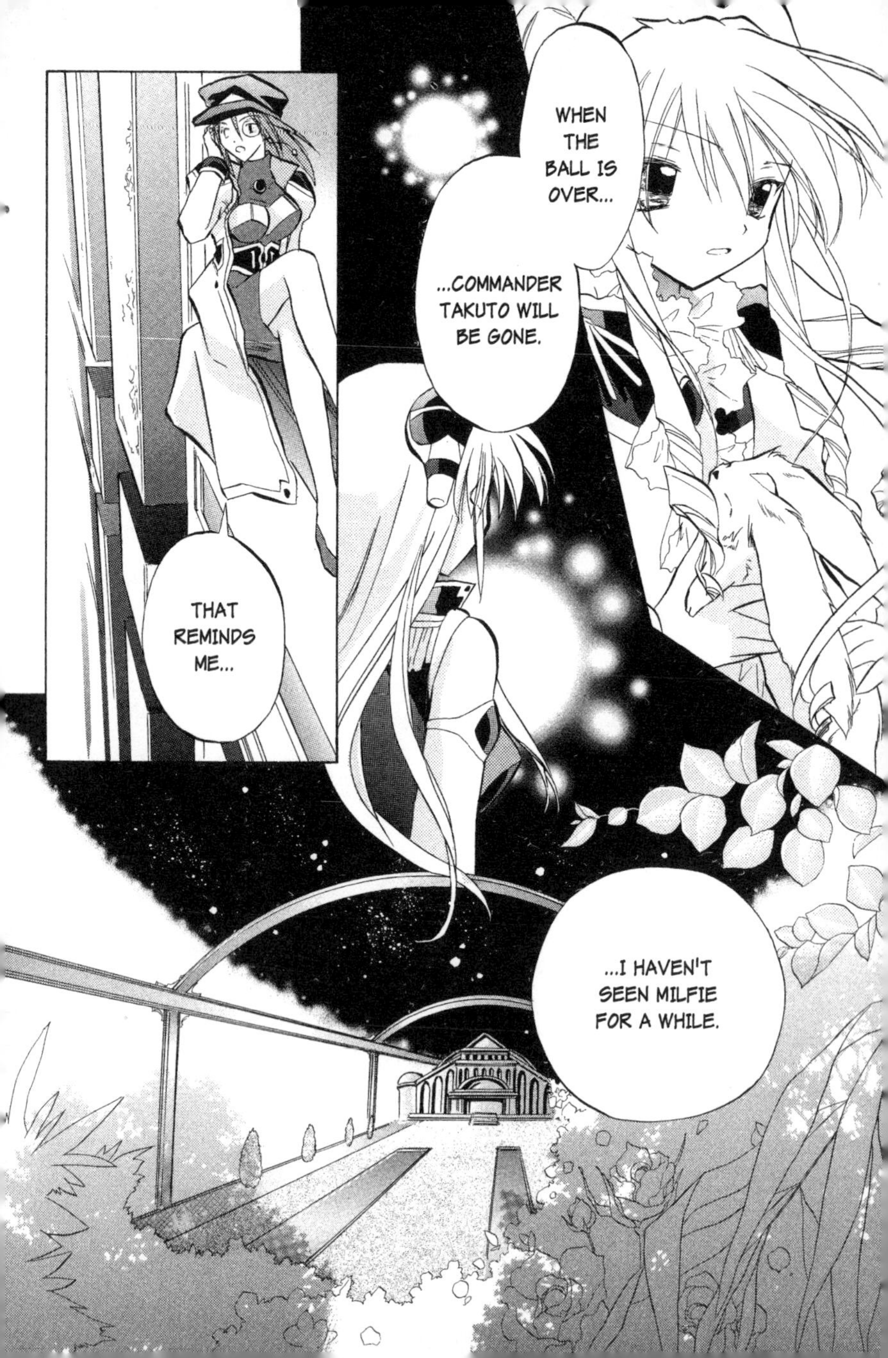
WHEN THE BALL IS OVER...
...COMMANDER TAKUTO WILL BE GONE.
THAT REMINDS ME...
...I HAVEN'T SEEN MILFIE FOR A WHILE.

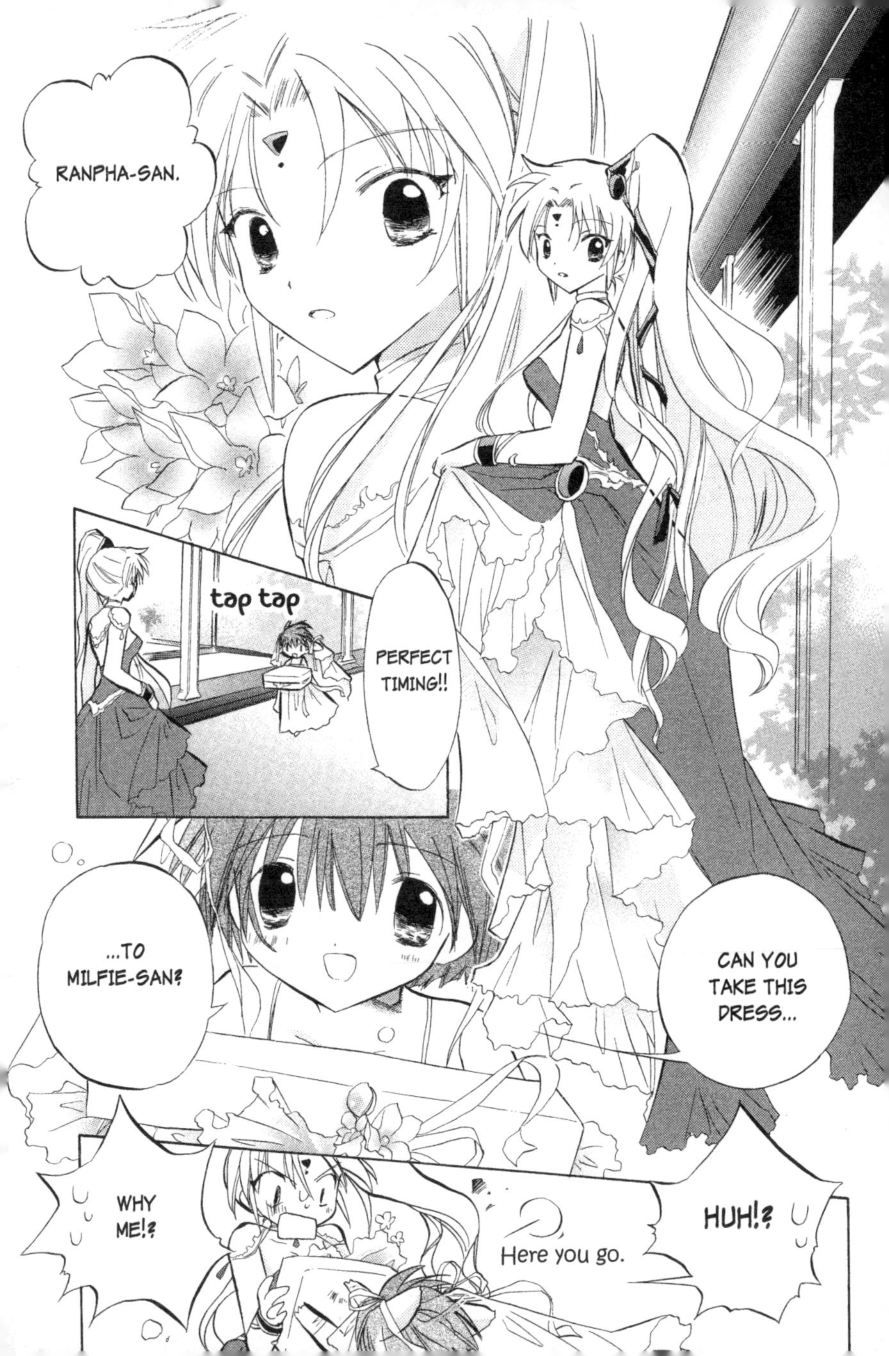
RANPHA-SAN.
tap tap
PERFECT TIMING!!
CAN YOU TAKE THIS DRESS...
...TO MILFIE-SAN?
HUH!?
Here you go.
WHY ME!?

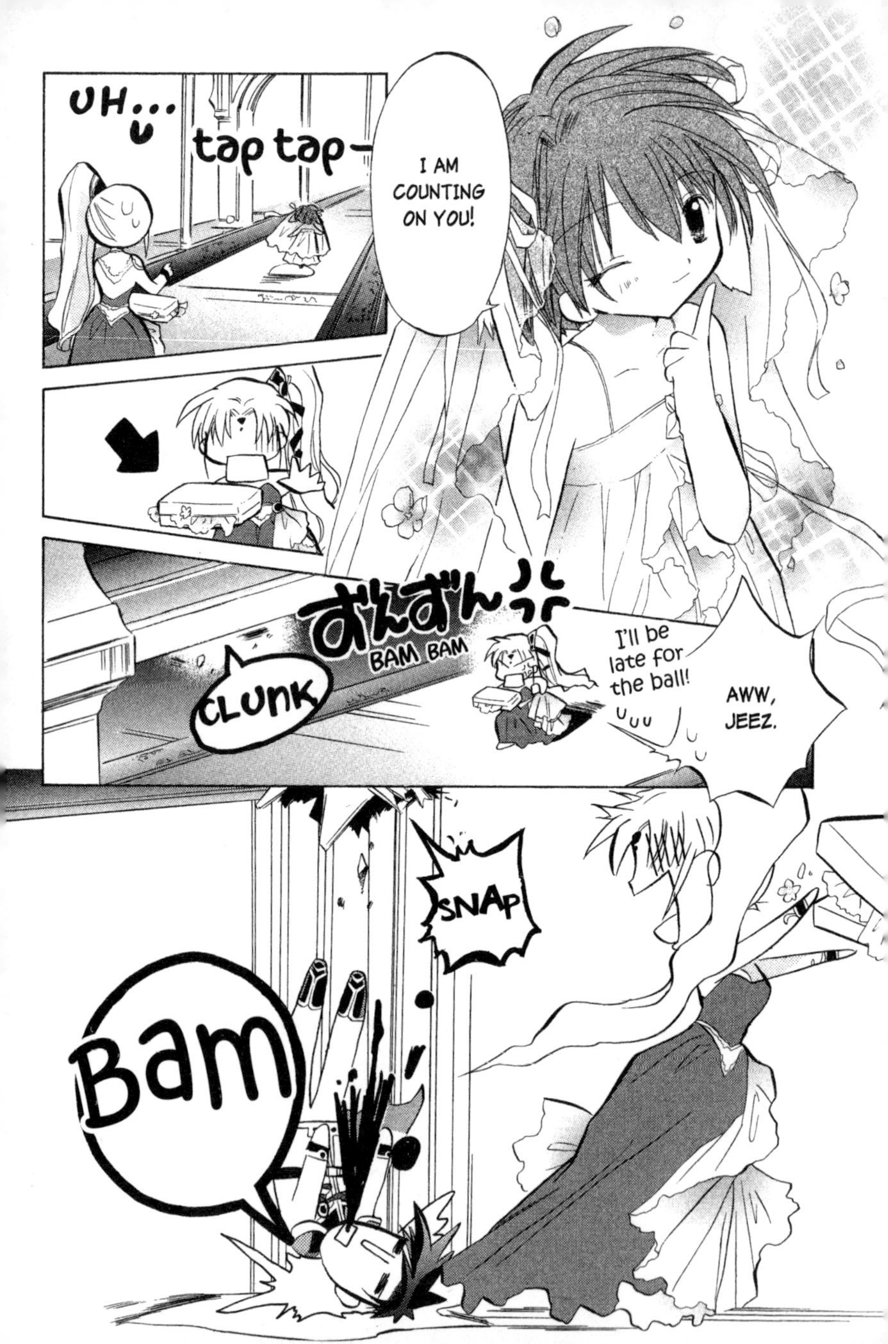
I AM COUNTING ON YOU!
UH...
tap tap—
AWW, JEEZ.
I'll be late for the ball!
ずんずん
BAM BAM
CLUNK
SNAP
Bam

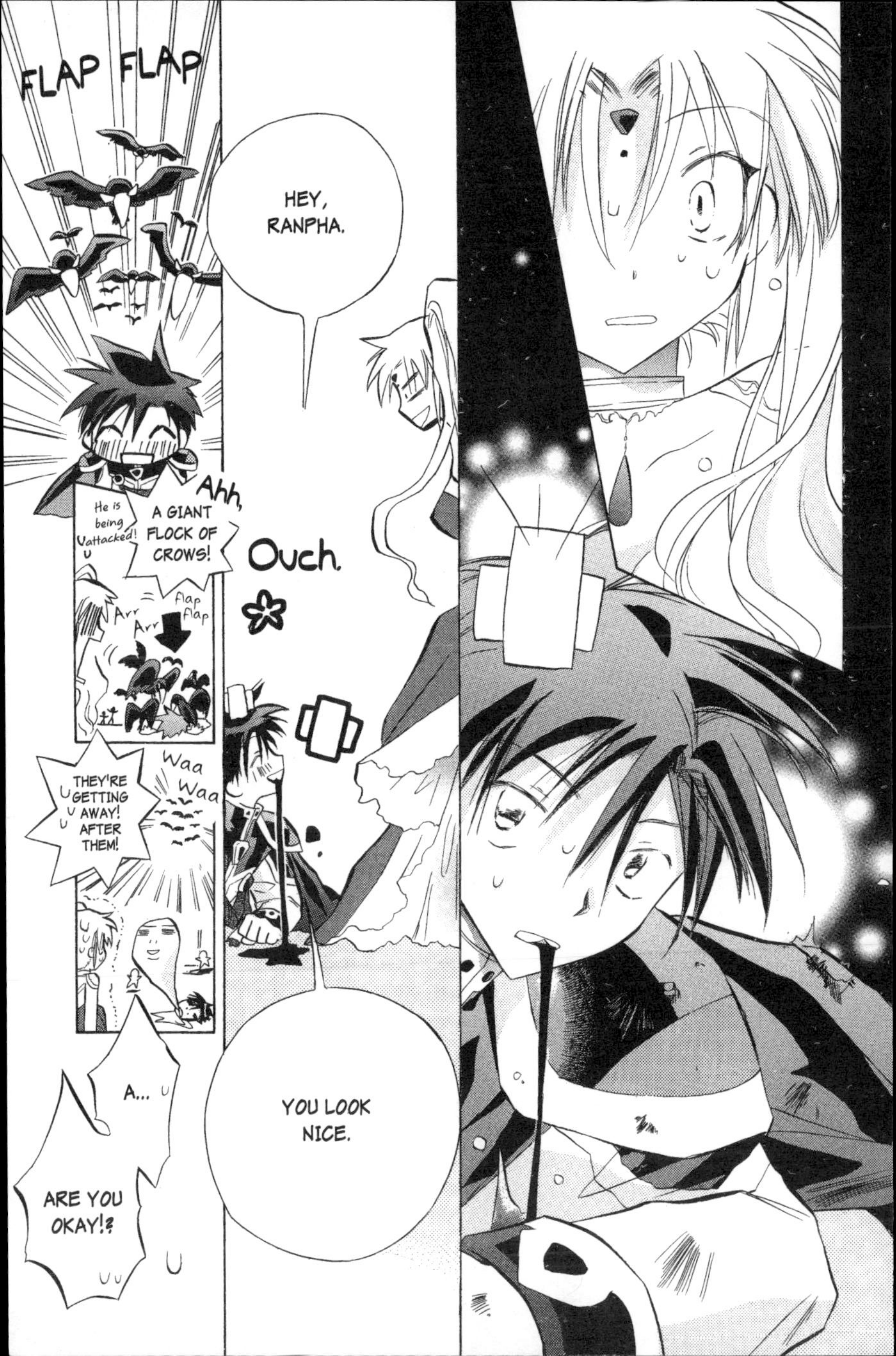
HEY, RANPHA.
Ouch.
YOU LOOK NICE.
FLAP FLAP
Ahh, A GIANT FLOCK OF CROWS!
He is being attacked!
Arr Arr
flap flap
THEY'RE GETTING AWAY! AFTER THEM!
Waa Waa
A...
ARE YOU OKAY!?

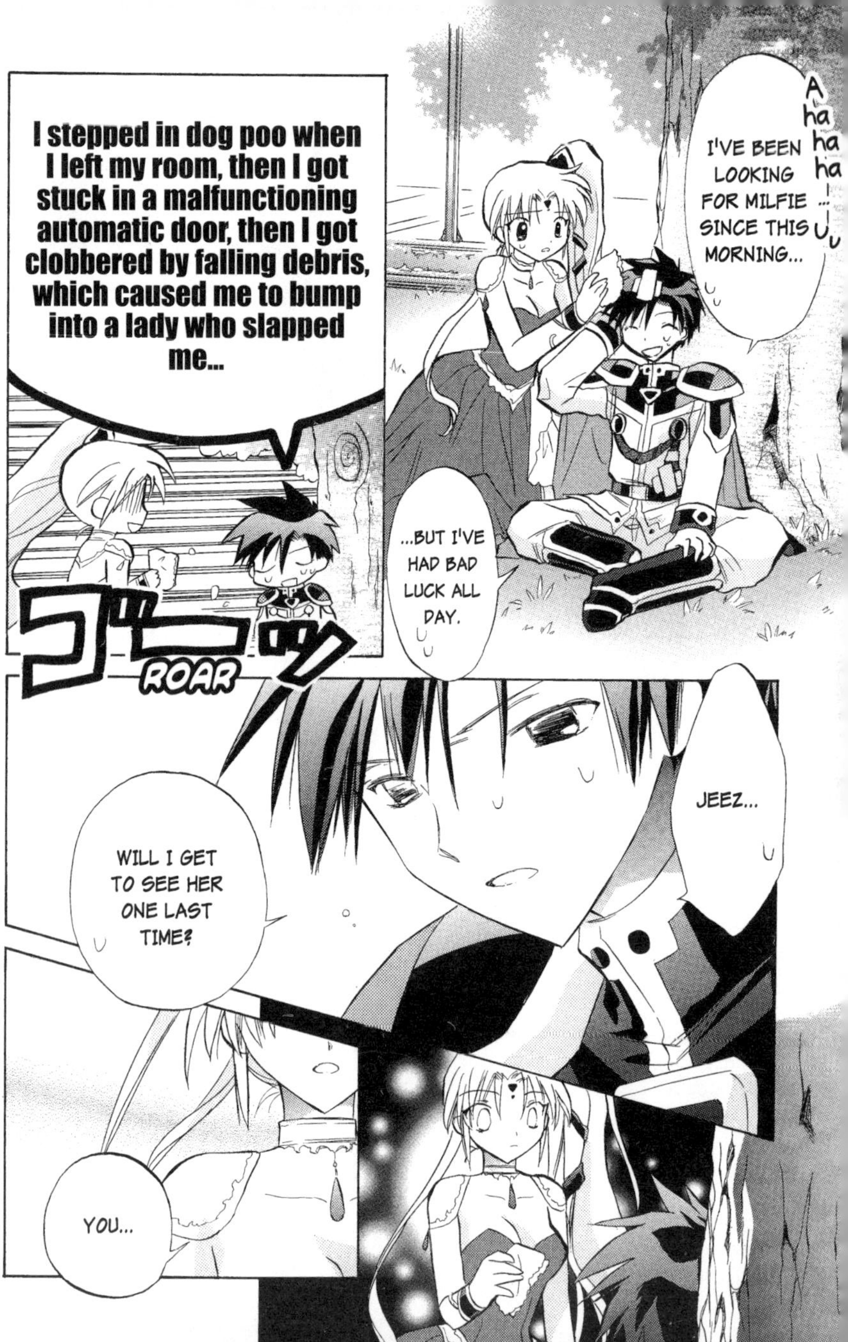
Ahahaha!
I'VE BEEN LOOKING FOR MILFIE SINCE THIS MORNING...
...BUT I'VE HAD BAD LUCK ALL DAY.
I stepped in dog poo when I left my room, then I got stuck in a malfunctioning automatic door, then I got clobbered by falling debris, which caused me to bump into a lady who slapped me...
ROAR
JEEZ...
WILL I GET TO SEE HER ONE LAST TIME?
YOU...

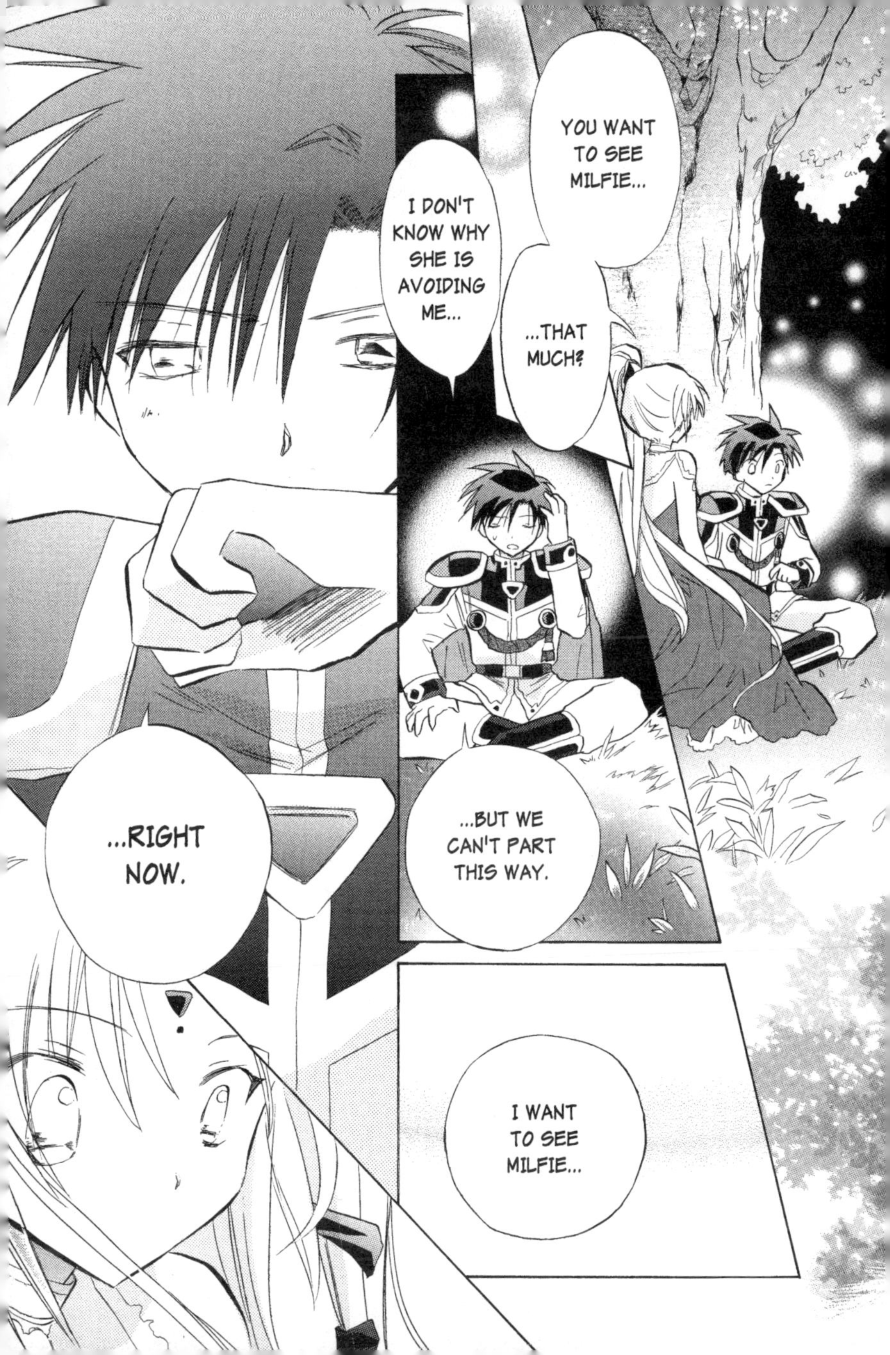
YOU WANT TO SEE MILFIE...
...THAT MUCH?
I DON'T KNOW WHY SHE IS AVOIDING ME...
...BUT WE CAN'T PART THIS WAY.
I WANT TO SEE MILFIE...
...RIGHT NOW.

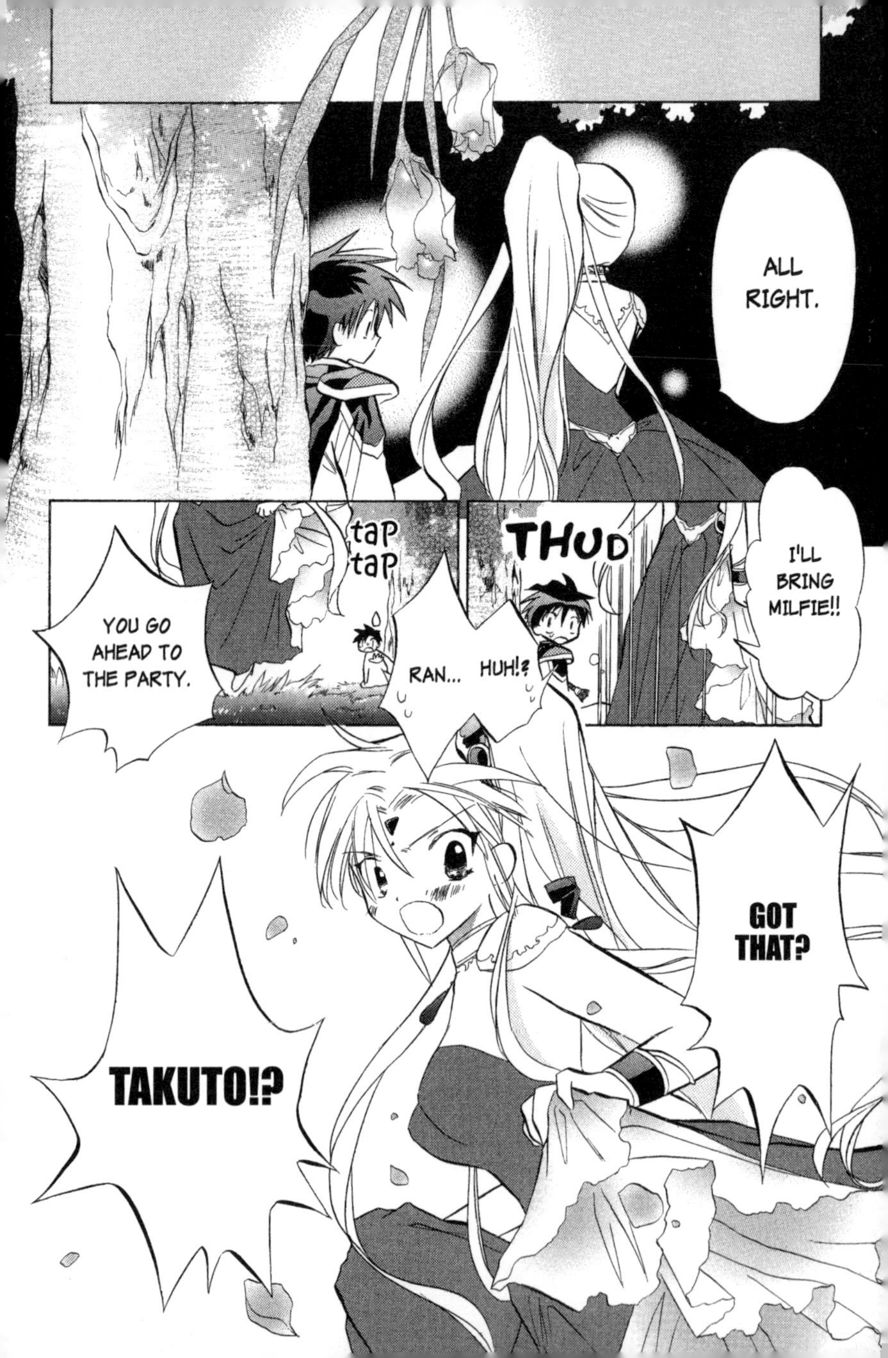
ALL RIGHT.
I'LL BRING MILFIE!!
THUD
HUH!?
tap tap
RAN...
YOU GO AHEAD TO THE PARTY.
GOT THAT?
TAKUTO!?

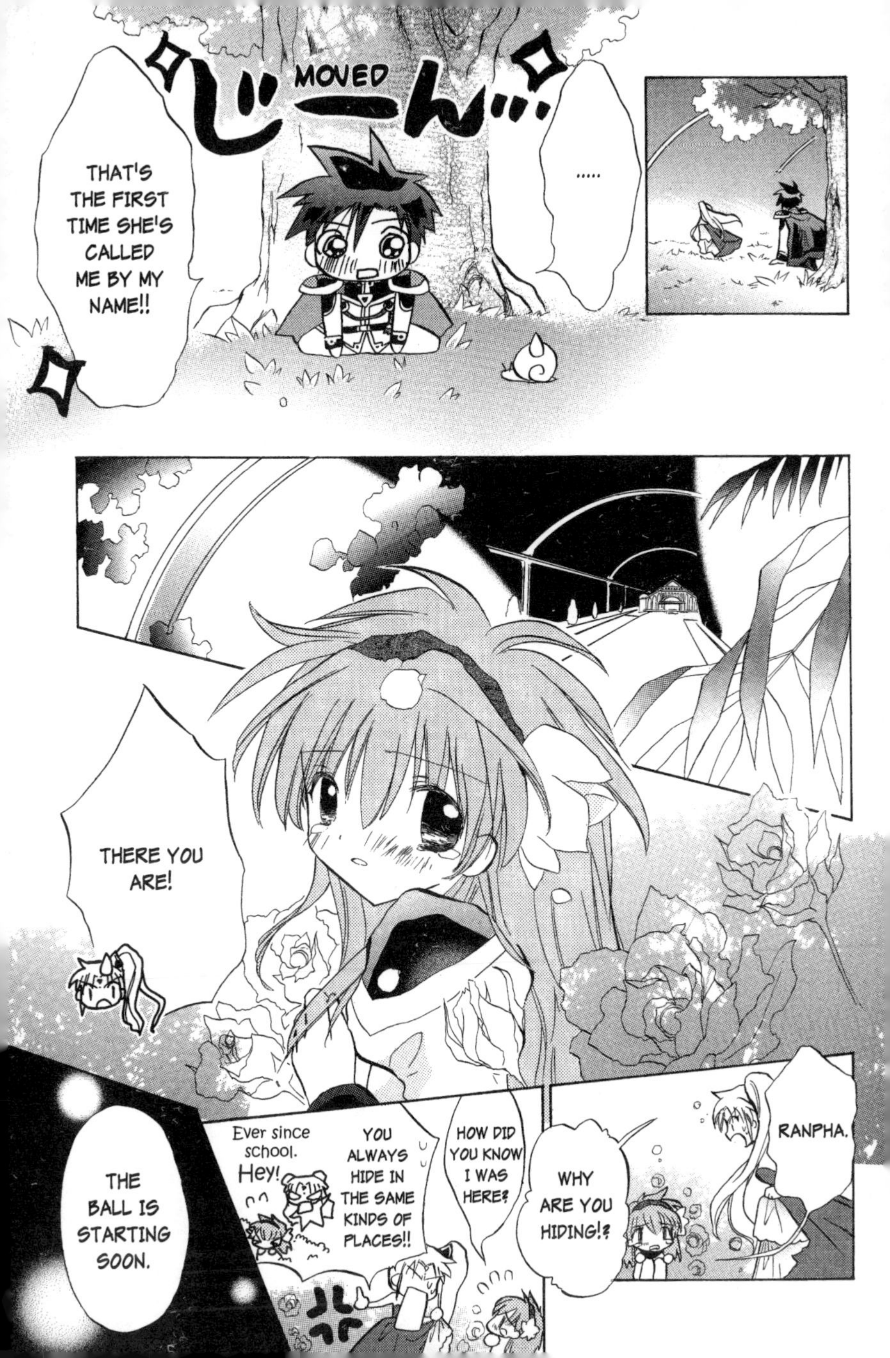
MOVED
じーん…
.....
THAT'S THE FIRST TIME SHE'S CALLED ME BY MY NAME!!
THERE YOU ARE!
RANPHA.
WHY ARE YOU HIDING!?
HOW DID YOU KNOW I WAS HERE?
YOU ALWAYS HIDE IN THE SAME KINDS OF PLACES!!
Ever since school.
Hey!
THE BALL IS STARTING SOON.

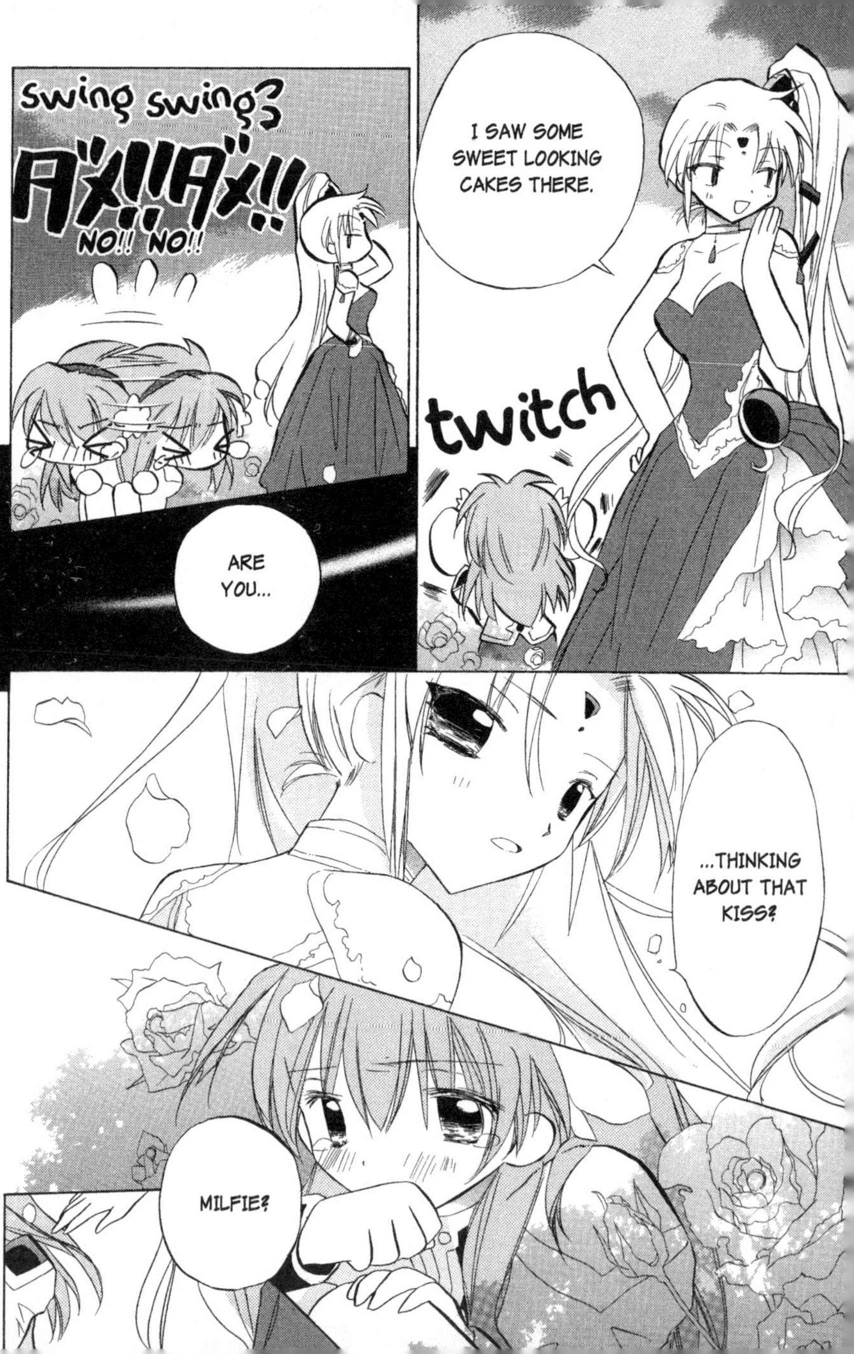
I SAW SOME SWEET LOOKING CAKES THERE.
twitch
swing swing?
ダメ!!ダメ!!
NO!! NO!!
ARE YOU...
...THINKING ABOUT THAT KISS?
MILFIE?

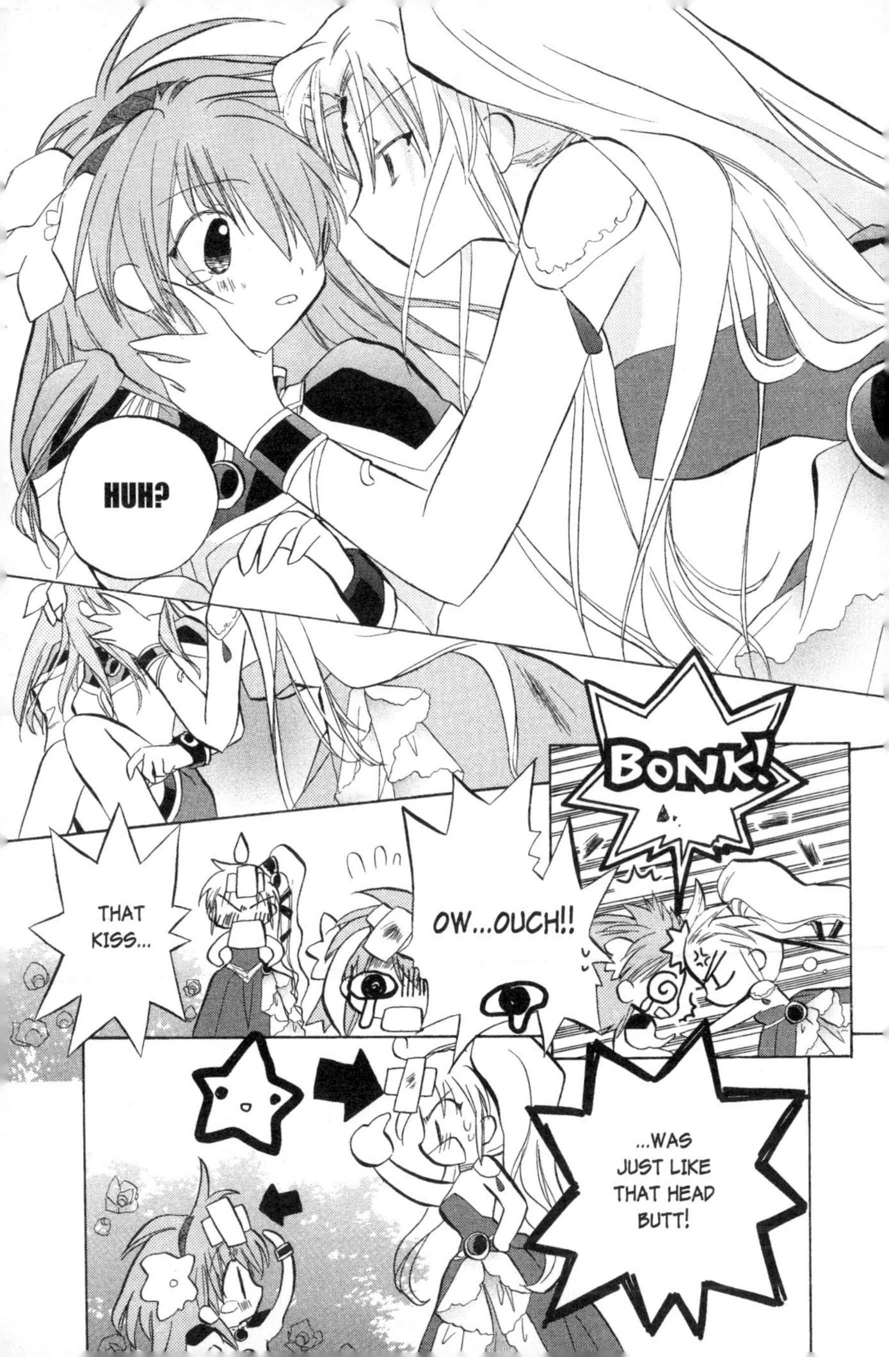
HUH?
BONK!
OW...OUCH!!
THAT KISS...
...WAS JUST LIKE THAT HEAD BUTT!

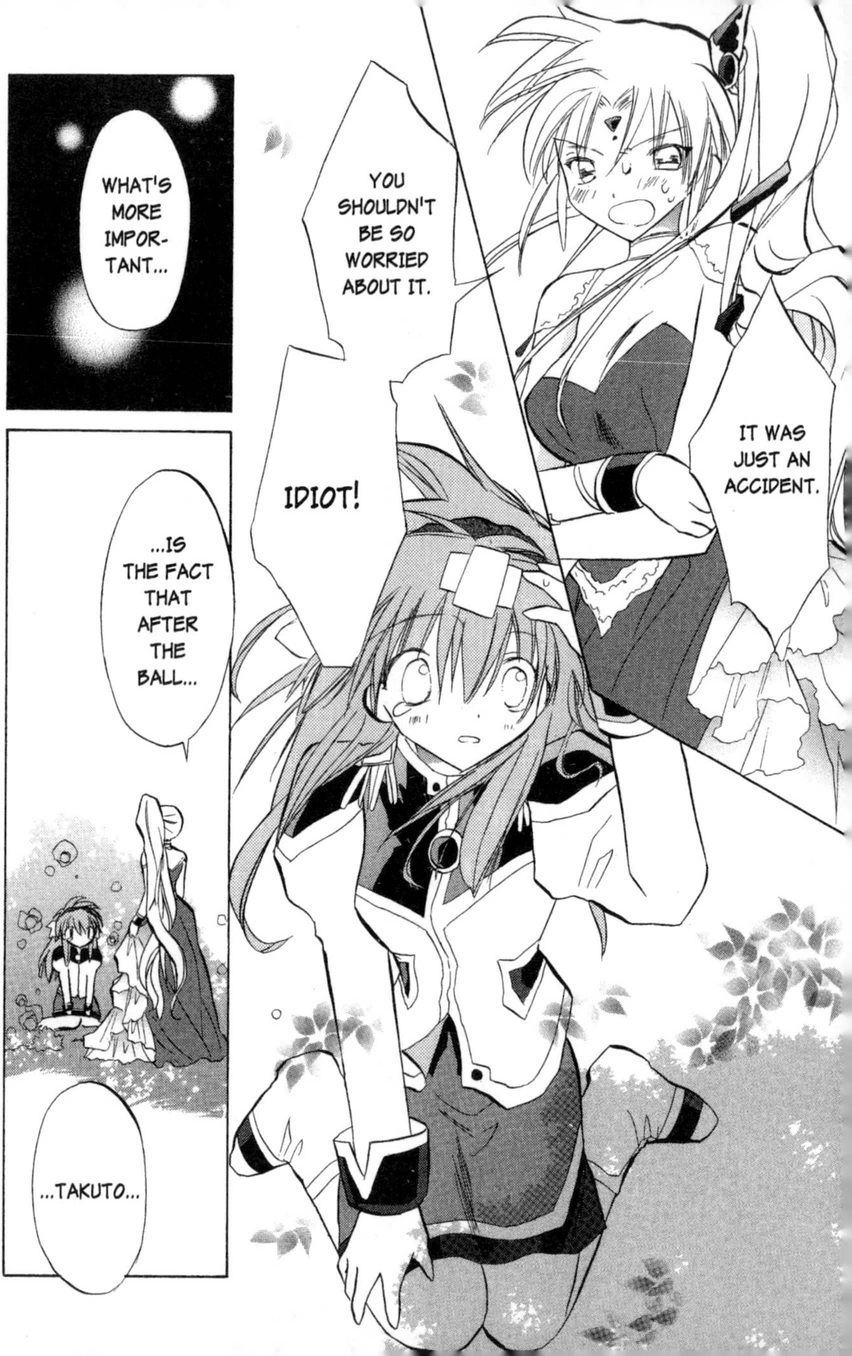
YOU SHOULDN'T BE SO WORRIED ABOUT IT.
IT WAS JUST AN ACCIDENT.
IDIOT!
WHAT'S MORE IMPOR-TANT...
...IS THE FACT THAT AFTER THE BALL...
...TAKUTO...

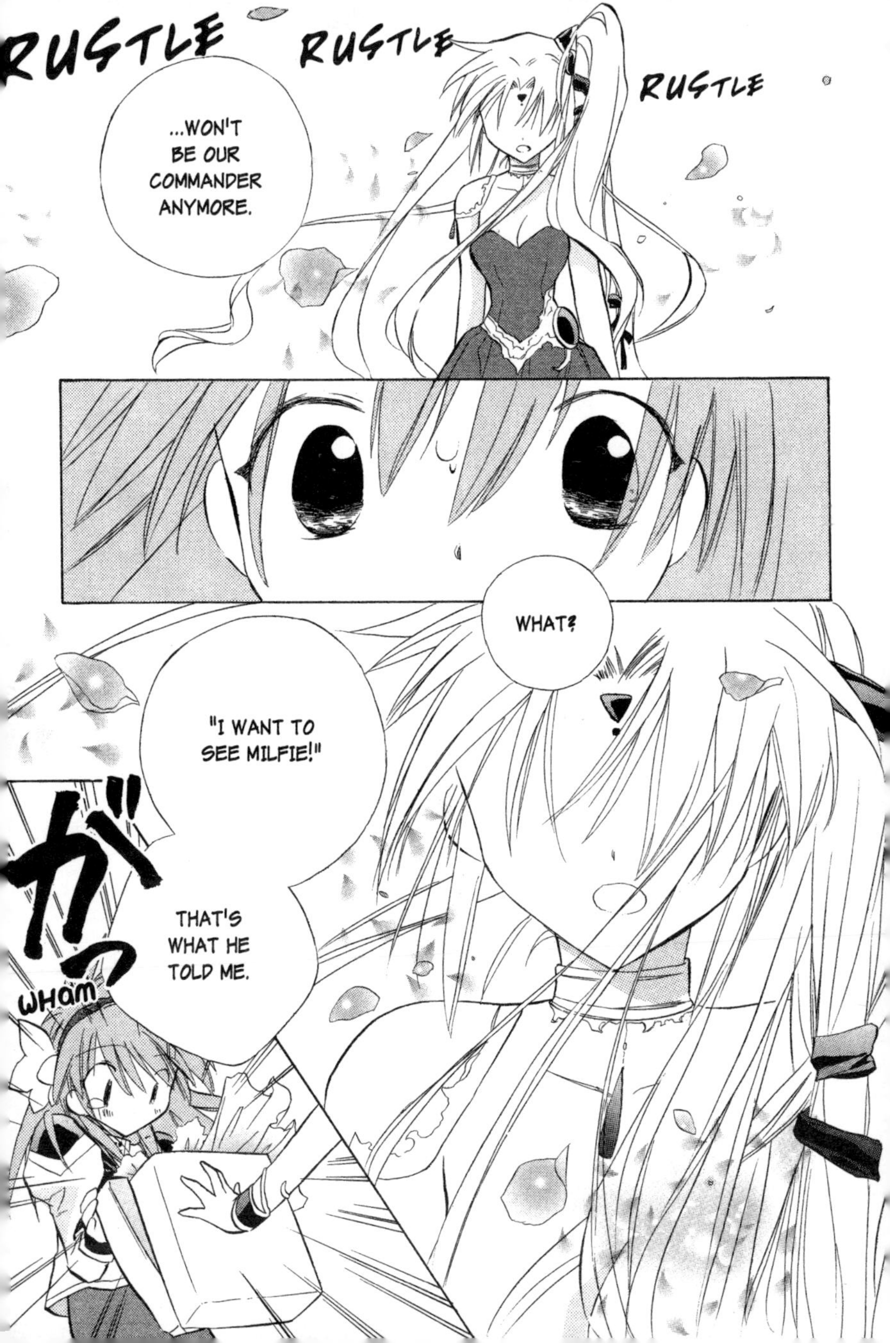
RUSTLE
RUSTLE
RUSTLE
...WON'T BE OUR COMMANDER ANYMORE.
WHAT?
"I WANT TO SEE MILFIE!"
THAT'S WHAT HE TOLD ME.
ガッ
WHAM

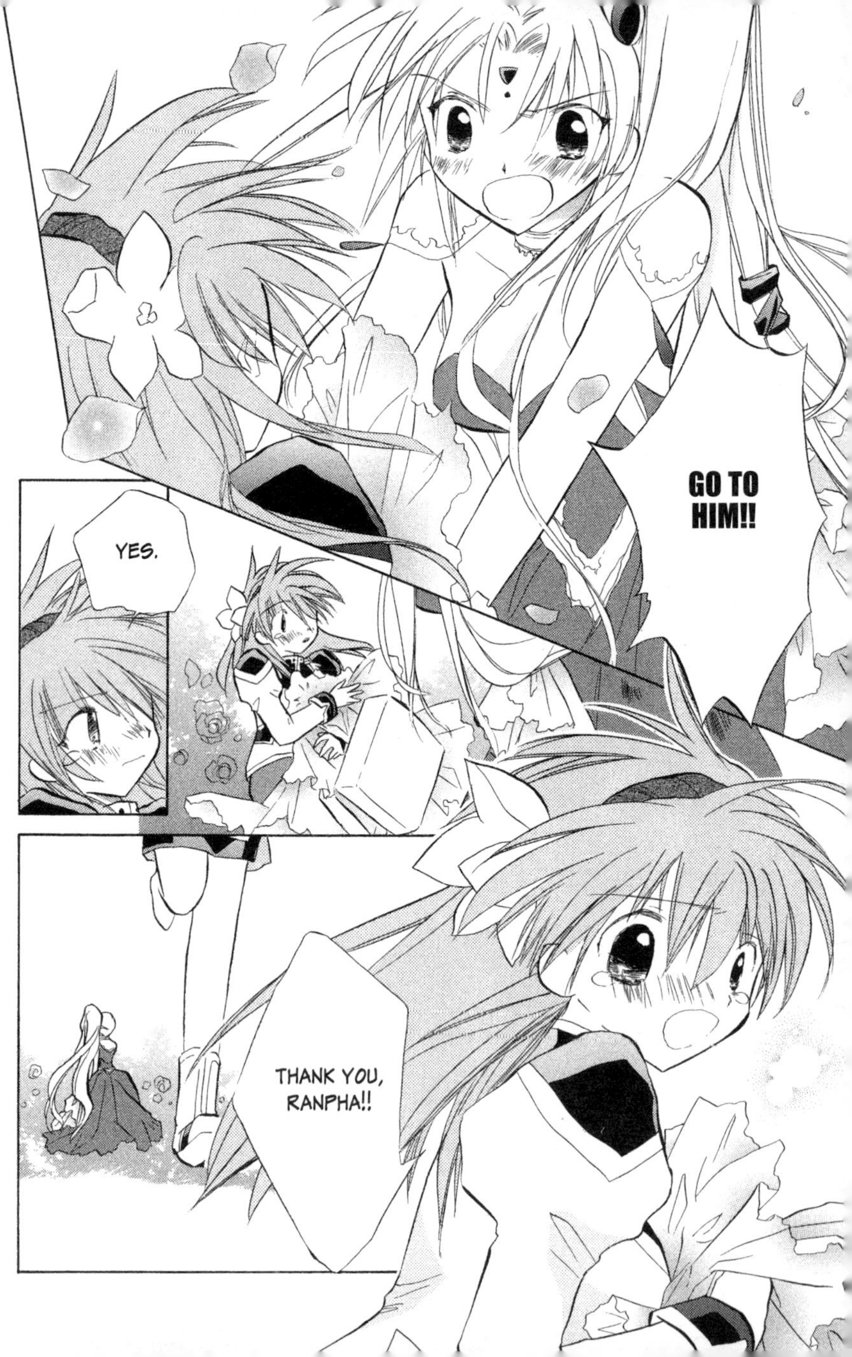
GO TO HIM!!
YES.
THANK YOU, RANPHA!!

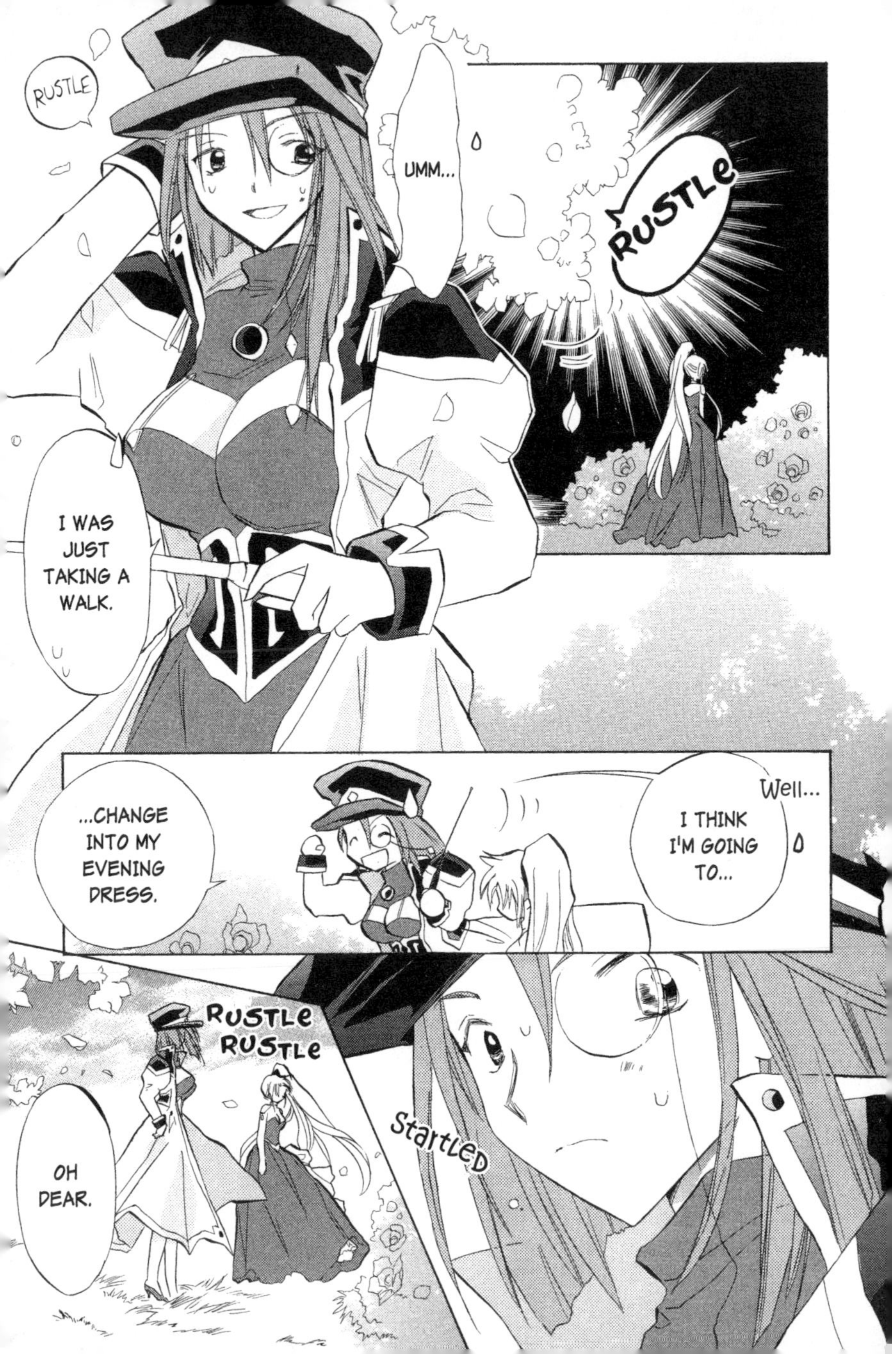
RUSTLE
UMM...
RUSTLE
I WAS JUST TAKING A WALK.
Well...
I THINK I'M GOING TO...
...CHANGE INTO MY EVENING DRESS.
Startled
RUSTLE RUSTLE
OH DEAR.

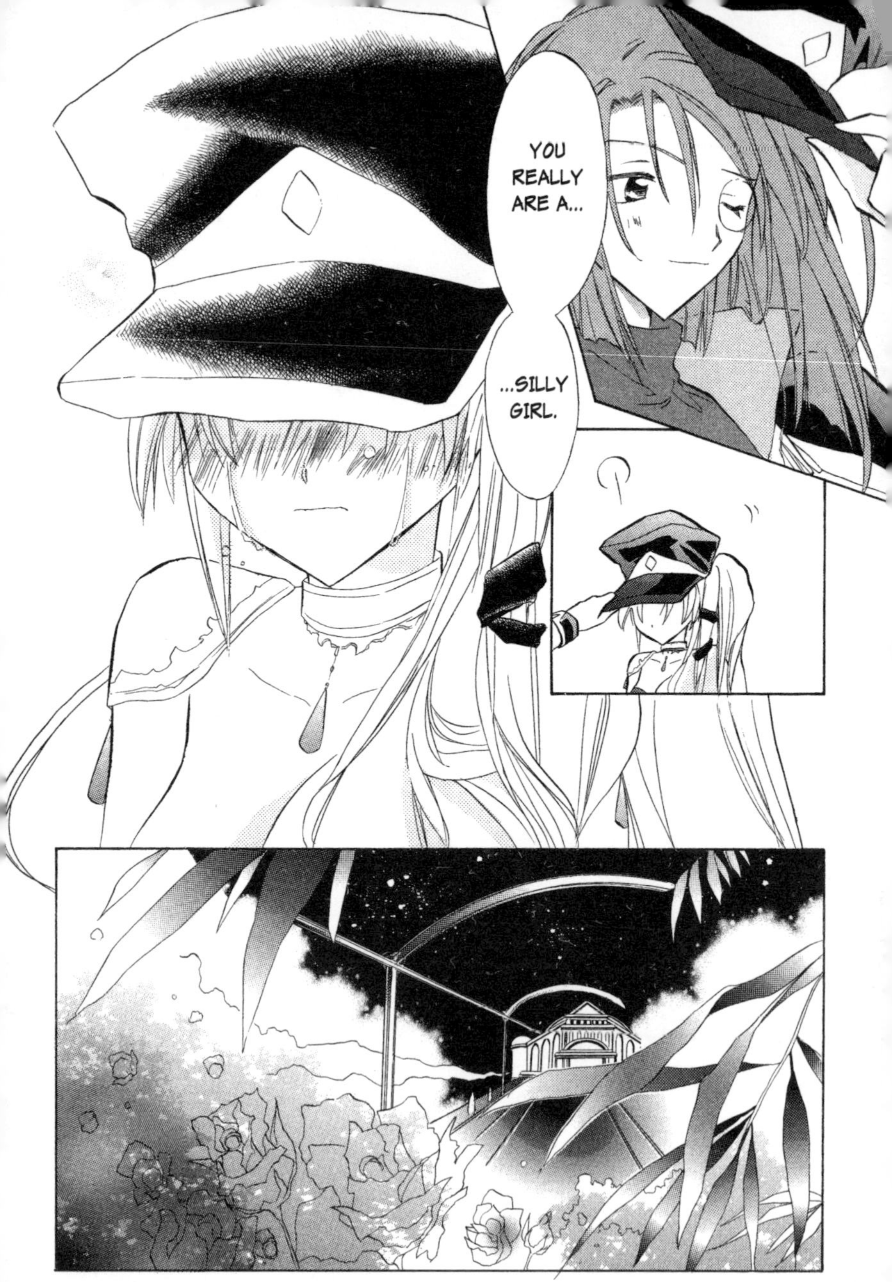
YOU REALLY ARE A...
...SILLY GIRL.

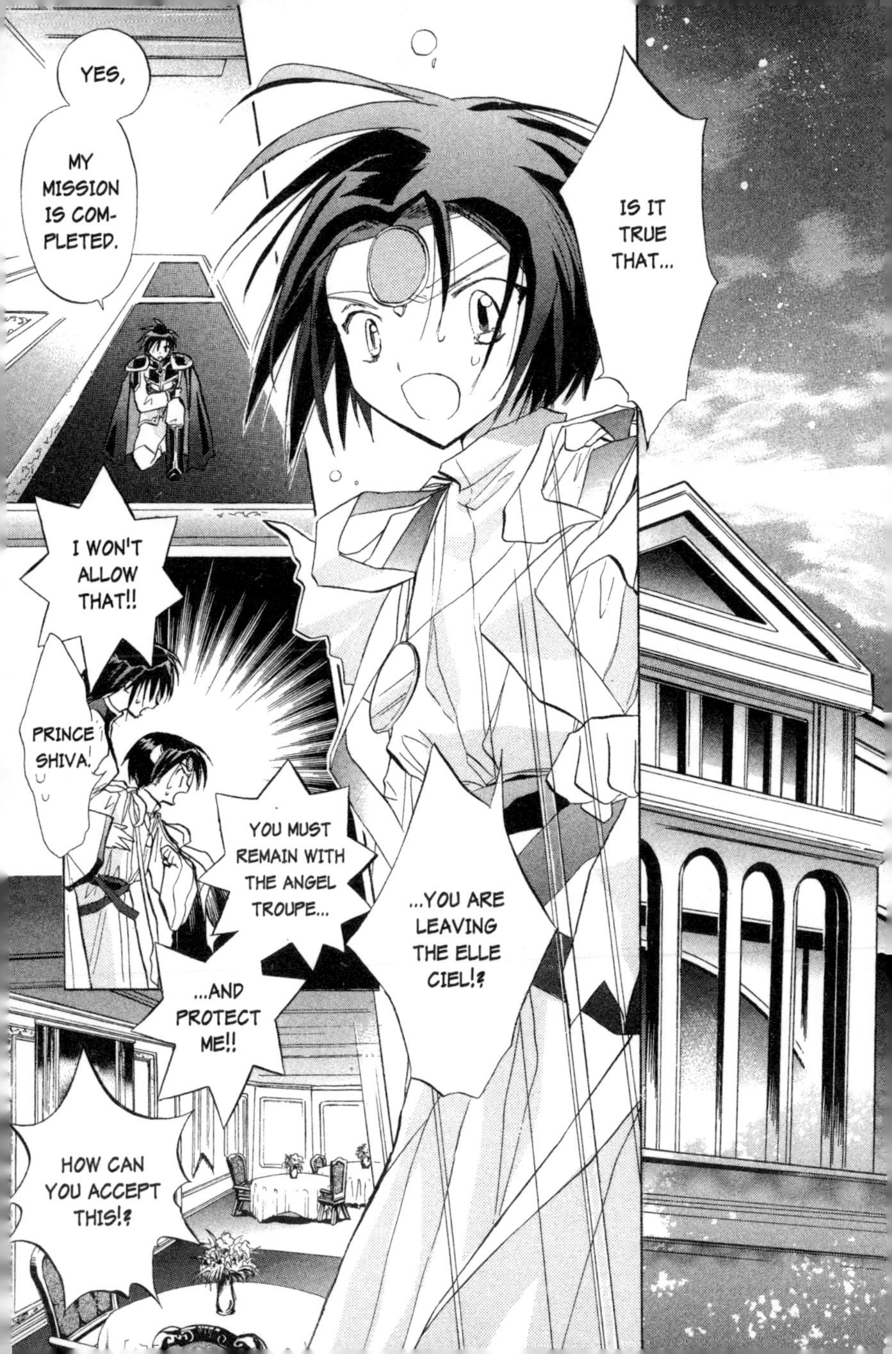
IS IT TRUE THAT...
...YOU ARE LEAVING THE ELLE CIEL!?
YES, MY MISSION IS COMPLETED.
I WON'T ALLOW THAT!!
PRINCE SHIVA!
YOU MUST REMAIN WITH THE ANGEL TROUPE...
...AND PROTECT ME!!
HOW CAN YOU ACCEPT THIS!?

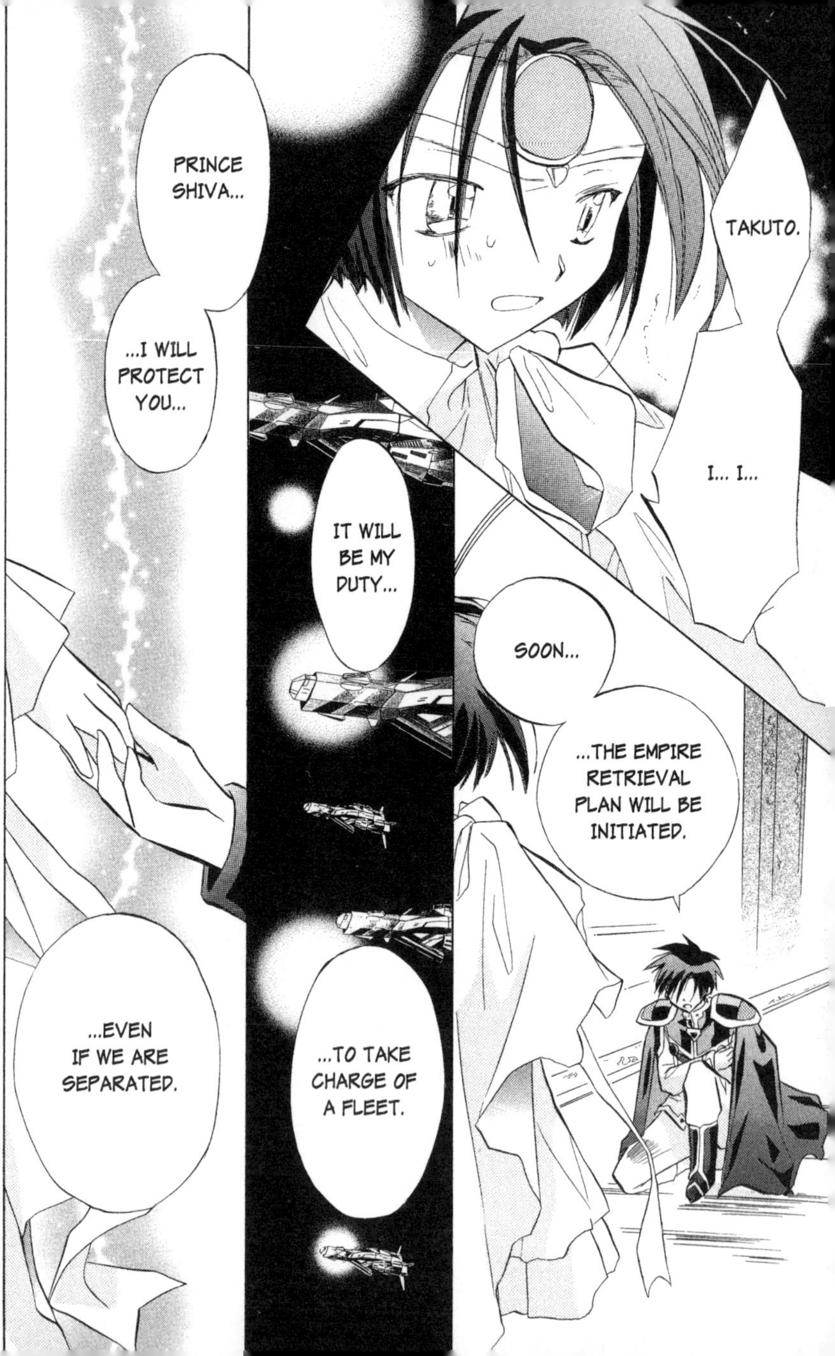
TAKUTO.
I... I...
SOON...
...THE EMPIRE RETRIEVAL PLAN WILL BE INITIATED.
IT WILL BE MY DUTY...
...TO TAKE CHARGE OF A FLEET.
PRINCE SHIVA...
...I WILL PROTECT YOU...
...EVEN IF WE ARE SEPARATED.

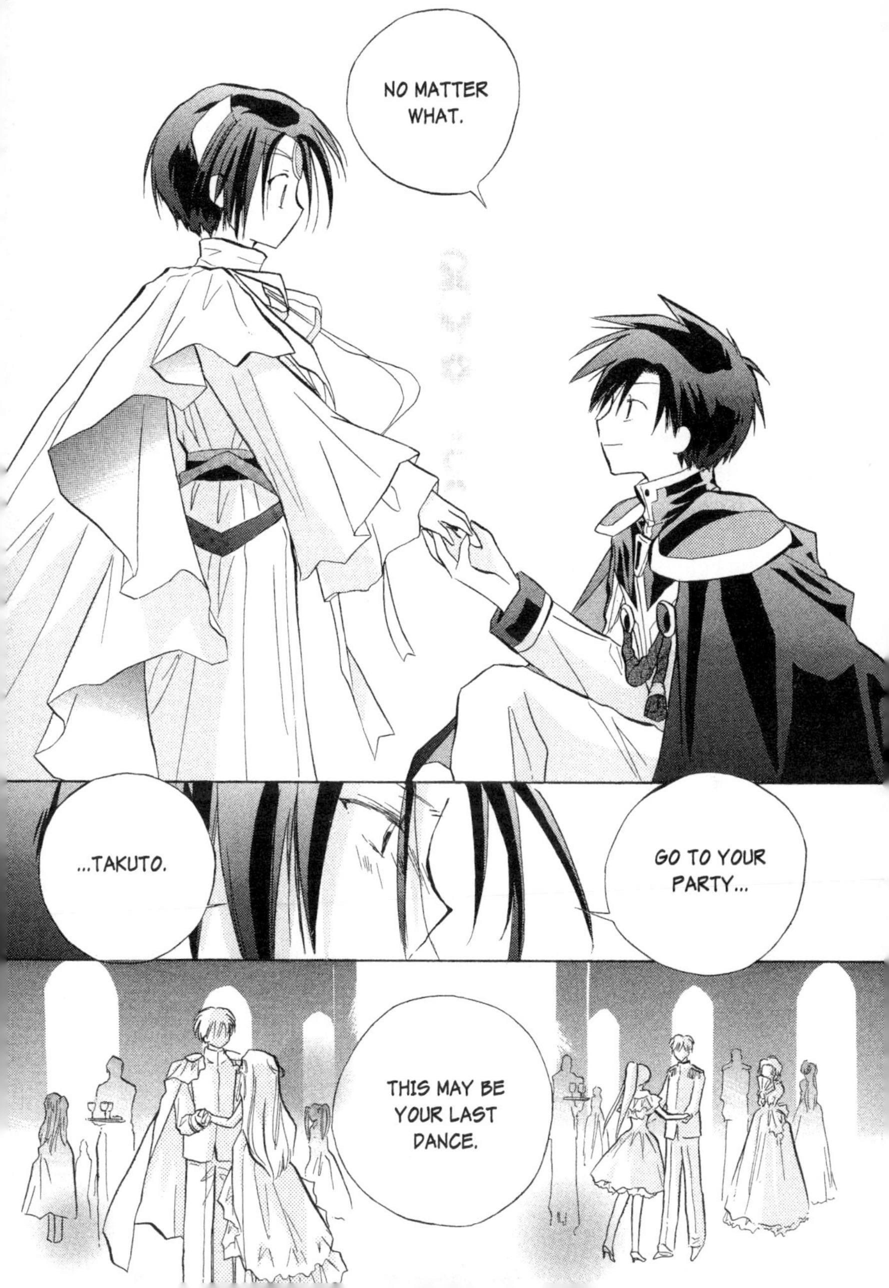
NO MATTER WHAT.
GO TO YOUR PARTY...
...TAKUTO.
THIS MAY BE YOUR LAST DANCE.

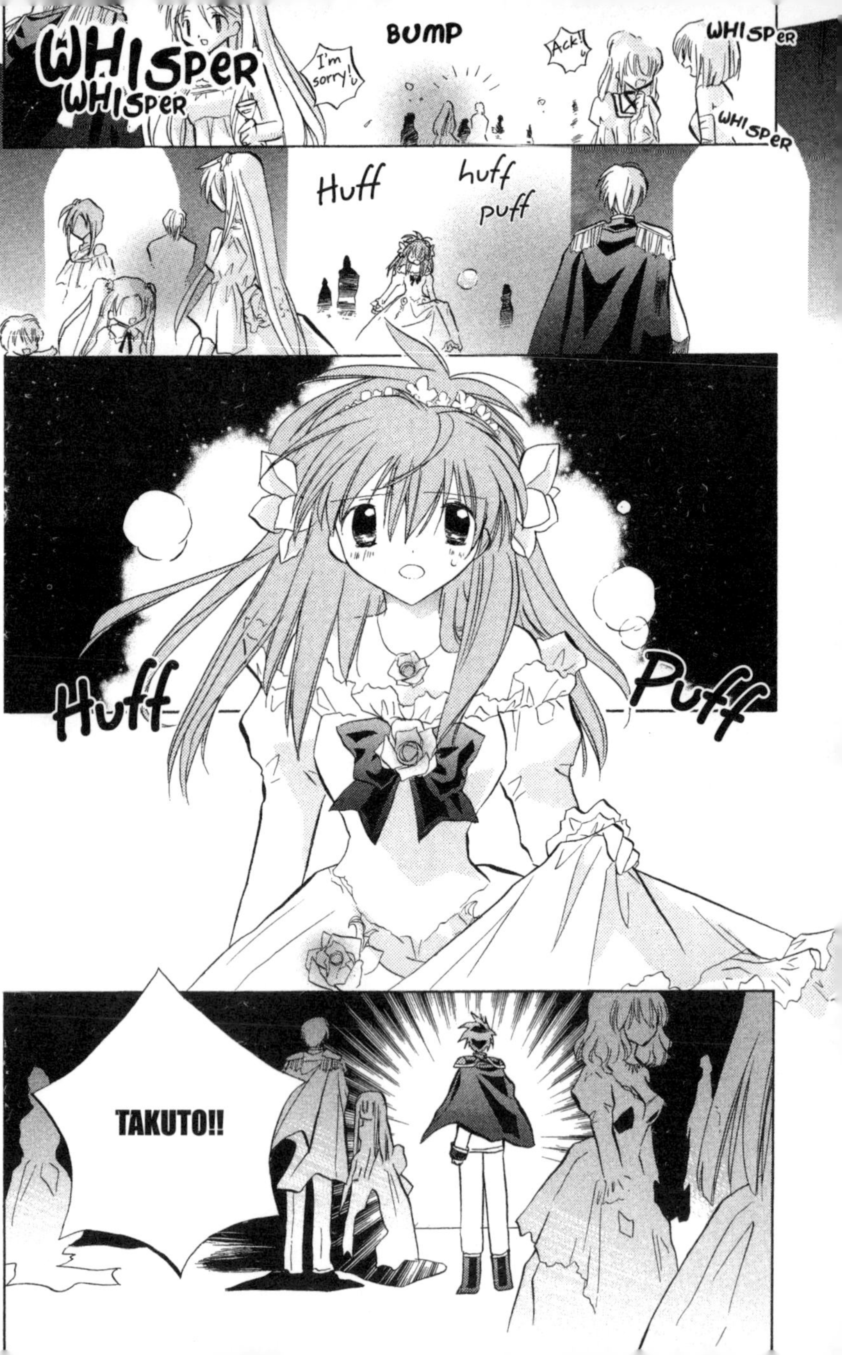
WHISPER
WHISPER
Ack!
BUMP
I'm sorry!
WHISPER
WHISPER
huff puff
Huff
Huff
Puff
TAKUTO!!

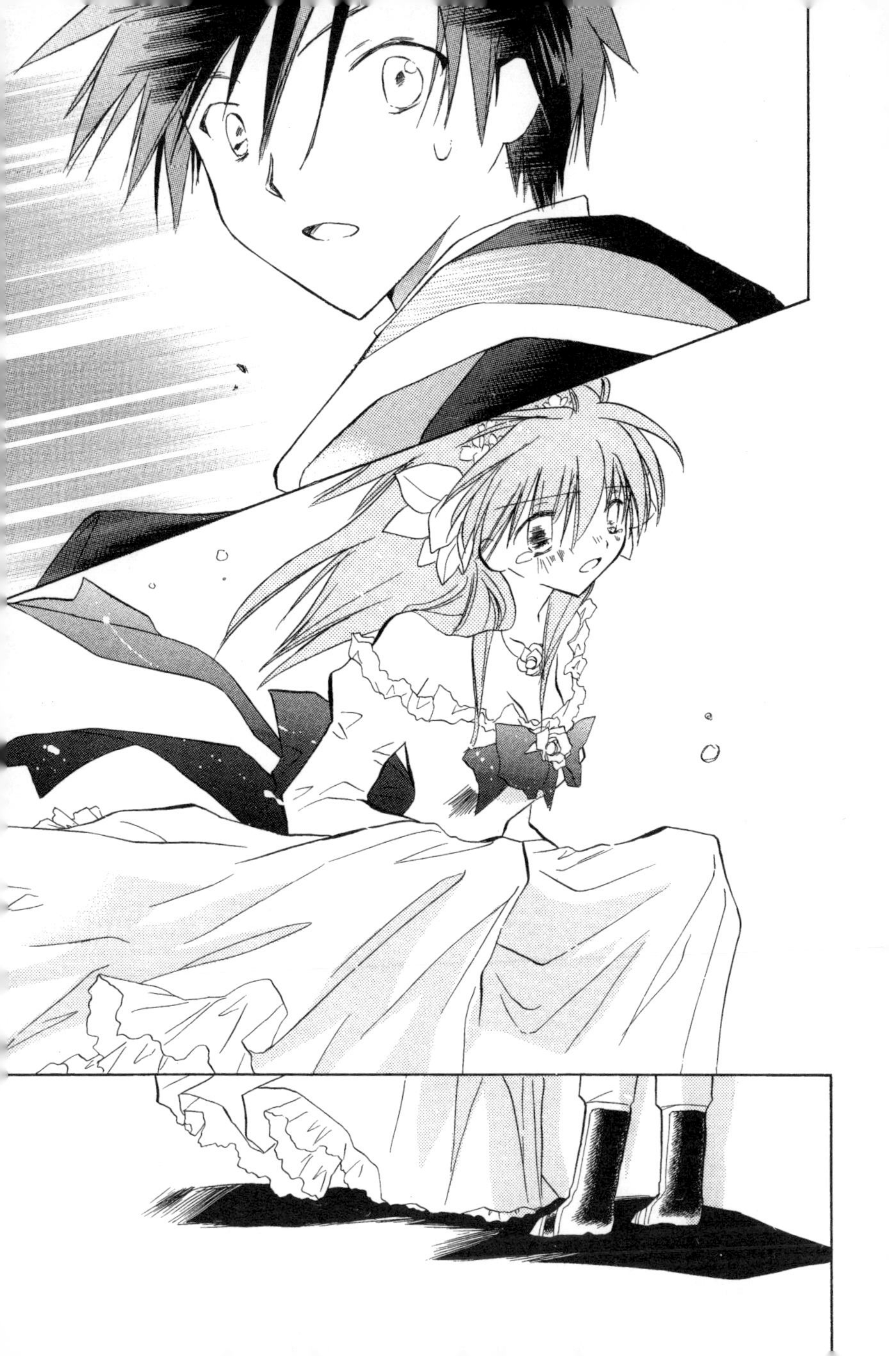

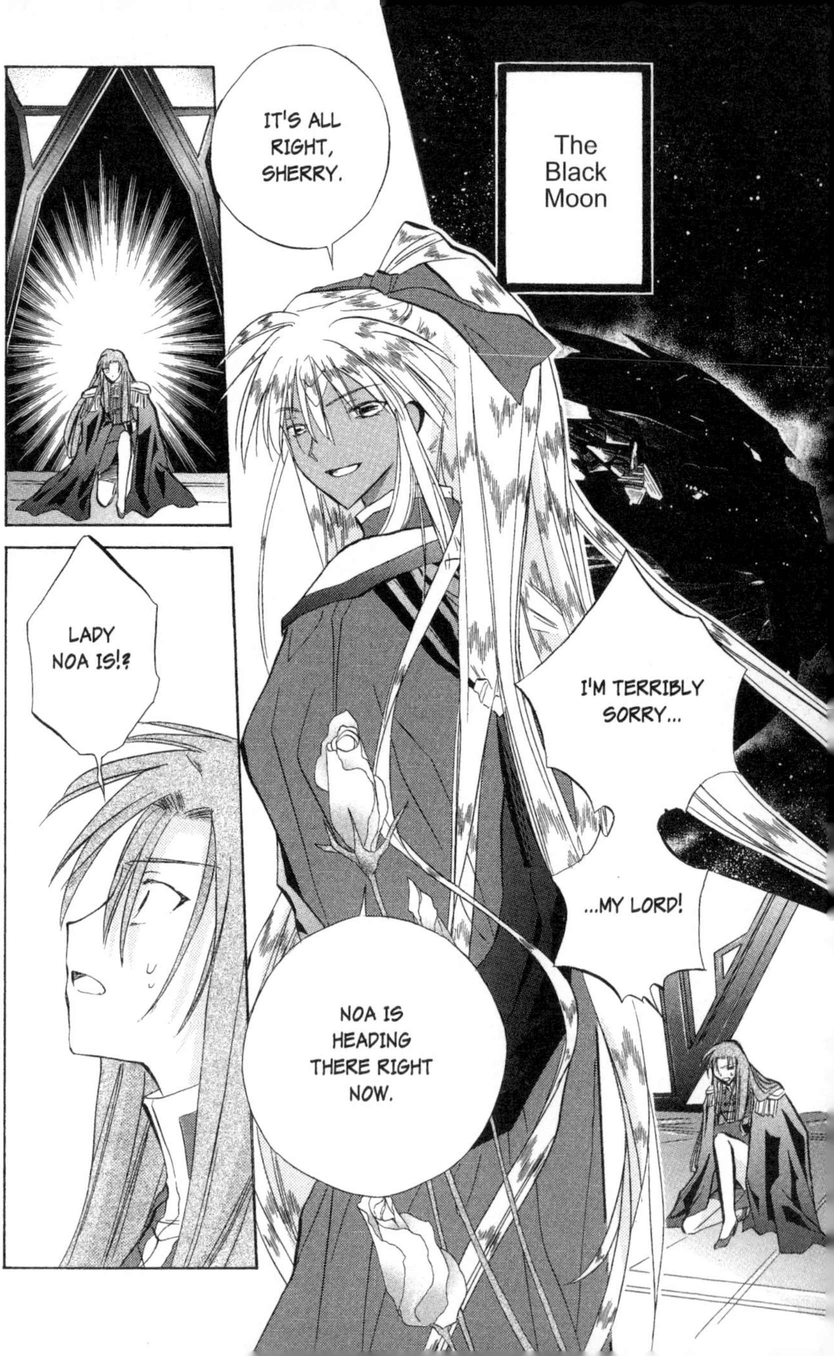
The Black Moon
I'M TERRIBLY SORRY...
...MY LORD!
IT'S ALL RIGHT, SHERRY.
NOA IS HEADING THERE RIGHT NOW.
LADY NOA IS!?

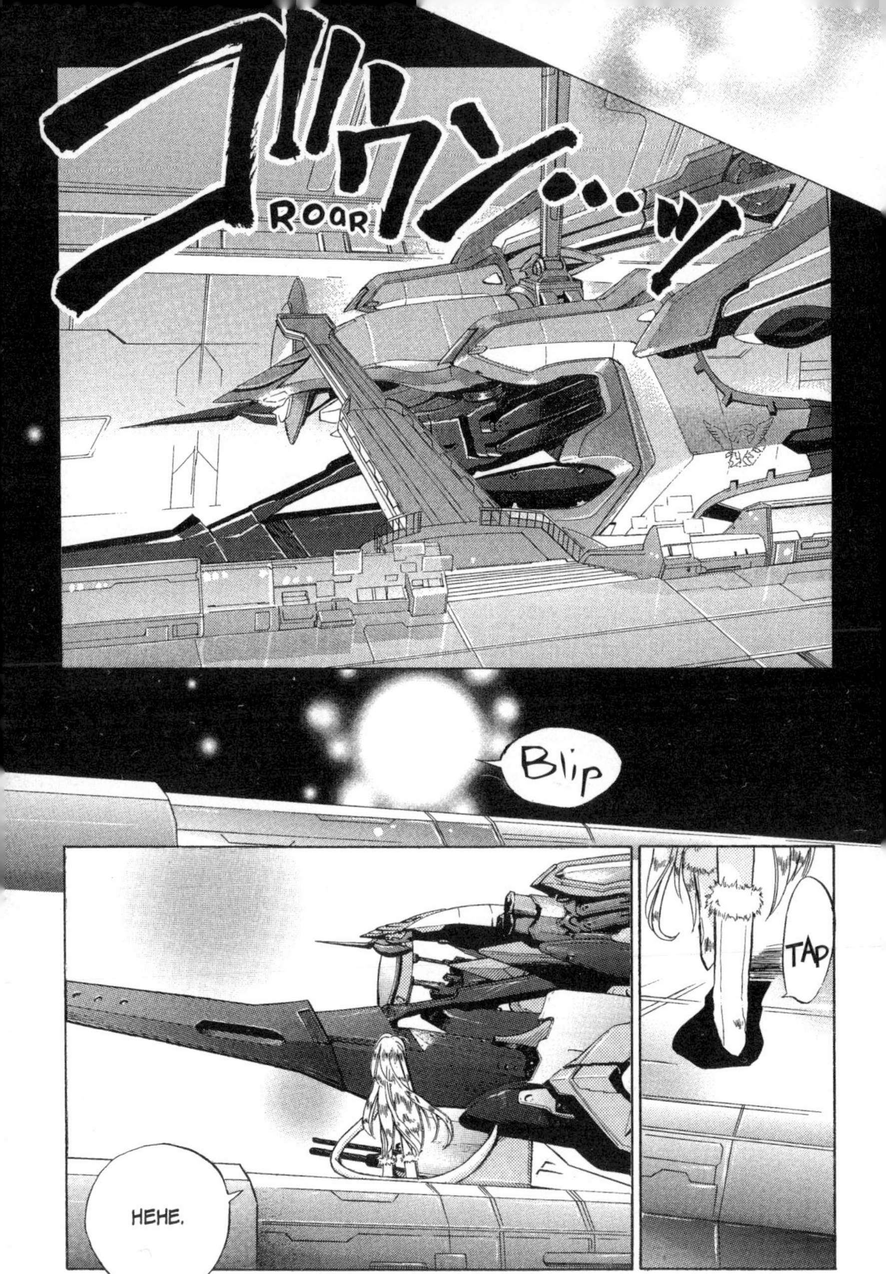
Roar
Blip
TAP
HEHE.

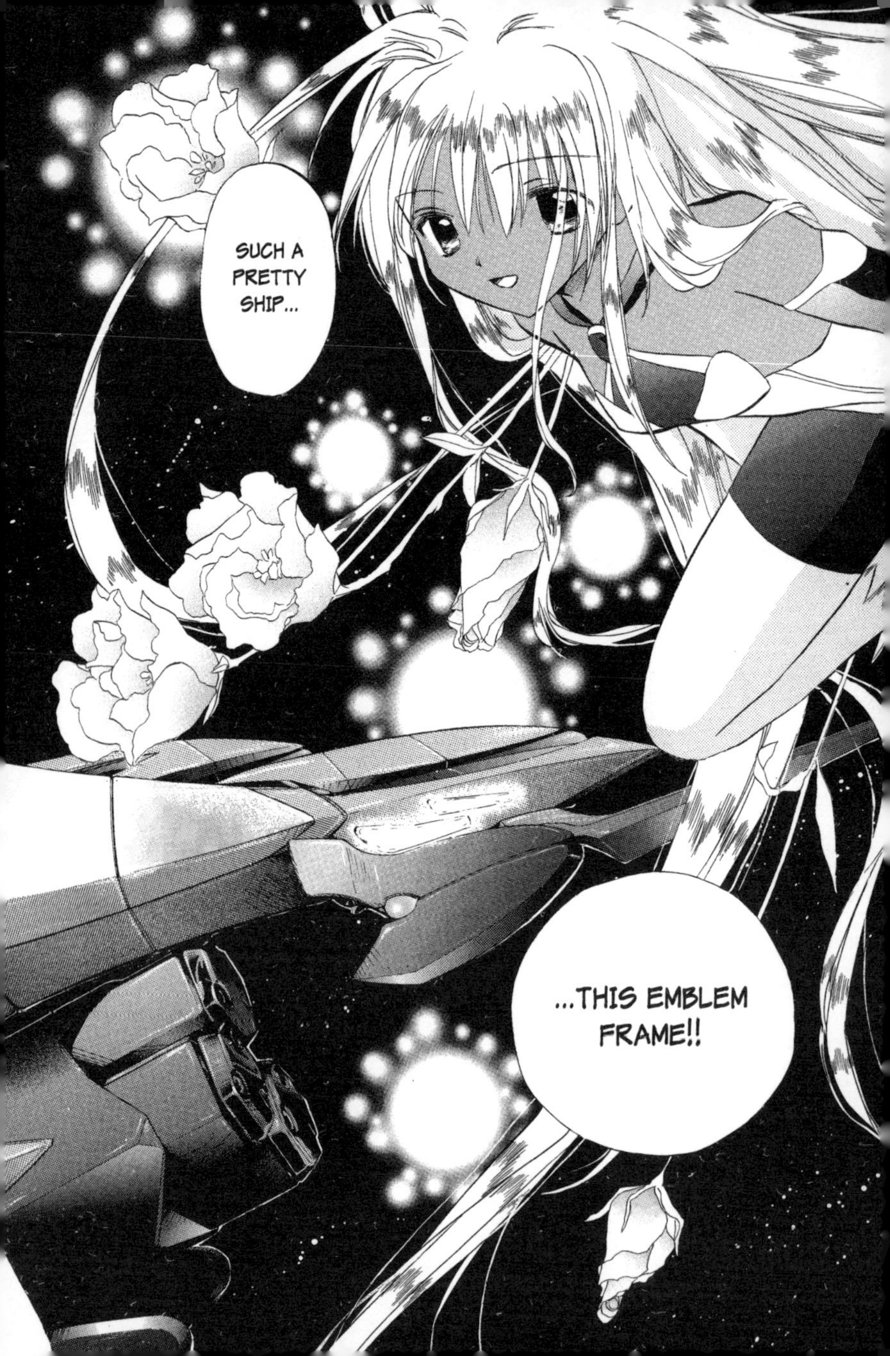
SUCH A PRETTY SHIP...
...THIS EMBLEM FRAME!!

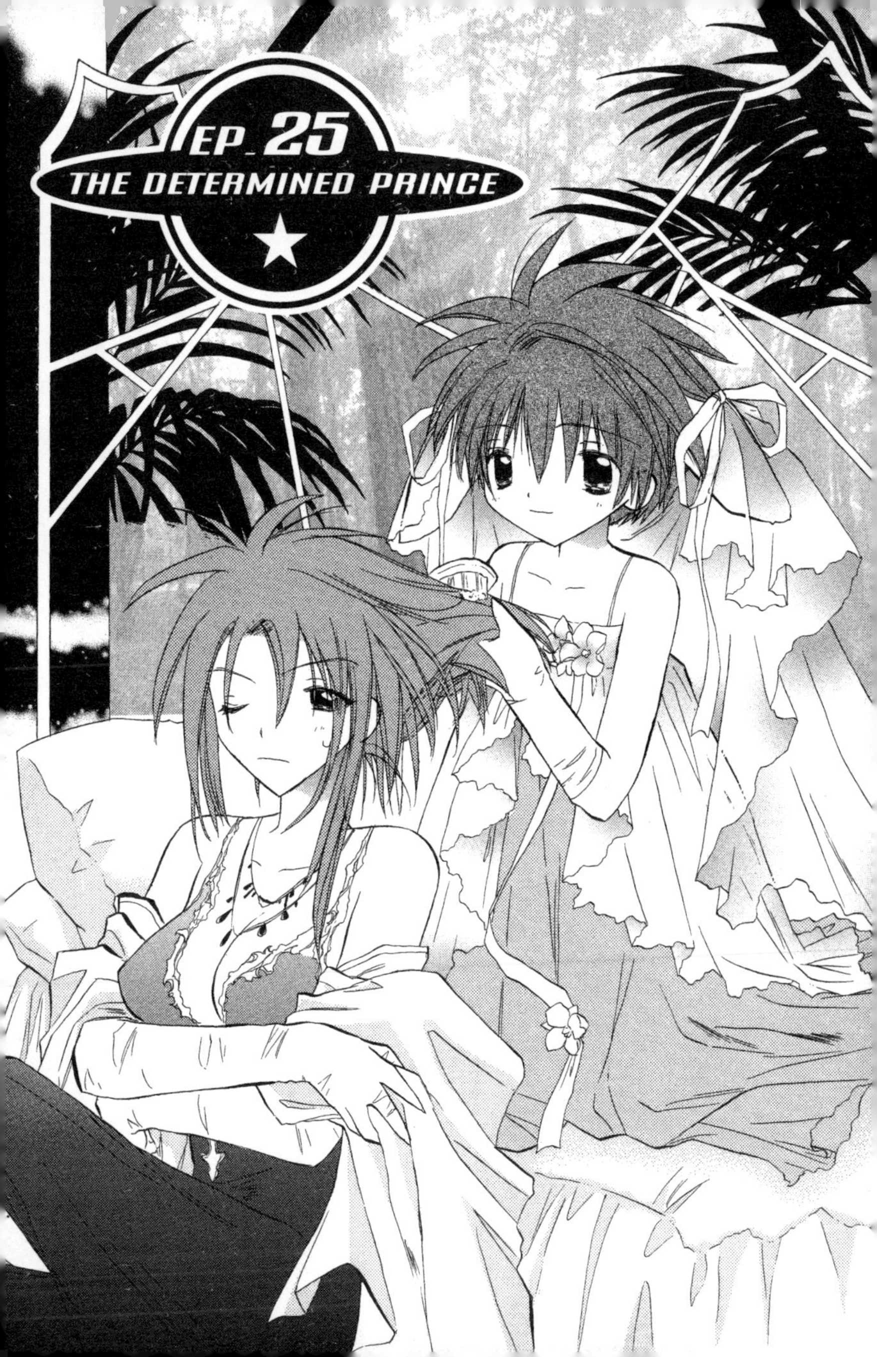
EP_25
THE DETERMINED PRINCE

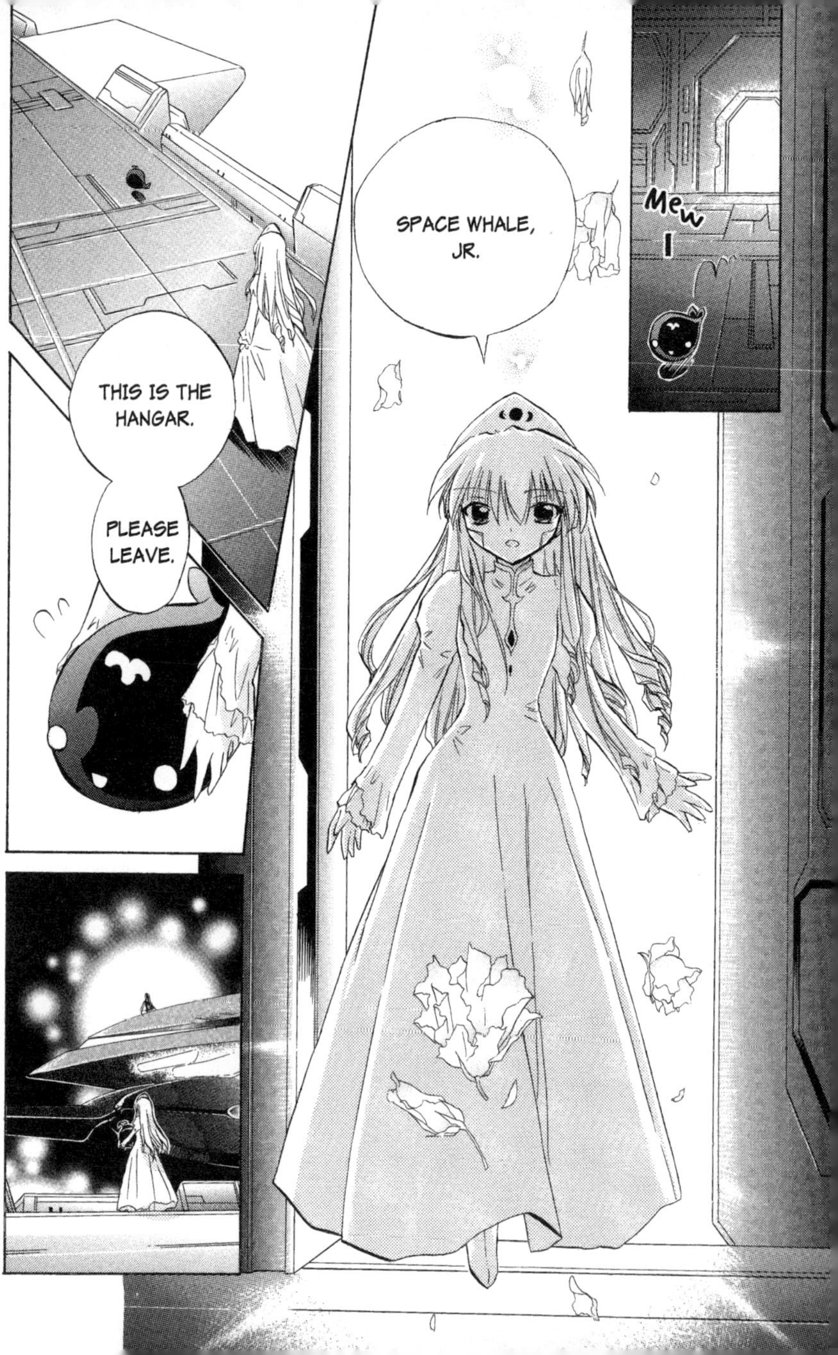
Mew
SPACE WHALE, JR.
THIS IS THE HANGAR.
PLEASE LEAVE.

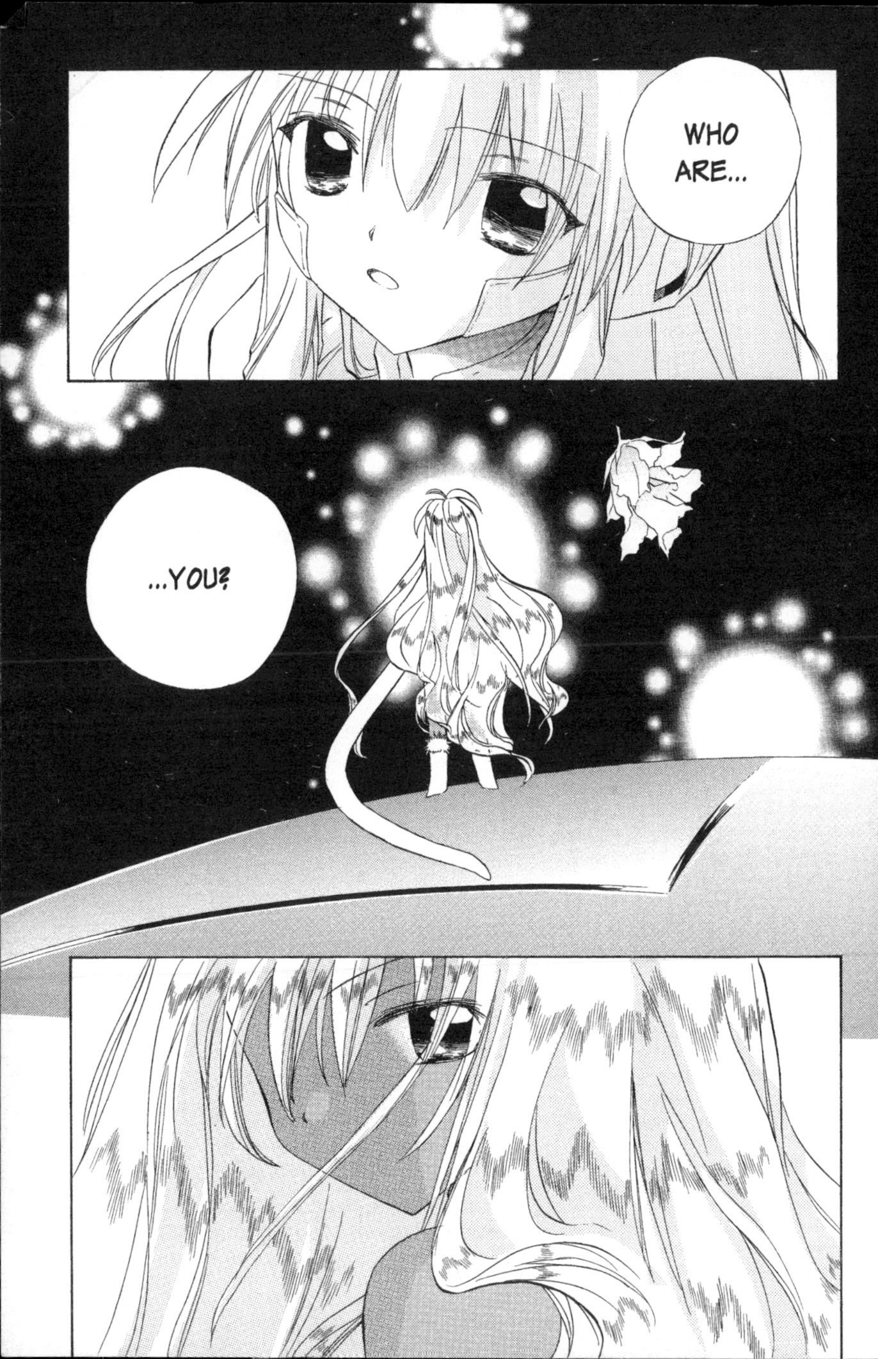
WHO ARE...
...YOU?

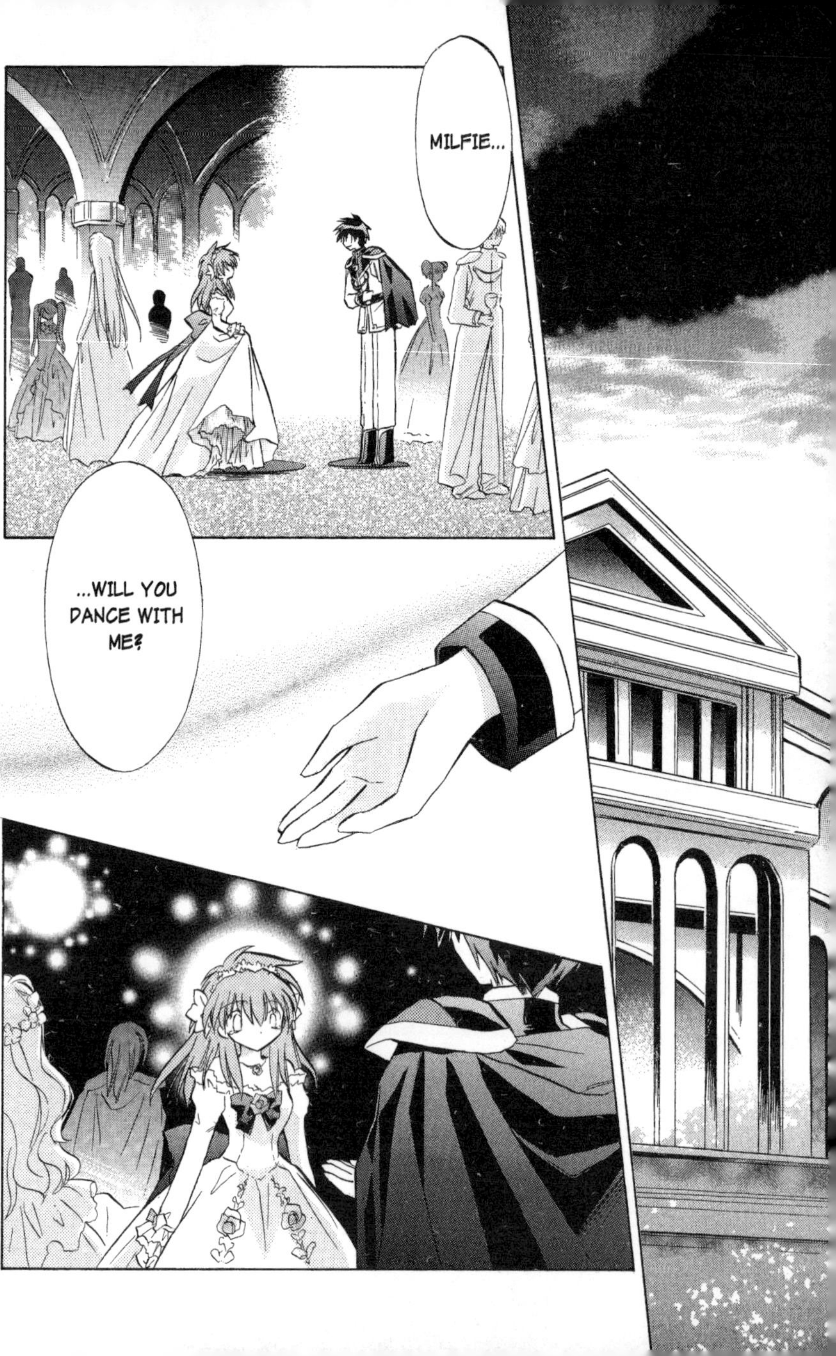
MILFIE...
...WILL YOU DANCE WITH ME?

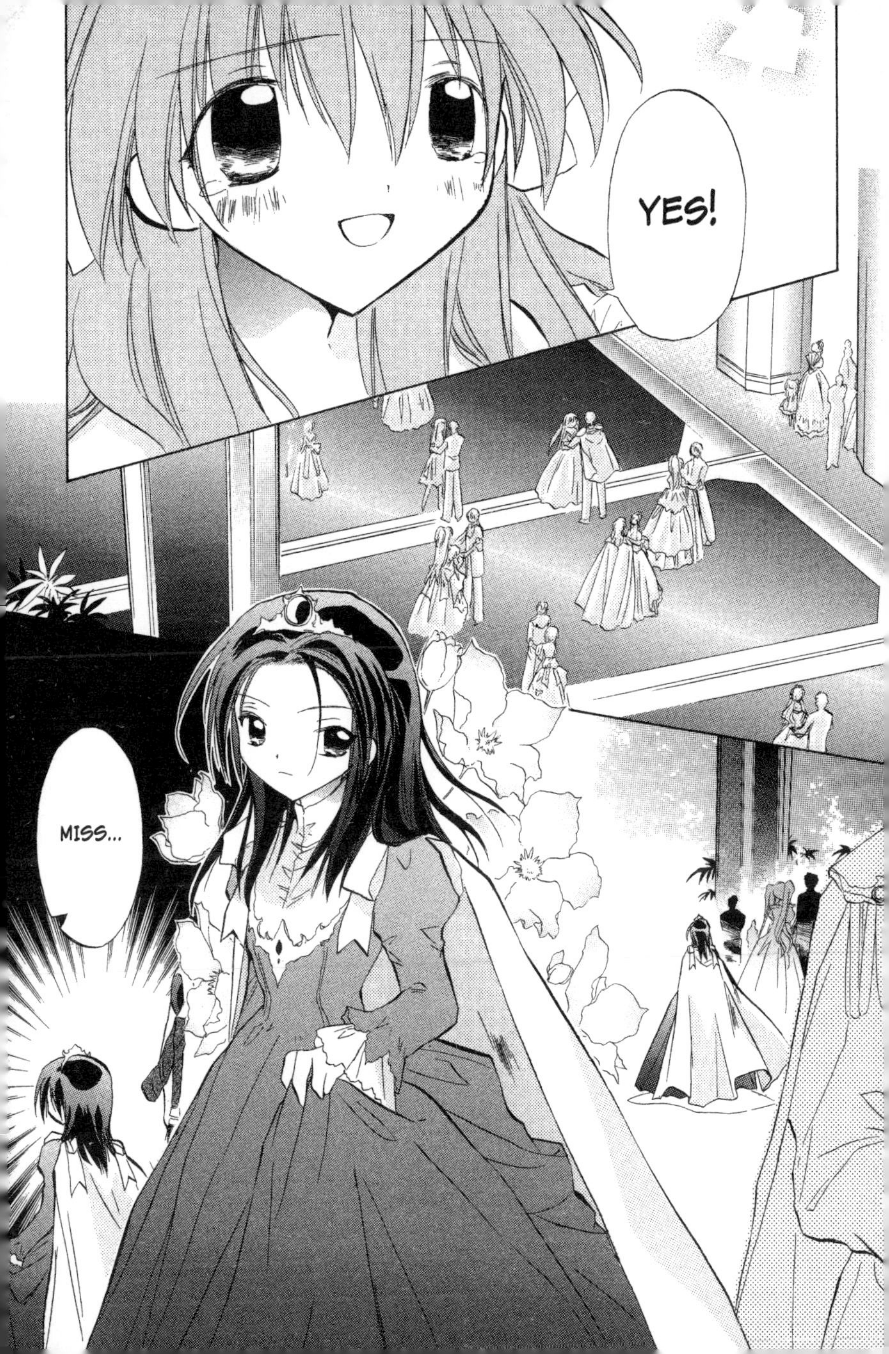
YES!
MISS...

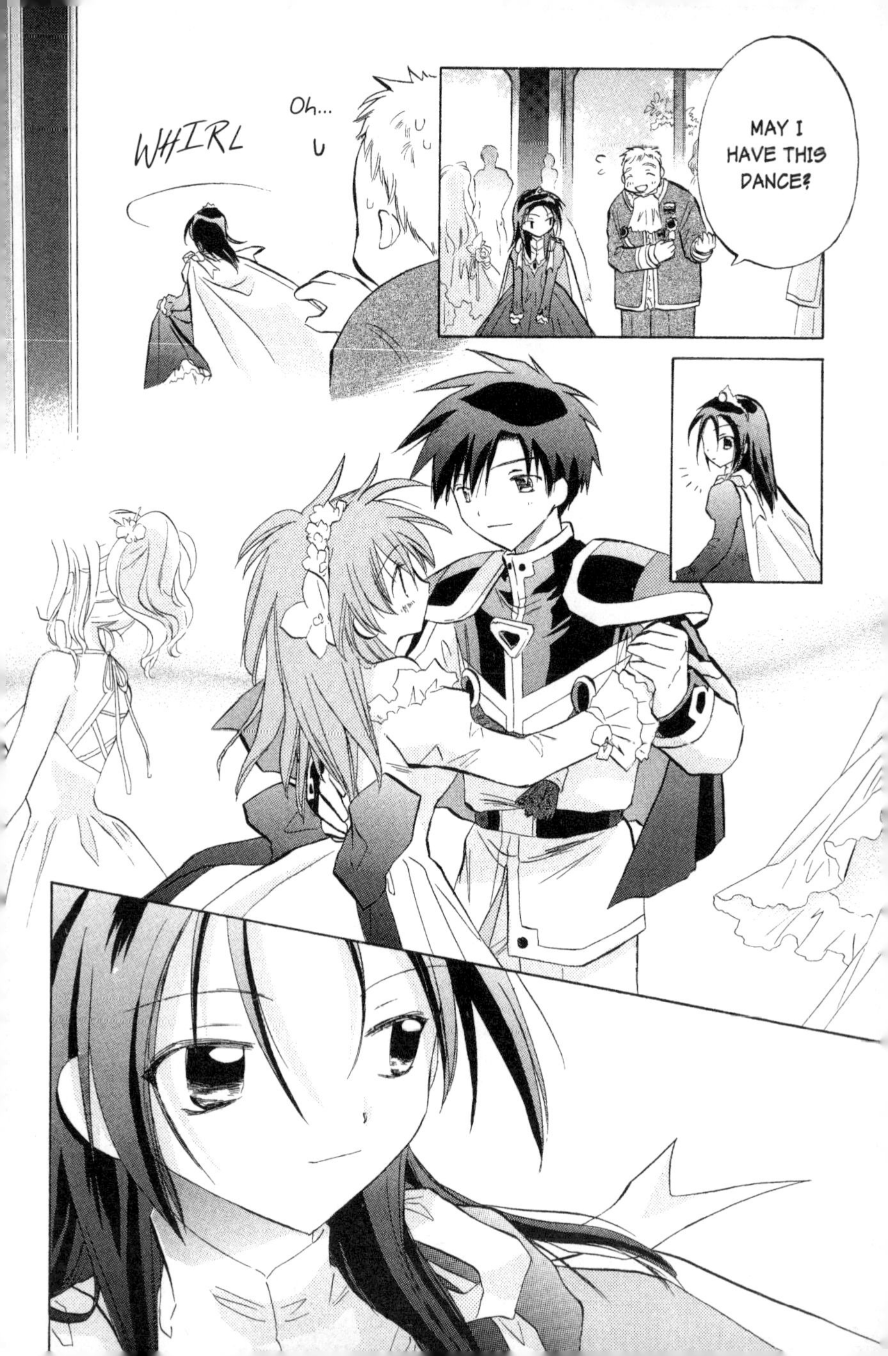
MAY I HAVE THIS DANCE?
Oh...
WHIRL

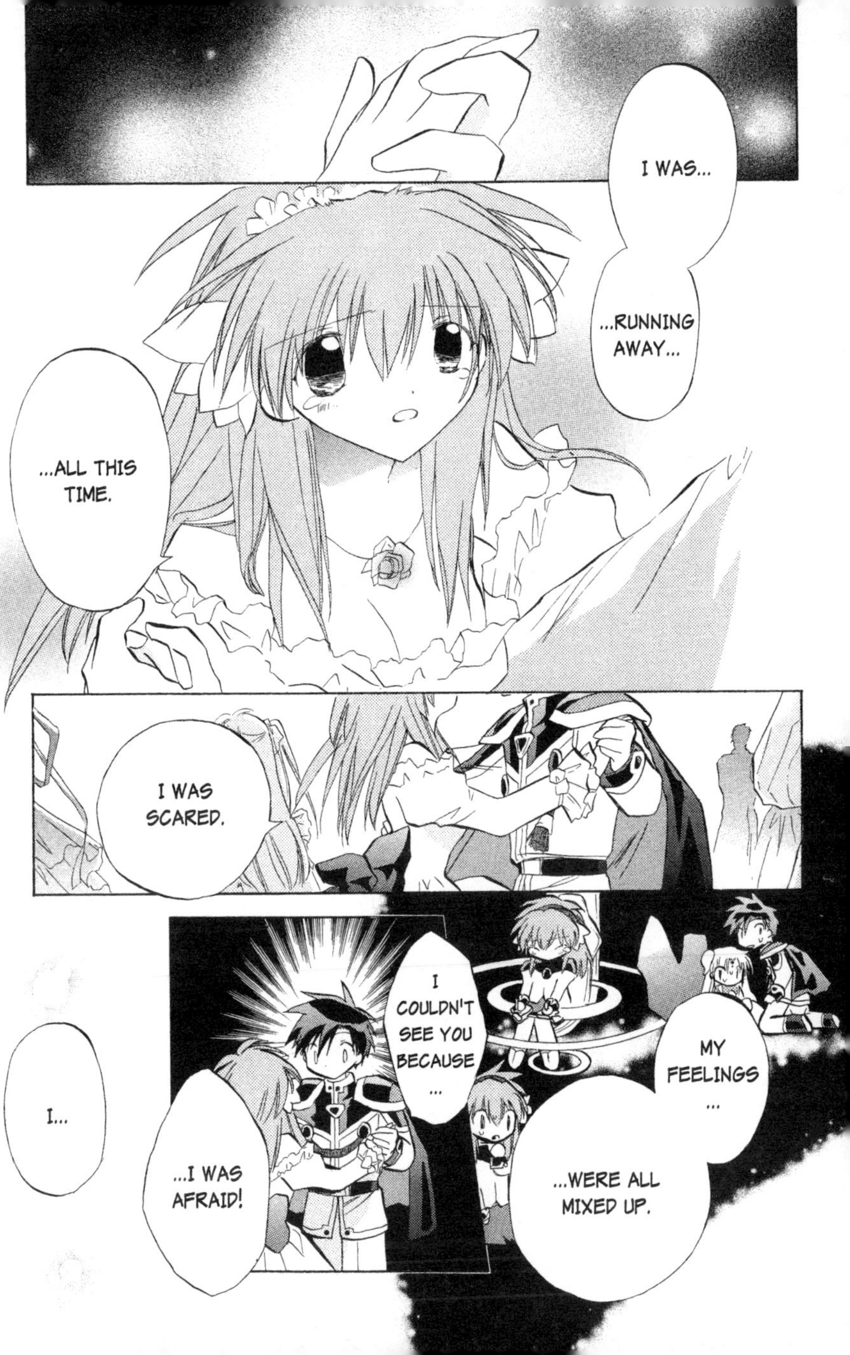
I WAS...
...RUNNING AWAY...
...ALL THIS TIME.
I WAS SCARED.
MY FEELINGS ...
...WERE ALL MIXED UP.
I COULDN'T SEE YOU BECAUSE ...
...I WAS AFRAID!
I...

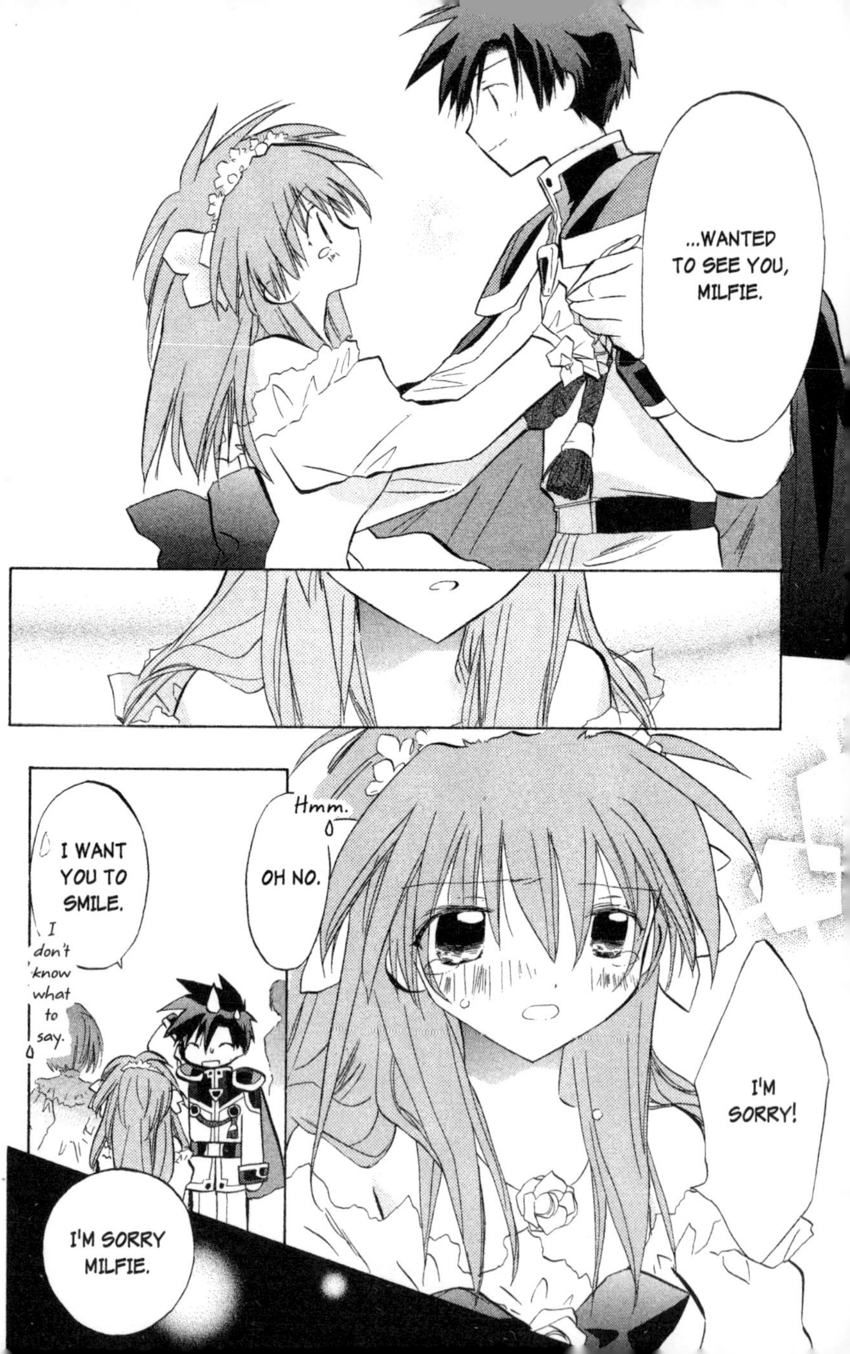
...WANTED TO SEE YOU, MILFIE.
I'M SORRY!
Hmm.
OH NO.
I WANT YOU TO SMILE.
I don't know what to say.
I'M SORRY MILFIE.

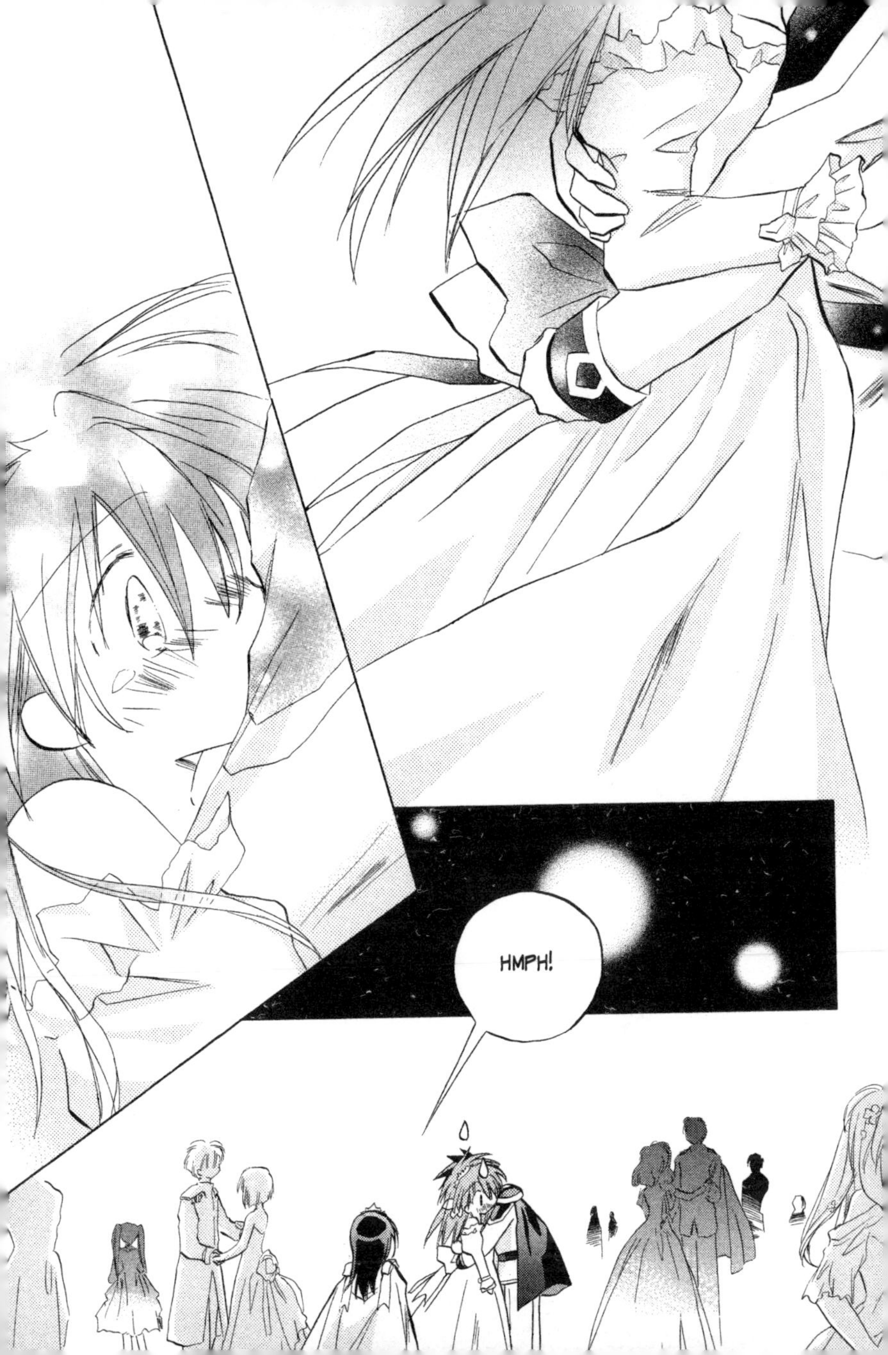
HMPH!

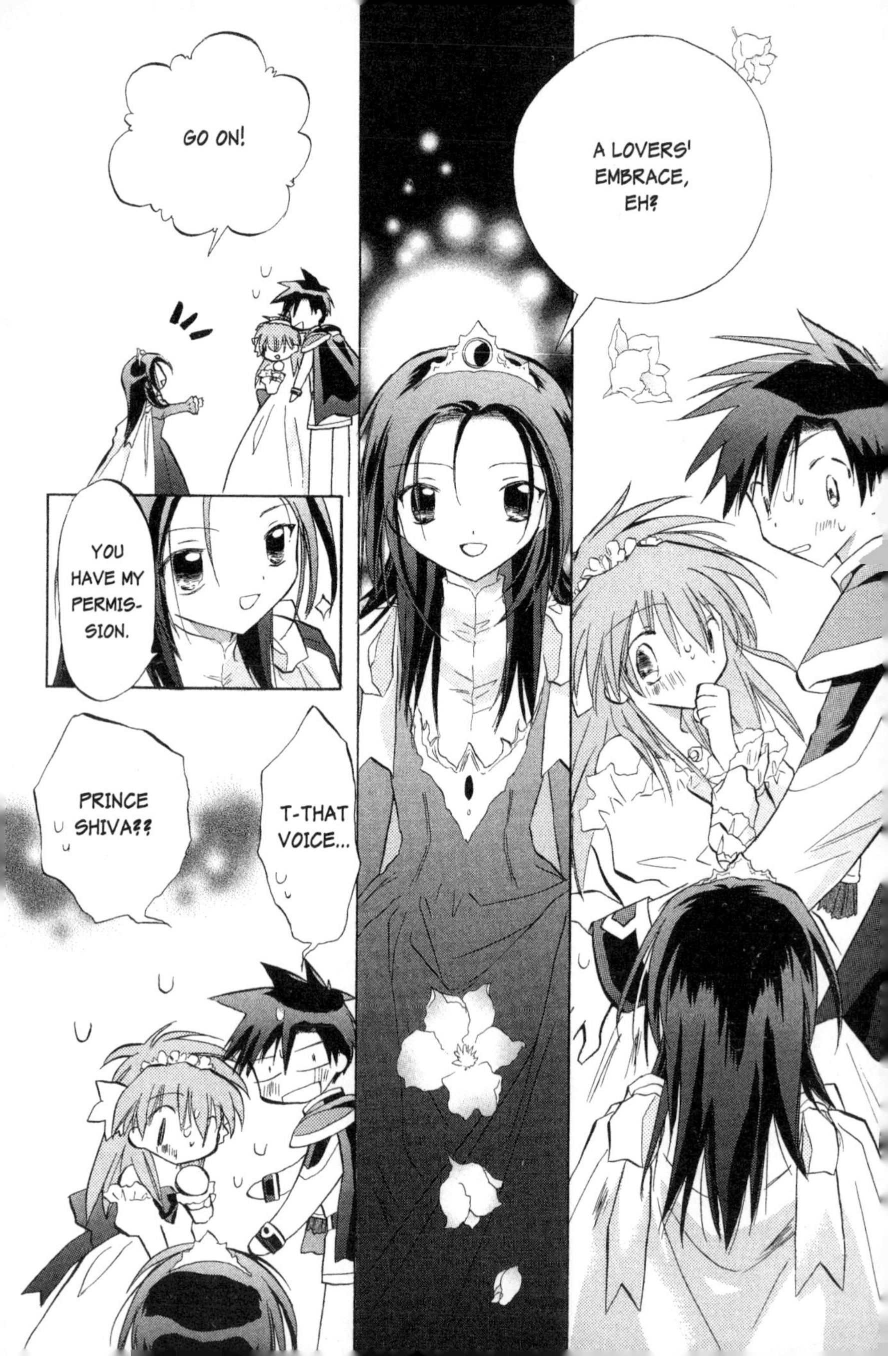
A LOVERS' EMBRACE, EH?
GO ON!
YOU HAVE MY PERMIS-SION.
T-THAT VOICE...
PRINCE SHIVA??

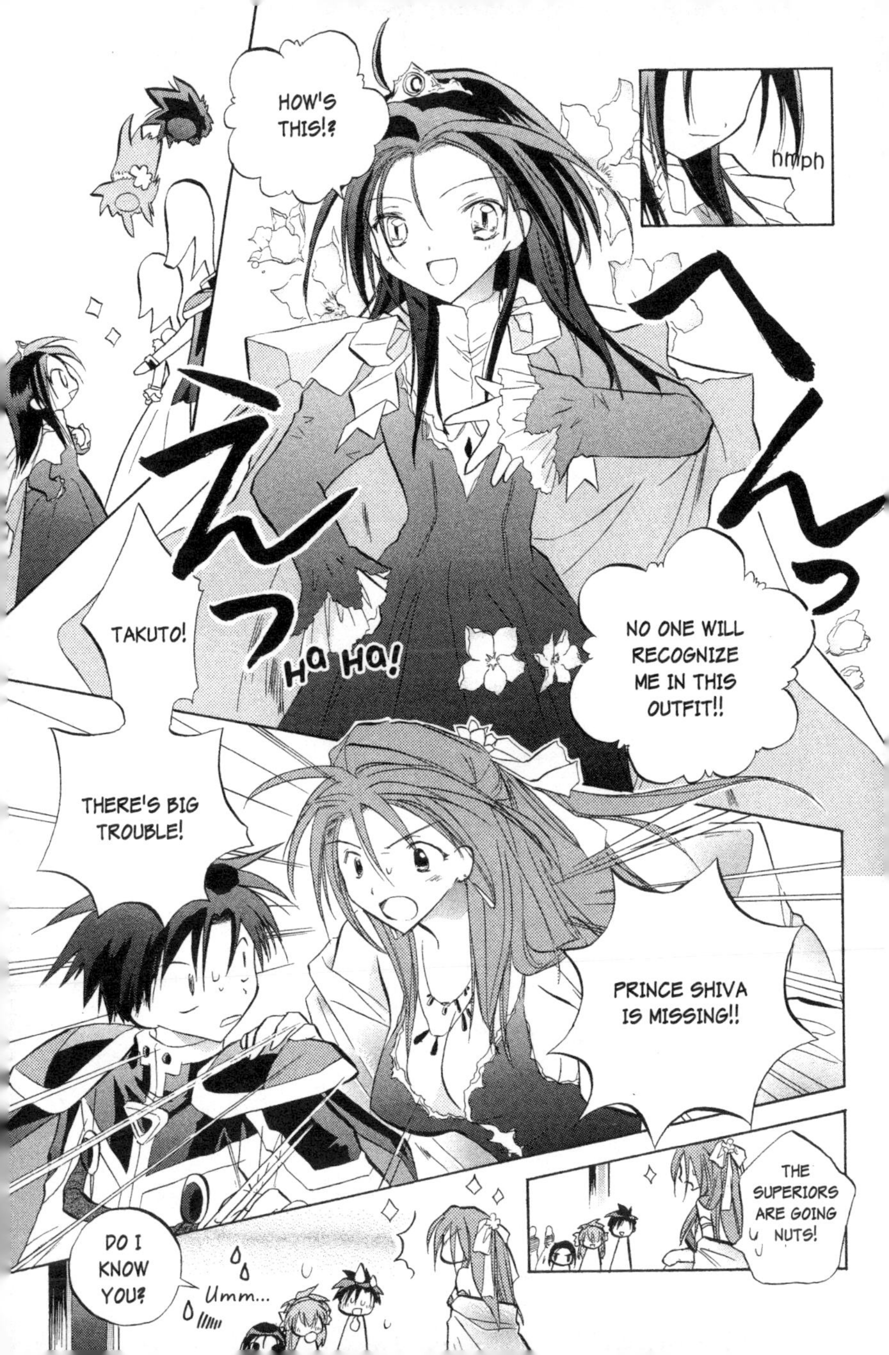
hmph
HOW'S THIS!?
NO ONE WILL RECOGNIZE ME IN THIS OUTFIT!!
えへんっ
Ha Ha!
TAKUTO!
THERE'S BIG TROUBLE!
PRINCE SHIVA IS MISSING!!
THE SUPERIORS ARE GOING NUTS!
Umm...
DO I KNOW YOU?

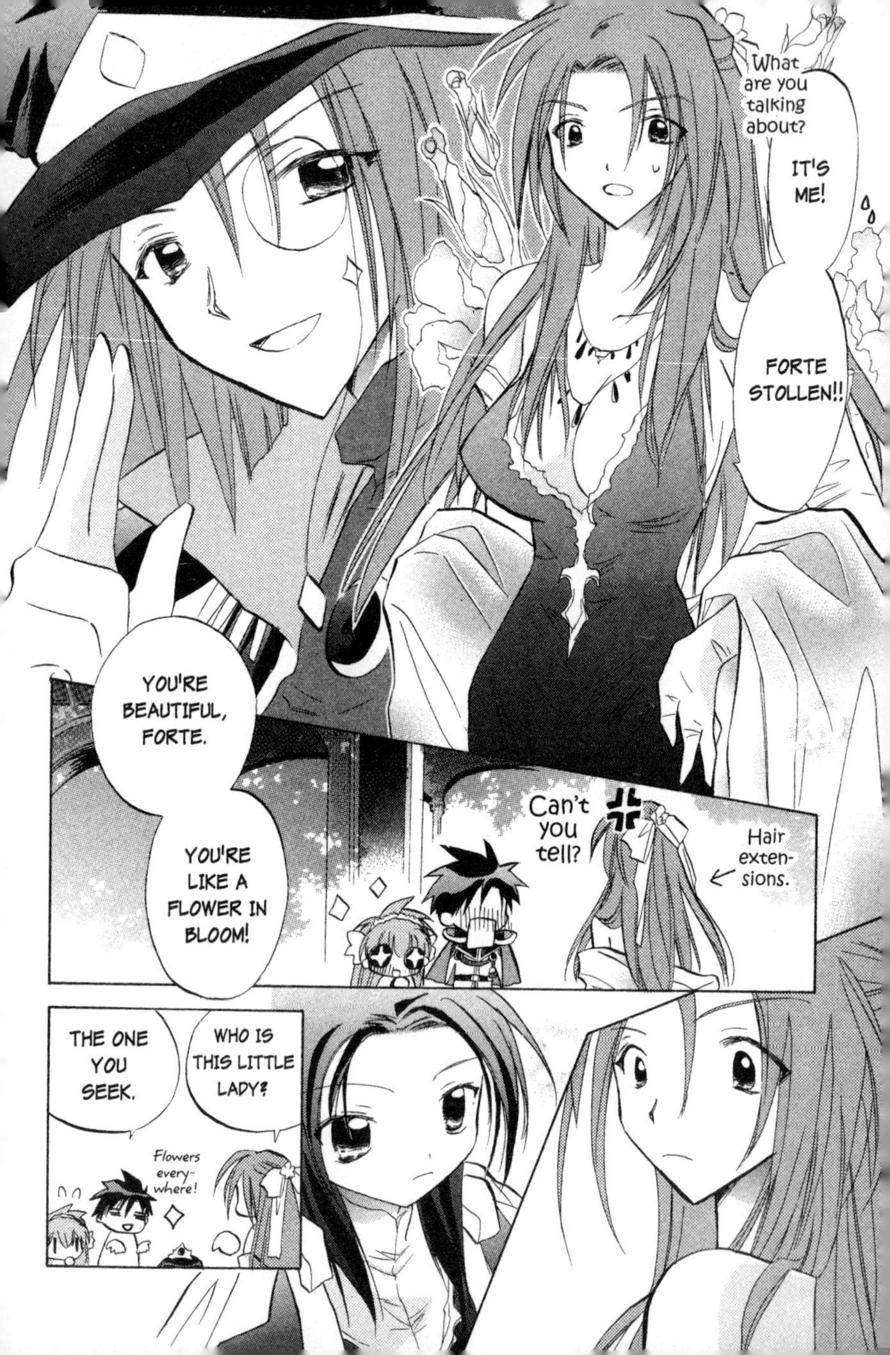

What are you talking about?
IT'S ME!
FORTE STOLLEN!!
YOU'RE BEAUTIFUL, FORTE.
YOU'RE LIKE A FLOWER IN BLOOM!
Hair extensions.
Can't you tell?
WHO IS THIS LITTLE LADY?
THE ONE YOU SEEK.
Flowers everywhere!

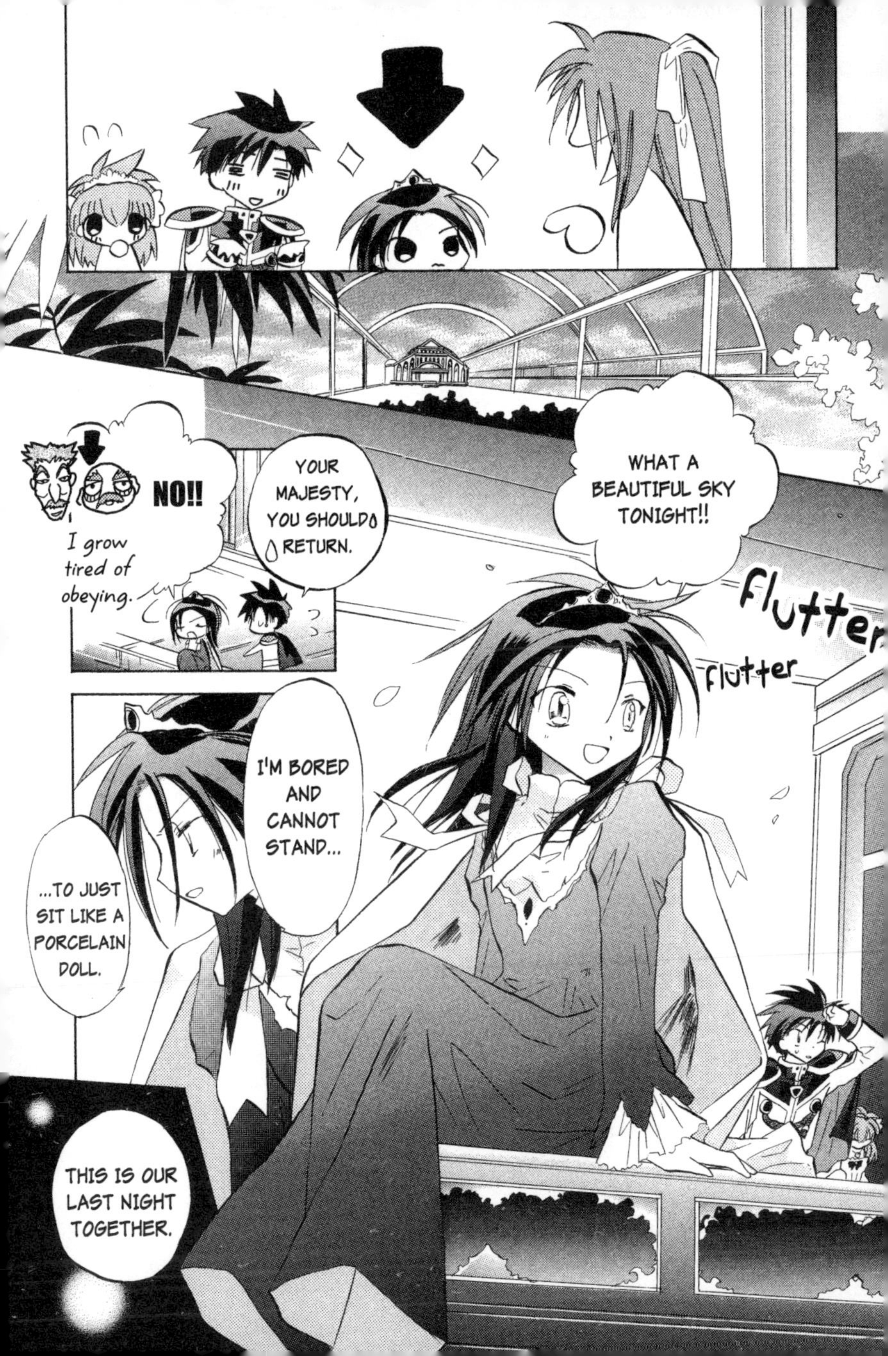
WHAT A BEAUTIFUL SKY TONIGHT!!
flutter
flutter
YOUR MAJESTY, YOU SHOULD RETURN.
NO!!
I grow tired of obeying.
I'M BORED AND CANNOT STAND...
...TO JUST SIT LIKE A PORCELAIN DOLL.
THIS IS OUR LAST NIGHT TOGETHER.

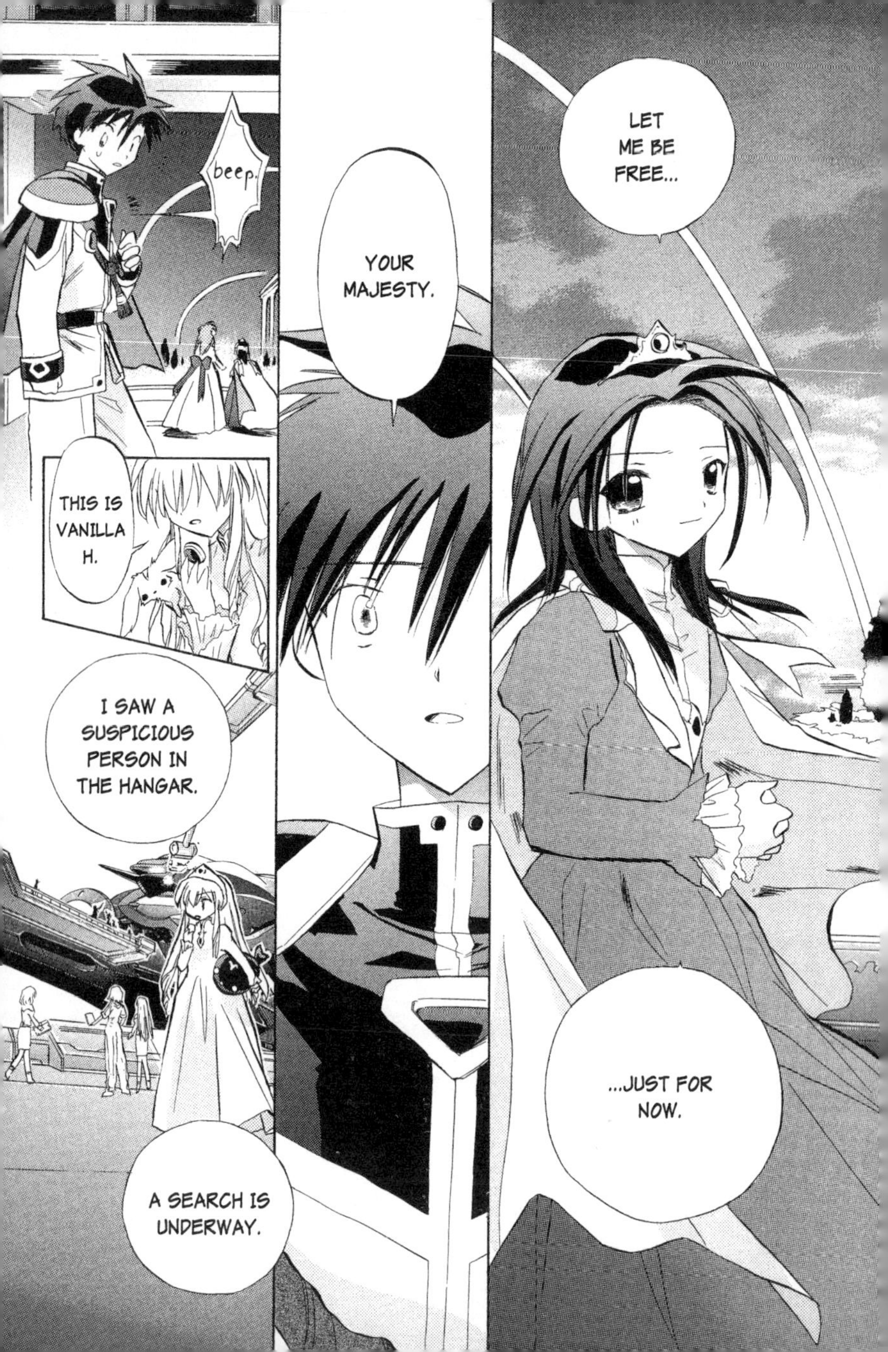
LET ME BE FREE...
...JUST FOR NOW.
YOUR MAJESTY.
beep.
THIS IS VANILLA H.
I SAW A SUSPICIOUS PERSON IN THE HANGAR.
A SEARCH IS UNDERWAY.

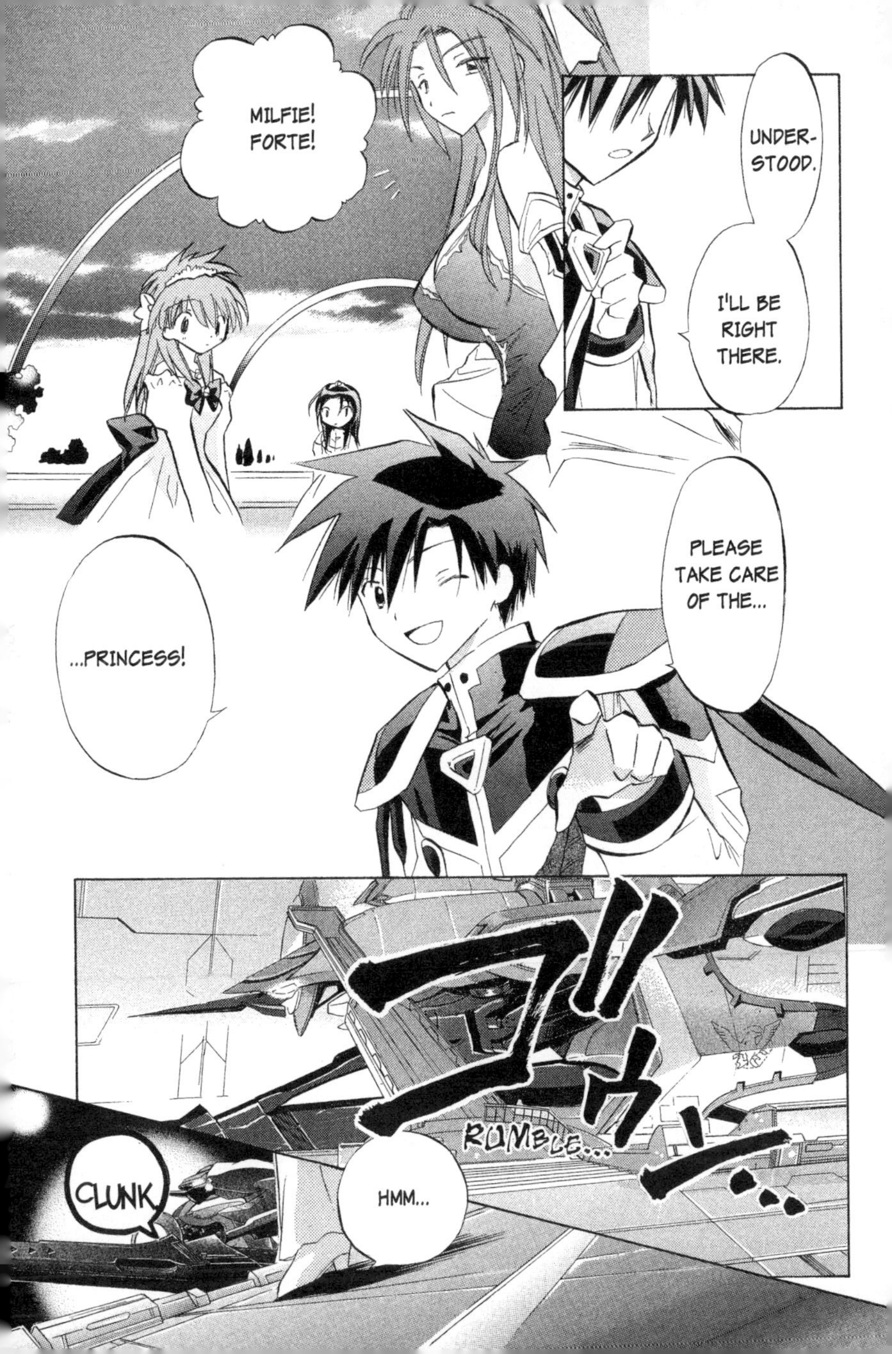
UNDER-STOOD.
I'LL BE RIGHT THERE.
MILFIE! FORTE!
PLEASE TAKE CARE OF THE...
...PRINCESS!
RUMBLE...
HMM...
CLUNK

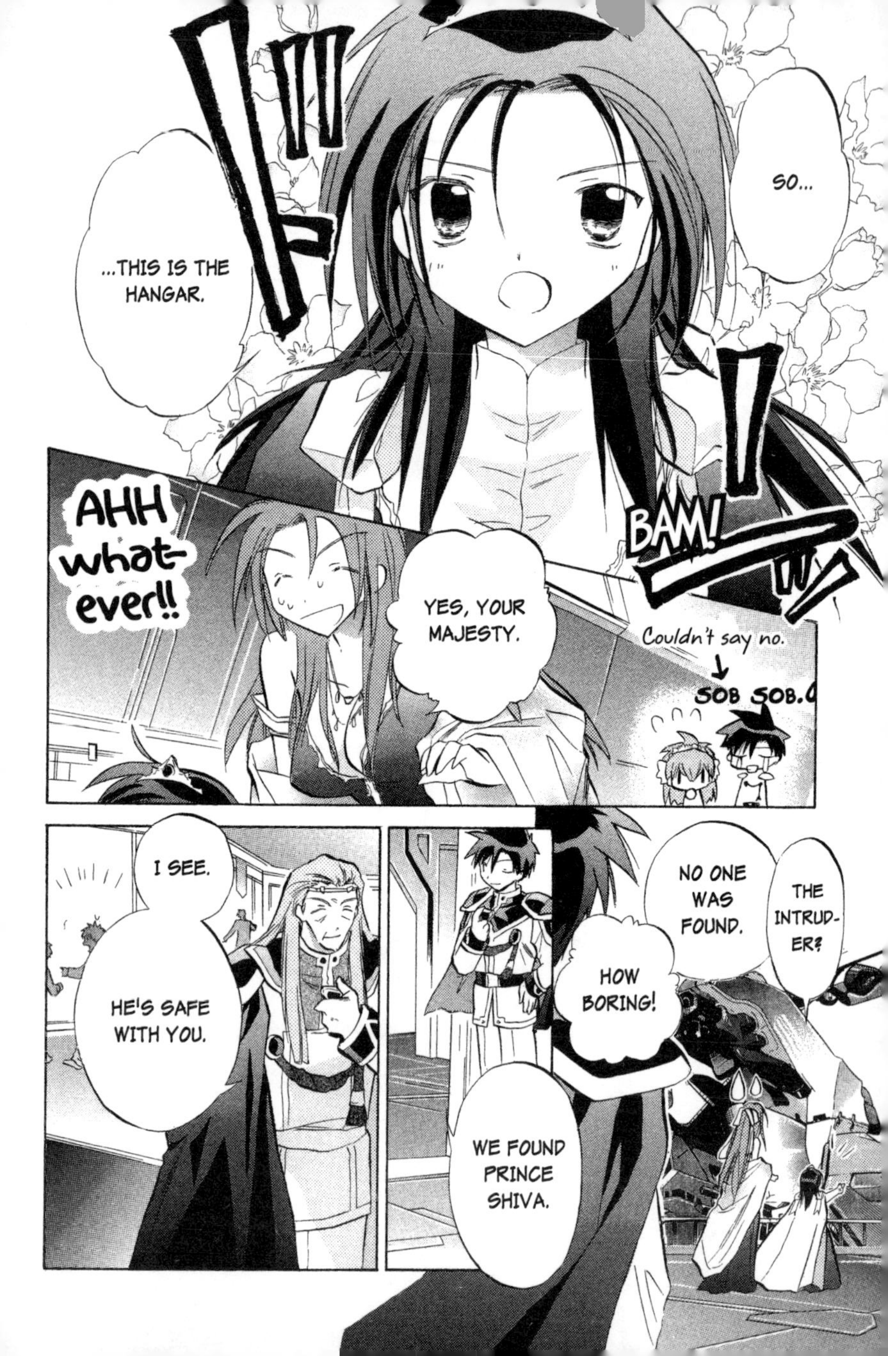
SO...
...THIS IS THE HANGAR.
BAM!
Couldn't say no.
SOB SOB.
YES, YOUR MAJESTY.
AHH whatever!!
THE INTRUDER?
NO ONE WAS FOUND.
HOW BORING!
WE FOUND PRINCE SHIVA.
I SEE.
HE'S SAFE WITH YOU.

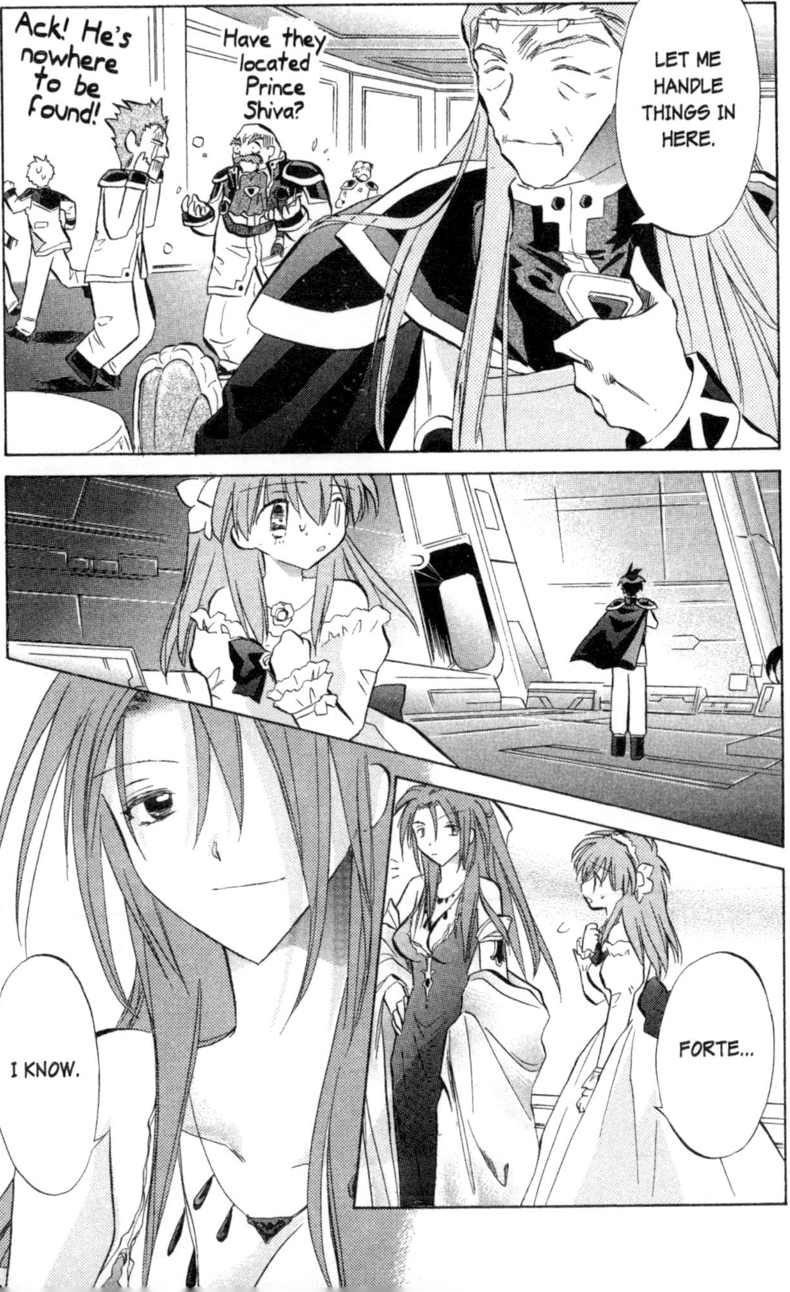
LET ME HANDLE THINGS IN HERE.
Have they located Prince Shiva?
Ack! He's nowhere to be found!
FORTE...
I KNOW.

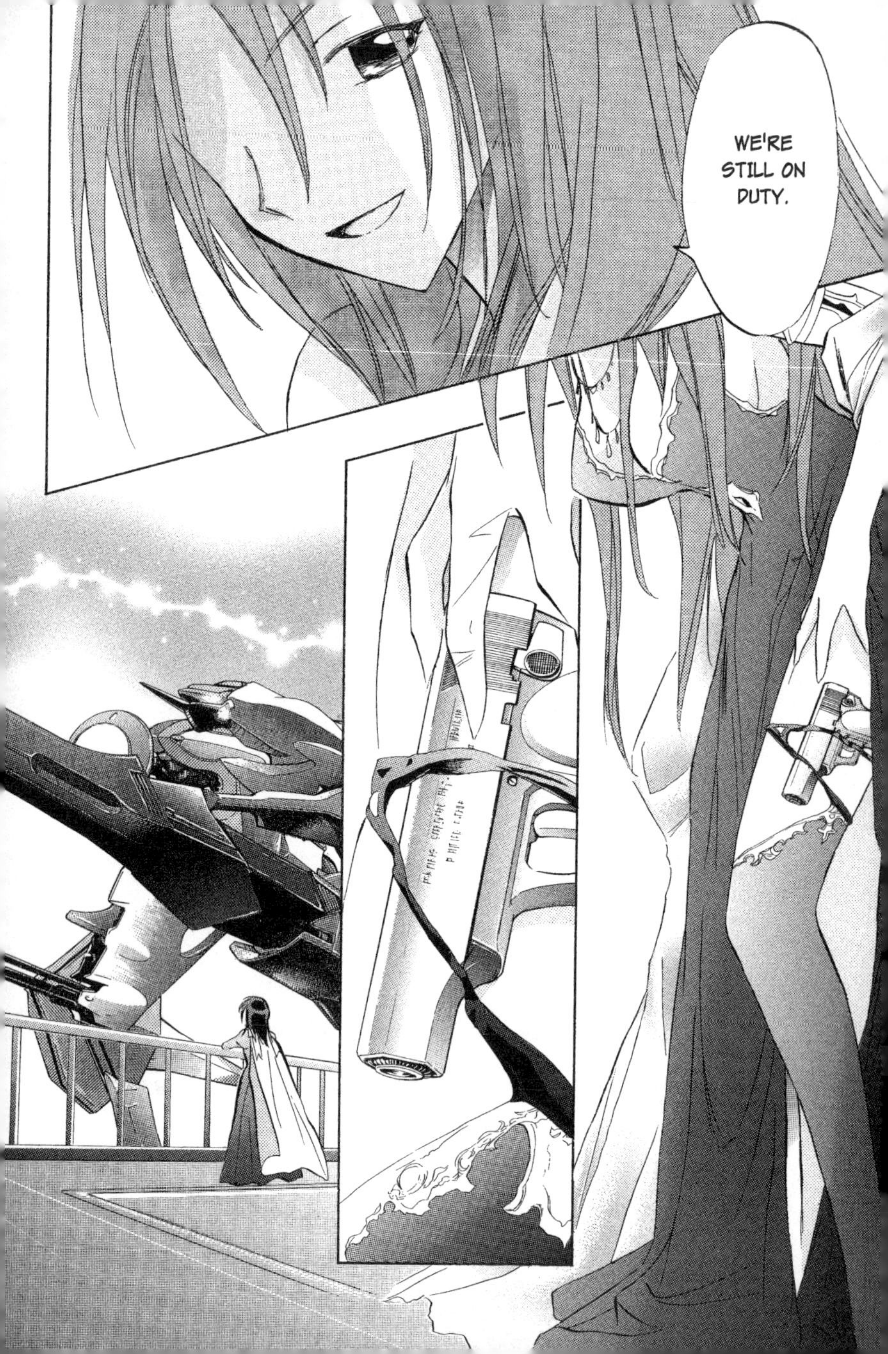
WE'RE STILL ON DUTY.

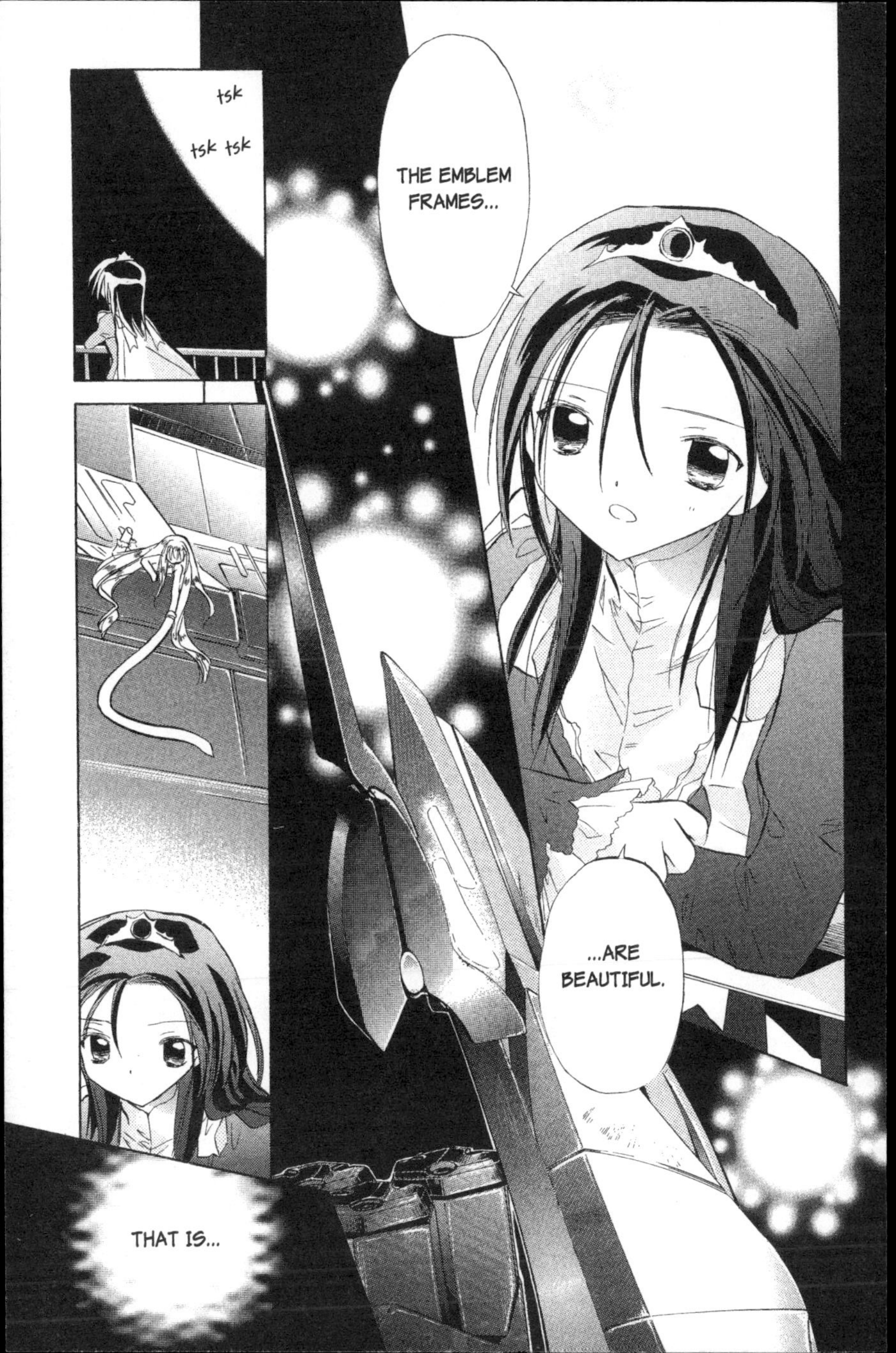
THE EMBLEM FRAMES...
...ARE BEAUTIFUL.
tsk
tsk tsk
THAT IS...

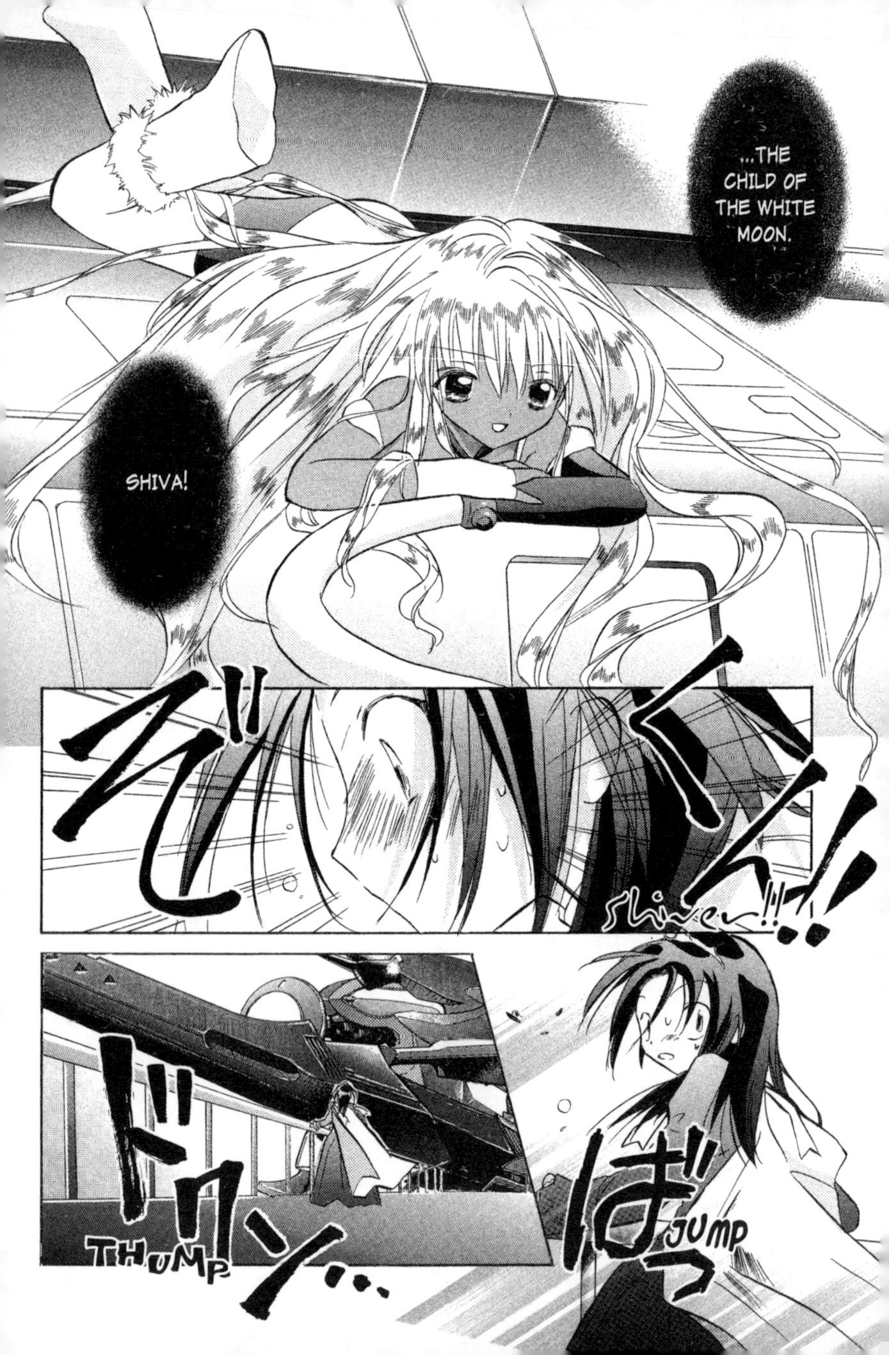
...THE CHILD OF THE WHITE MOON.
SHIVA!
ぞくん!!
shiver!!!
ぱっ
JUMP
THUMP

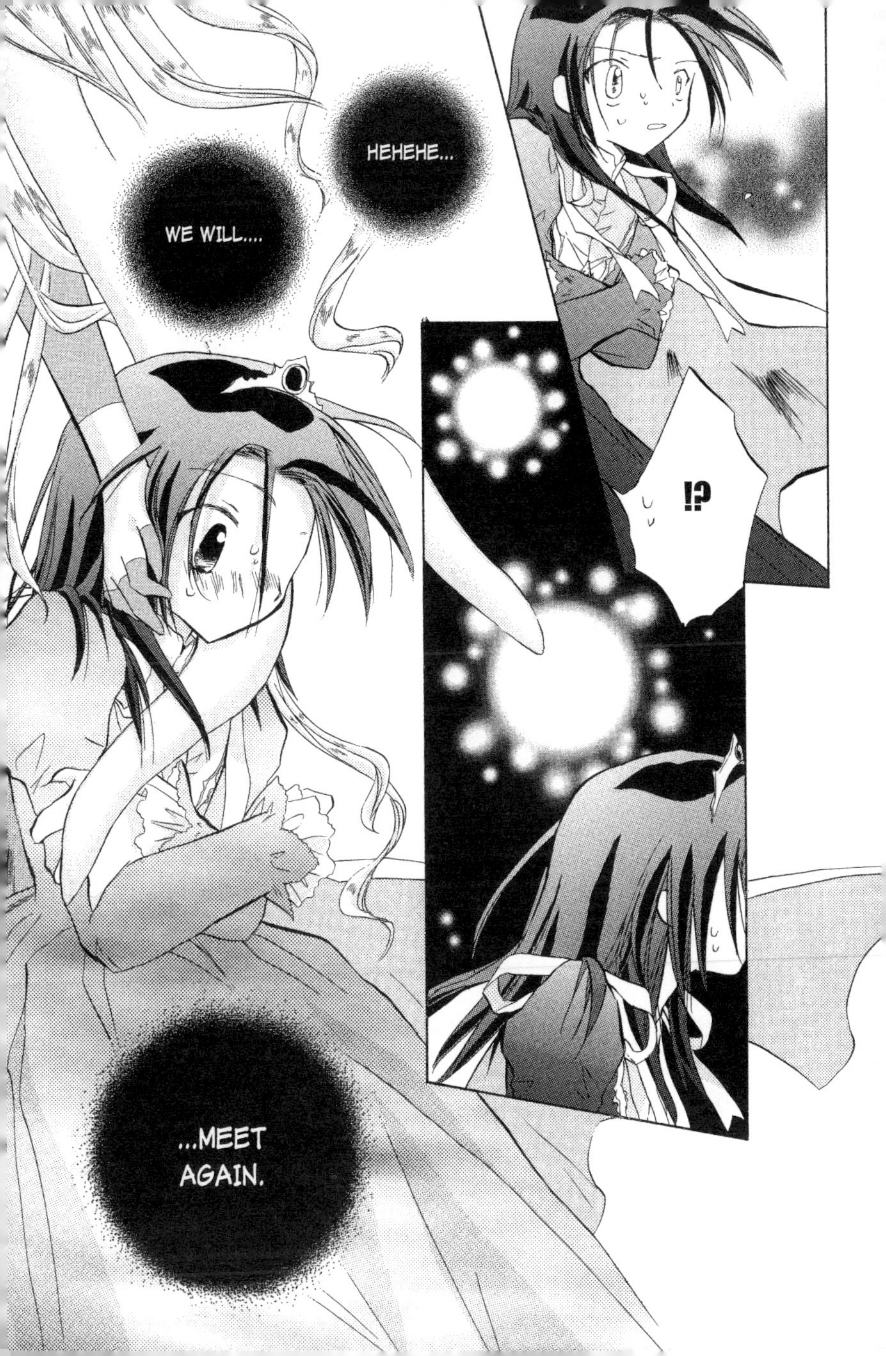
!?
HEHEHE...
WE WILL....
...MEET AGAIN.

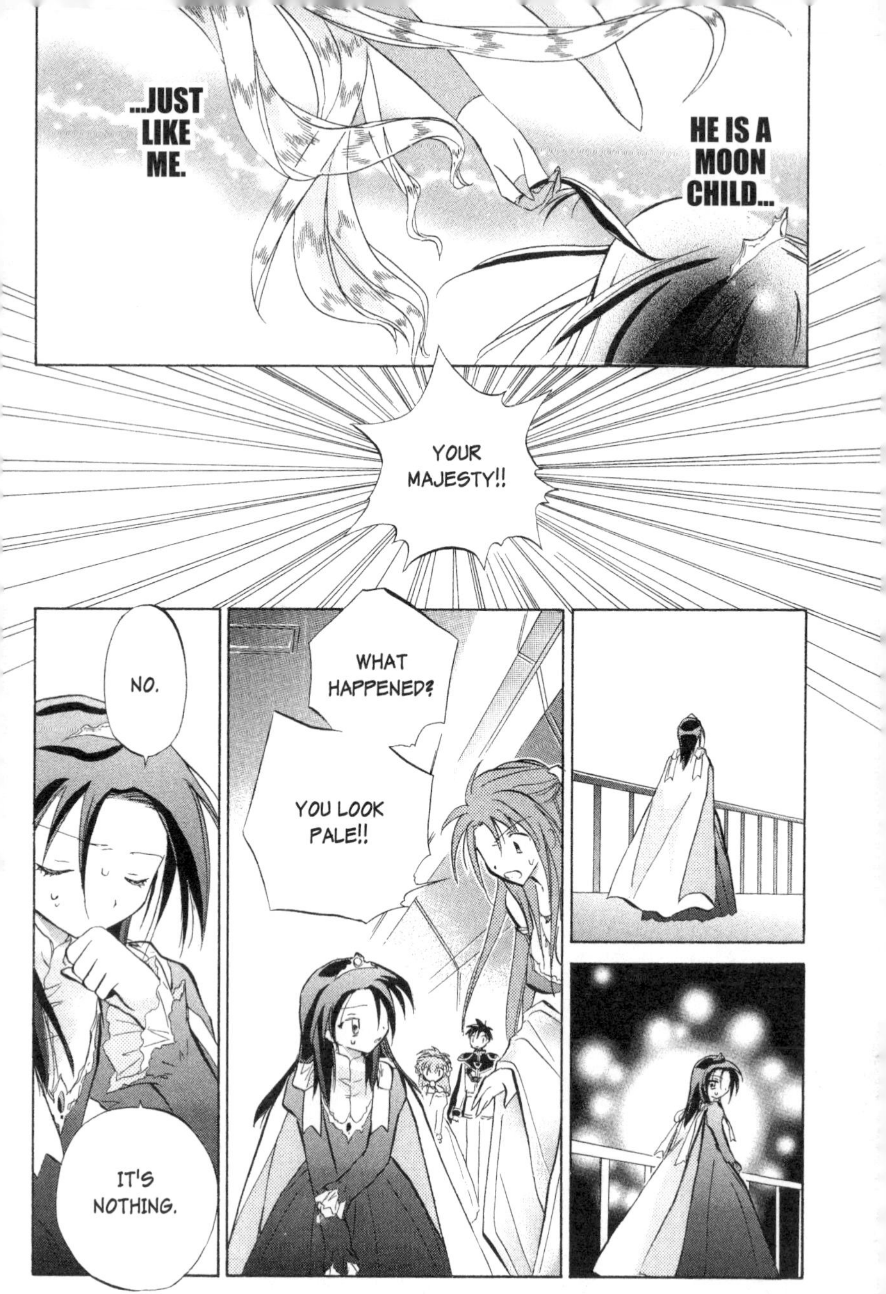
HE IS A MOON CHILD...
...JUST LIKE ME.
YOUR MAJESTY!!
WHAT HAPPENED?
YOU LOOK PALE!!
NO.
IT'S NOTHING.

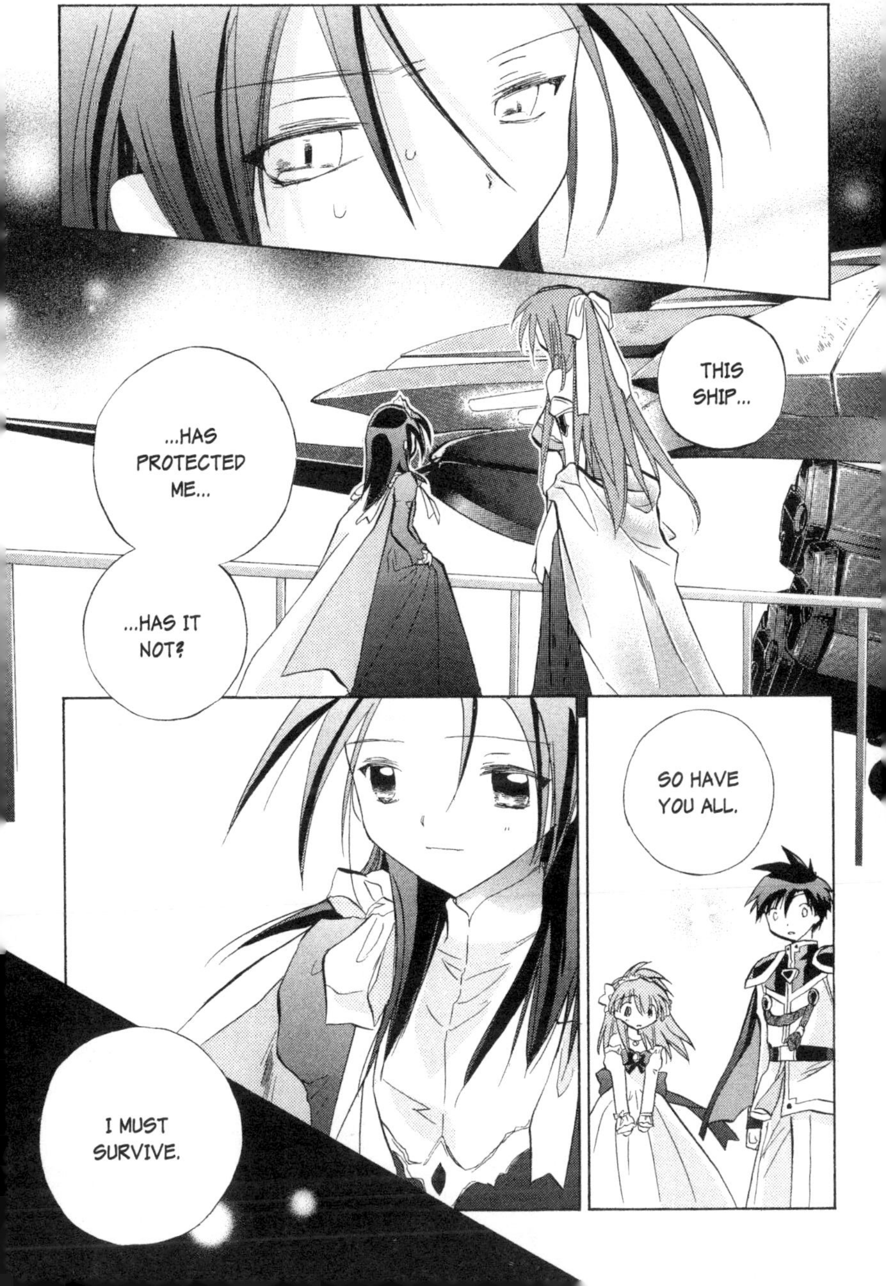
THIS SHIP...
...HAS PROTECTED ME...
...HAS IT NOT?
SO HAVE YOU ALL.
I MUST SURVIVE.

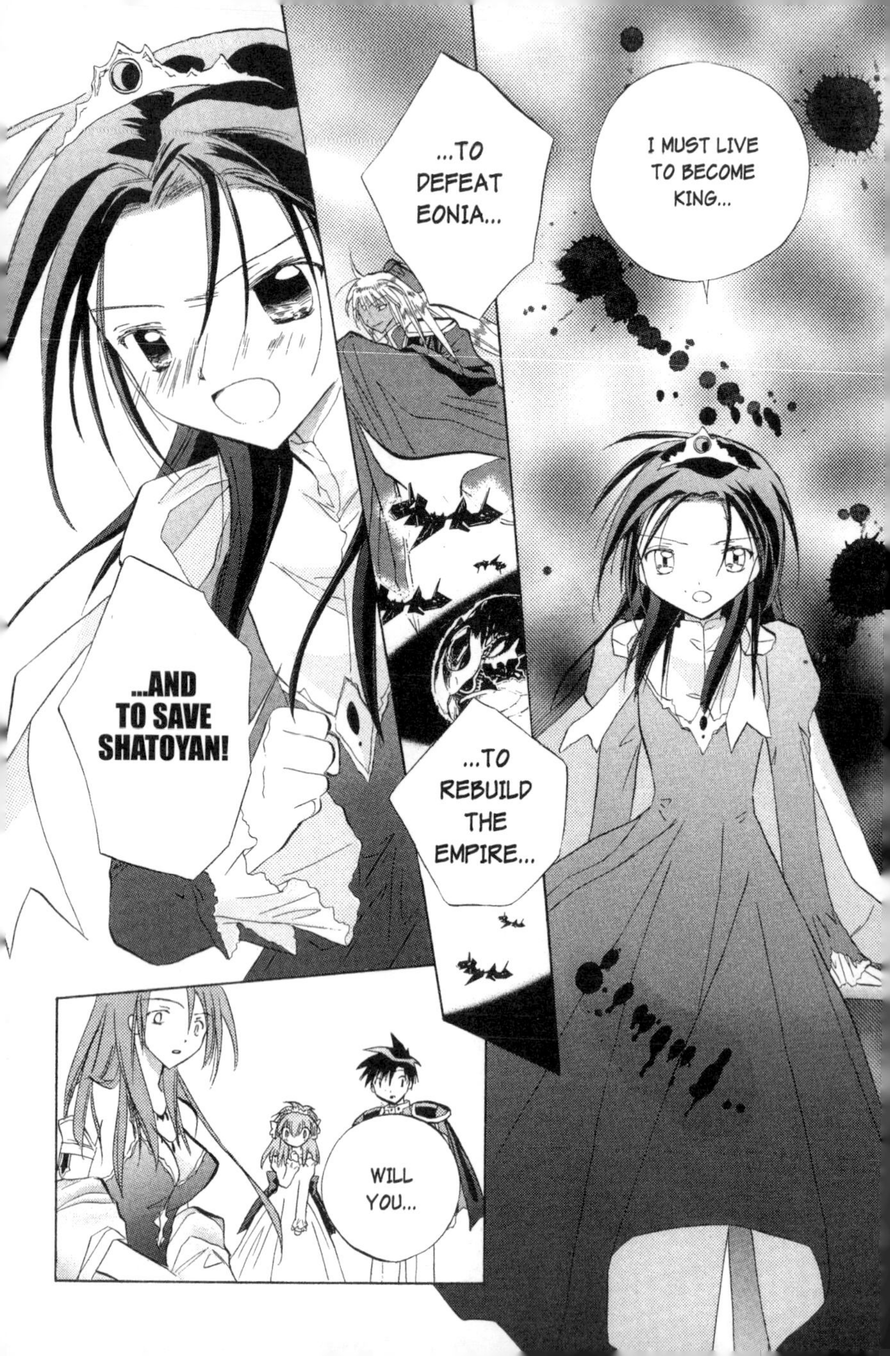
I MUST LIVE TO BECOME KING...
...TO DEFEAT EONIA...
...TO REBUILD THE EMPIRE...
...AND TO SAVE SHATOYAN!
WILL YOU...

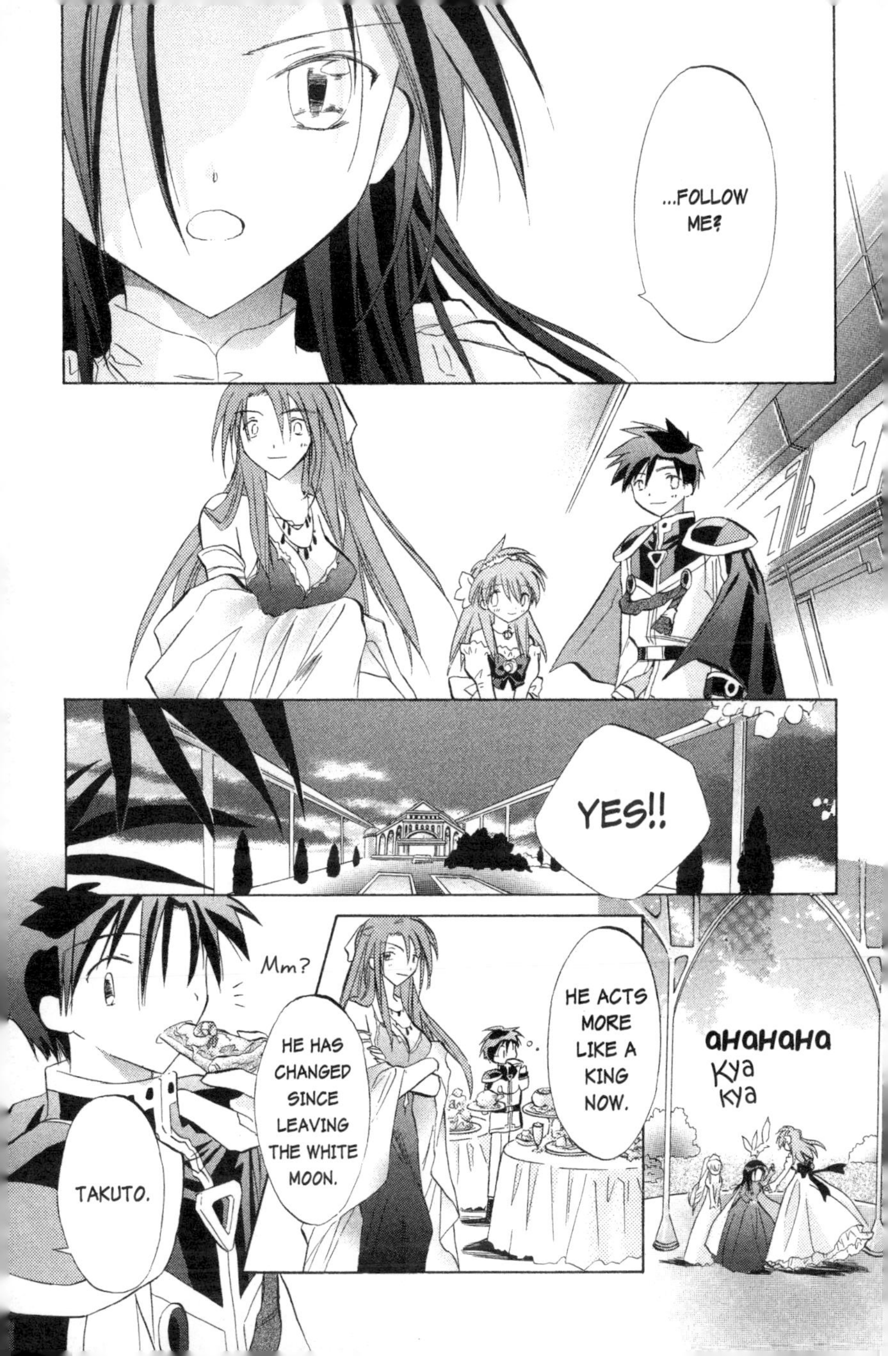
...FOLLOW ME?
YES!!
ahahaha
Kya kya
HE ACTS MORE LIKE A KING NOW.
HE HAS CHANGED SINCE LEAVING THE WHITE MOON.
Mm?
TAKUTO.

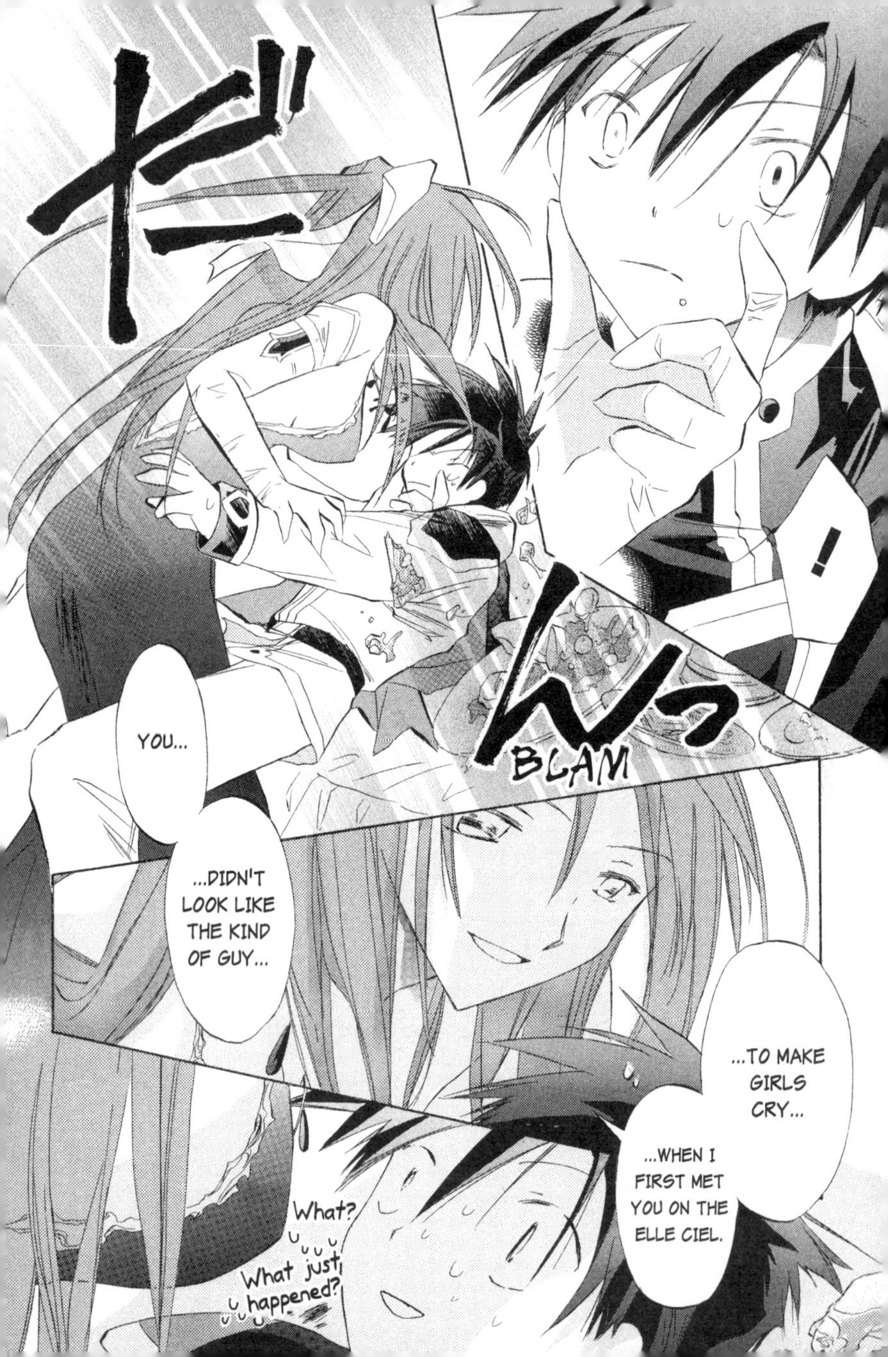
!
BLAM
YOU...
...DIDN'T LOOK LIKE THE KIND OF GUY...
...TO MAKE GIRLS CRY...
...WHEN I FIRST MET YOU ON THE ELLE CIEL.
What?
What just happened?

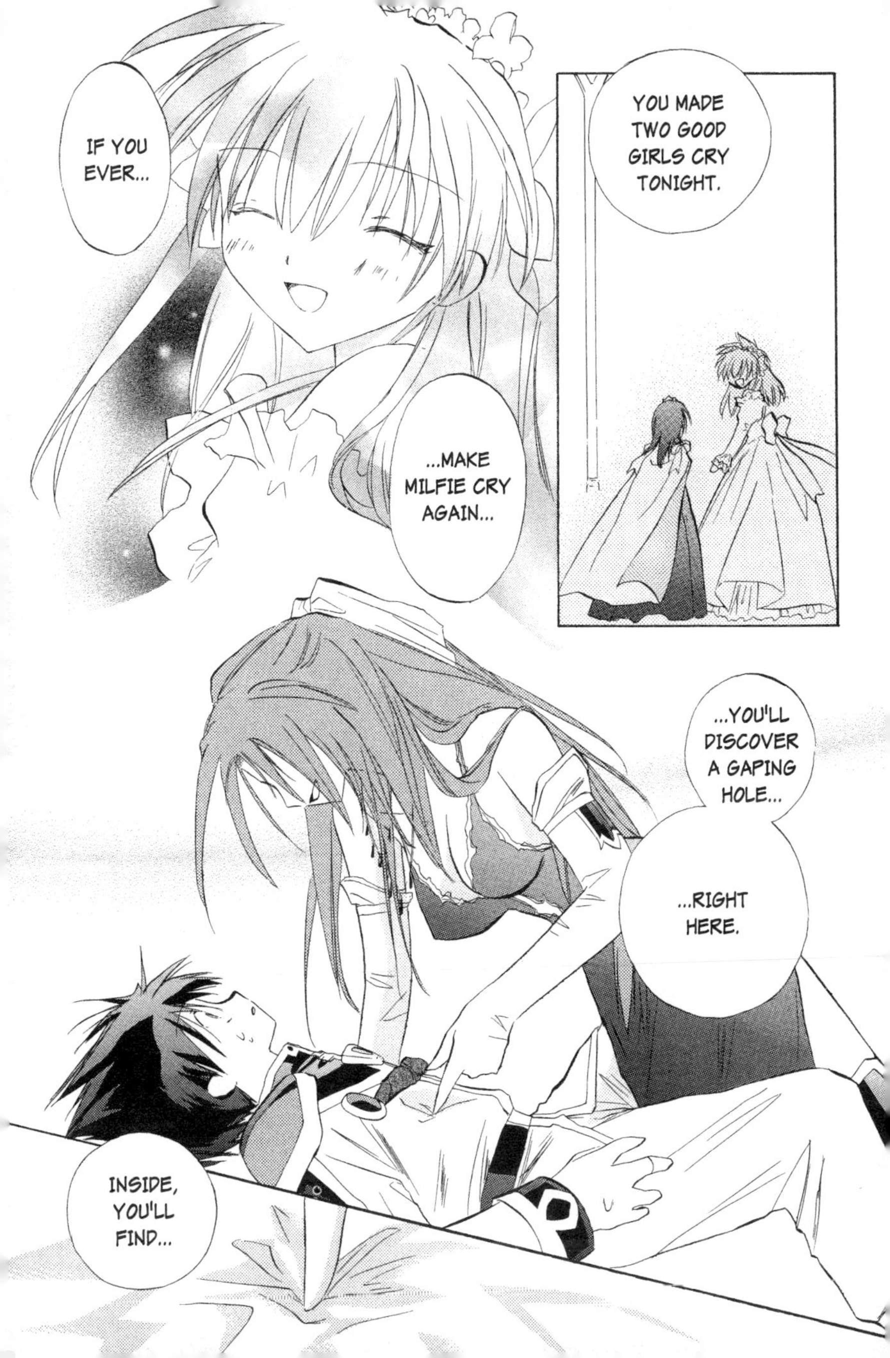
YOU MADE TWO GOOD GIRLS CRY TONIGHT.
IF YOU EVER...
...MAKE MILFIE CRY AGAIN...
...YOU'LL DISCOVER A GAPING HOLE...
...RIGHT HERE.
INSIDE, YOU'LL FIND...

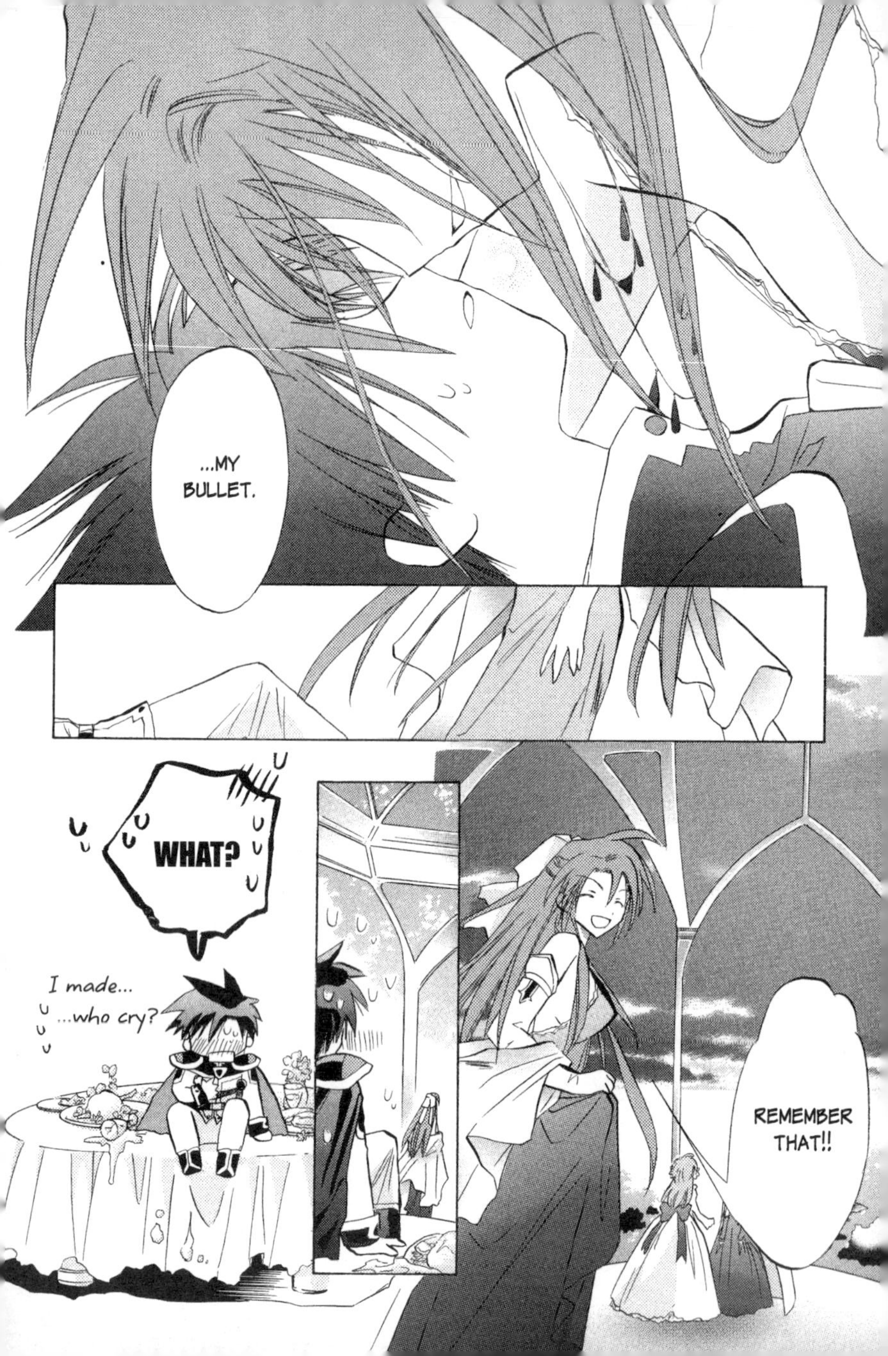
...MY BULLET.
REMEMBER THAT!!
WHAT?
I made...
...who cry?

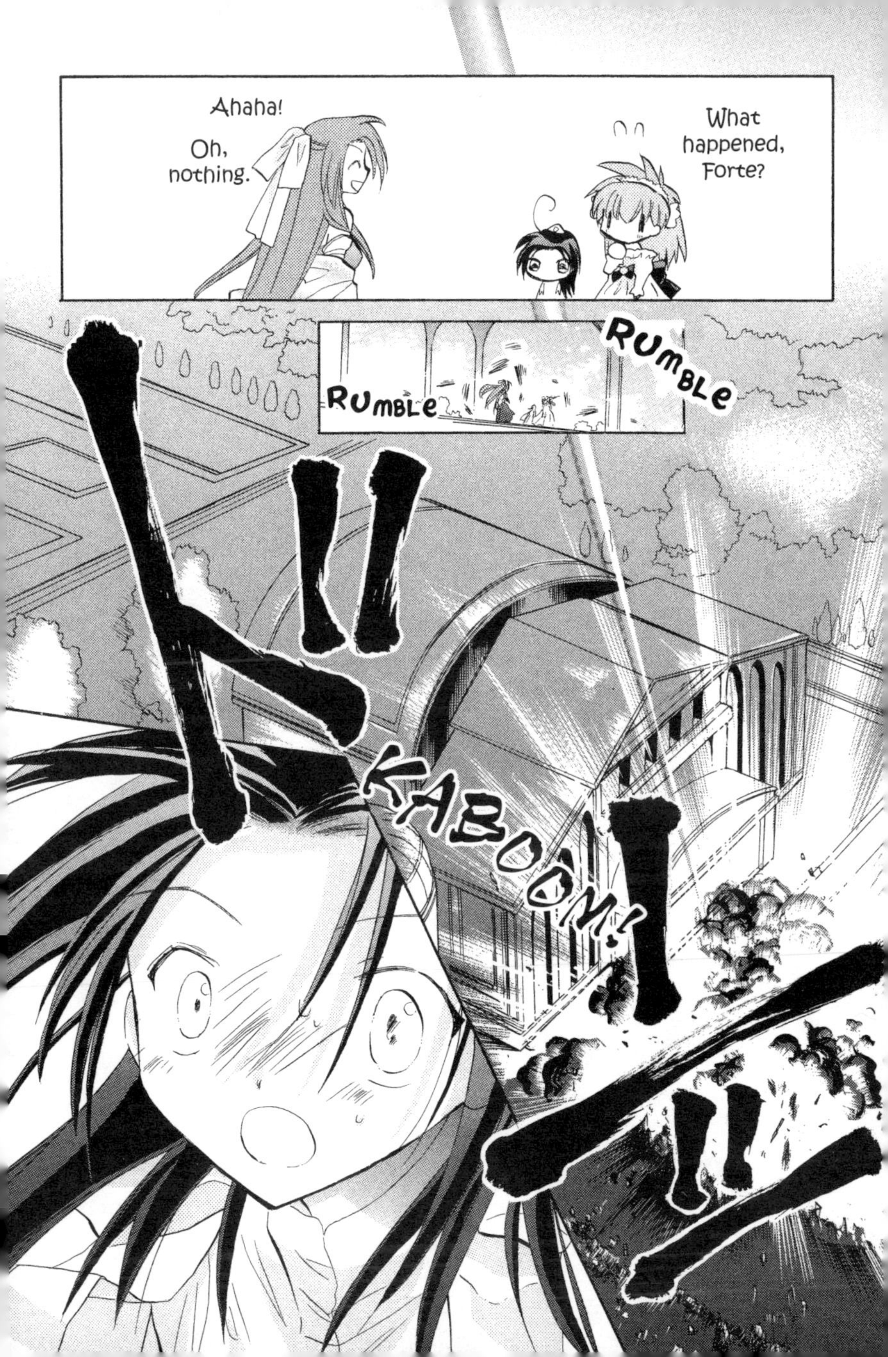
What happened, Forte?
Ahaha!
Oh, nothing.
RUMBLE
RUMBLE
KABOOM!

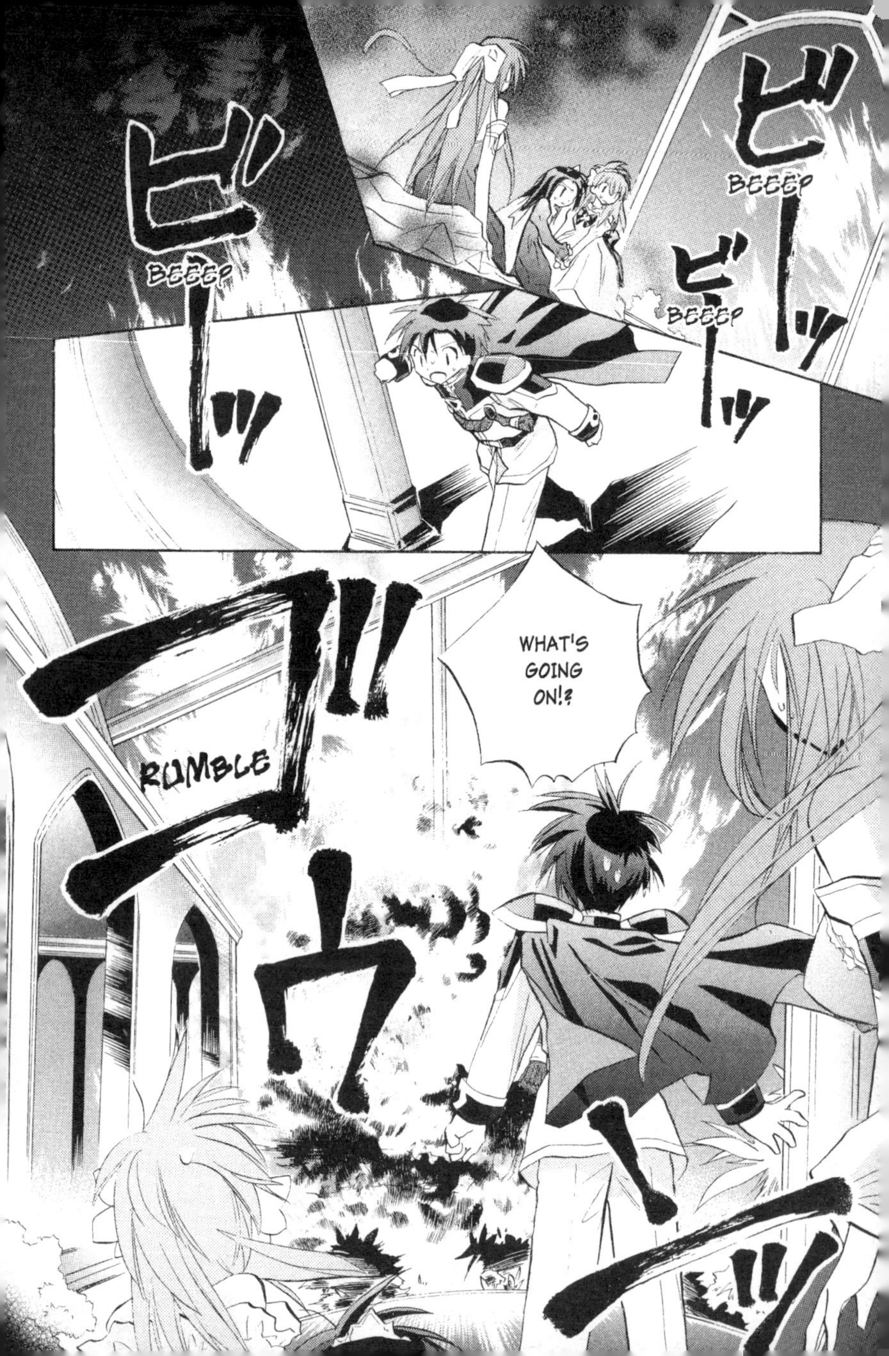
ビーッ
BEEEP
ビーッ
BEEEP
ビーッ
BEEEP
WHAT'S GOING ON!?
ゴウーッ
RUMBLE

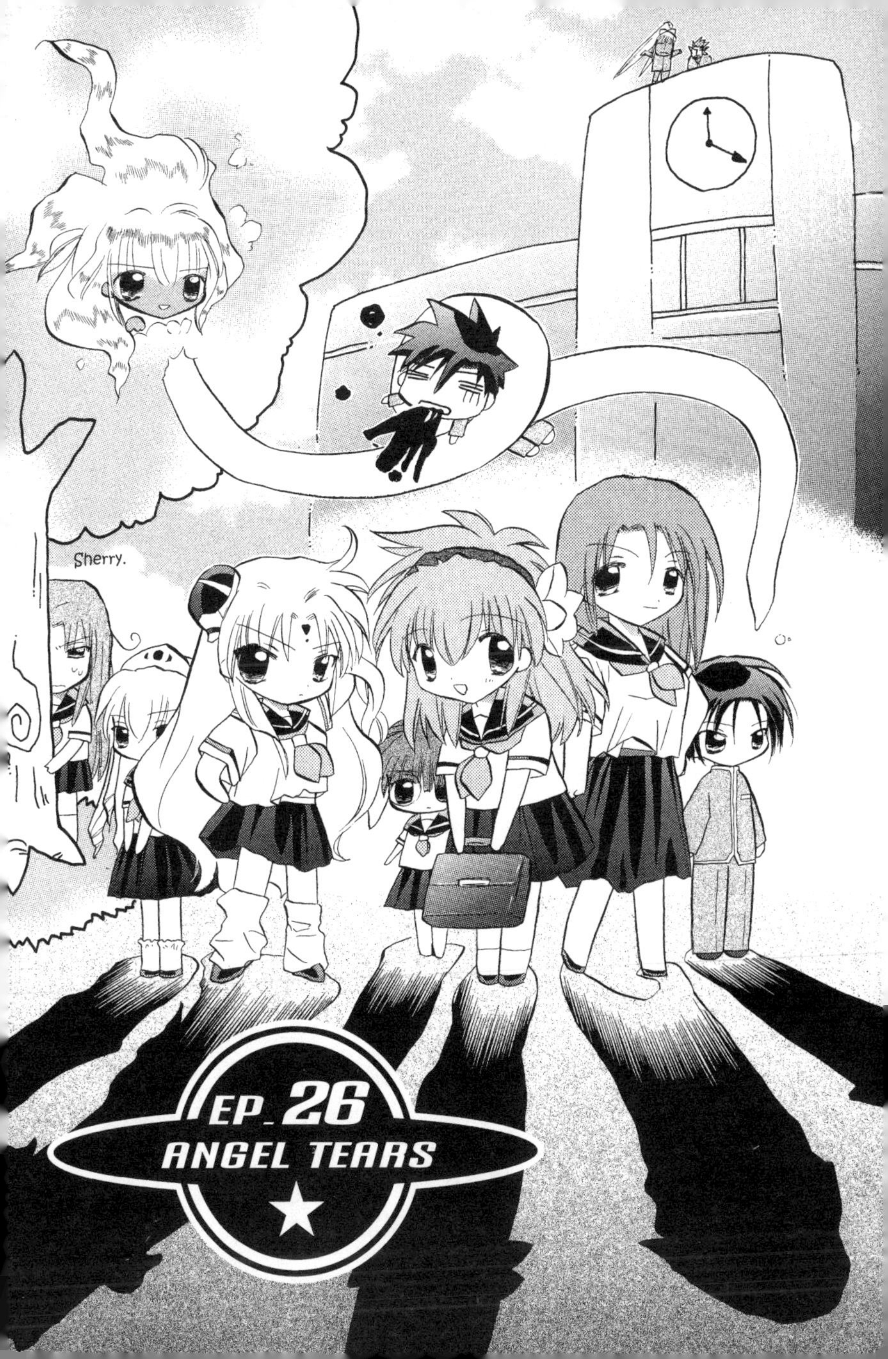
Sherry.
EP_26
ANGEL TEARS

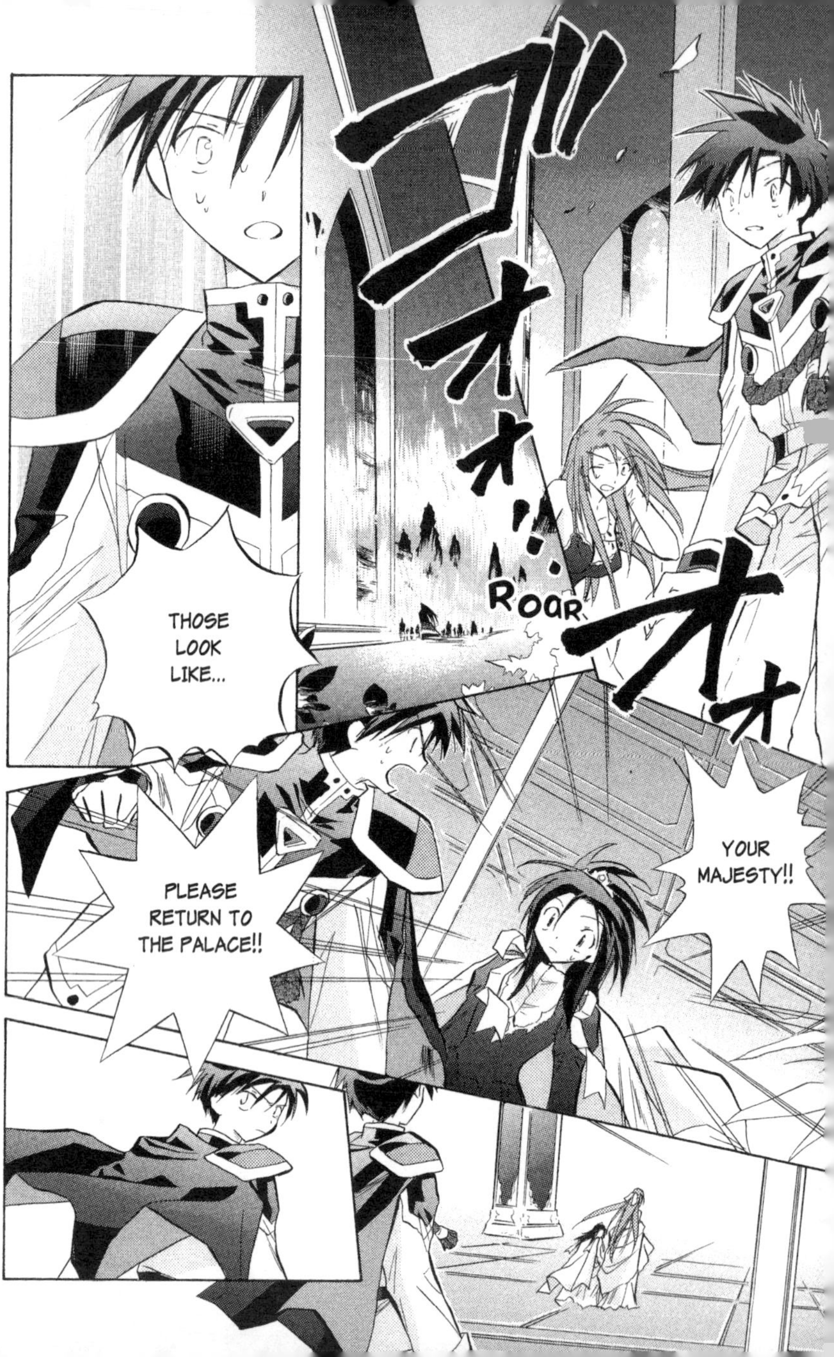
ゴオオ!!
ROAR
オォ
THOSE LOOK LIKE...
YOUR MAJESTY!!
PLEASE RETURN TO THE PALACE!!

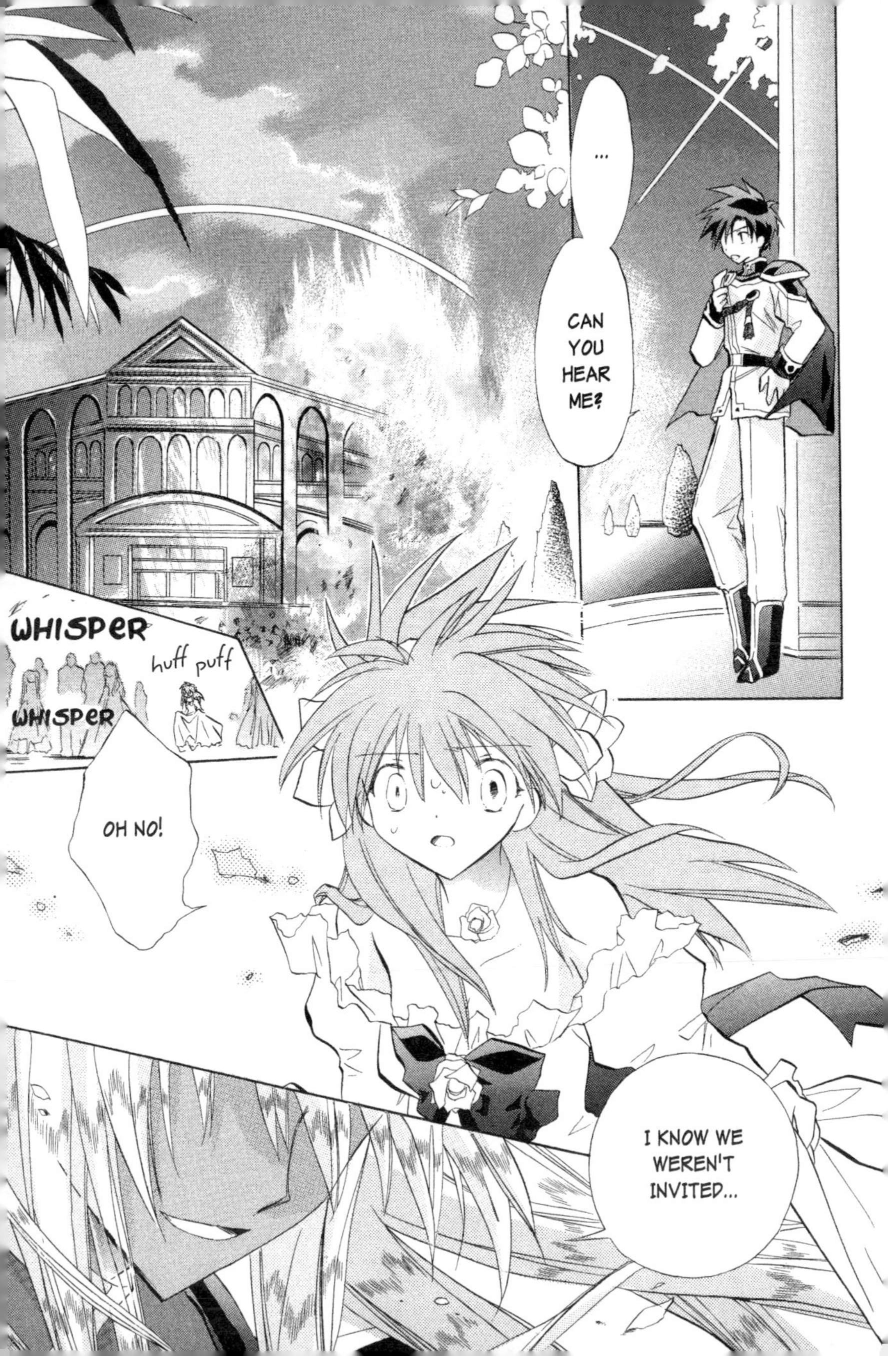
...
CAN YOU HEAR ME?
WHISPER
huff puff
WHISPER
OH NO!
I KNOW WE WEREN'T INVITED...

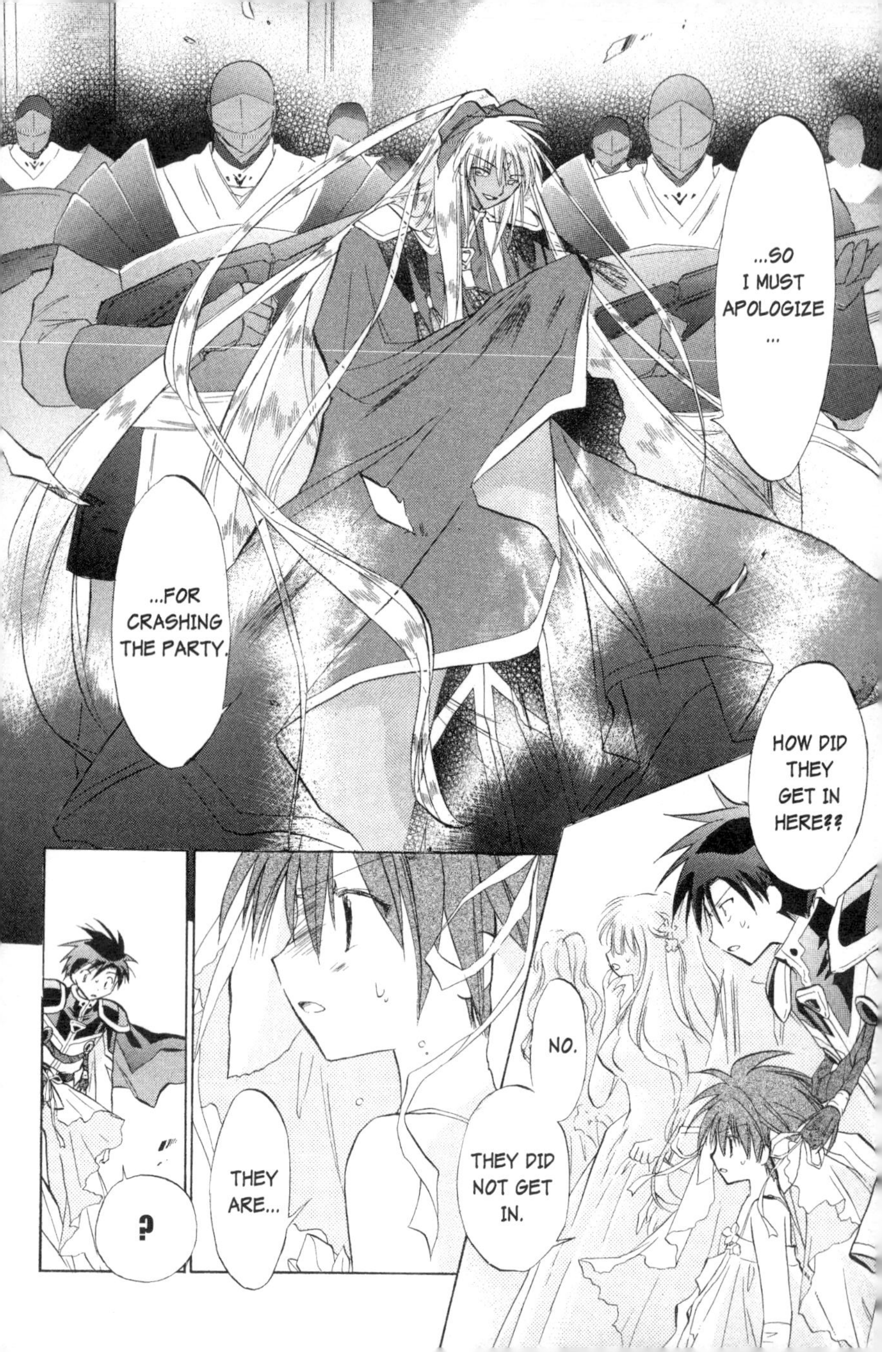

...SO I MUST APOLOGIZE ...
...FOR CRASHING THE PARTY.
HOW DID THEY GET IN HERE??
NO.
THEY DID NOT GET IN.
THEY ARE...
?

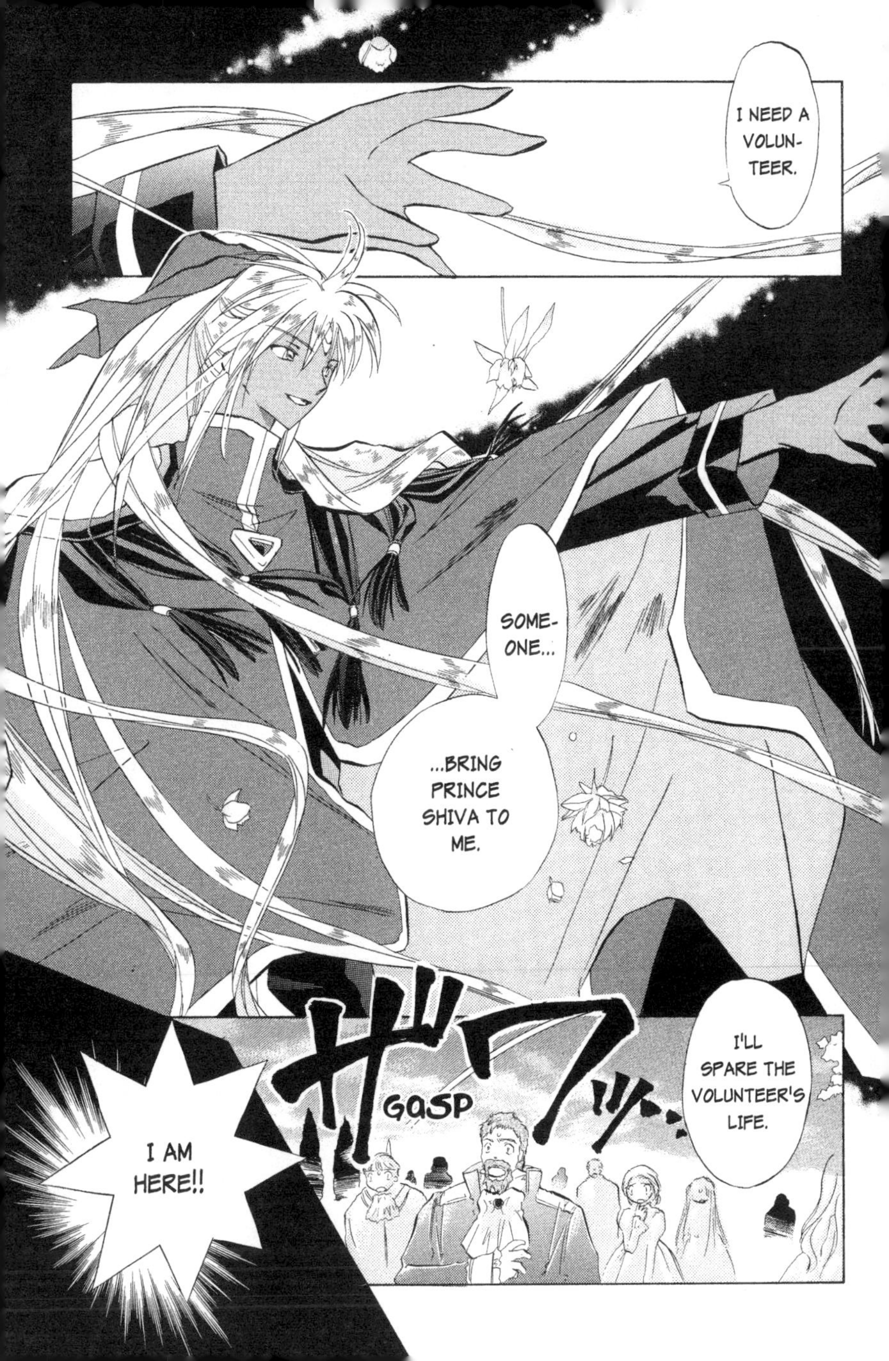
I NEED A VOLUN-TEER.
SOME-ONE...
...BRING PRINCE SHIVA TO ME.
I'LL SPARE THE VOLUNTEER'S LIFE.
ザワッ
GASP
I AM HERE!!

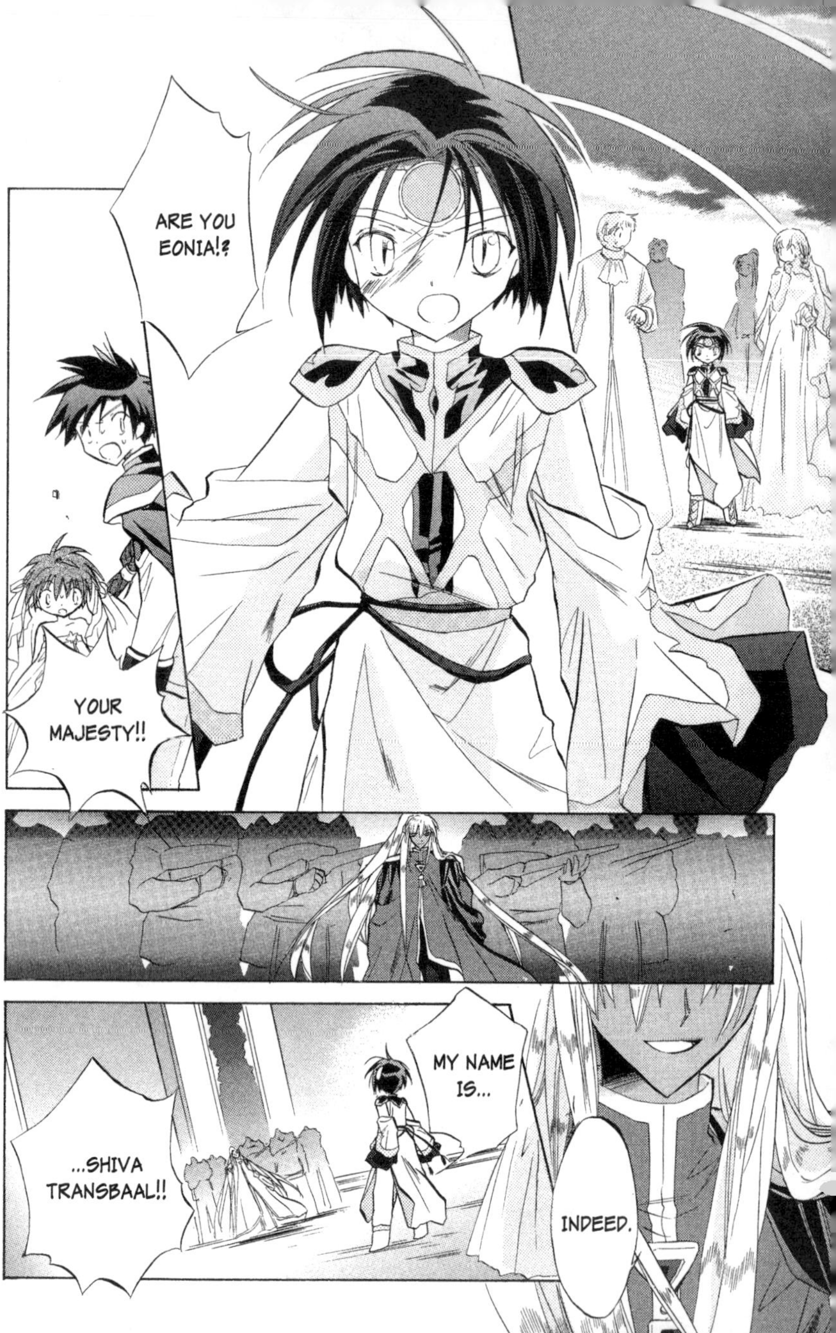
ARE YOU EONIA!?
YOUR MAJESTY!!
INDEED.
MY NAME IS...
...SHIVA TRANSBAAL!!

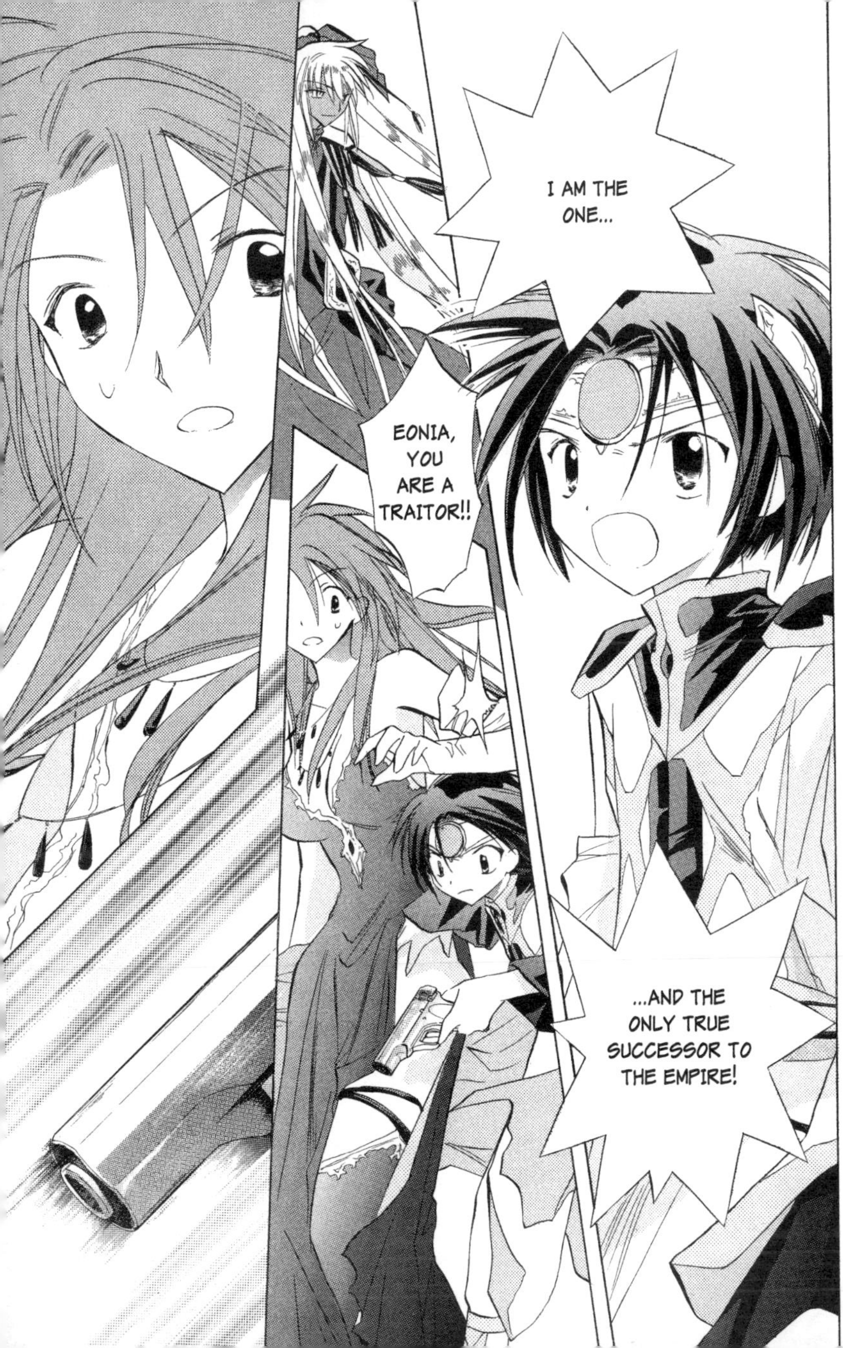
I AM THE ONE...
...AND THE ONLY TRUE SUCCESSOR TO THE EMPIRE!
EONIA, YOU ARE A TRAITOR!!

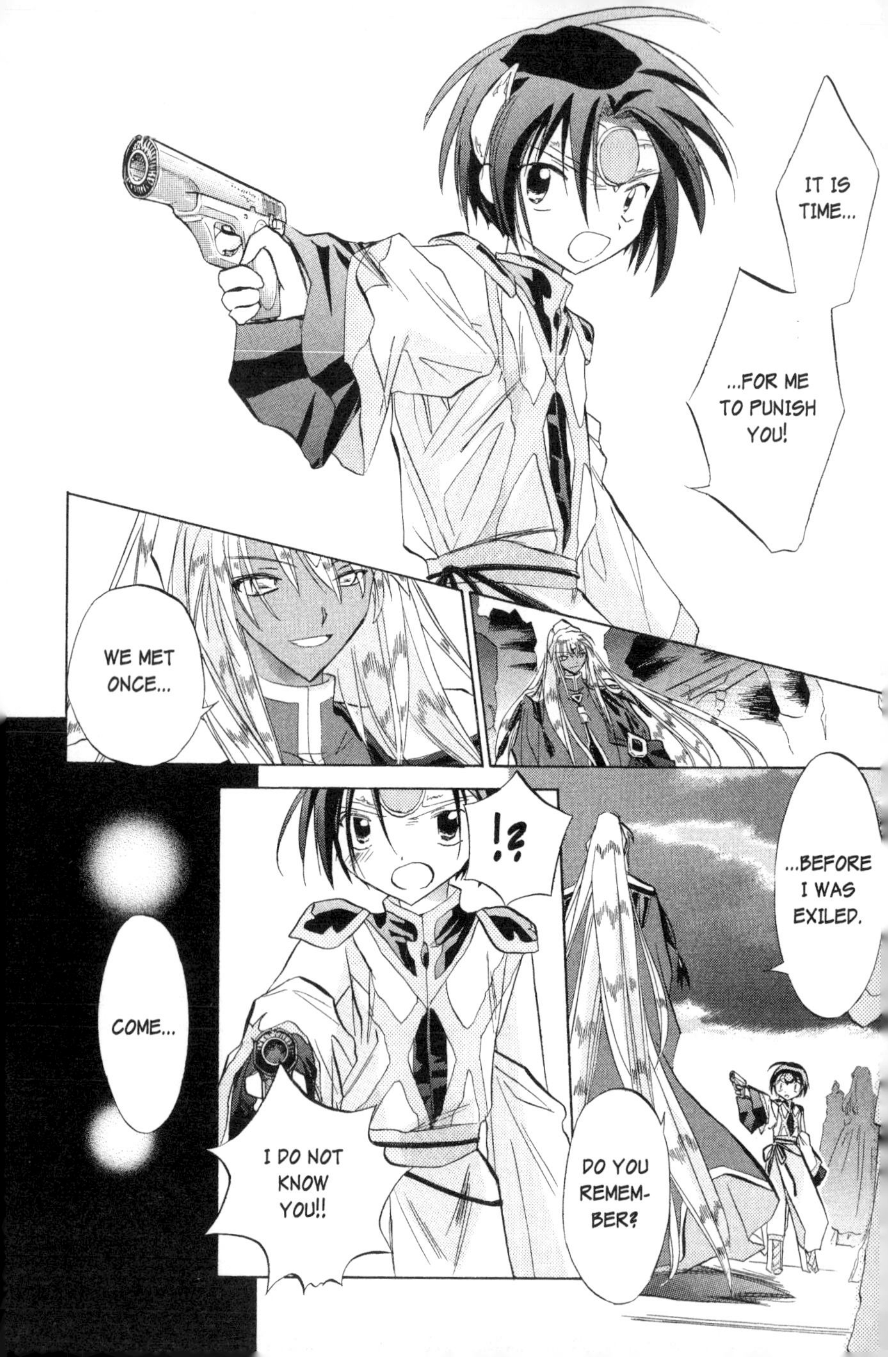
IT IS TIME...
...FOR ME TO PUNISH YOU!
WE MET ONCE...
...BEFORE I WAS EXILED.
DO YOU REMEM-BER?
!?
I DO NOT KNOW YOU!!
COME...

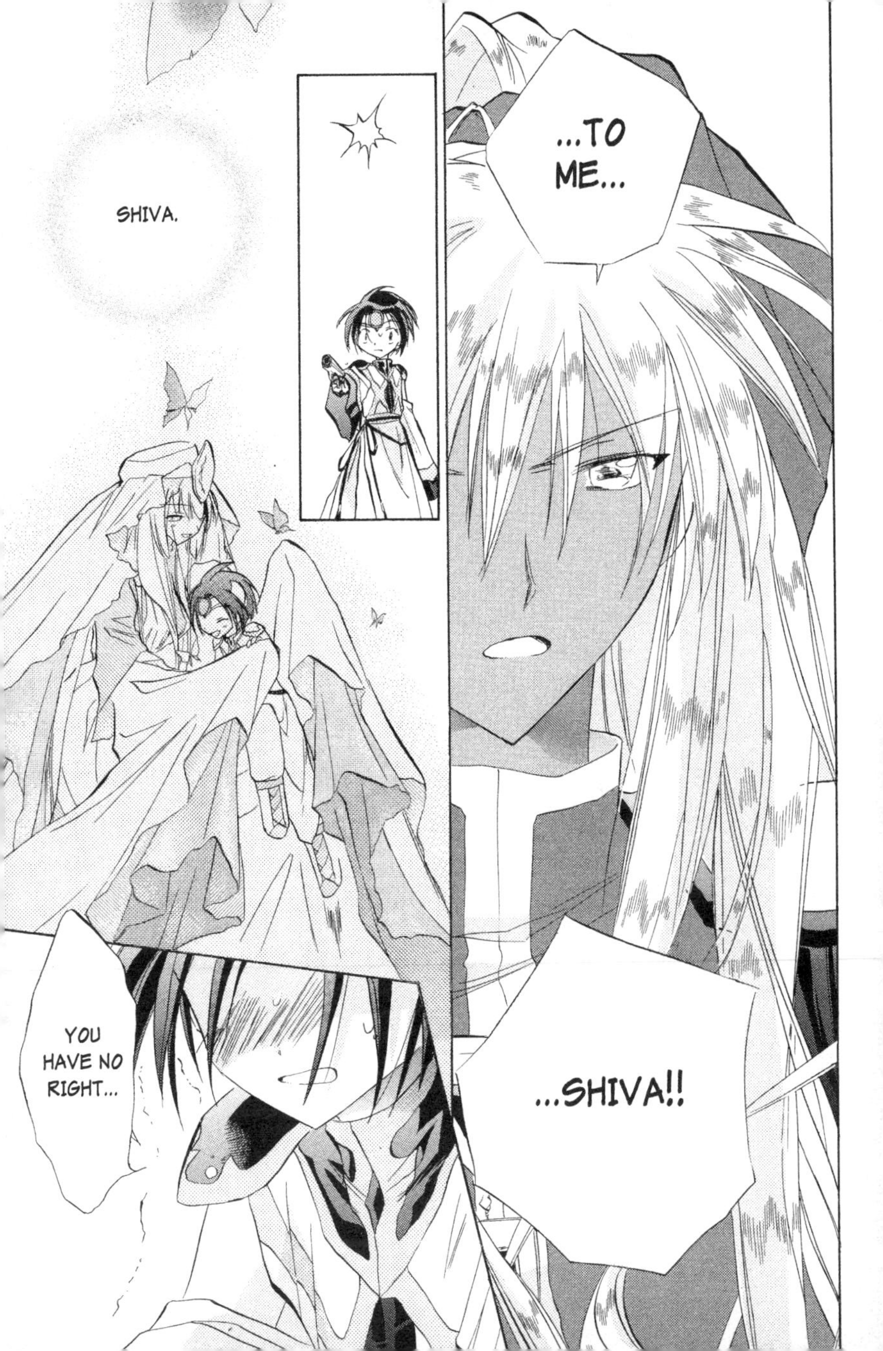
SHIVA.
YOU HAVE NO RIGHT...
...TO ME...
...SHIVA!!

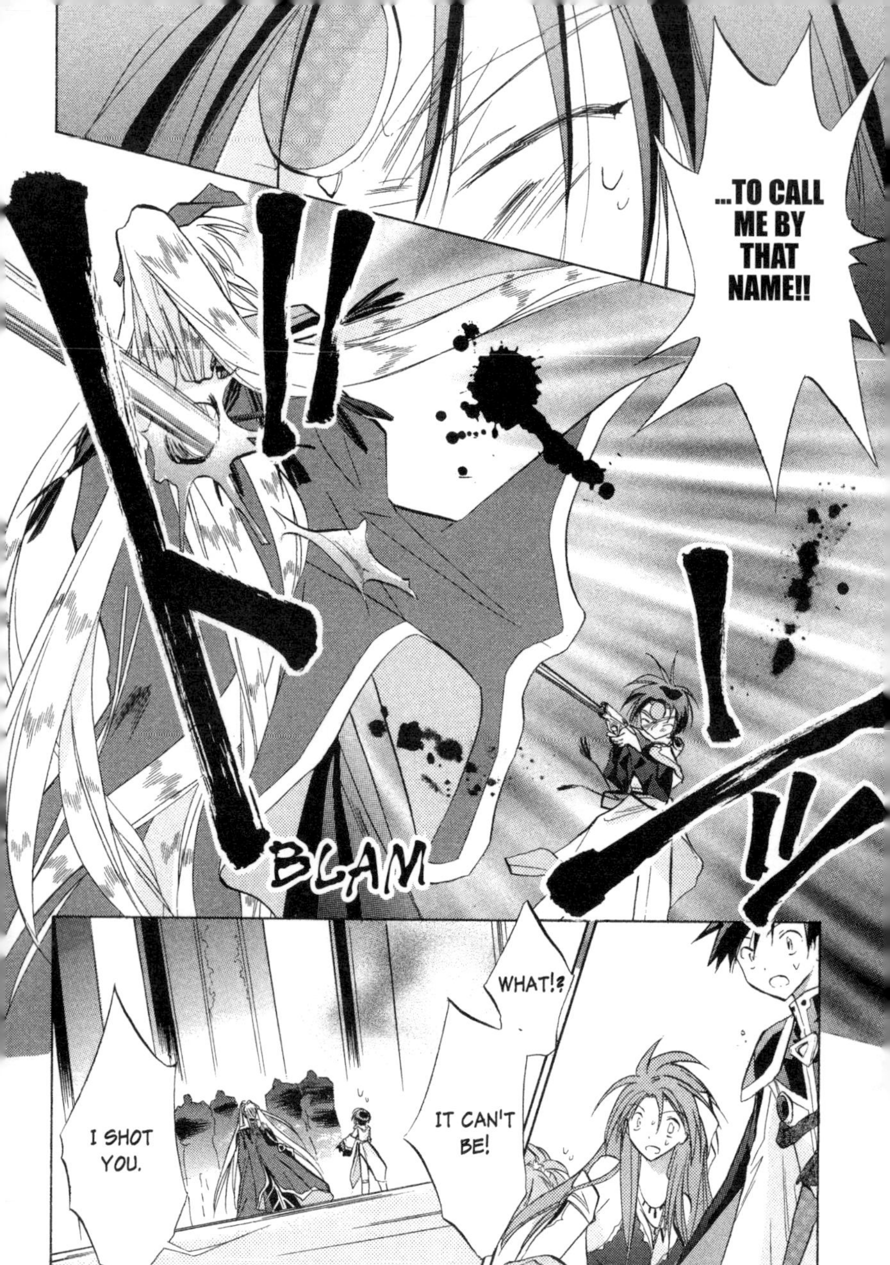
...TO CALL ME BY THAT NAME!!
BLAM
WHAT!?
IT CAN'T BE!
I SHOT YOU.

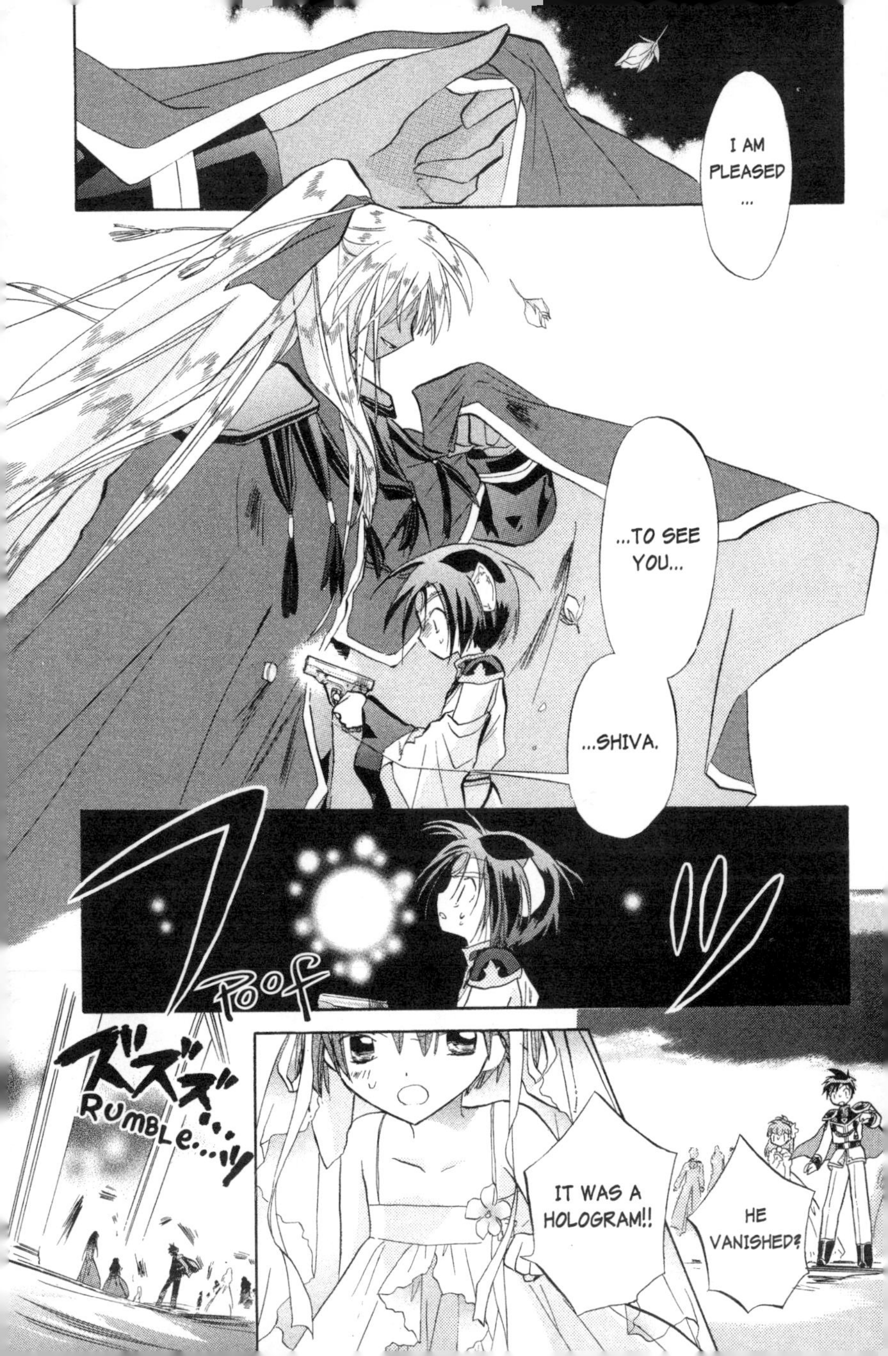
I AM PLEASED ...
...TO SEE YOU...
...SHIVA.
Poof
HE VANISHED?
IT WAS A HOLOGRAM!!
ズズズ
RUMBLE...!!

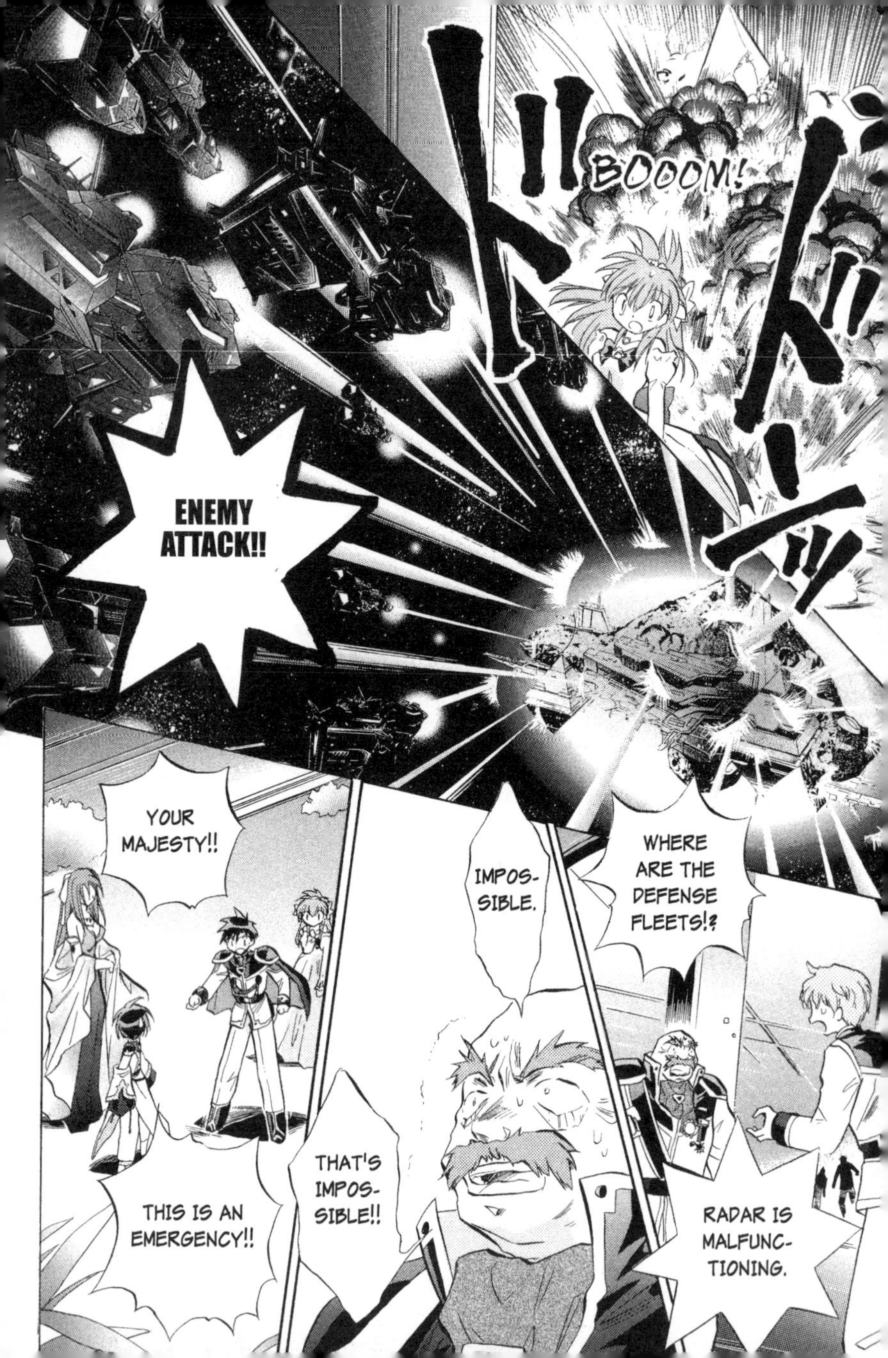
BOOOM!
ENEMY ATTACK!!
WHERE ARE THE DEFENSE FLEETS!?
RADAR IS MALFUNCTIONING.
IMPOSSIBLE.
THAT'S IMPOSSIBLE!!
YOUR MAJESTY!!
THIS IS AN EMERGENCY!!

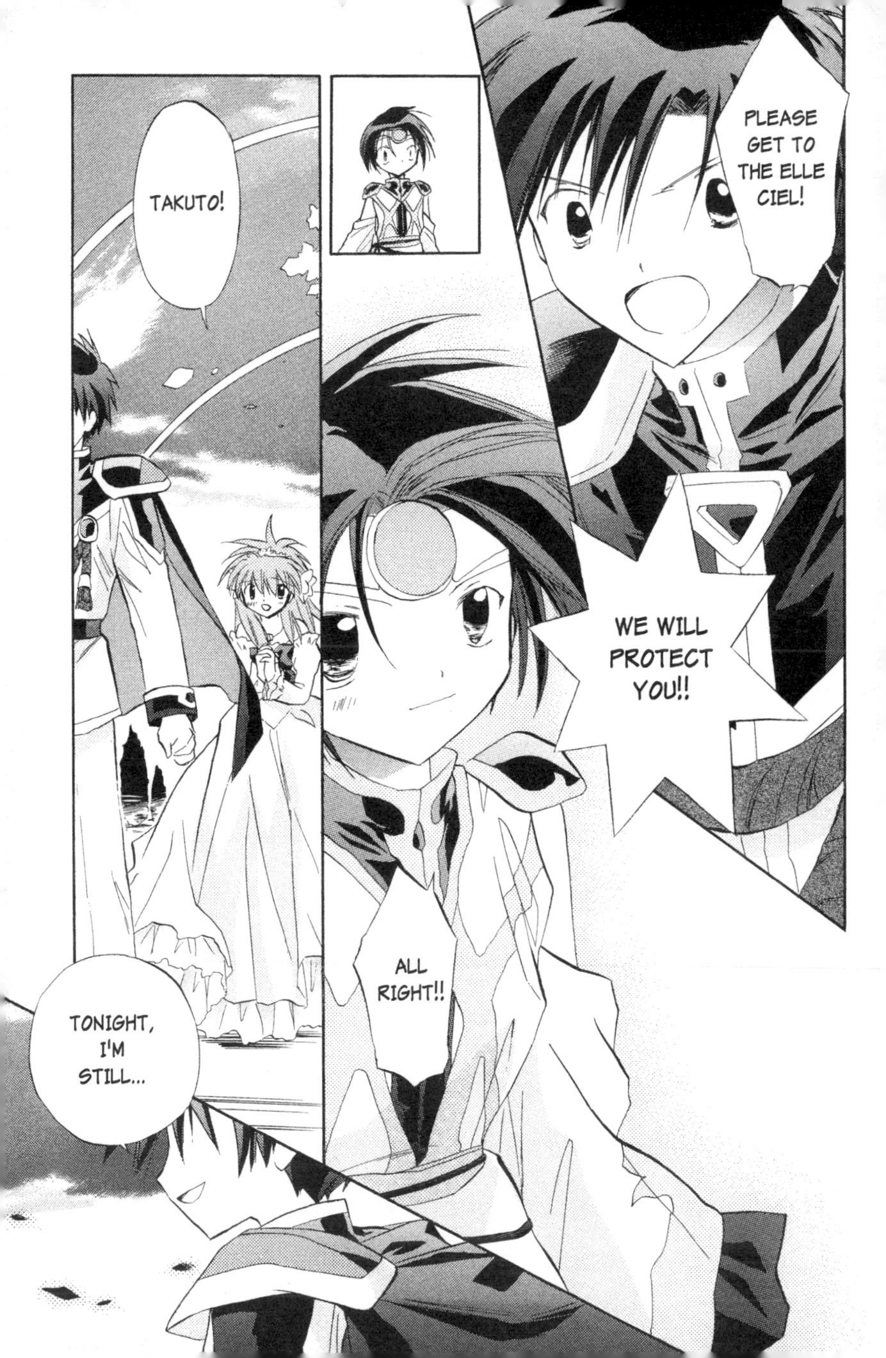
PLEASE GET TO THE ELLE CIEL!
WE WILL PROTECT YOU!!
ALL RIGHT!!
TAKUTO!
TONIGHT, I'M STILL...

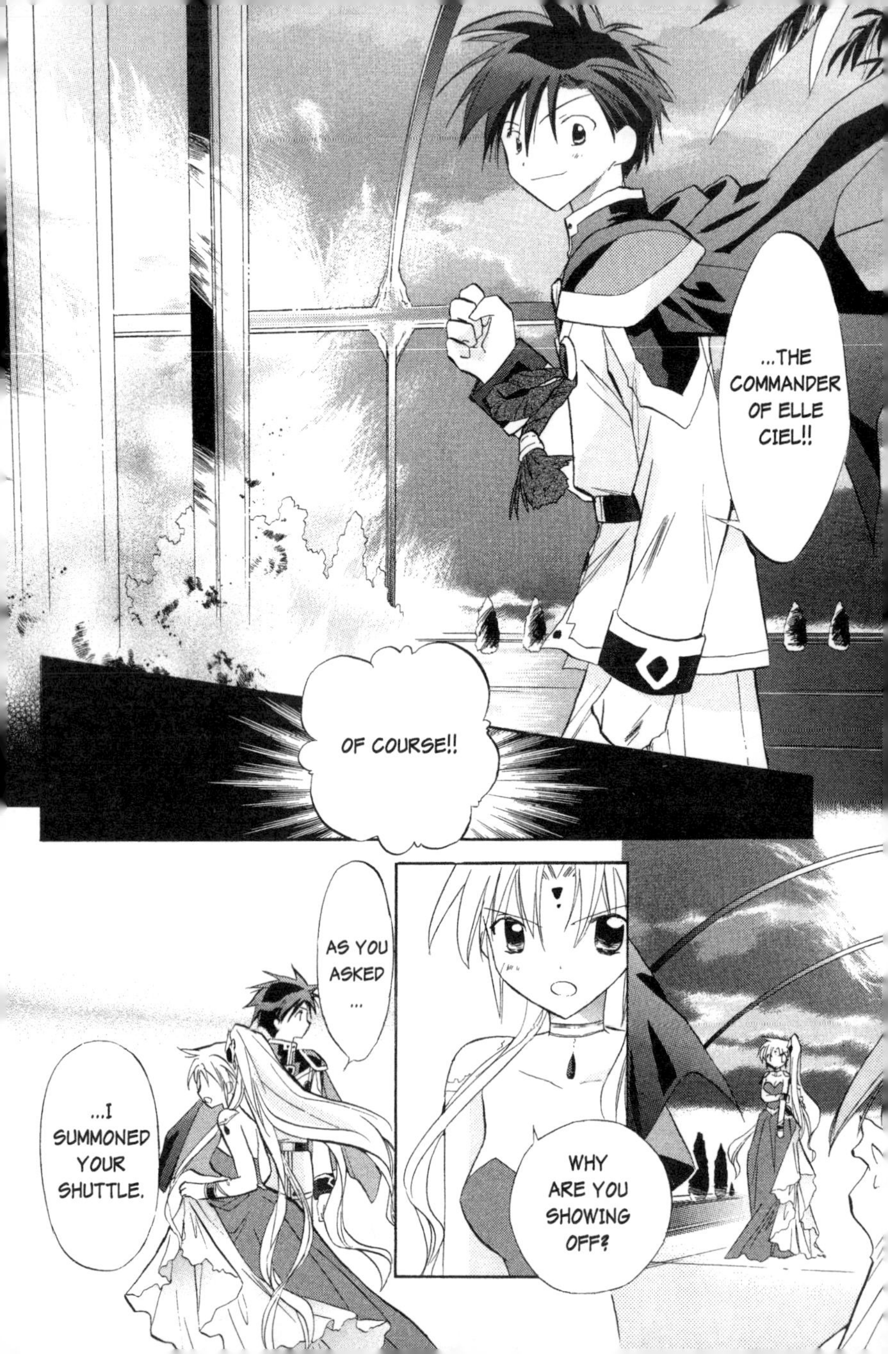
...THE COMMANDER OF ELLE CIEL!!
OF COURSE!!
WHY ARE YOU SHOWING OFF?
AS YOU ASKED ...
...I SUMMONED YOUR SHUTTLE.

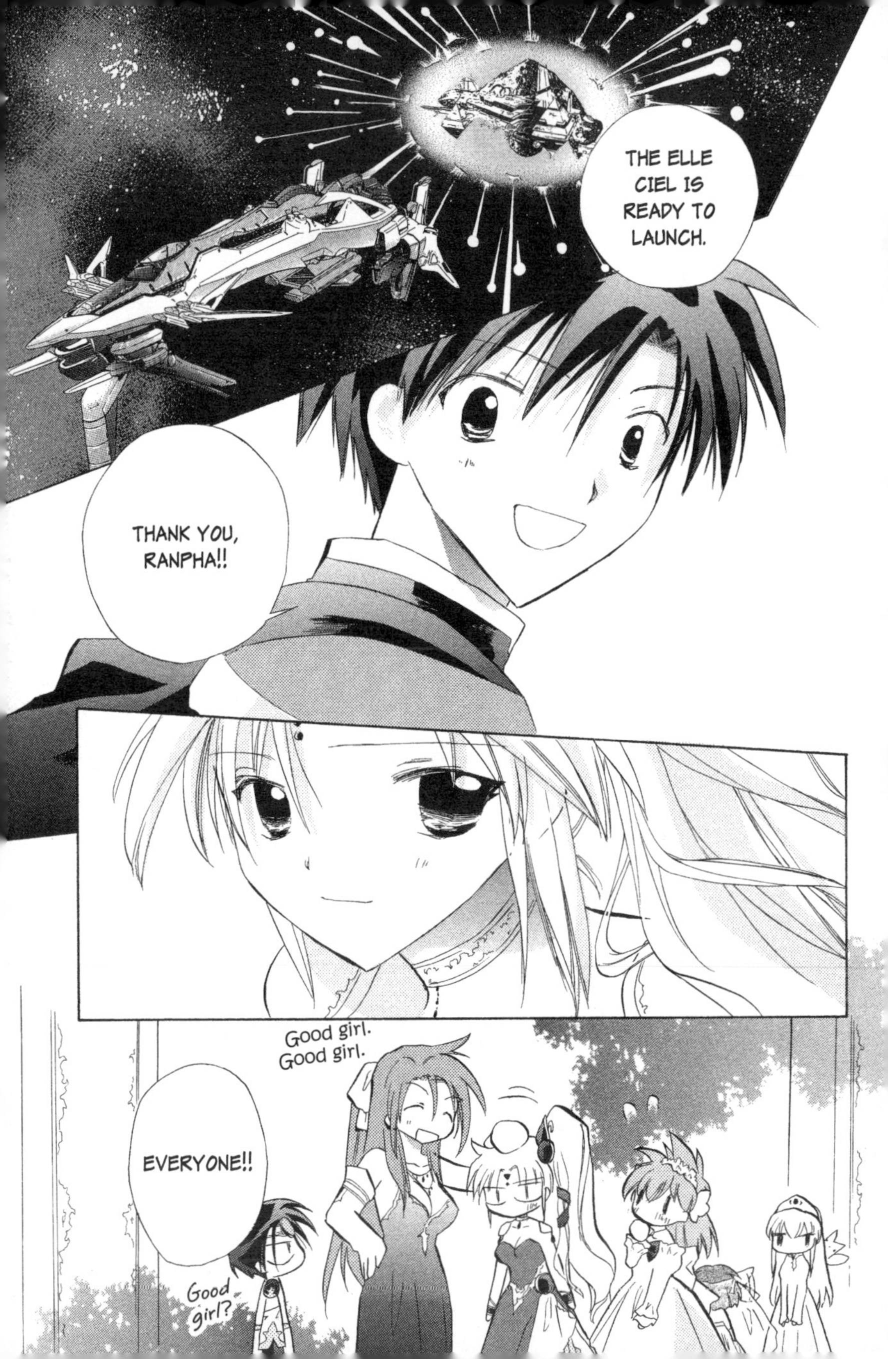
THE ELLE CIEL IS READY TO LAUNCH.
THANK YOU, RANPHA!!
Good girl. Good girl.
EVERYONE!!
Good girl?

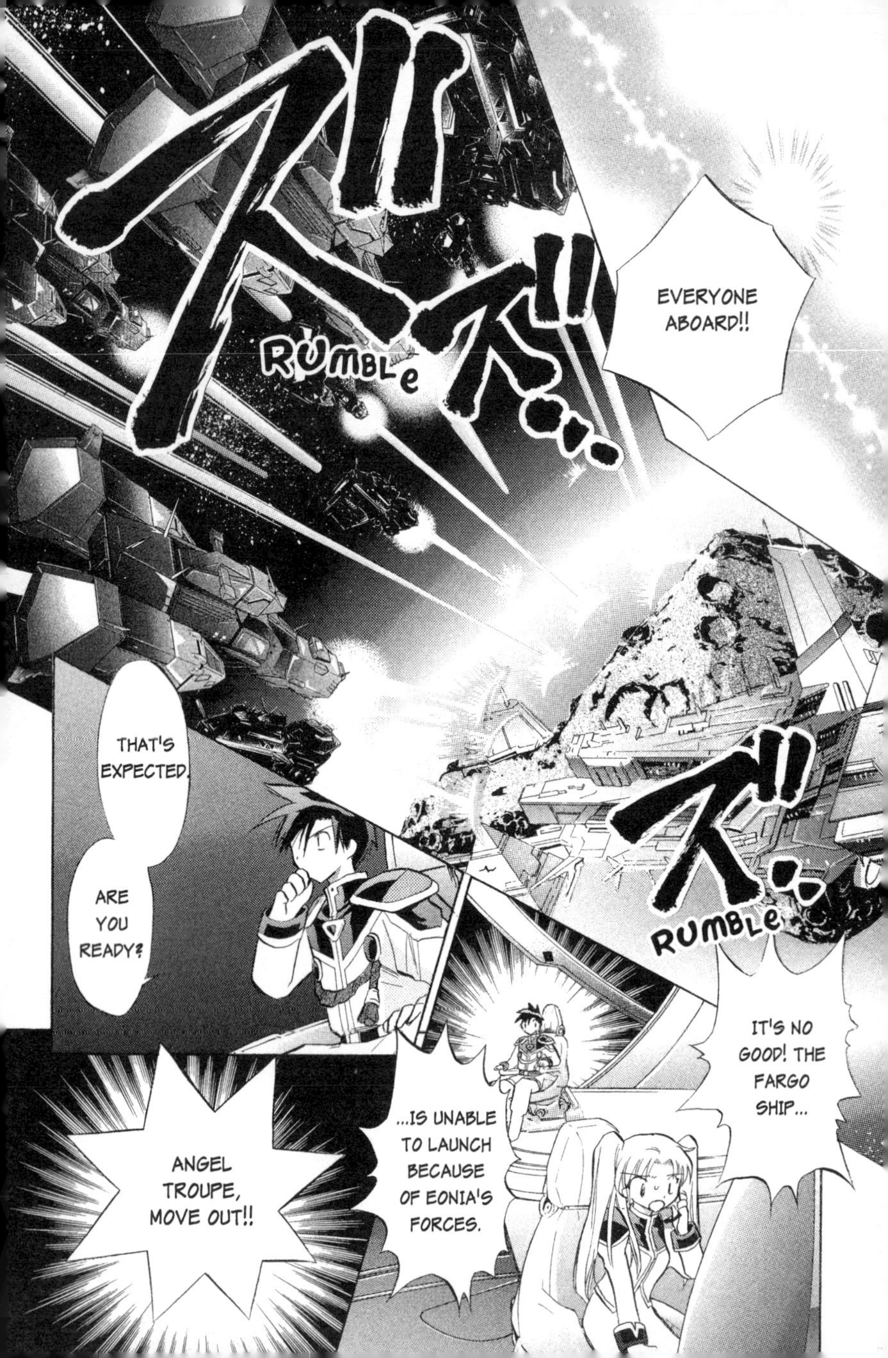
EVERYONE ABOARD!!
RUMBLE
RUMBLE
IT'S NO GOOD! THE FARGO SHIP...
...IS UNABLE TO LAUNCH BECAUSE OF EONIA'S FORCES.
THAT'S EXPECTED.
ARE YOU READY?
ANGEL TROUPE, MOVE OUT!!

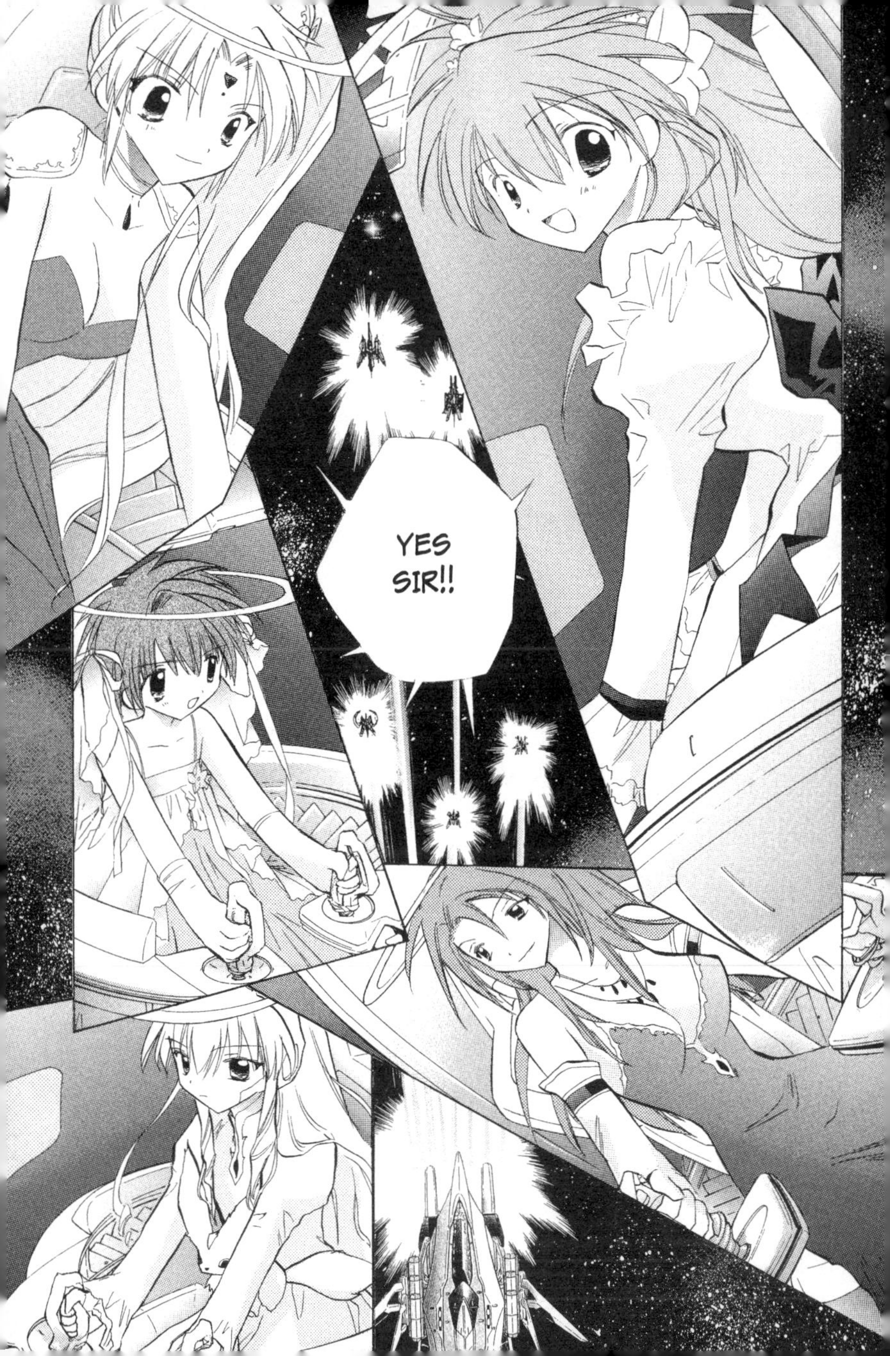
YES SIR!!

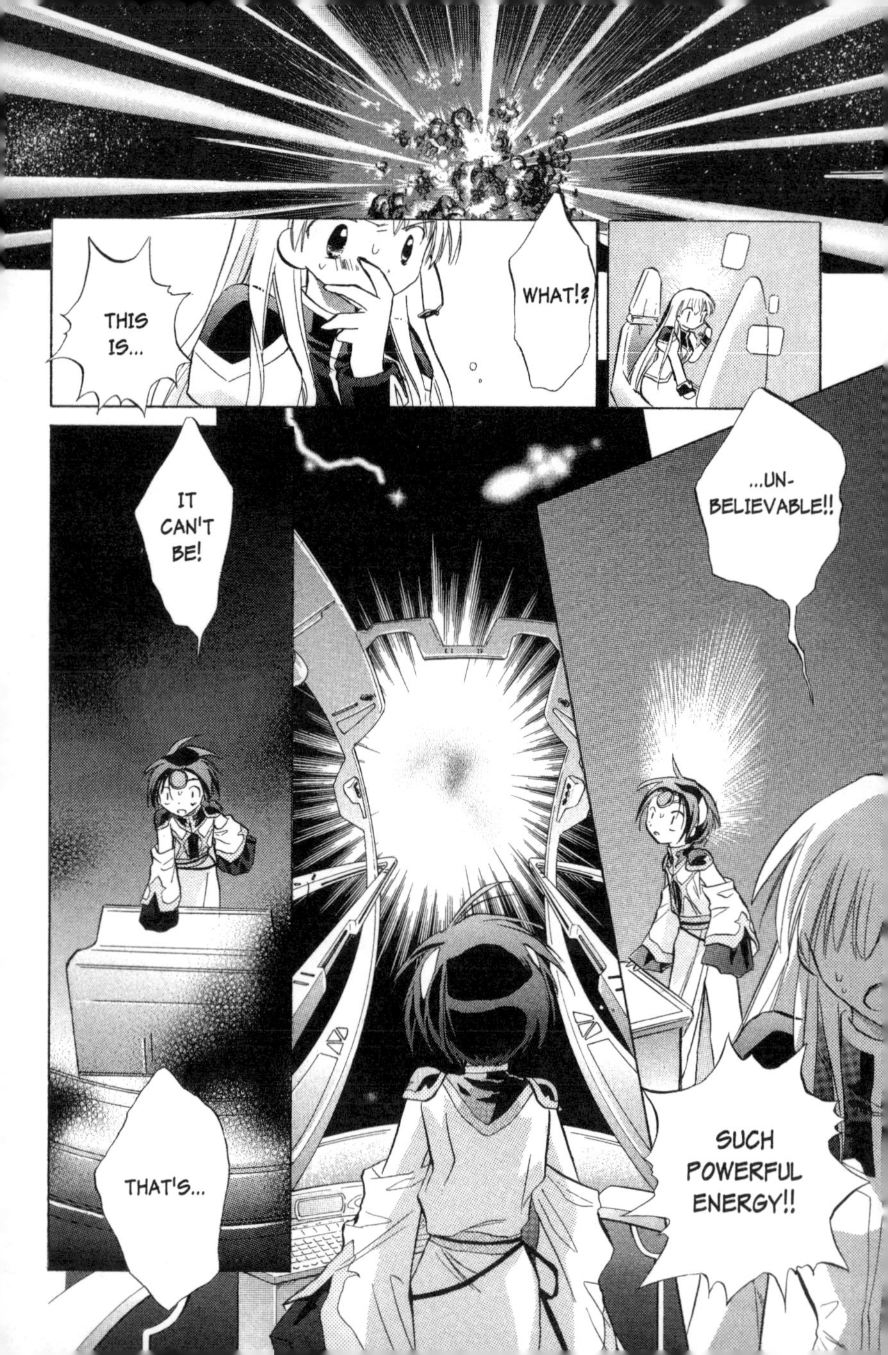
WHAT!?
THIS IS...
...UN-BELIEVABLE!!
SUCH POWERFUL ENERGY!!
IT CAN'T BE!
THAT'S...

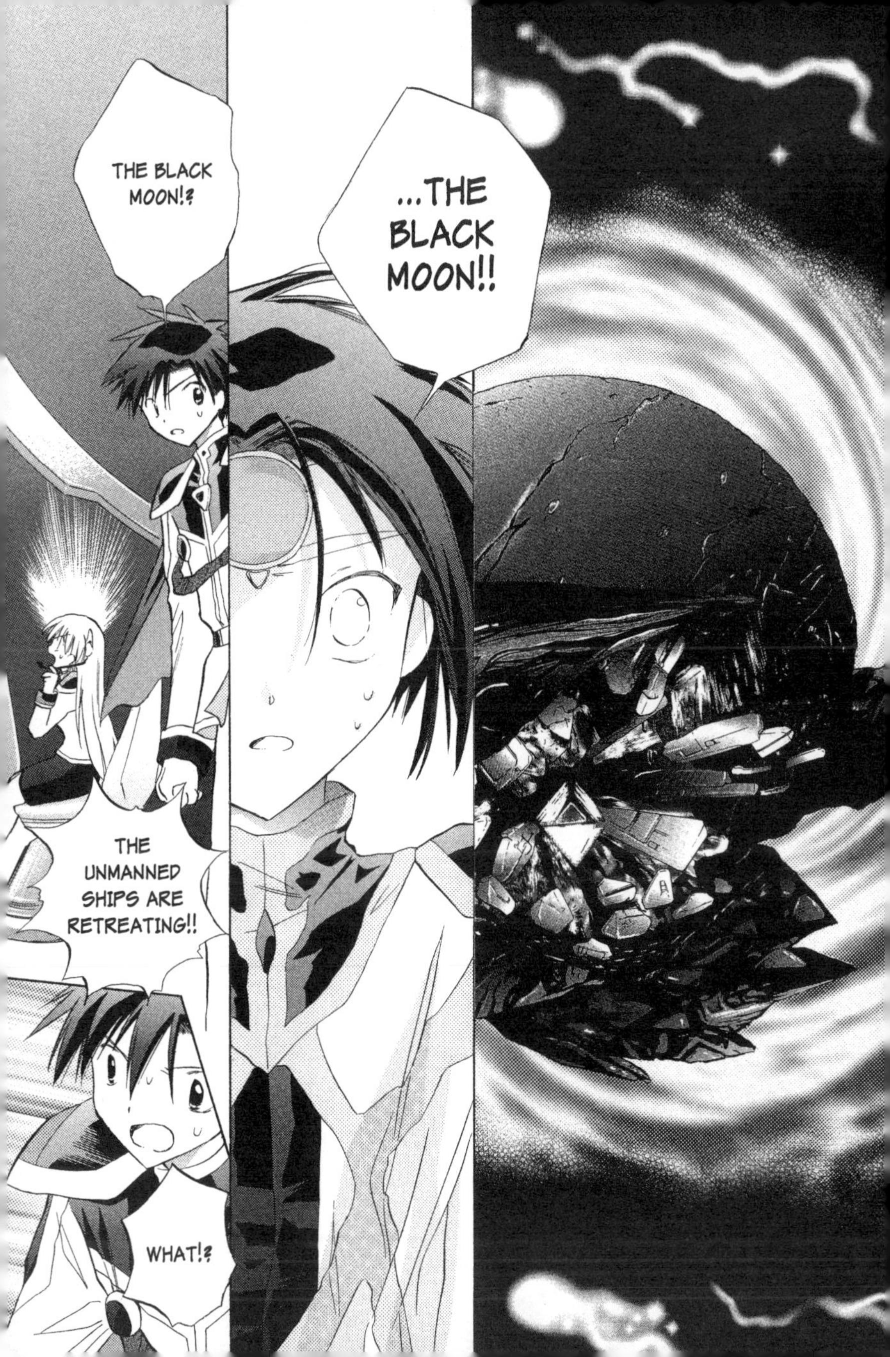

...THE BLACK MOON!!
THE BLACK MOON!?
THE UNMANNED SHIPS ARE RETREATING!!
WHAT!?

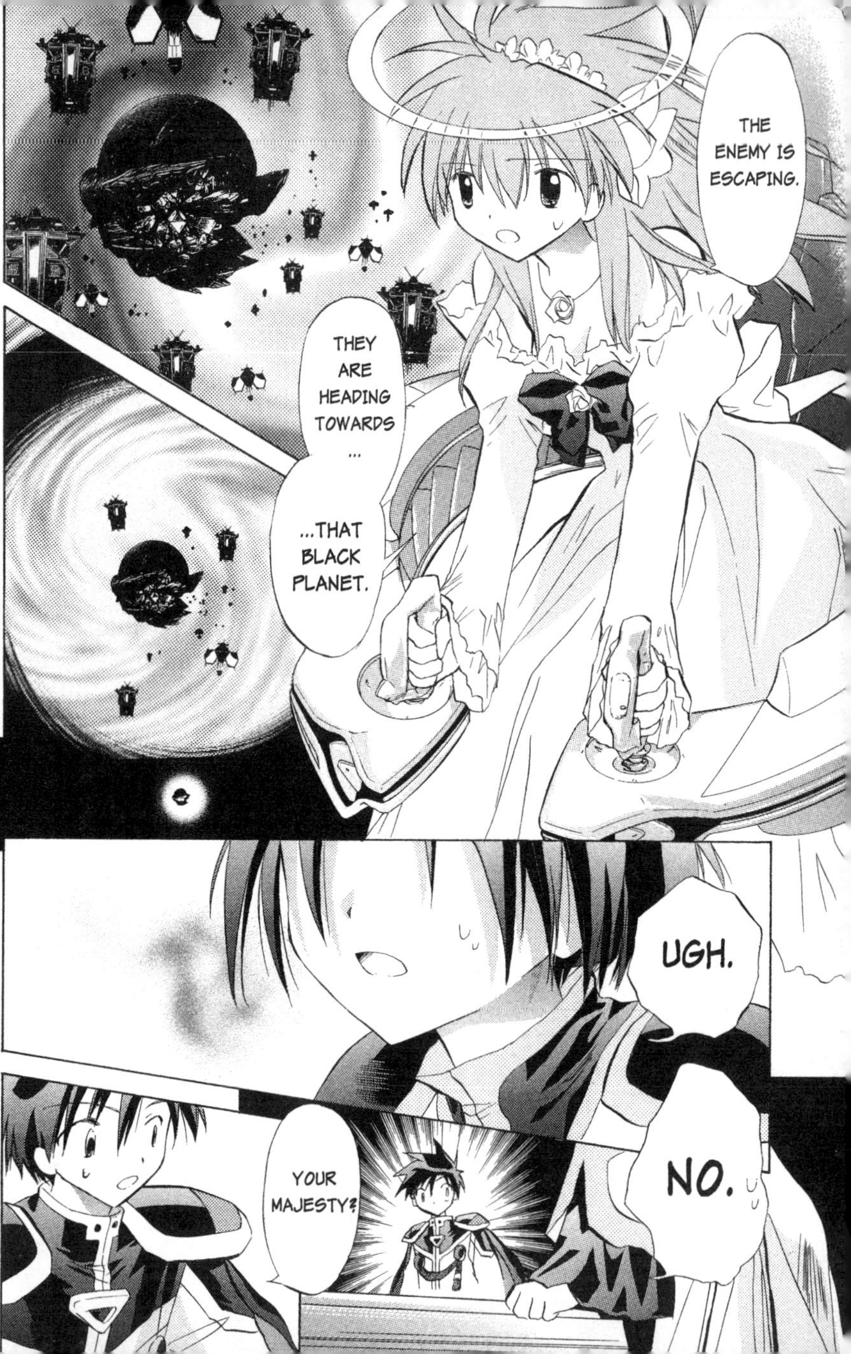
THE ENEMY IS ESCAPING.
THEY ARE HEADING TOWARDS ...
...THAT BLACK PLANET.
UGH.
NO.
YOUR MAJESTY?

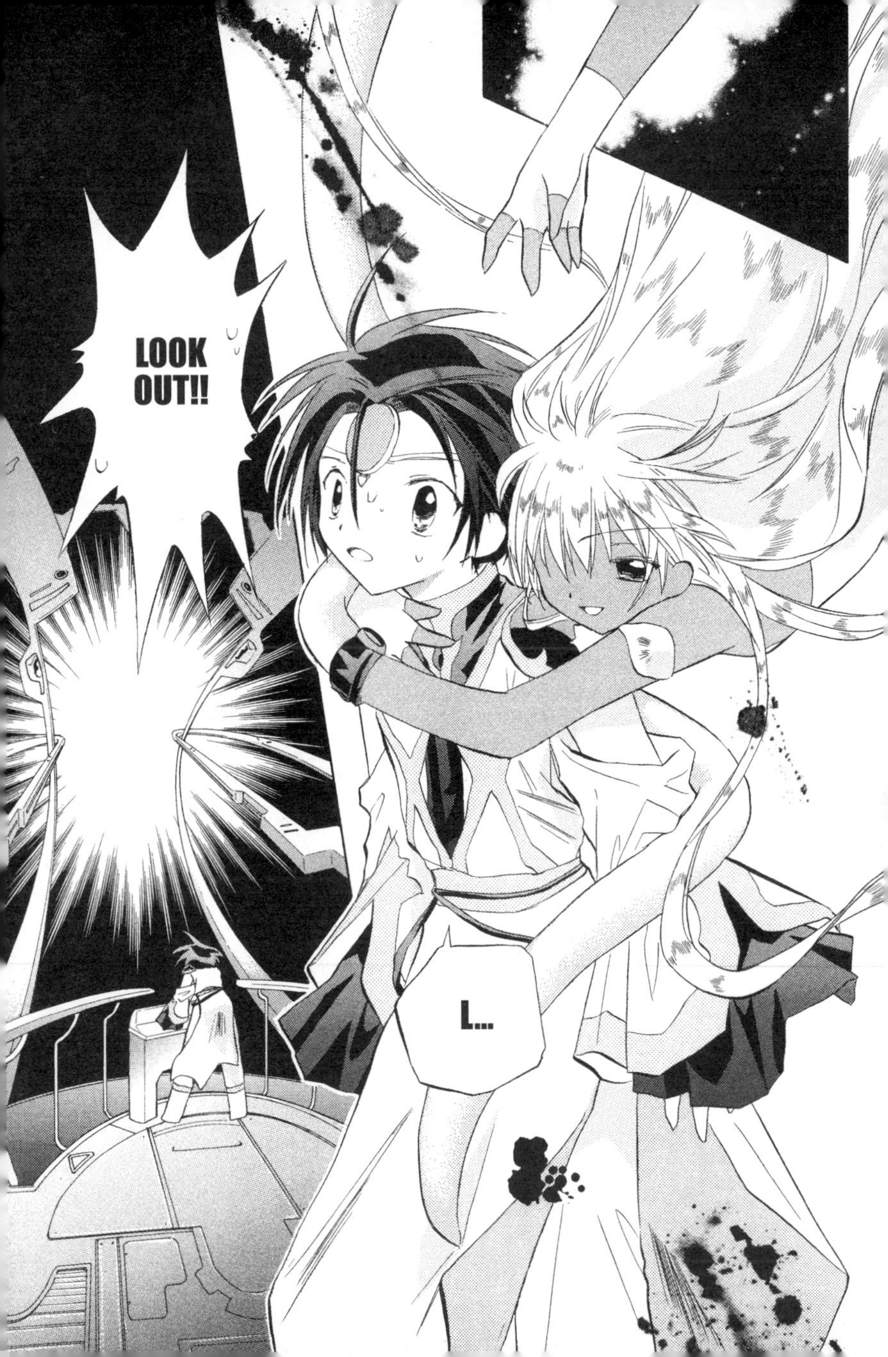
LOOK OUT!!
I...

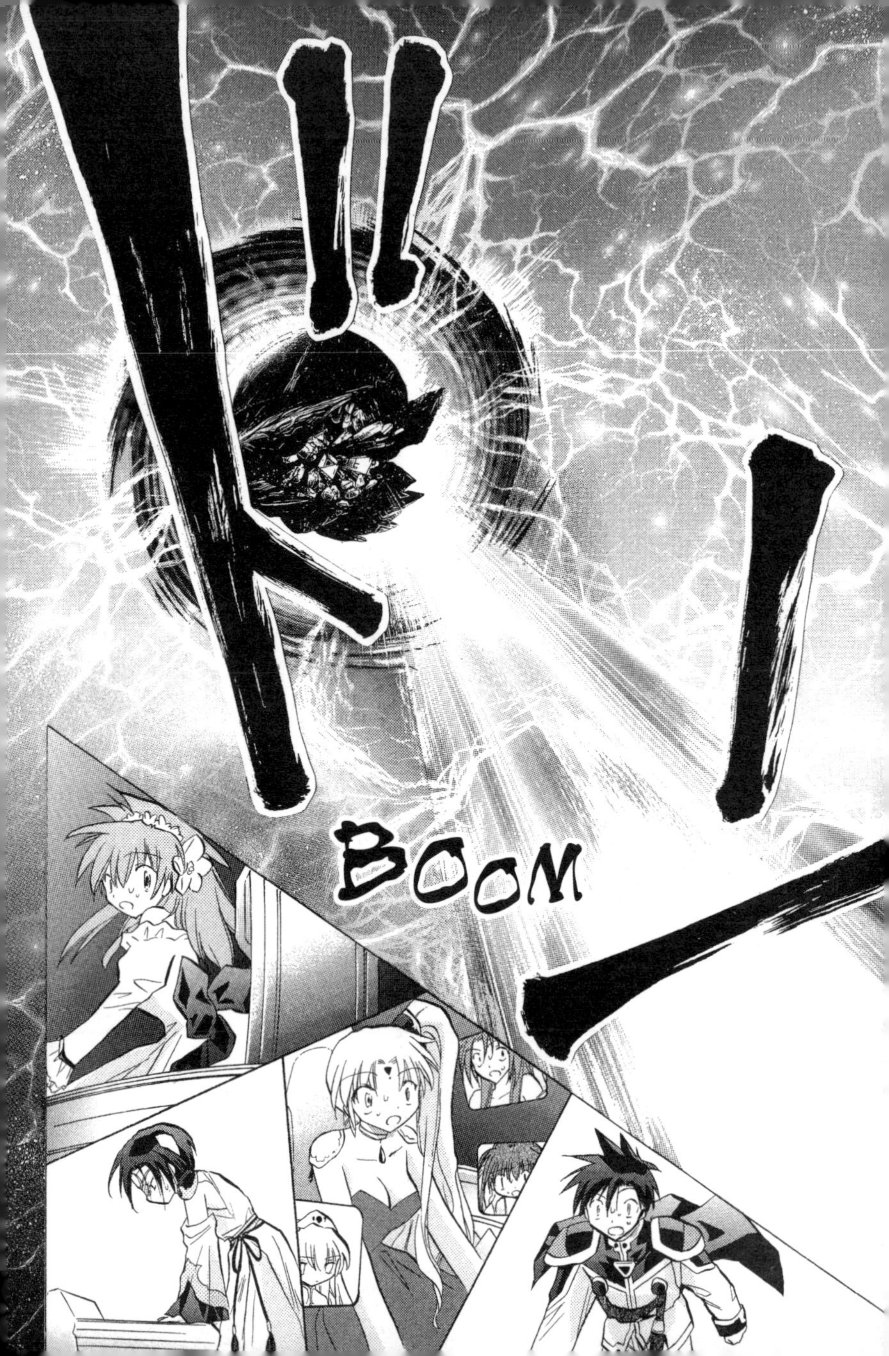
BOOM

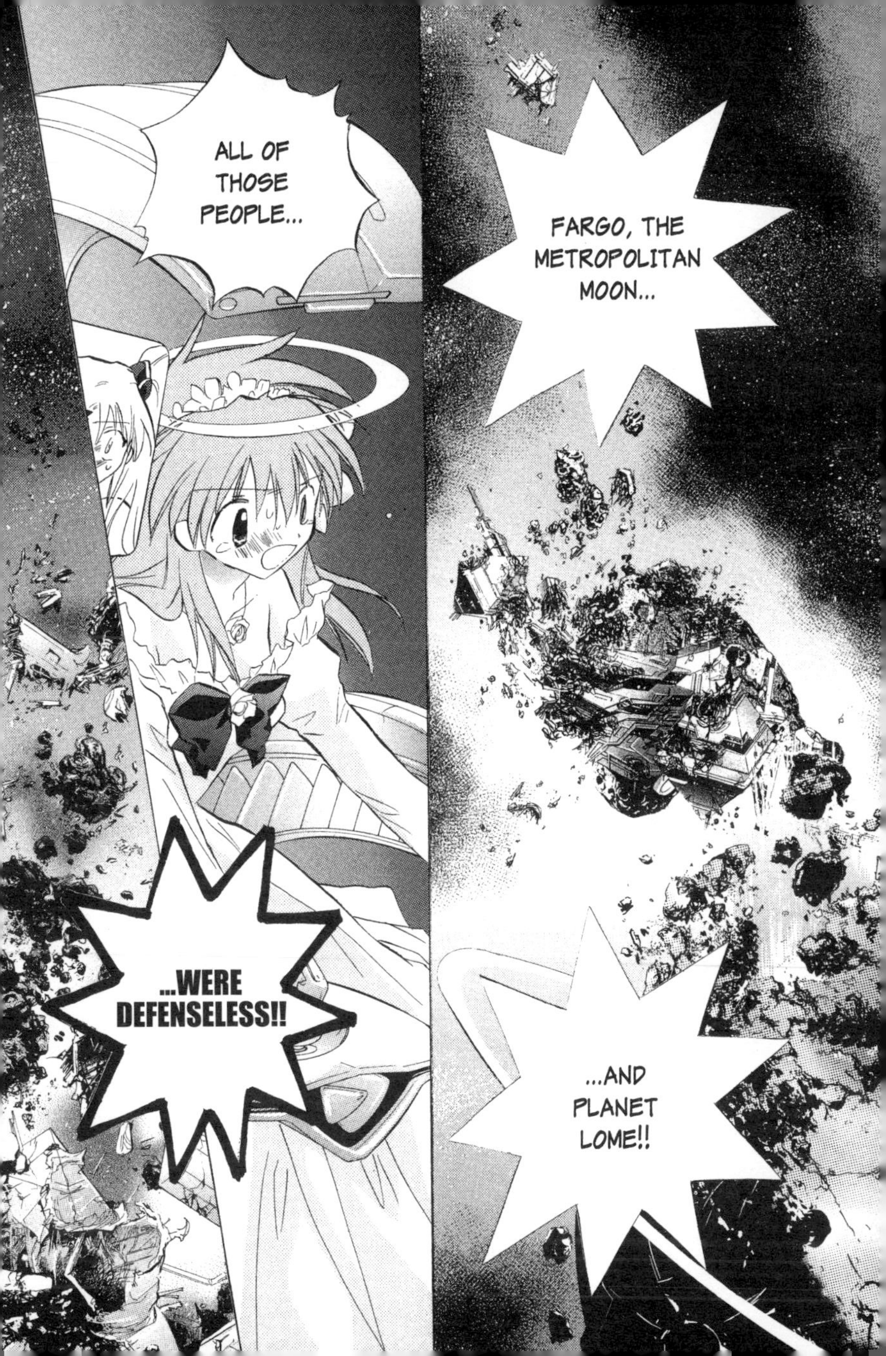
FARGO, THE METROPOLITAN MOON...
...AND PLANET LOME!!
ALL OF THOSE PEOPLE...
...WERE DEFENSELESS!!

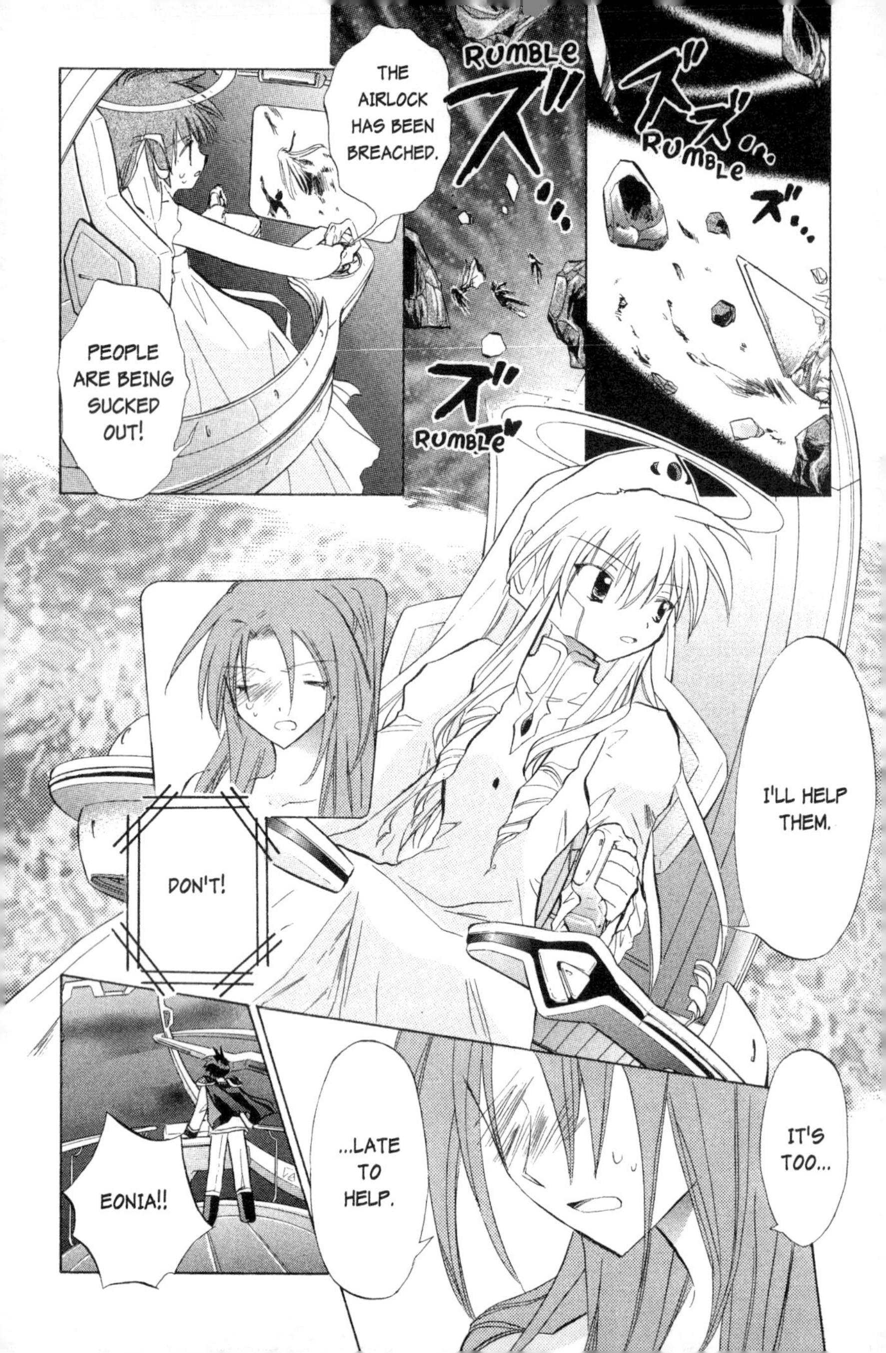

RUMBLE
ズズ...
RUMBLE
ズ...
RUMBLE
ズ...
RUMBLE
ズ
THE AIRLOCK HAS BEEN BREACHED.
PEOPLE ARE BEING SUCKED OUT!
I'LL HELP THEM.
DON'T!
IT'S TOO...
...LATE TO HELP.
EONIA!!

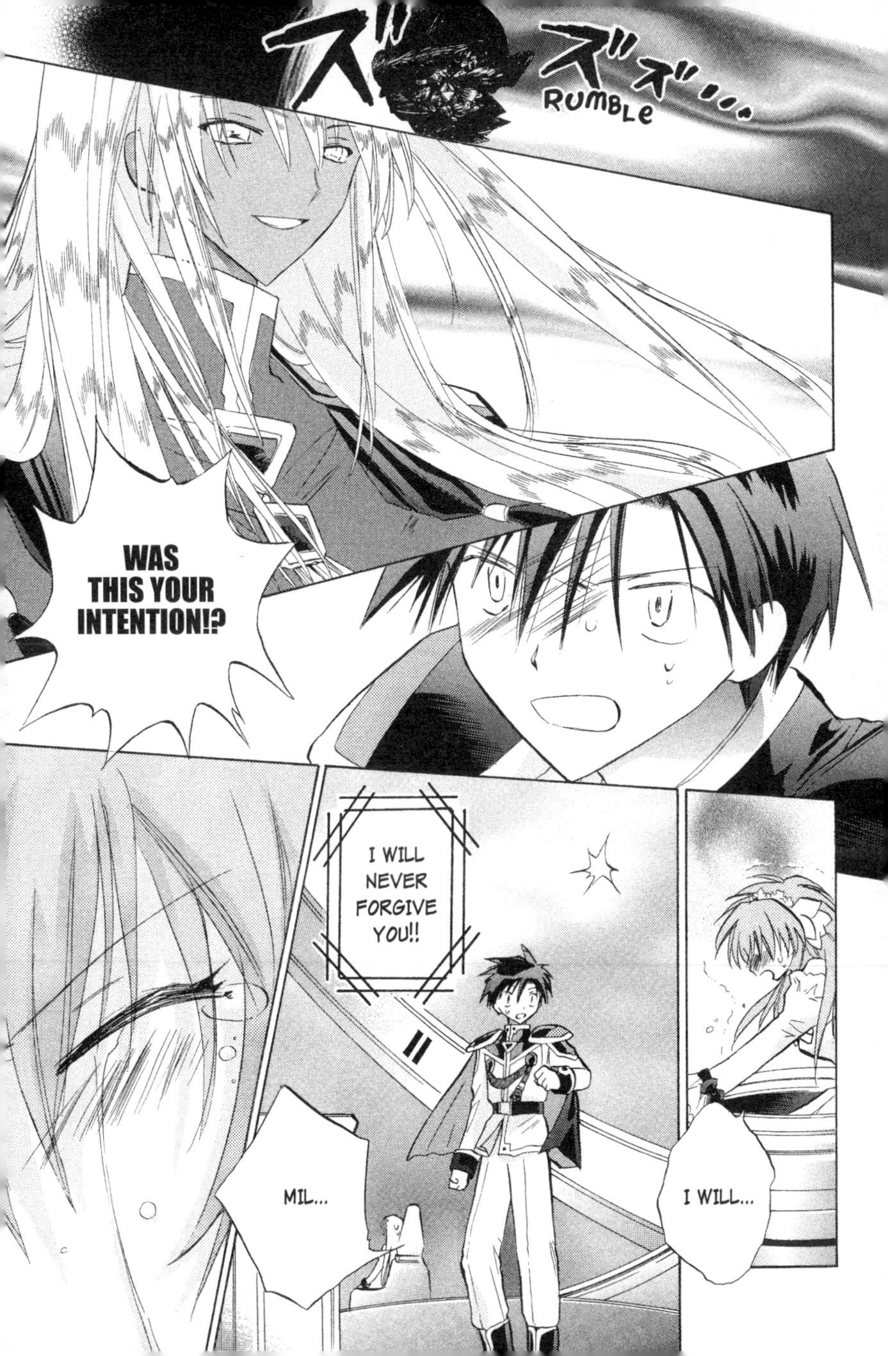
ズズズ…
RUMBLE
WAS THIS YOUR INTENTION!?
I WILL...
I WILL NEVER FORGIVE YOU!!
MIL...

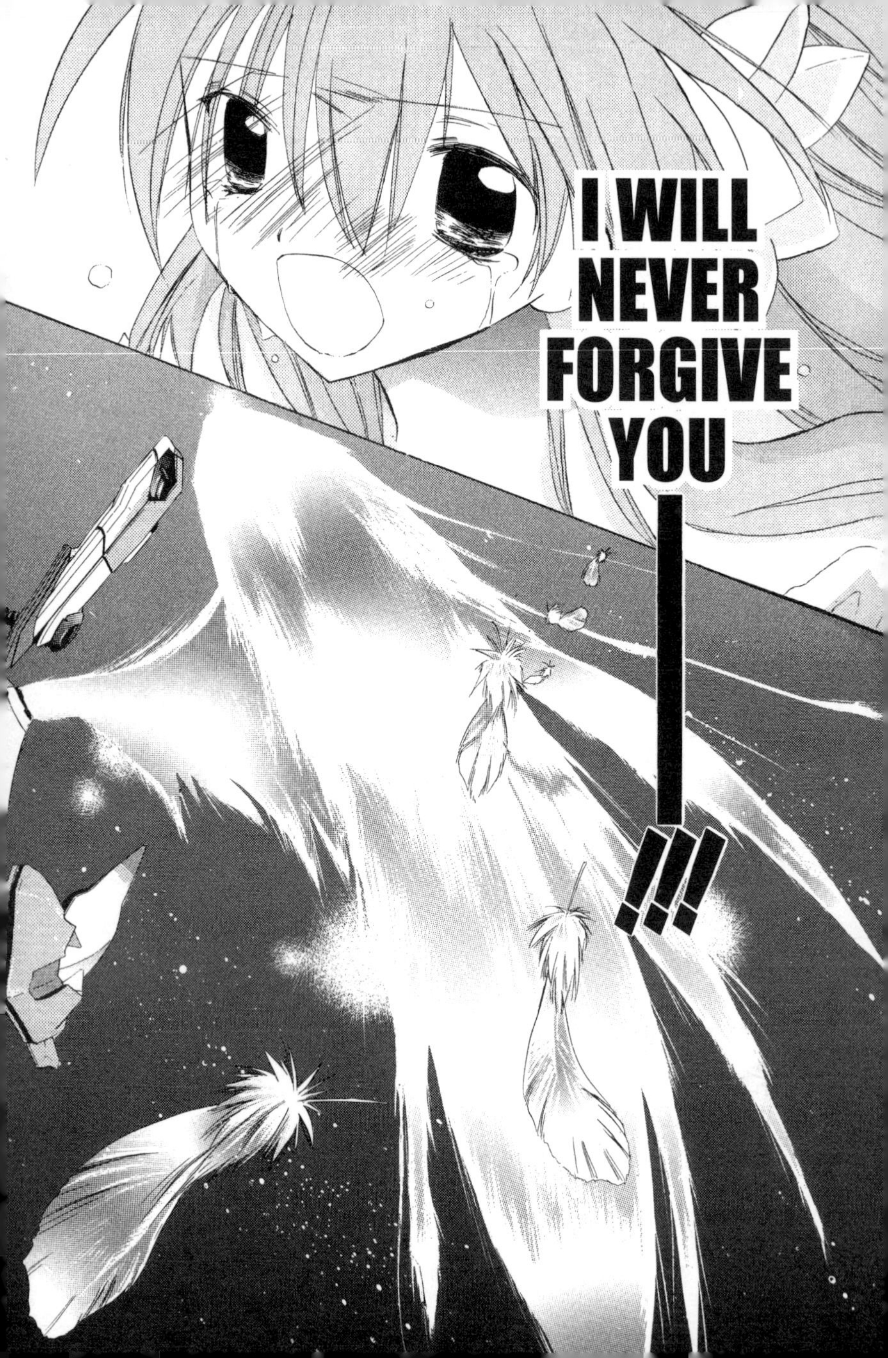
I WILL NEVER FORGIVE YOU―!!!

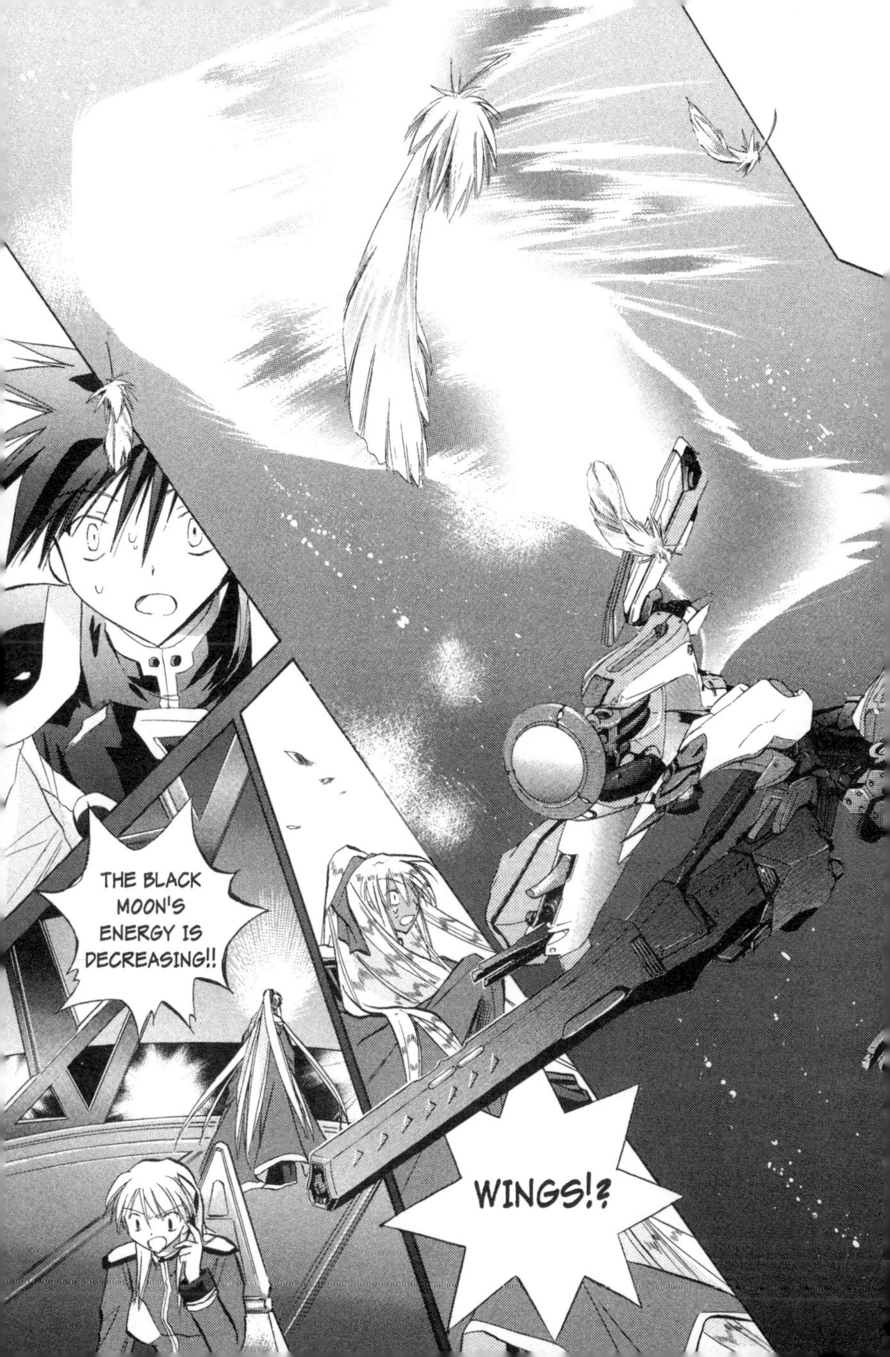
WINGS!?
THE BLACK MOON'S ENERGY IS DECREASING!!

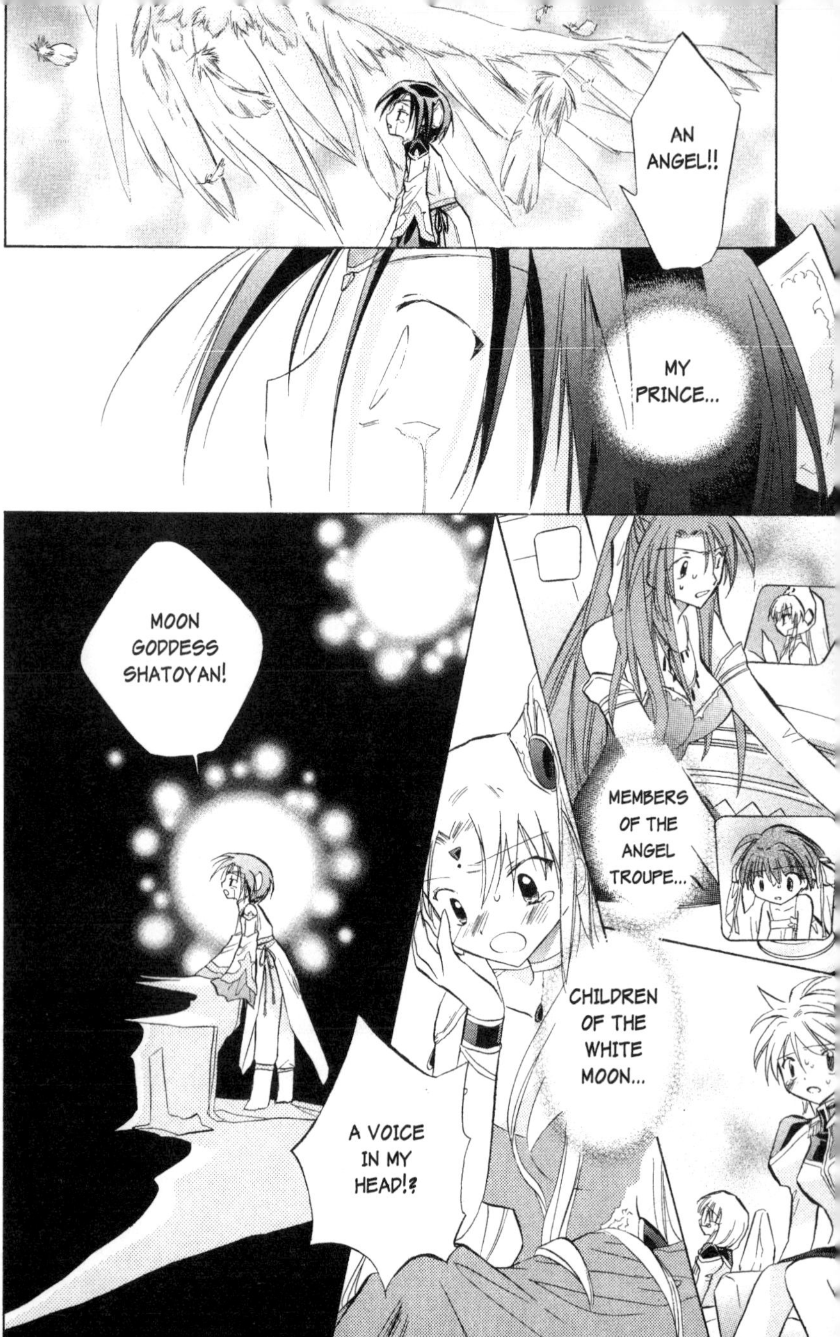
AN ANGEL!!
MY PRINCE...
MEMBERS OF THE ANGEL TROUPE...
CHILDREN OF THE WHITE MOON...
A VOICE IN MY HEAD!?
MOON GODDESS SHATOYAN!

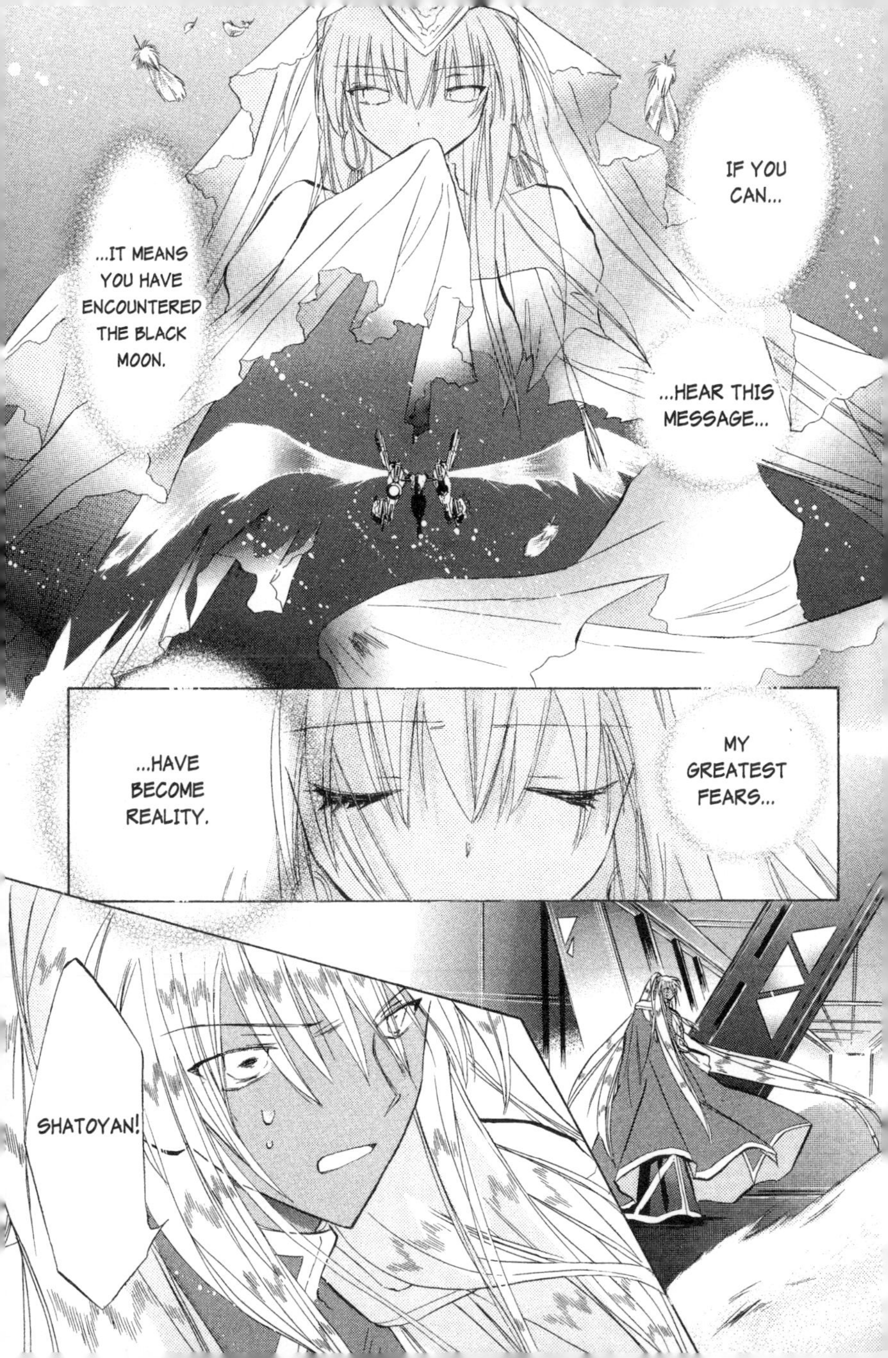
IF YOU CAN...
...HEAR THIS MESSAGE...
...IT MEANS YOU HAVE ENCOUNTERED THE BLACK MOON.
MY GREATEST FEARS...
...HAVE BECOME REALITY.
SHATOYAN!

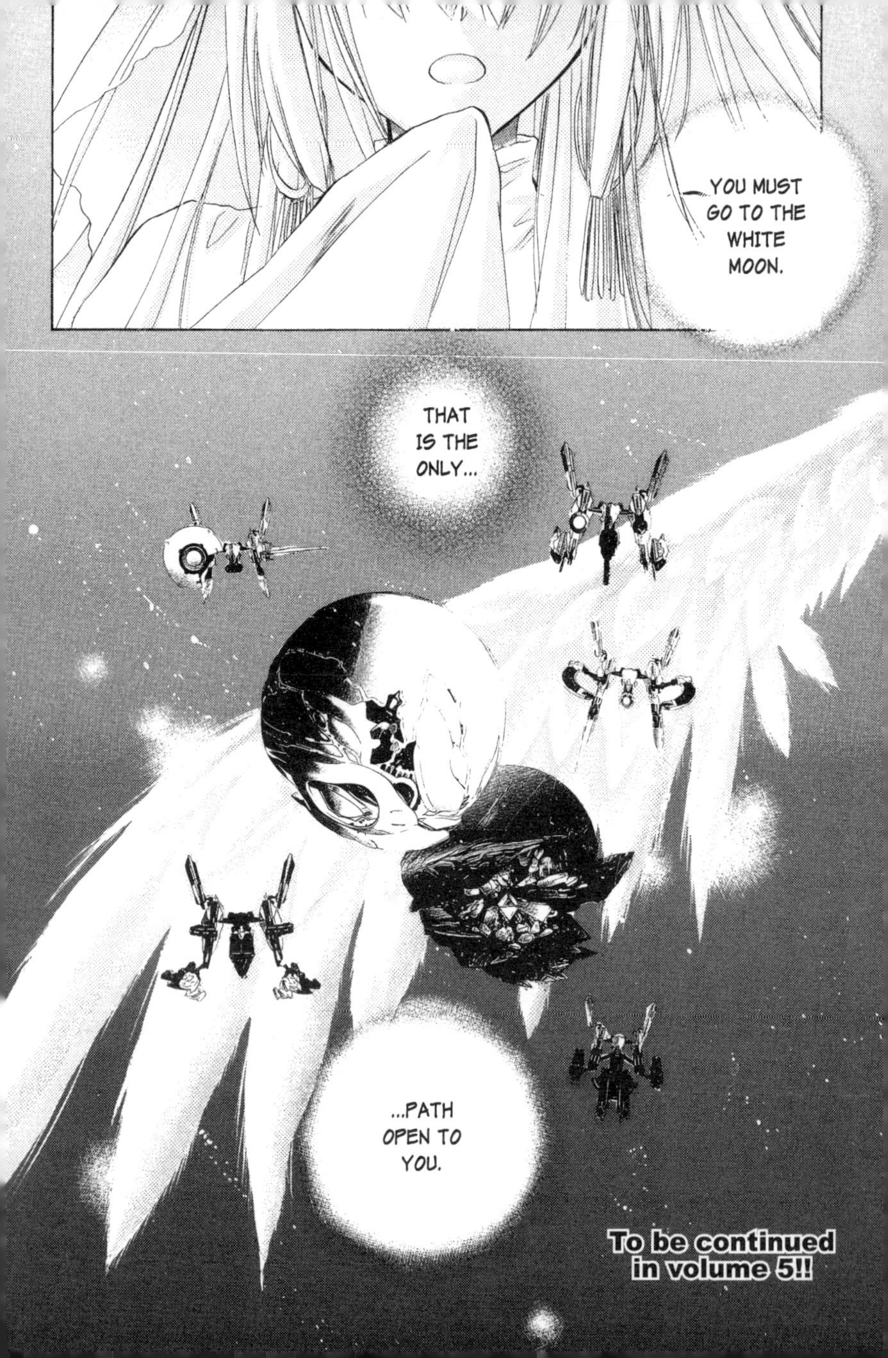
—YOU MUST GO TO THE WHITE MOON.
THAT IS THE ONLY...
...PATH OPEN TO YOU.
To be continued in volume 5!!

●SPECIAL THANKS●

<CONTENT CHECK & IDEA>
Ryo Mizuno

<RESOURCE FOR SPACESHIP, ETC>
IKUSABUNE

<SPACESHIP DESIGN>
Kokoro Takei

<COLOR CGS>
Michiru Yamazaki

●MAIN STAFF●

Mieko Araki   Kaori Satou
Kyoko Tarasawa

A Bonus Page

I took a survey.

"How would you like to see Forte dressed?"

"Cross-dressing" was the #1 response.

As a host.◇

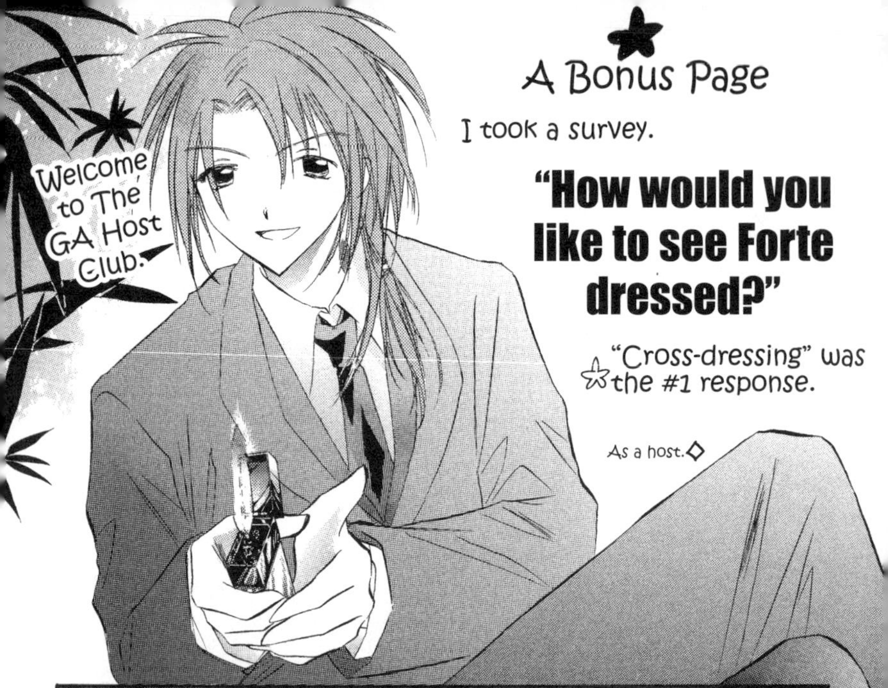
Welcome to The GA Host Club.

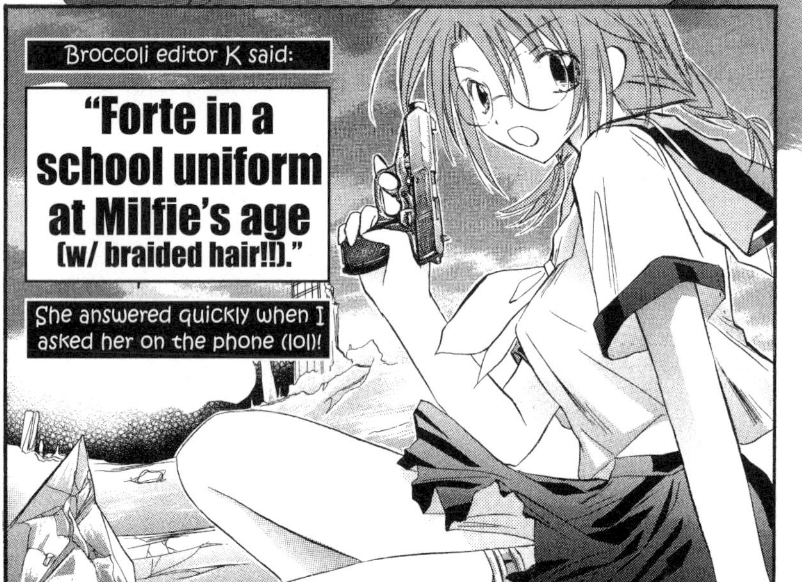
Broccoli editor K said:
"Forte in a school uniform at Milfie's age (w/ braided hair!!)."
She answered quickly when I asked her on the phone (lol)!

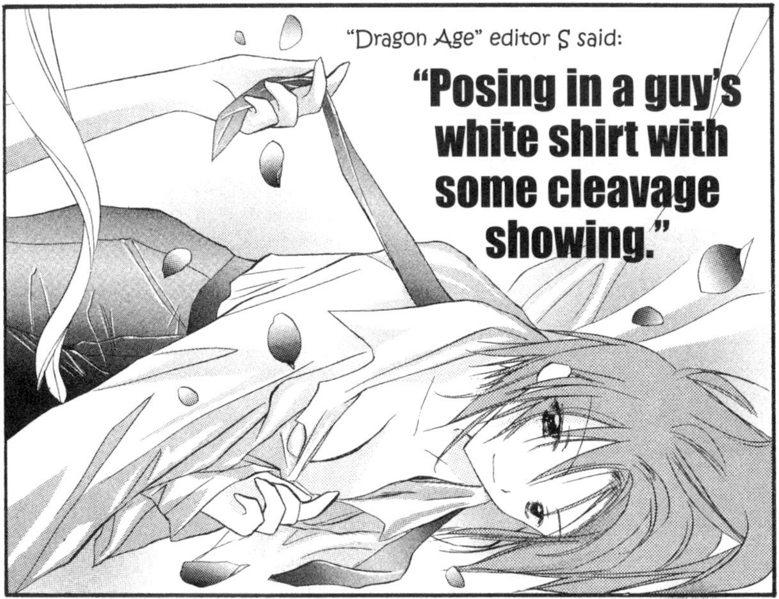
"Dragon Age" editor S said:
"Posing in a guy's white shirt with some cleavage showing."

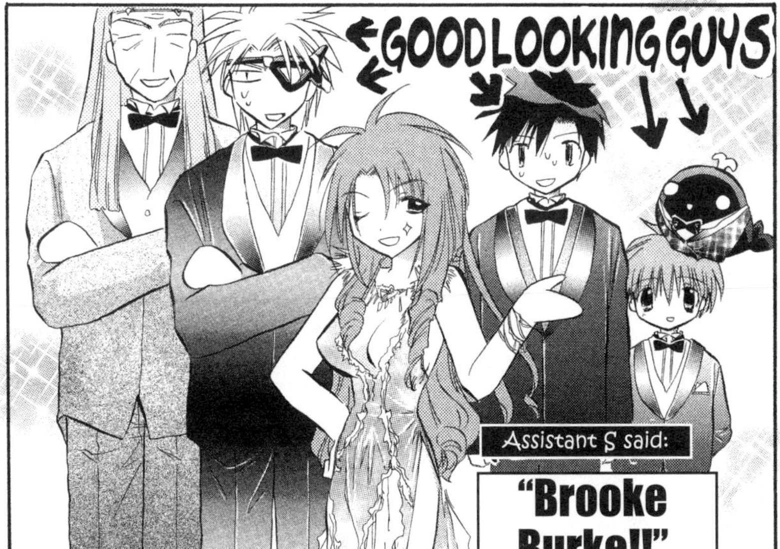
GOOD LOOKING GUYS
Assistant S said:
"Brooke Burke!!"

Oh my...

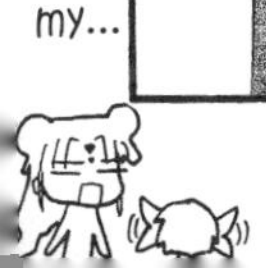

•Afterword•

★ Many people helped me to draw this manga. Thank you all so much. I'll keep making manga at my own pace. (I-I'm so slow that people yell at me...) Hopefully, I can take things slowly one step at a time. Your support makes me truly happy.

Be seeing you.

Kanan

October 2003

← Bonus four-panel manga.

★

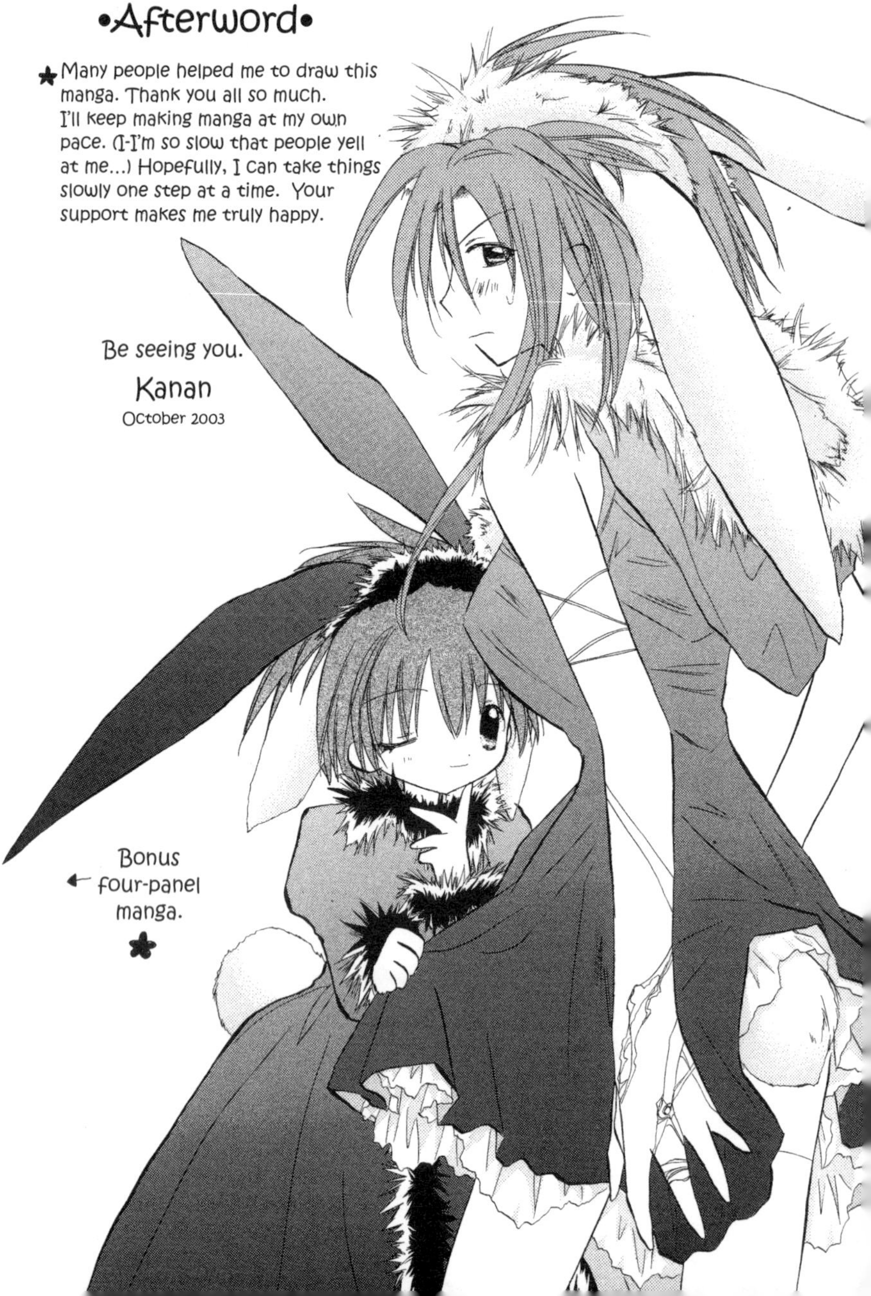

Little Mint Riding Hood

by Kanan

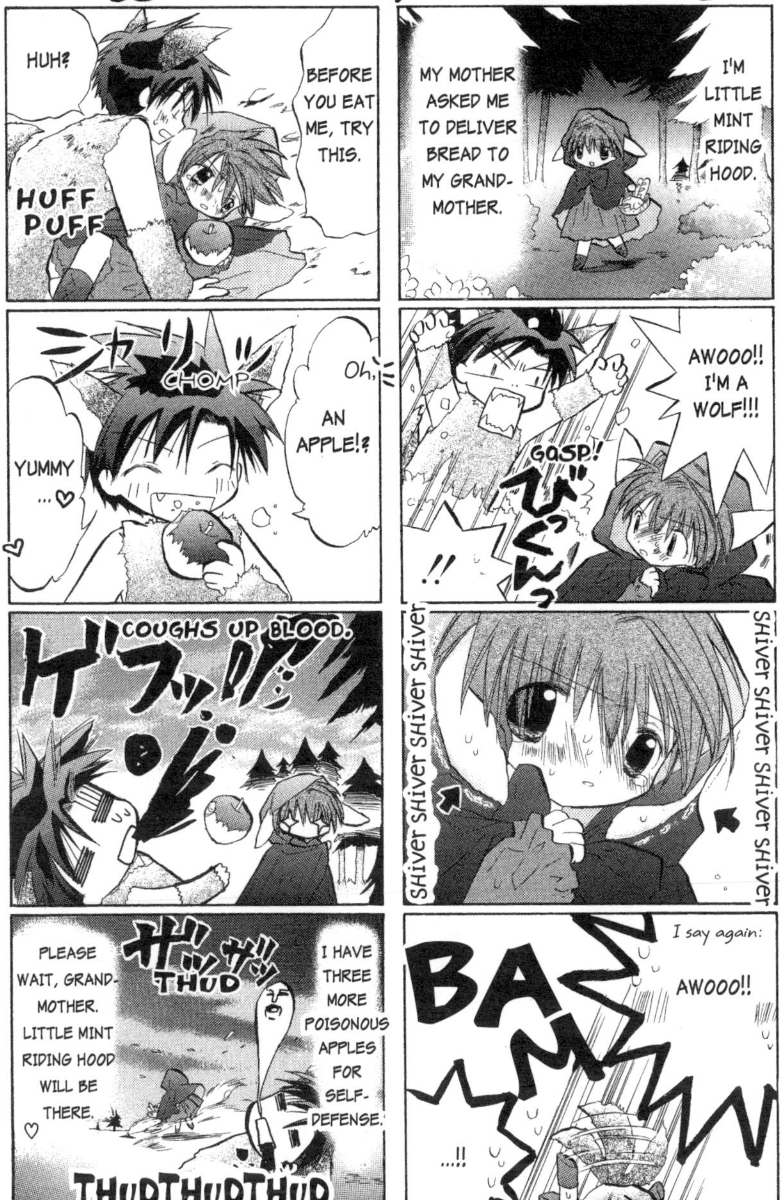
I'M LITTLE MINT RIDING HOOD.
MY MOTHER ASKED ME TO DELIVER BREAD TO MY GRANDMOTHER.
BEFORE YOU EAT ME, TRY THIS.
HUH?
HUFF PUFF
AWOOO!! I'M A WOLF!!!
GASP!
びくんっ
!!
Oh,
AN APPLE!?
シャリ
CHOMP
YUMMY ...♥
SHIVER SHIVER SHIVER
SHIVER SHIVER SHIVER
COUGHS UP BLOOD.
ゲフッ
I say again:
AWOOO!!
BAM
...!!
I HAVE THREE MORE POISONOUS APPLES FOR SELF-DEFENSE.
ザッ ザッ
THUD
PLEASE WAIT, GRANDMOTHER. LITTLE MINT RIDING HOOD WILL BE THERE. ♡
THUDTHUDTHUD

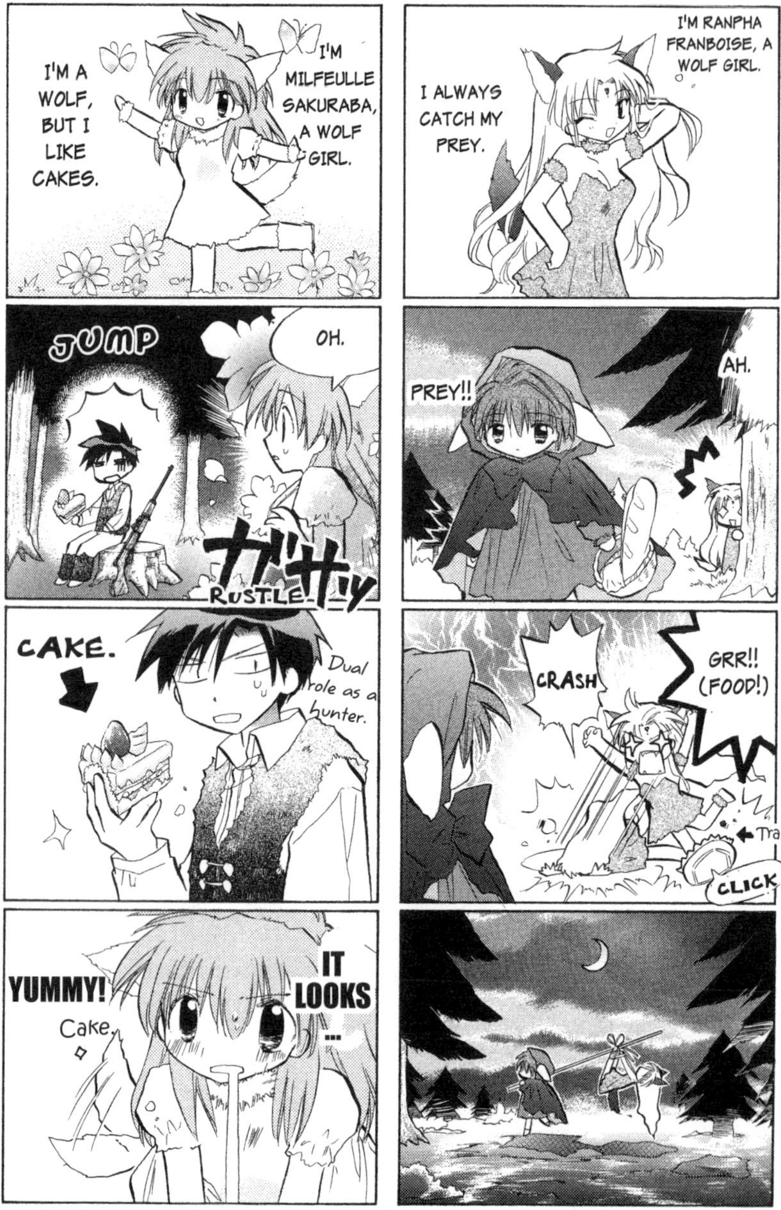
I'M RANPHA FRANBOISE, A WOLF GIRL.
I ALWAYS CATCH MY PREY.
AH.
PREY!!
GRR!! (FOOD!)
CRASH
Trap
CLICK
I'M MILFEULLE SAKURABA, A WOLF GIRL.
I'M A WOLF, BUT I LIKE CAKES.
OH.
JUMP
ガサッ
RUSTLE
CAKE.
Dual role as a hunter.
IT LOOKS ...
YUMMY!
Cake.

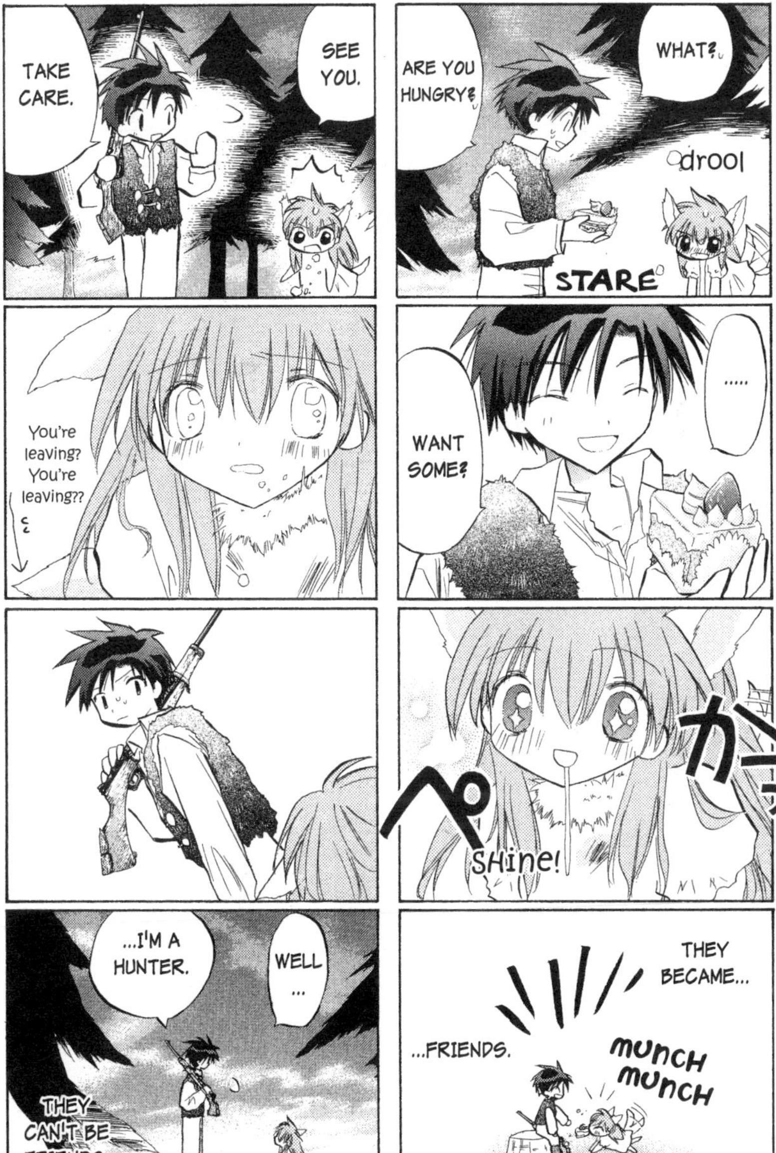
WHAT?
ARE YOU HUNGRY?
drool
STARE
SEE YOU.
TAKE CARE.
.....
WANT SOME?
You're leaving? You're leaving??
か
ぺ
SHine!
THEY BECAME...
...FRIENDS.
munch munch
WELL ...
...I'M A HUNTER.
THEY CAN'T BE FRIENDS.

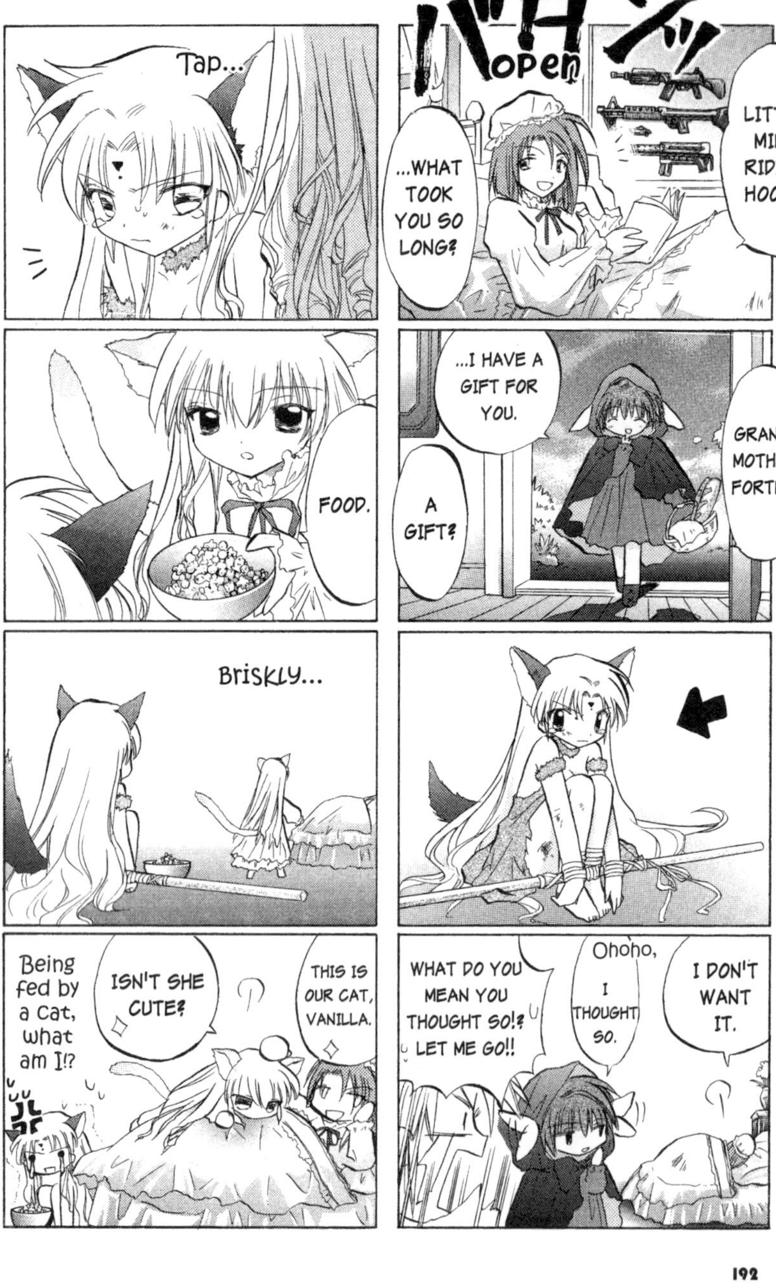
バタンッ
open
LITTLE MINT RIDING HOOD...
...WHAT TOOK YOU SO LONG?
Tap...
GRAND-MOTHER FORTE...
...I HAVE A GIFT FOR YOU.
A GIFT?
FOOD.
Briskly...
I DON'T WANT IT.
Ohoho,
I THOUGHT SO.
WHAT DO YOU MEAN YOU THOUGHT SO!? LET ME GO!!
THIS IS OUR CAT, VANILLA.
ISN'T SHE CUTE?
Being fed by a cat, what am I!?

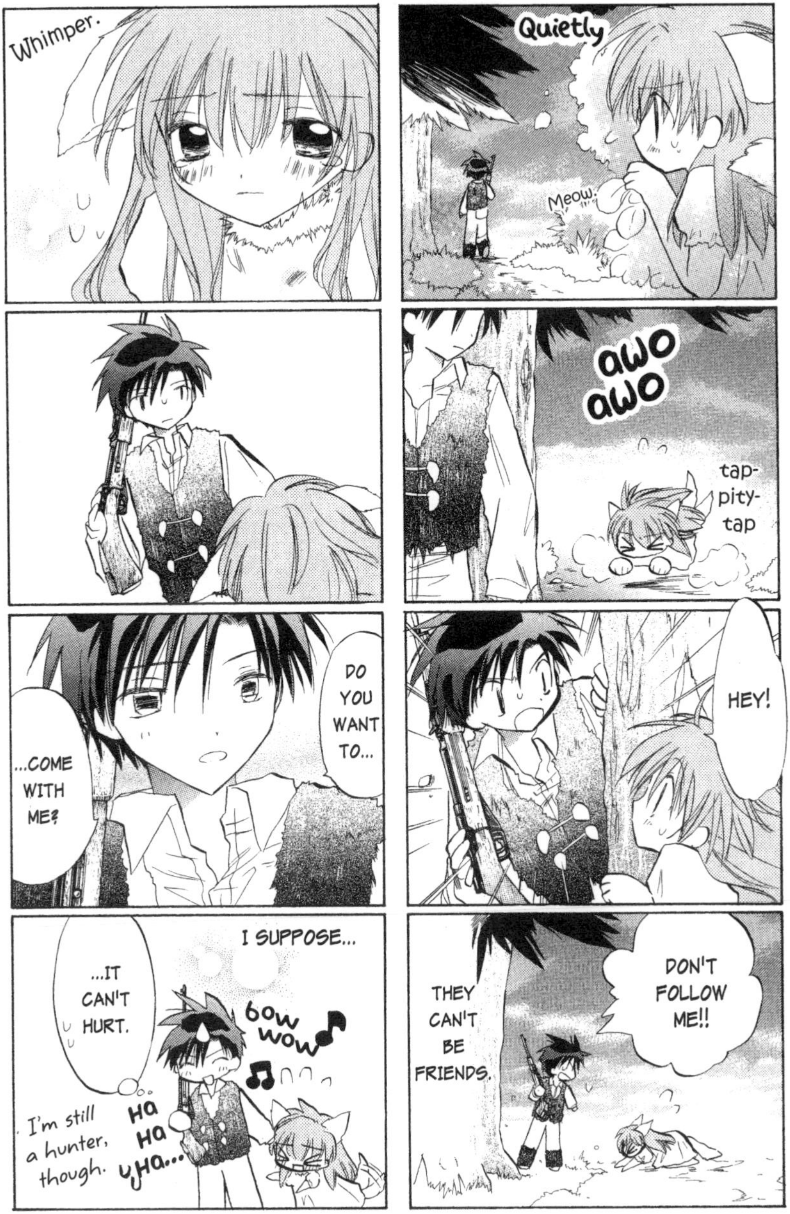
Quietly
Meow.
Whimper.
awo awo
tap-pity-tap
HEY!
DO YOU WANT TO...
...COME WITH ME?
DON'T FOLLOW ME!!
THEY CAN'T BE FRIENDS.
I SUPPOSE...
...IT CAN'T HURT.
bow wow
HA HA HA...
I'm still a hunter, though.

See you in Volume 5!

My brother's
drawings.

My brother has a job in the
medical field, and he doesn't
usually draw manga, but
sometime he scribbles while
he's on the phone. This looks
kind of realistic and scary,
but he's good!! Am I a sucker
for my brother?
You bet I am!

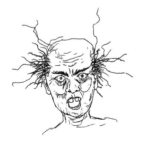

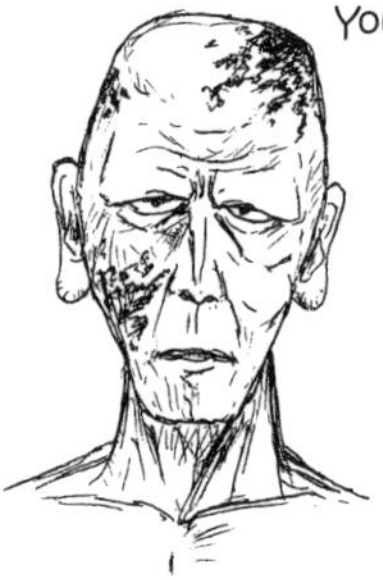

Galaxy Angel™

ギャラクシーエンジェル

5

BROCCOLI BOOKS DELUXE
Galaxy Angel
5
BY Kanan

THE ANGEL TROUPE FEELS THE PRESSURE AS EONIA'S FORCES DRAW EVER CLOSER, SPREADING A REIGN OF TERROR ACROSS THE GALAXY. WHEN EONIA'S LEGIONS EXECUTE A DEVASTATING ATTACK ON A MILITARY ENVOY, THE ANNIHILATION IS SO COMPLETE THAT ONLY ONE SURVIVOR REMAINS – CHITOSE. PLEDGING TO FIGHT AGAINST EONIA WITH ALL HER STRENGTH, SHE JOINS FORCES WITH THE ANGEL TROUPE. BUT EVEN WITH THE AID OF ITS NEWEST ALLY, THE DECK IS STACKED AGAINST THE TROUPE AS THEY STRIVE TO DELIVER PRINCE SHIVA SAFELY TO THE WHITE MOON AND UNCOVER ITS MYSTERIOUS SECRET.

VOLUME 5 WILL BE AVAILABLE THIS COMING JANUARY AT YOUR LOCAL BOOKSTORES!

HERE IS A PREVIEW PAGE TO GIVE YOU A SNEAK PEEK!

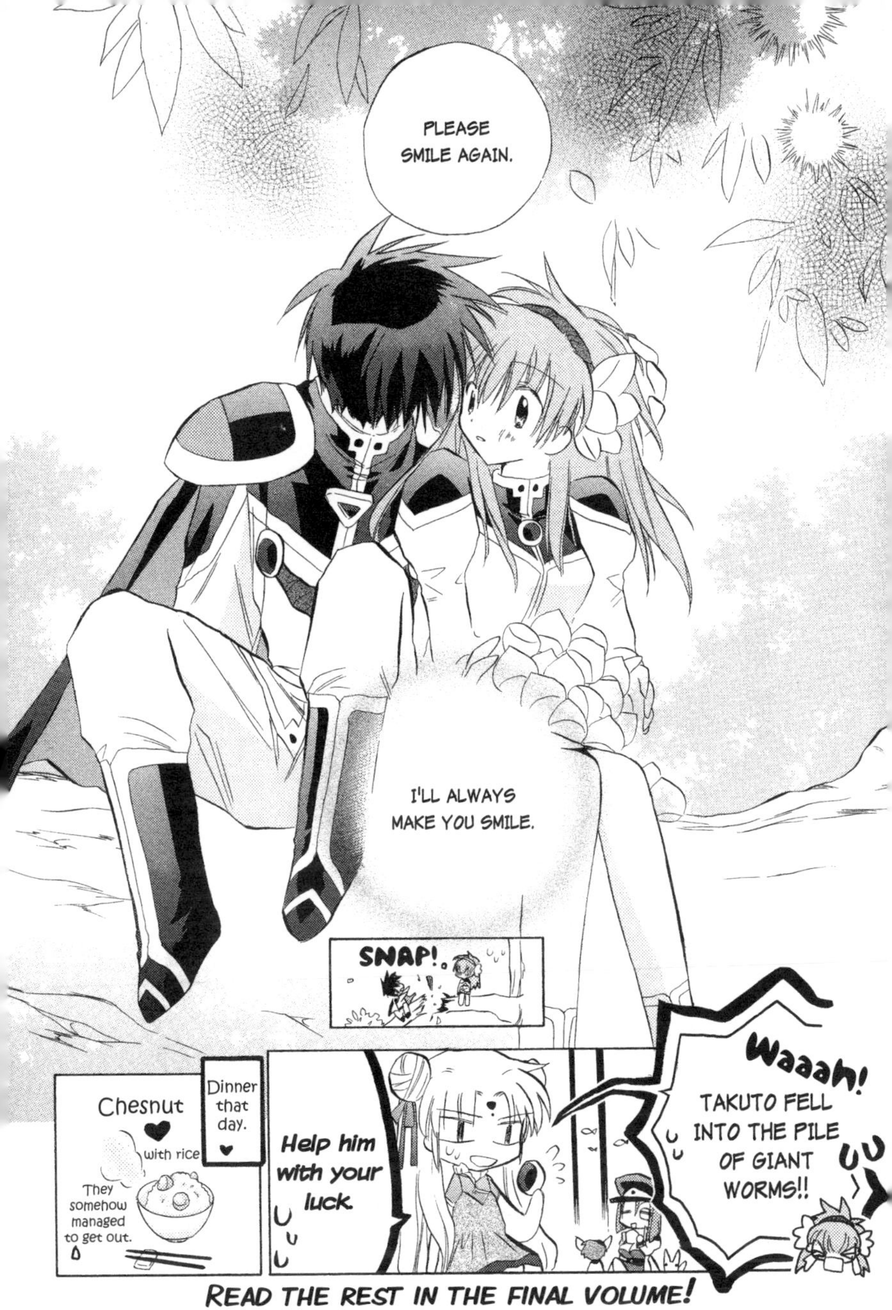
PLEASE SMILE AGAIN.
I'LL ALWAYS MAKE YOU SMILE.
SNAP!
Waaaah!
TAKUTO FELL INTO THE PILE OF GIANT WORMS!!
Help him with your luck.
Dinner that day.
Chesnut
with rice
They somehow managed to get out.

READ THE REST IN THE FINAL VOLUME!

Mint Blancmanche

Mint seems to be smiling all the time, but she is really a shrewd and slick character who doesn't back down on important matters. She is the only daughter of the Blancmanche Conglomerate, one of the wealthiest families of the galaxy. Due to her strict education, she is adept at strategy and information analysis. It can be said that she is the "brain" of the Angel Troupe. In addition, she has the extraordinary gift of telepathy, which she can use to read people's inner thoughts. This gift has its downside, however, and has caused her to become somewhat distrustful. Mint enjoys artificially flavored and colored junk food, character cosplay and other costumes, and bizarre fashions.

Age: 16
Rank: Second Lieutenant
Height: 4'1"

Favorite food:
Junk food with lots of artificial flavoring and color

Hobbies:
Cosplay (although she keeps it a secret)

Special abilities:
Reading minds

GA-002 Trick Master

This Emblem Frame is outfitted with a remote-controlled pod-unit called "Flier," suited for long-range attacks. It possesses powerful radar for widespread reconnaissance and is very effective at information analysis. Trick Master is often used as a mobile command center.

Length: 120'9"
Width: 123'4"
Height: 57'1"

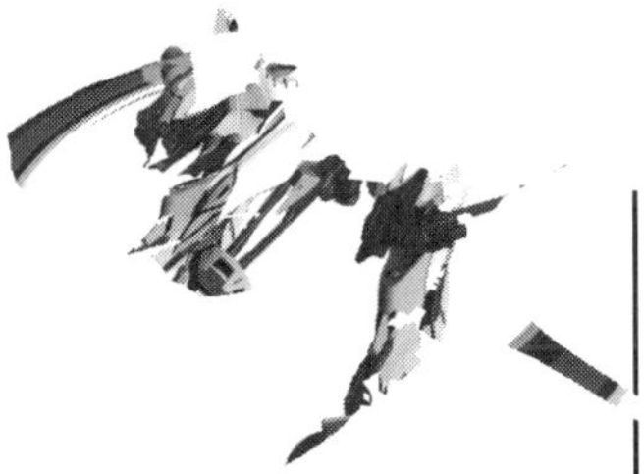

Favorite food:
N/A

Hobbies:
N/A

Special abilities:
N/A

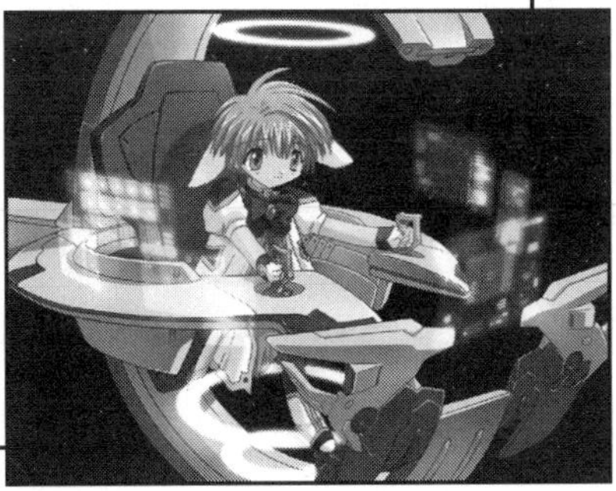

Prince Shiva

Shiva is the lone surviving prince of the Transbaal Kingdom and first heir to the throne. He was raised by Shatoyan on the White Moon. During the coup d'etat, he was forced to flee with the Angel Troupe.

Age: 10
Hobbies: Chess

Moon Goddess Shatoyan

She is the resident of the White Moon and is known as the "Moon Goddess." The people see her as a religious figure to be worshipped, and she is thought of as the one who brings prosperity to the kingdom. During the coup d'etat, she refused to be subjected to Eonia's rule. She authorized the use of the ceremonial ship Elle Ciel to assist Prince Shiva's escape from the White Moon. After Shiva fled, she used the Lost Technology to set up a barrier around the White Moon. Only a woman as powerful as the Goddess herself can break the seal.

Age: Unknown
Special abilities: To provide love and affection to people

Luft Weizen

He is the general of the Imperial Force, and he also holds the honorary title of Special Guardian Division Satellite Defense Fleet Commander. During the turmoil of the coup d'etat, he was appointed by Shatoyan to be the commander of the Elle Ciel. He was also Takuto's instructor at the Academy.

Although he is easily in the top five military commanders of the Imperial Force, he feels unsuited to command the Angel Troupe and calls upon Takuto to become commander.

Age: unknown (in his 50s)

Siegfried G. DeMoyer

Siegfried is the supreme commander of the Second Division of the Imperial Army. He is an influential aristocrat based in Lome and the center of the anti-Eonia faction. His skills in battle are unknown.

Age: 63

Camus O. Laphroaig

Camus is the leader of Eonia's mercenary team, the "Hell Hounds." He is an effeminate and narcissistic pretty boy. He persistently chases after Milfeulle with words of love, bestowing upon her luxurious gifts composed mostly of sadistic attacks. Camus may be a lunatic weirdo, but he is an elite pilot.

Age: unknown (late twenties)

Riserva Chianti

As a self-described member of the "noble elite," Riserva coldly looks down upon people. He harbors an ill feeling against the only daughter of the Blancmanche Conglomerate, and insults Mint as a member of the "nouveau riche." It is unknown whether he is as aristocratic as he claims.

Age: unknown (late teens)

Red Eye

A man of few words, he fights ceaselessly in never-ending loneliness. Little is known about his background, but the scars running across his body imply his rough past. His fighting skills are of a professional level, which makes him a great rival for Forte.

Age: unknown (late teens)

Vermouth Matin

A member of the Hell Hounds, he is an annoying brat who constantly talks smack to his enemies. He always tries to get a rise out of the stoic Vanilla, but has never succeeded. He is a geek who is into mechanics.

Age: unknown (mid teens)

Guinness Stout

Guinness is an annoying, hot-blooded, macho jock. He has his eye on Ranpha and her kung fu abilities and describes her as his "life-long rival."

Age: unknown (early twenties)

DVDs by ◼️ Synch-Point

AquarianAge
the movie

The danger caused by the ERASER fleet has been eliminated thanks to the combined powers of the ARAYASHIKI, DARK-LORE, E.G.O., and WIZ-DOM factions. But a new threat looms in the horizon. Calling themselves the POLESTAR EMPIRE, they seek to take over the world by any means. Now it is up to five young women to come to terms with themselves and accept their true calling...

I'm Gonna Be An Angel!

On his way to school, Yuusuke stumbles upon a naked Noelle sleeping in the forest. Now, everyone's calling him her husband! But Yuusuke already has a crush on his classmate Natsumi. To make matters worse, Noelle's family of monsters has moved into his house. On top of that, the evil Dispel, who is trying to kidnap Noelle, sends all sorts of creatures after her. Wrestlers, catgirls, and aliens... Oh my!

Di Gi Charat™

Di Gi Charat (Dejiko for short) is an alien hybrid-cat-eared girl with the ambition of becoming a superstar on planet Earth. However, the cost of living is quite high in Tokyo. Luckily she gets both work and housing at an anime chain store called Gamers, and quickly becomes popular with the fans who shop there. But this is only the beginning of her misadventures!

For more information visit:
www.bro-usa.com

STOP!
YOU'RE READING THE WRONG WAY!

This is the end of the book! In Japan, manga is generally read from right to left. All reading starts on the upper right corner, and ends on the lower left. American comics are generally read from left to right, starting on the upper left of each page. In order to preserve the true nature of the work, we printed this book in a right to left fashion. Those who are unfamiliar with manga may find this confusing at first, but once you start getting into the story, you will wonder how you ever read manga any other way!

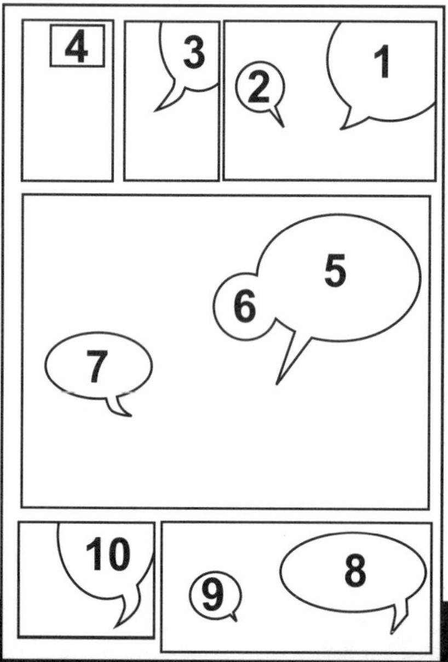
1
2
3
4
5
6
7
8
9
10

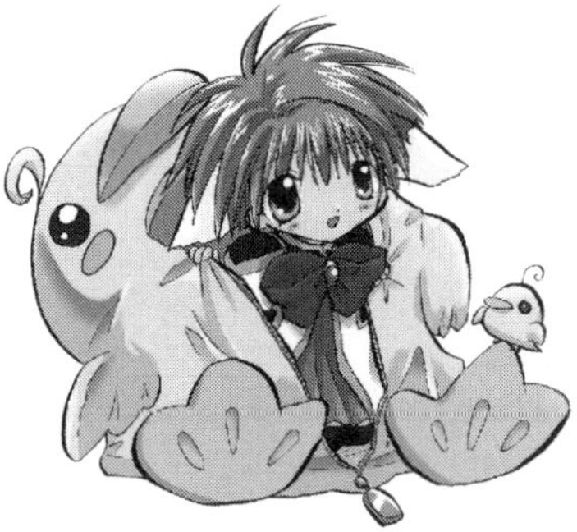